Ancient Effigy Mound Landscapes of Upper Midwestern North America

Ancient Effigy Mound Landscapes of Upper Midwestern North America

Robert A. Birmingham and Amy L. Rosebrough

AMERICAN LANDSCAPES

American Landscapes is an imprint of Oxbow Books

Published in the United Kingdom in 2025 by
OXBOW BOOKS
81 St Clements, Oxford OX4 1AW

and in the United States by
OXBOW BOOKS
1950 Lawrence Road, Havertown, PA 19083

Paperback Edition: ISBN 978-1-78570-087-3
Digital Edition: ISBN 978-1-78570-088-0

A CIP record for this book is available from the British Library

Library of Congress Control Number: 2024949877

Printed and bound in the United Kingdom by CPI Group (UK) Ltd, Croydon, CR0 4YY
Typeset in India by DiTech Publishing Services

For a complete list of titles, please contact:

UNITED KINGDOM
Oxbow Books
Telephone (0)1226 734350
Email: oxbow@oxbowbooks.com
www.oxbowbooks.com

UNITED STATES OF AMERICA
Oxbow Books
Telephone (610) 853-9131, Fax (610) 853-9146
Email: queries@casemateacademic.com
www.casemateacademic.com/oxbow

Oxbow Books is part of the Casemate Group

Front cover: Wisconsin Department of Natural Resources aerial photograph

Contents

1

The effigy mounds of the Upper Midwest

Long before the appearance of urban societies and associated monumental architecture, many traditional communities of the world engaged in types of monument building related to the supernatural that remain somewhat mysterious but, nevertheless, represent the role that religious beliefs played in the emergence of complex societies. Familiar examples are the giant stone megalithic structures of the European Neolithic period, the 11,000 year old Göbekli Tepe temple complex in Turkey, and, in a different continent, the immense 2000 year old Hopewell earthworks of Ohio in the present United States (Lynott 2014). Lesser known is another spectacular example of ancient monument building in the Upper Midwestern region of the United States centered on the state of Wisconsin, where thousands of earth sculptures were molded from the natural landscape as an integral part of a ceremonial complex that swept the region in the 1st millennium AD.

The building of mounds had a long history in this region, beginning *ca* 800 BC with large conical or round mounds covering burial pits from only that part of a population that occupied higher status than others. However, after *ca* AD 600, mound building exploded across the landscape, eventually taking a radically different form. People now turned the natural terrain into vast ceremonial landscapes of sometimes huge earthen representations, or effigies, of birds, mammals, serpents, supernatural beings, human beings, and other forms that most often contained burials, although now of just one or few individuals (Figs 1.1 and 1.2). A few burials have also been found outside of mounds and this emphasizes the use of these ceremonial landscape areas as cemeteries for social groups. Archaeologists now refer to the phenomenon as the Effigy Mound Ceremonial Complex.

In many cases, the new mounds surrounded large conical burial mounds made in previous times, indicating a continuing use of sanctified places but, quickly, effigy mound construction spread to many other places not previously used for such purposes. This unparalleled wave of ceremonial mound building resulted in a 'multitude of extraordinary figures raised like embossed ornaments over the whole of this country' as one early 19th century visitor observed before modern settlement and farming destroyed many of the mounds (Locke 1840).

By the time this great wave of ceremonial activity waned, about AD 1100, it is estimated that over 15,000 mounds had been built at over 1000 locations, often spreading out over huge areas of land. At least 3200 of these were effigies, many

Fig. 1.1 (*opposite*) Above: LiDAR image of the Marching Bear Mound Group at Effigy Mounds National Monument, Iowa (produced by William Romain); below: Wisconsin Department of Natural Resources aerial photograph of the group on a high hill north of the Wisconsin River in Richland County that is a part of the Eagle Township cluster. The grouping is affectionately known to local people as 'Frank's Hill' after landowner Frank Schadewald, who cared for the mounds until his death in 2013.

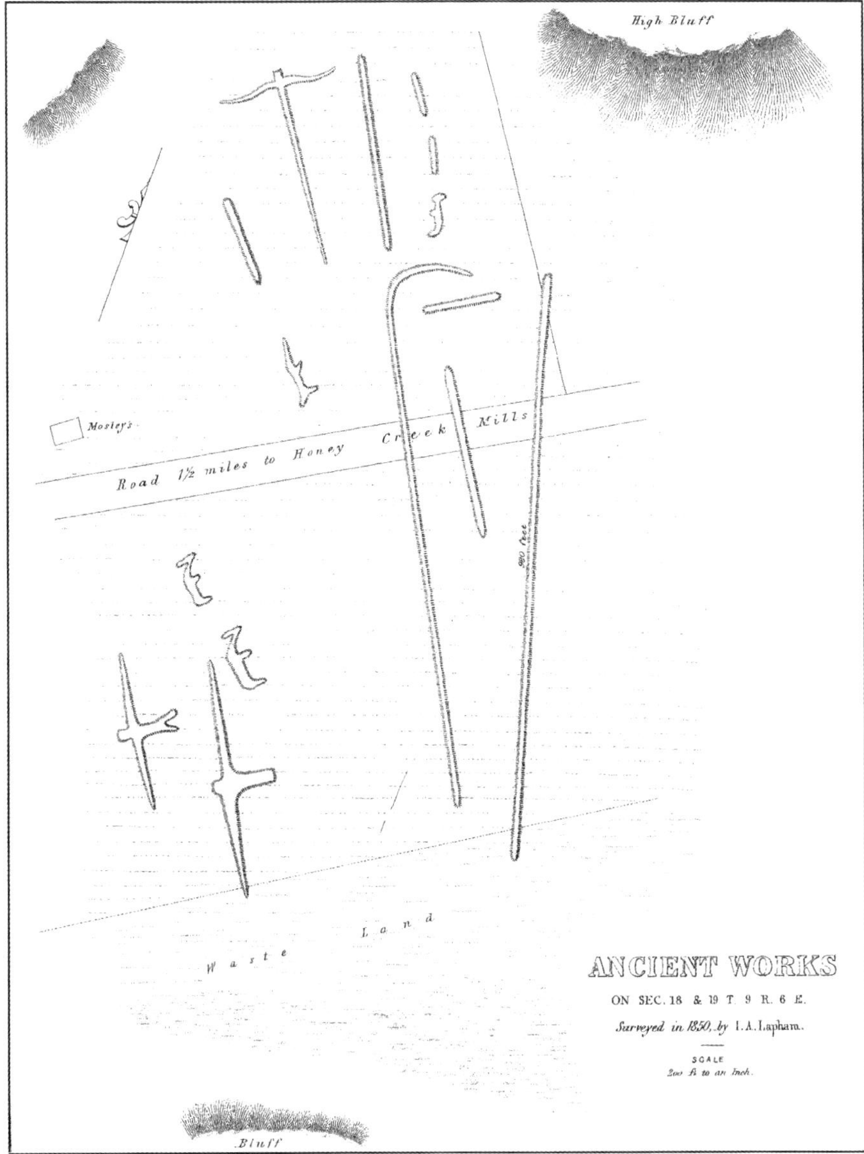

Fig. 1.2 Increase Lapham's map of large effigy mounds at the Mosely site, now destroyed, near the Wisconsin River (from Lapham 1855).

recognizable as animals and supernatural beings important in the traditions and belief systems of more recent Native people, such as the eagle-like Thunderbirds, rulers of the air; hawks; bears, often viewed as representing the earth and earthly order; and long-tailed supernatural creatures that inhabit a watery Underworld and are variously called Underground Water Panthers or simply Water Spirits by more recent Midwestern tribes. Many more are very long, tapering linear forms, sometimes curved, that almost certainly are snakes – another animal associated with the Underworld in the cultural traditions of Native people throughout the Americas (Birmingham 2010, 39, 178; see also papers in Diaz-Granados 2023). Other common forms found among the effigy mounds are short, linear mounds and the ubiquitous small conical or round mounds. While these new mound forms continued to be used as burial places, Native people were now putting their supernatural beliefs, and quite possibly even their clan-based social systems derived from these beliefs, on the surface of the ground using ritual practices appropriate to different populations over large areas.

Fig. 1.3 (*opposite*) Map of the Upper Midwest showing the location of effigy mound groups (by Amy Rosebrough).

The effigy mound region

Ancient people elsewhere in the Mississippi River drainage system and beyond occasionally made large earthen (and sometimes stone) animal effigies but nowhere are mounds found in such concentrations as in the Upper Midwest effigy mound region (Fig. 1.3). Separated in time and not culturally related to the Upper Midwestern mounds, those made elsewhere share the same themes, such as great celestial birds and supernatural watery Underworld creatures, supporting a conclusion that the Upper Midwestern effigy mounds had their roots in a long-time belief structure widespread in North America.

The effigy mound region covers the whole of southern Wisconsin and small parts of adjacent Iowa, Minnesota, and Illinois. A few outlying effigy mounds are found in northern Wisconsin but not in the large clusters found in the south. This mound region closely corresponds to a pre-settlement ecological zone consisting of a mosaic of oak savannas (prairie grasses and scattered oak trees), prairies, and southern mesic and oak forests (Curtis 1959; Finley 1976) that was rich with easily obtained wild food resources, especially large herds of deer. The region also encompasses many major water bodies – rivers, streams, and lakes – that provided aquatic foods such as fish, clams, and wild rice.

The productivity of this zone greatly increases when one factors in a favorable environment and climate for corn cultivation and other types of gardening and agriculture. The growing season for this zone meets the 140-day minimum growing season needed for successful maize horticulture. Immediately to the north, this productive zone grades into a cooler climate with northern coniferous forests that was not as abundant in wildlife and had less agricultural potential. To the south, in Illinois, and west into Minnesota, lie vast tall grass prairies that, again, were not as rich in food resources, except for bison found on the western prairies that begin the Great Plains. The effigy mound region is bounded on the east by Lake Michigan, one of the Great Lakes.

The already bountiful natural resources in the effigy mound region were much enhanced by climatic warming along with sufficient moisture, beginning about AD 600, as modeled by the University of Wisconsin Climate Research Center (Bryson and Bryson 2000), that had been preceded by a long period of cool and wet weather ending in a sharp, long drought about AD 400. The warming peaked during a climatic episode called the Noe-Atlantic or the Medieval Warm Climate between AD 800 and 1200, so called because it was first well documented for early medieval times in Europe where it led to population increases, ample harvests, expansion of trade and deep sea fishing, and large scale building construction (Fagan 2008). During this time, Scandinavian Vikings spread westward to Greenland and Iceland and, briefly,

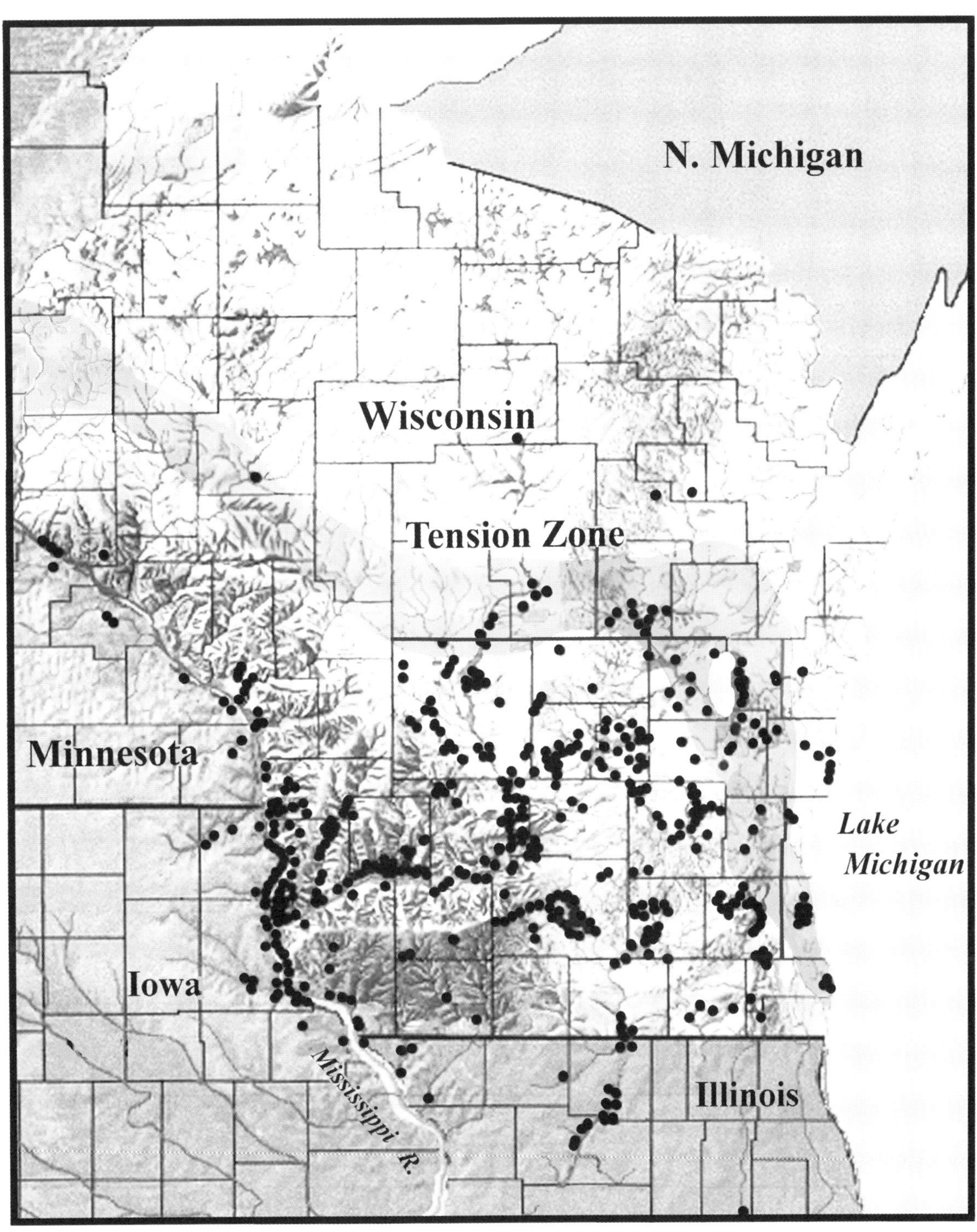
N. Michigan
Wisconsin
Tension Zone
Minnesota
Lake Michigan
Iowa
Mississippi R.
Illinois

a settlement in Newfoundland. A number of complex societies saw florescence in many parts of the world during this time, among which was the Mississippian civilization in mid-continental North America with its central city of Cahokia on the Mississippi River in southern Illinois, although other historical factors were involved, like the long trajectory of increasing cultural complexity in prior times. Between AD 1050 and 1200, the Mississippians expanded north into the effigy mound region, changing the culture of effigy builders through several processes of cultural contact. Some former effigy mound people even joined Mississippian communities.

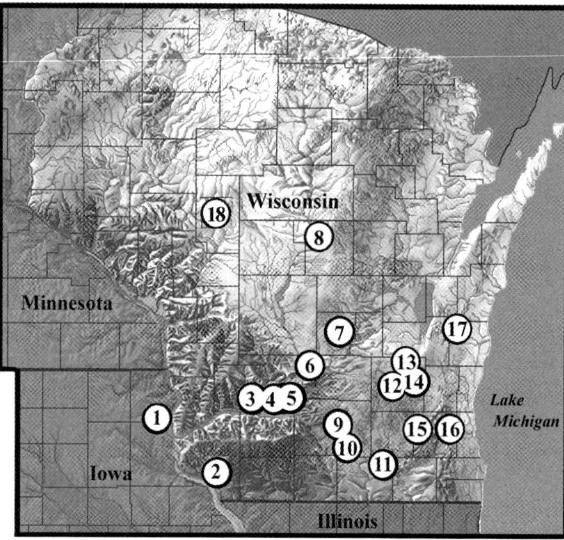

Fig. 1.4 Location of mound groups mentioned in text: 1) Effigy Mounds National Monument; 2) Raisbeck; 3) Eagle Township; 4) Twin Lizard; 5) Mosely; 6) Kingsley Bend; 7) Kratz; 8) Sanders; 9) Mendota State Hospital and Woodward Shores groups; 10) Gilman; 11) Maple; 12) Nitschke; 13) Kolterman; 14) Clark's Wood; 15) Regula; 16) School Section; 17) Henschel; 18) Lizard Mound.

In the Upper Midwest, climate change enabled expansion in the range of deer, long the major food resource in the region (Cleland 1966, 33–4), and the long summers no doubt contributed to the incorporation of corn horticulture into the region from the south to hunting and gathering economies. The increase in availability of food resources is correlated with the growth of a large human population, most notably in the effigy mound region, where some areas become 'packed with people' as settlements grew even to upland areas away from major bodies of water (Theler and Boszhardt 2006; Birmingham 2010). Some of the largest or densest effigy mound landscapes recorded, such as the Eagle Township mound cluster, the Raisbeck mounds in southwestern Wisconsin, the Mendota State Hospital Mound Group in the Four Lakes mound district in central Wisconsin, and the Nitschke Mound Group in eastern Wisconsin, developed or reached their zenith between 900 and 1200, as indicated by either radiocarbon dates or other direct evidence (Fig. 1.4). The growing population in western Wisconsin likely stressed resources leading to over-hunting and collapse of deer herds, and the demise of the effigy mound cultures in that area, as proposed by Theler and Boszhardt (2006).

Late Woodland effigy mound tradition

The effigy mound tradition belongs to a period or stage called Late Woodland by archaeologists and dates between AD 500 and 1200 (see Table 1, on p. 47), a time marked by several other changes from the preceding Middle Woodland stage/period in the Upper Midwest (*ca* 100 BC–AD 400) that was characterized by mound building in the form of large conical mounds and was culturally influenced by participation in the widespread Hopewell trade and ceremonial complex emanating from Ohio that brought many different peoples of eastern North America into

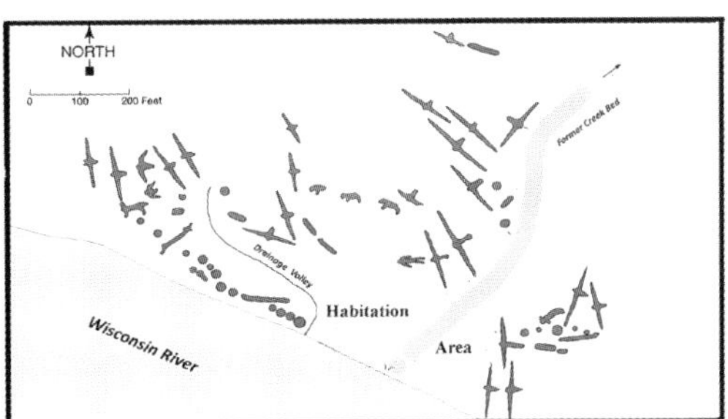

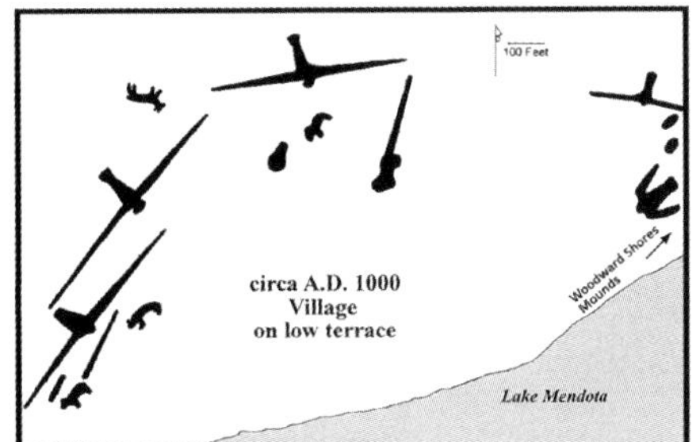

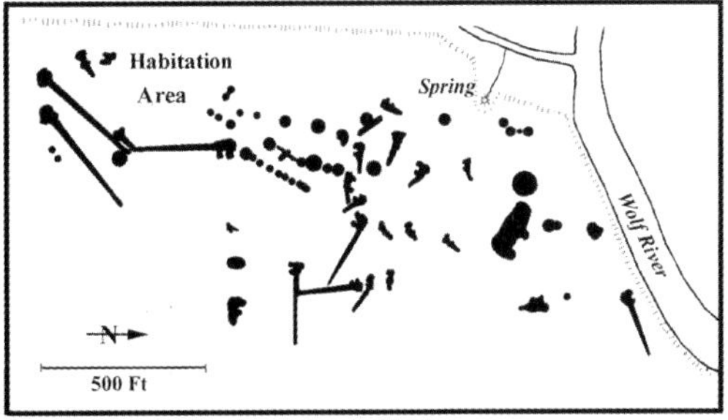

Fig. 1.5 Upper: habitation sites at the Eagle Township cluster on the Wisconsin River; middle: the Mendota Mental Health Hospital Mound Group on Lake Mendota in south-central Wisconsin (see Chapter 5); lower: the Sanders site in central Wisconsin.

contact. The bow and arrow used for hunting and warfare first came into use during the Late Woodland and new elaborate forms of pottery appeared with complex decorations made by impressing cords into wet clay. Populations dramatically increased and it is during the Late Woodland that we see in the Upper Midwest a shift, after AD 900, from a hunting and gathering subsistence pattern that had supported human life for many thousands of years to one that incorporated maize or corn horticulture. This, in turn, led to the formation of small villages and, later, villages that were sometimes fortified by timber stockades indicating a trend towards conflict. At the same time, a new form of domestic structure – a small, bark covered, pit house with a long entrance way – makes its first appearance in the archaeological record of the region.

The relationship between effigy mounds and settlement areas is still not well understood because few archaeological surveys have been conducted around most surviving effigy mound groupings. Evidence thus far shows that villages were maintained at some important ceremonial centers, such as at the Eagle Township effigy mound landscape along the Wisconsin River, the Sanders Mound Group along the Wolf River, and the Mendota State Hospital Mound Group near modern-day Madison in south-central Wisconsin (Hurley 1975; Birmingham 2010, 17, 124–6; Fig. 1.5; see Chapter 5), while a short-lived temporary camp has been identified at the Nitschke Mound Group in eastern Wisconsin (Clauter 2011). Extensive surveys around one small, isolated effigy mound group along a creek near Lake Waubesa in Wisconsin found no evidence of habitation or even subsequent use of the area (Birmingham 2010). It is apparent that mound building played different roles in the overall settlement, subsistence, and ceremonial systems, and quite probably these roles changed as the settlement and subsistence patterns changed with the shift to more reliance on growing crops. Unfortunately, relatively few effigy mounds have been directly dated because most were excavated prior to the development of radiocarbon dating. Many more radiocarbon dates have been obtained from Late Woodland habitation sites with pottery vessels similar to those found in some mounds (Stoltman and Christiansen 2000).

The Late Woodland people who made the effigy mounds do not seem to have been part of a single political entity but, rather, comprised many local social groups who shared the Effigy Mound Ceremonial Complex that perhaps integrated them into a confederacy. One of us (AR) has identified as many as 25 sub-regions or localities within the broader effigy mound region, often separated by large expanses of land, that differ in mound forms or mound form styles (Rosebrough 2010; 2014). There are also differences in ceramic styles across the region that are not consistent with one homogenous population (Boszhardt 1996; Rosebrough 2010; Clauter 2011). Villages at several major effigy mound ceremonial centers may even represent places where local leaders lived (Birmingham 2010, 126).

Burials in the mounds are sometimes accompanied by a few grave goods aside from pottery: a clay pipe and a few other utilitarian or personal decorative items but, in most cases, there is nothing. This would seemingly suggest that were no great differences in social status among the effigy mound people, but this would discount the facility into which interments were made – the effigy mound itself. Not only are the mound forms different but some mounds are very much larger than others and, from this, we can assume that people interred in the mounds occupied a social status different from others. Since mounds contain burials of men, women, and children of all ages it can be further assumed that the status differences were inherited along kinship lines rather than achievements of the individuals in life.

Certainly, the construction of some of the larger effigy mounds indicates the ability to control a large amount of human labor and time, but the social-political structure of the effigy mound people remains uncertain. One feasible model is a type of society called chiefdoms where there are powerful leaders (chiefs) that held high status. In classic anthropological social system theory, kinship group (ie, clan) ranking is a characteristic of complex chiefdom societies as opposed to egalitarian tribes and bands or stratified class and urban based state societies (Service 1962). According to this model, characteristics of a chiefdom include social ranking of kinship groups and a redistributive economy where a central agent – the Chief – takes in food and goods and then redistributes these to others of the society. Chiefdoms are believed to have characterized many parts of North America at the time of European contact and some are believed to have existed among the Middle Woodland cultures of the Midwestern part of the country that preceded the effigy mound builders. However, such models have been criticized for being rooted in ideas of culture evolution based on analogy of biological evolution which is not appropriate. Further, some archaeological work has cast doubt on even the existence of a chiefdom as previously conceived because it does not fit the archaeological facts, as argued by Mississippian culture scholar Timothy Pauketat (2007), whose extensive research failed to find evidence of such a social-political and economic structure in the archaeological record. However, Robert Cainero (2010) disputes Pauketat's findings, emphasizing that socially ranked chiefdoms are well documented in the ethno-historic record among various Native peoples in the southeastern region of what is now the United States. So the matter remains in dispute.

But did the effigy mound people have a ranked social-political system where people occupied different statuses? The very existence of effigy mound landscapes of varying sizes and mound types illustrates social differences. Huge eagle or Thunderbird mounds exist at many sites (see subsequent chapters) and so any interments found below the mounds would be expected to be of people with high status. However, as mentioned, analysis of many excavated burials from effigy mounds shows little evidence of status differences in the form of grave offerings that are generally simple or non-existent. Rosebrough (2010) has proposed that mound construction itself reflects a ranking whereby religious or other leaders gained social prestige by the control and demonstration of arcane knowledge involved. She identifies a form of 'masked' or hidden ranking.

There is little evidence from mounds and habitation sites of external relationships in the form of trade for exotic prestige or other non-perishable goods from other regions, unlike within the preceding long succession of cultures extending back thousands of years. Earlier Middle Woodland mounds and sites in the effigy mound region have produced a variety of foreign and exotic items, such as stone tools and projectile points made of fine stone from other regions, along with copper, silver, obsidian, grizzly bear teeth, seashell, and even silver (cf. McKern 1931; Stevenson *et al.* 1997, 157–66). Long before that, vast quantities of copper tools and ornaments were moved around in what is now eastern Wisconsin and the Upper Peninsula of Michigan between 4000 and 1500 BC (Pleger and Stoltman 2009).

The effigy mound peoples formed a distinct cultural expression different from surrounding areas that lasted for hundreds of years. However, after AD 1000 and, apparently, when some were still practicing effigy mound rituals, Late Woodland cultures became increasing influenced by the expansion of a new people from the south in modern-day Illinois, the Mississippians, who had formed a complex culture complete with a capital city in southern Illinois, now called Cahokia (Iseminger 2010). Artifacts from later Woodland sites show that the Mississippians lived among the Woodland people or that close trade relationships had been established (Stoltman 2000; Stoltman and Christiansen 2000).

Effigy mound construction

Effigy mounds vary greatly in size. Typical is the Raisbeck mound group in southwestern Wisconsin, the largest grouping of preserved effigy mounds where there are 40 animal effigies among a total of 125, including conical and linear mounds. The effigies mainly range between 62 and 181 ft (*ca* 19–55 m) in maximum length (Broihahn and Rosebrough 2014, 255–62). However, many elsewhere were enormous. The largest surviving mound is an eagle or Thunderbird on the north shore of Lake Mendota at Madison, Wisconsin, that is part of the vast Four Lakes effigy mound landscape (see Chapter 5). It has a wingspan of 624 ft (*ca* 190 m; see Fig. 5.7, below). A virtually identical but even larger bird, with a wingspan of a quarter of mile (0.4 km), once flew across a plateau at the large effigy mound landscape known as the Eagle Township cluster along the Wisconsin River in southwestern Wisconsin (Birmingham and Eisenberg 2000, 64–5). The mound had been plowed down by generations of farmers but mound researcher, professor James Scherz of the University of Wisconsin discovered a 1968 aerial photo that showed its footprint or soil shadow, along with other long gone mounds, appearing as slight soil differences with the surrounding land. Other mounds in the shape of Water Spirits (Fig. 1.6) and probable snakes have lengths of over 700 ft (213+ m). The 'Great Bear' at Effigy

Fig. 1.6 The body of a Water Spirit mound at the Regula site in southeastern Wisconsin (photograph: Kurt Sampson).

Mounds National Monument is 137 ft long, 70 ft wide, and over 3 ft in height (*ca* 41.8 × 21.3 × 0.9 m). In contrast, effigy mounds at the Kletzien Mound Group (deer, water spirits, bears) at Sheboygan on the far northeastern edge of the effigy mound region, are unusually small. Most are under 60 ft (18.3 m) in length and some as small as 37 ft (11.3 m) long and 20 ft (6.1 m) wide (McKern 1930). Obviously, the people associated with this remote site on the fringe of the effigy mound region spent little time in mound construction as compared with people elsewhere.

Whatever the size, the mounds tend to be so low that they merge seamlessly into the surrounding landscape and, therefore, are many times more difficult to see for the casual observer. Some erosion over time would be expected but most mounds were built in areas such as oak savannas where prairie grasses would have anchored the soil, greatly retarding erosion processes. While the mound groupings certainly represent territories of individual communities they would not have been highly visible to outsiders. New mounds are believed to have been added to groupings at intervals, perhaps annually or at some other propitious occasion.

The most common mode of interment within the mounds was in the form of disarticulated bone bundles indicating that the corpse had long since decomposed before burial, so it is apparent that the death of the individual was not itself necessary to stimulate immediate mound construction. Examination of the skeletal remains of individuals excavated in the past showed indications of both 'defleshing', where remaining flesh had been scraped off, and exposure to the air for long periods of time (eg, Cornelison 2013, 264–5). This most likely resulted from an initial 'sky burial' where corpses had been placed on scaffolds until the body decayed to bones: a custom well documented for Native peoples of the Great Plains and elsewhere.

There is also a high incidence of fleshed burials in a flexed, foetal position. However, even here there are indications that burial did not immediately follow death since some corpses are so tightly flexed as to indicate that some decomposition had taken place (Goldstein 1995, 114–15). In fewer cases, the dead were disposed of as piles of burned or cremated bone although burning had taken place elsewhere and not at the grave pit.

The mounds were evidently made by scraping the surrounding area with small hand tools such as celts and deer antlers to mold or sculpt the mound form. No large tools have yet been identified but these could have been made of wood that would decay and disappear. Barrow areas for dirt are not generally found around the mounds, and the scraping and sculpturing, as opposed to piling dirt dug from holes, seems to have been a conscious effort to conform the mounds to the local topography, creating the impression that they are rising from the earth rather than superimposed on it. It is often difficult to see where a mound ends and the natural surface begins.

Archaeological excavations of mounds, most conducted in the early 20th century, show that in some cases mound construction began with sod being removed in the shape of the intended effigy and that the following rituals extended over a length of time with the making of ritual fires. When inhumations were made, as they most often were, the remains of the dead were placed on the ground or buried in small, shallow pits. Other evidence of ritual activities are occasional arrangements of rocks and clay receptacles or 'altars', and ritual fires (Fig. 1.7). Large concentrations of food remains – butchered and burned animal bone – accompanied the burial of the dead at Kolterman and Nitschke I mound groups in eastern Wisconsin, suggesting that ritual feasting sometimes accompanied mound building ceremonies with the food remains buried as offerings (McKern 1930; Wittry and Bruder 1955).

While completed effigy mounds reflect some customs that vary from area to area, there are common ritual practices that demonstrate the sharing of ceremonial protocols throughout the effigy mound region (Rosebrough and Birmingham 2004; Birmingham 2010, 38–9; Birmingham and Rosebrough 2017). For example, there is a clear tendency for mounds to be built consistent with orientation of the natural topography upon which they were built (Fig. 1.8). Mounds many times orient roughly parallel or perpendicular to land forms. There is also a common tendency for animal mounds to be built with legs downslope, and with heads

Fig. 1.7 Cross-section of a typical effigy mound (painting by Amy Rosebrough. Wisconsin Historical Society Image ID 120472).

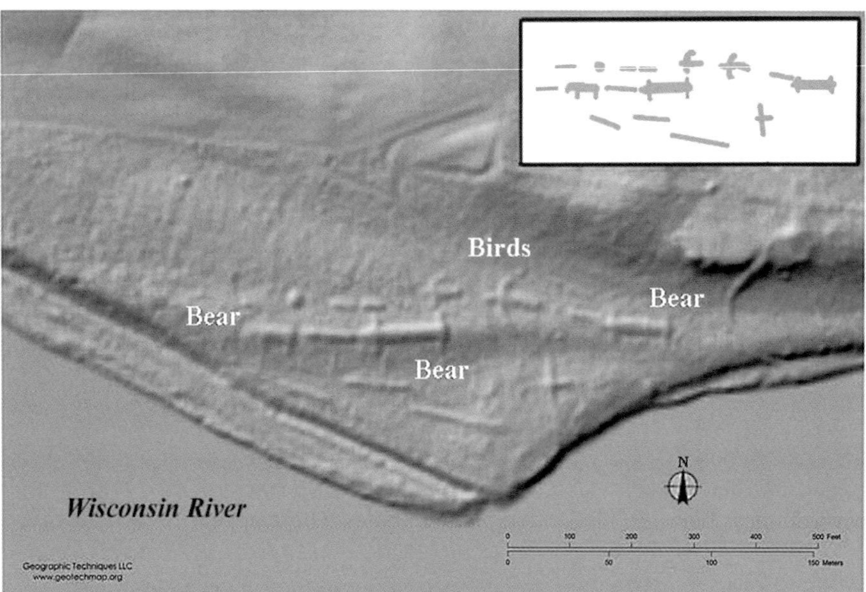

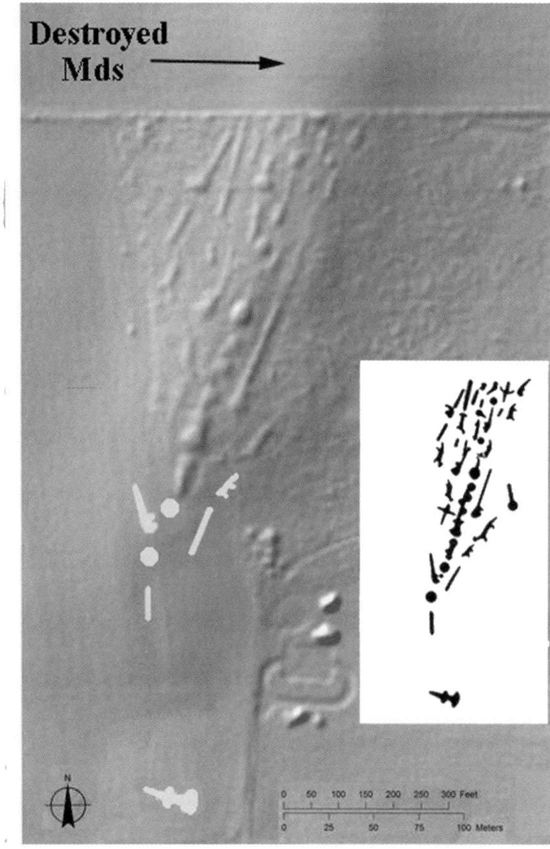

Fig. 1.8 LiDAR images from WisconsinView website (https://wisconsinview.org/) showing how orientations of mounds frequently follow the local topography. Above: the Twin Lizard Mound group along the Wisconsin River; below: the Nitschke Mound Group in southeastern Wisconsin.

downstream when located along streams and rivers. Adding to these patterns is the insight that effigy mound forms throughout the region were made in two perspectives, either in profile or flattened, as though looking down on the form, or up in the case of flying birds (Hall 1993; Birmingham 2010; Fig. 1.9). Under what circumstances a certain perspective was chosen is uncertain and an interesting area of future research but this common pattern, along with the others, argues strongly for the existence of religious practitioners such as a region-wide medicine society whose members, as in more recent times, would have been invested with the types of arcane and undoubtedly sacred knowledge necessary to undertake the proper rituals.

Conical and short linear mounds are commonly found in effigy mound groups and, in the case of conicals, are often more numerous than the effigies. At some sites, larger conical mounds were constructed in much earlier times. In other cases, such as at the Raisbeck, Kratz, and Nitschke mound groups in Wisconsin, single conical mounds located at prominent locations within the mound groupings covered mass burials of individual bone bundles. These appear to have initiated

Fig. 1.9 Examples of profiled and aerial perspectives of effigy mounds.

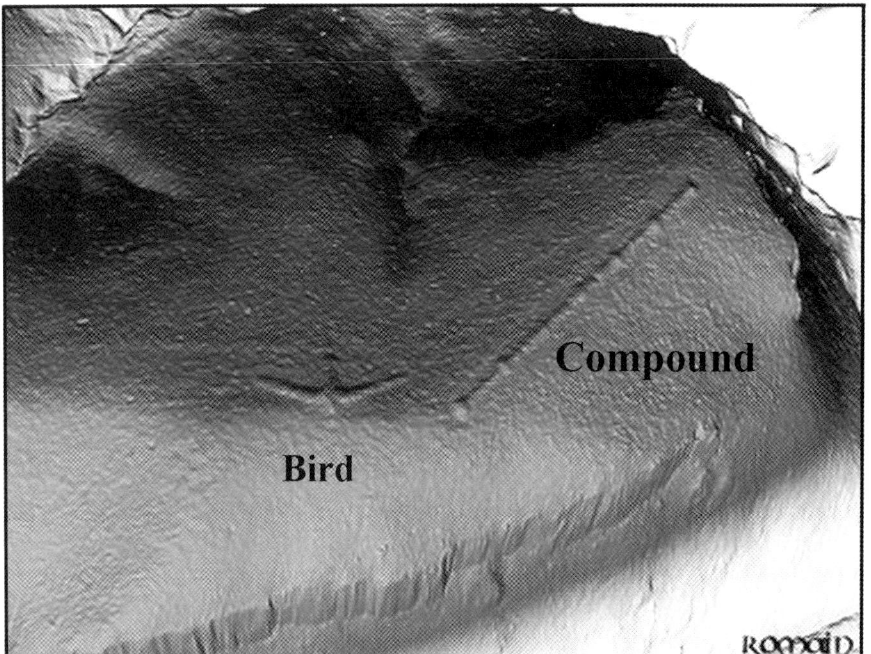

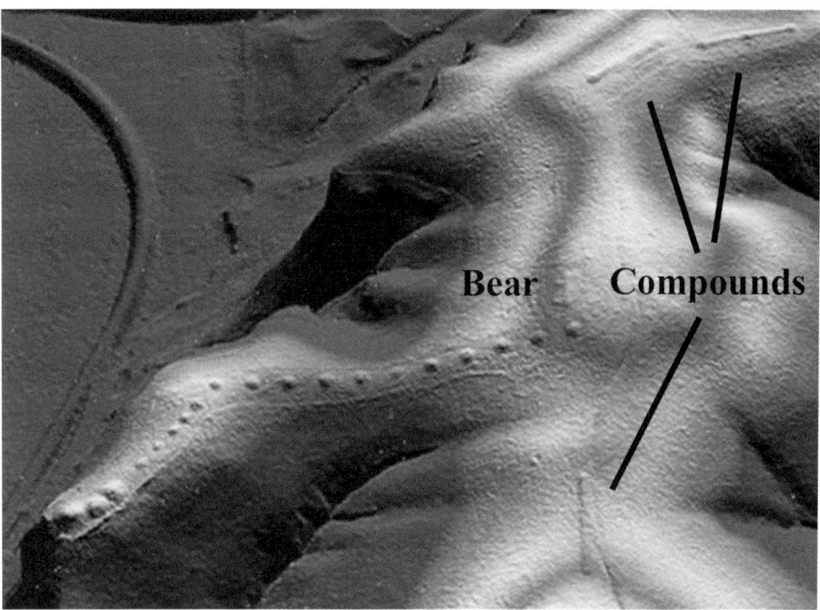

Fig. 1.10 LiDAR images of chain or compound mounds at Effigy Mounds National Monument. Above: showing seven joined conical mounds; below: compound mounds with three linked conicals (courtesy of William Romain).

new mound construction as the Effigy Mound Ceremonial Complex expanded into locations not previously used for mound building or cemeteries. The dead had been taken from previous resting places to establish a new place for the ancestors, linking people to the new land. Numerous smaller, conical burial mounds with fewer burials are frequently arranged in lines or otherwise segregated from the effigy mounds at the highest or most prominent locations, indicating a different ceremonial function and/or status of those interred.

Among the most mysterious of mound forms are compound mounds – strings of small conical mounds jointed by linear ridges – believed to have been built in the initial phase of development of effigy mound landscapes, which are found primarily in the western part of the effigy mound region near the Mississippi River, including in Effigy Mounds National Monument (Fig. 1.10). The number of conical mounds varies but most common are sets of three and nine suggesting that these numbers had special meaning (Rosebrough 2010, 1279–863).

Mound arrangements and distribution

Effigy mound groupings vary in size from just a few mounds to hundreds, although mounds in many larger groups have been destroyed by modern land use. Examples of the range of mound group sizes are provided throughout this book. Among the largest *intact* mound groups is the Clarence Raisbeck site in southwestern Wisconsin with 125 mounds, 40 of which are animal effigies (Broihahn and Rosebrough 2014). In the vast Four Lakes effigy mound landscape in south-central Wisconsin, mound locations range from single examples to over 50 (Birmingham 2010; see Chapter 5).

In 1892 Lewis recorded 900 mounds as the Harpers Ferry Great Mound Group on a sandy terrace of the Mississippi River in Iowa in the area of the Effigy Mounds National Monument. Most were small, dome-shaped conical mounds, but several were effigy mounds. If Lewis's count was accurate, it would represent the single greatest concentration of Native American mounds in North America. In more recent times, scholars have cast doubt on the existence of this great mound group or, at least, one of such huge size. Recent investigations have concluded that what Lewis saw was actually a landscape dominated by naturally formed mounds or Mima mounds found in many prairie area in the Midwest and other places, but also that Lewis may have suspected this because nearly all were omitted from his mound totals for Iowa (Finney and Johnson 2010).

The individual groupings tend to be located on high ground – on bluffs or terraces overlooking major rivers, streams, lakes, and large wetlands, where they are often associated with springs (Birmingham 2010, 38) – the sources of water and therefore life itself in traditions of Native Americans and other societies around the world. There are significance exceptions such as the Lizard Mound group in eastern Wisconsin, which is arranged on an upland plateau some distance from large bodies of water but, here too, there are springs in the vicinity. In some areas, effigy mound groupings are so dense that they form virtually continuous giant landscapes. One famous example is at the Effigy Mounds National Monument where groupings of effigy and earlier mounds stretch for 3 miles (nearly 5 km). An even larger mound landscape is a chain of lakes around modern Madison, Wisconsin, in the center of the effigy mound region where effigy and other mounds occupy virtually every high area along the edges of the lakes (Birmingham 2010). A summary description of that vast landscape is presented in Chapter 5 as a key example of a well-studied, ceremonial landscape.

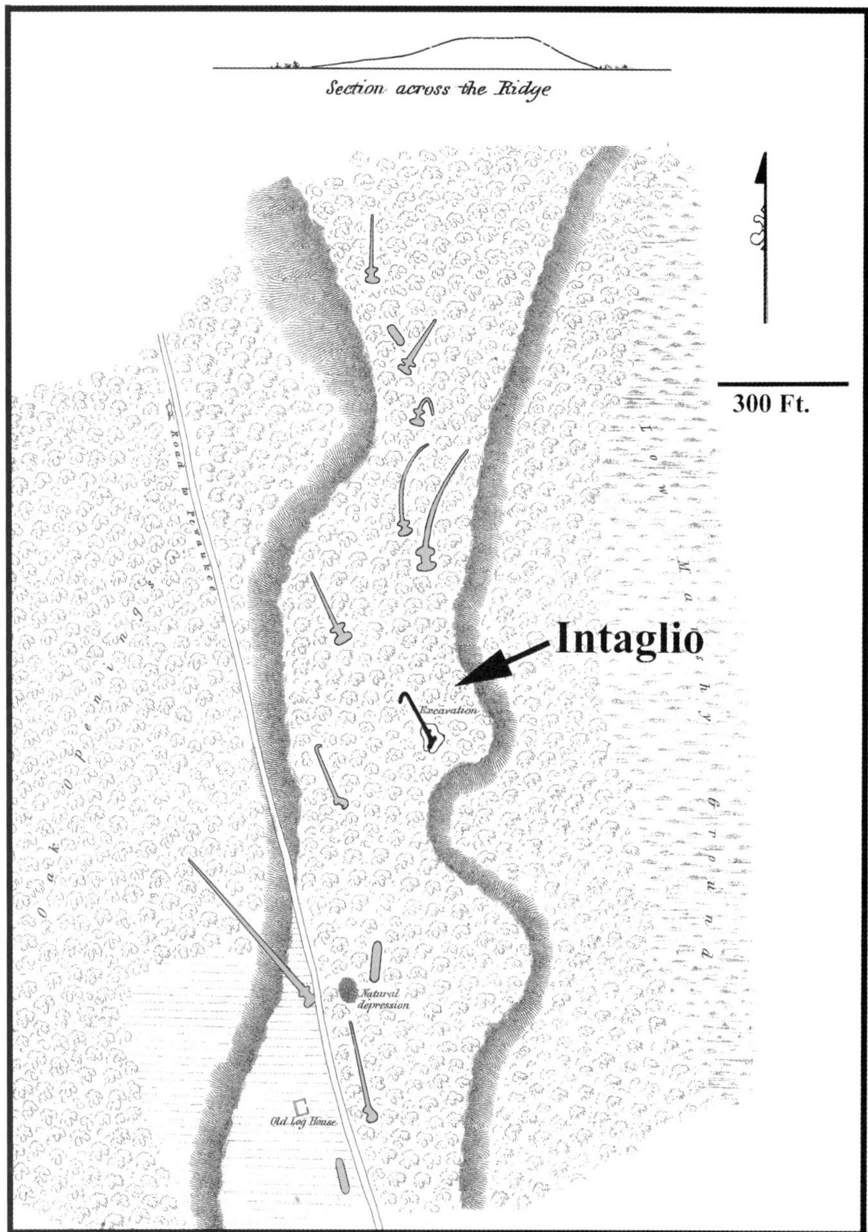

Fig. 1.11 Water Spirit intaglio among long-tailed Water Spirit mounds located on a ridge surrounded by wetlands at the School Section site in southeastern Wisconsin (Lapham 1855, pl. xxiii).

As with similar monument building elsewhere, such as the megalithic structures in Europe, England, and Ireland, effigy mounds clearly incorporate death rituals into the broader ceremonials. The use of the effigy mounds as burial places is only part of the story. The various mound forms are sometimes clearly arranged on the landscape to reflect the layered realms of the world they represent: air, earth, and water (or Upper, Middle, and Lower Worlds) and the forms themselves positioned on the landscape to animate effigy forms: birds fly up and down slopes and bears march across hills, changing direction with the topography as shown

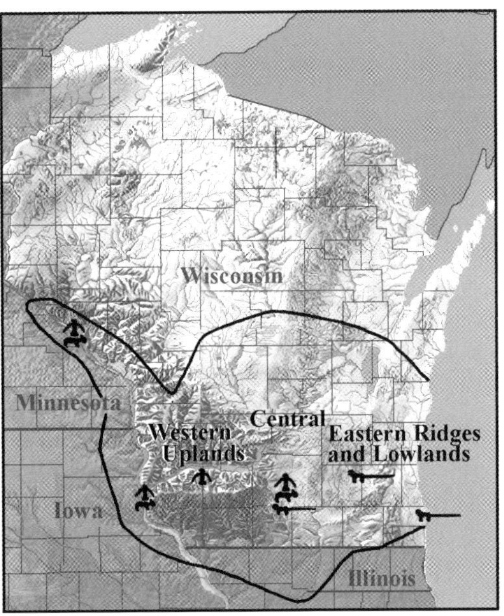

Fig. 1.12 Geographic sub-regions showing the most common effigy mound forms in each.

in Figure 1.1. Long-tailed Water Spirits crawl to or from water sources, as do long mounds interpreted as snakes also associated with water in Native traditions (see, for instance Figs 5.8, 5.31, 5.42). Further animation can be seen among some mammal mounds where the legs are bent as though the animal is walking or running (Birmingham 2010, fig. 4.1).

In 11 recorded cases, all in the eastern or central part of the effigy mound region, effigies appear in the form of non-burial 'intaglios' – the reverse of mounds dug into the earth rather than rising above it (Fig. 1.11). This further demonstrates that effigy mound landscapes went beyond burial of the dead and into the broader religious beliefs of the people who built them. Appropriately, most are in the same form as the Water Spirit mounds and Water Spirits occupy the watery Underworld in Native traditions.

These various types of ritual activities and systemic arrangements indicate that burial of the dead was only part of broader ceremonies and not the sole purpose; effigy mounds were not simply elaborate grave markers. Observing that effigy mounds were much more than tombs, the late Robert Hall (1993, 51) described them as 'monumental expressions of the cosmology of the builders and represented the division of the world into the earth/water and sky divisions'. He suggested that this dualism in worldview may indicate the presence of moieties in effigy mound societies – a two-part kinship arrangement with social rules requiring marriage of individual into the opposite moiety. Based on the relationship of mound forms to the animal and supernatural being ancestors in the beliefs of more recent Native people, as well as the animated nature of effigy mound landscapes, it is further proposed that effigy mound ceremonial landscapes were perceived by their builders as *living* landscapes derived in three dimensions from the underlying cosmological structure that comprises a worldview – that is, part of the cosmographic ordering of the landscape by which people sought to explain their place in the world.

The mounds may have been built for different specific ceremonial purposes but all generally included the burial of the dead as part of the repertoire of activities. Through the act of sculpting the effigy from the earth and associated rituals, undoubtedly supervised by religions specialists, principal spirits were brought into earthly existence at the places they inhabited to renew the world and, in so doing, the dead were also reborn into a spirit world, carried there by their spirit ancestors (Birmingham 2010, 201–2). In this sense, effigy mound landscapes can be viewed as places of continuous re-creation and transformation.

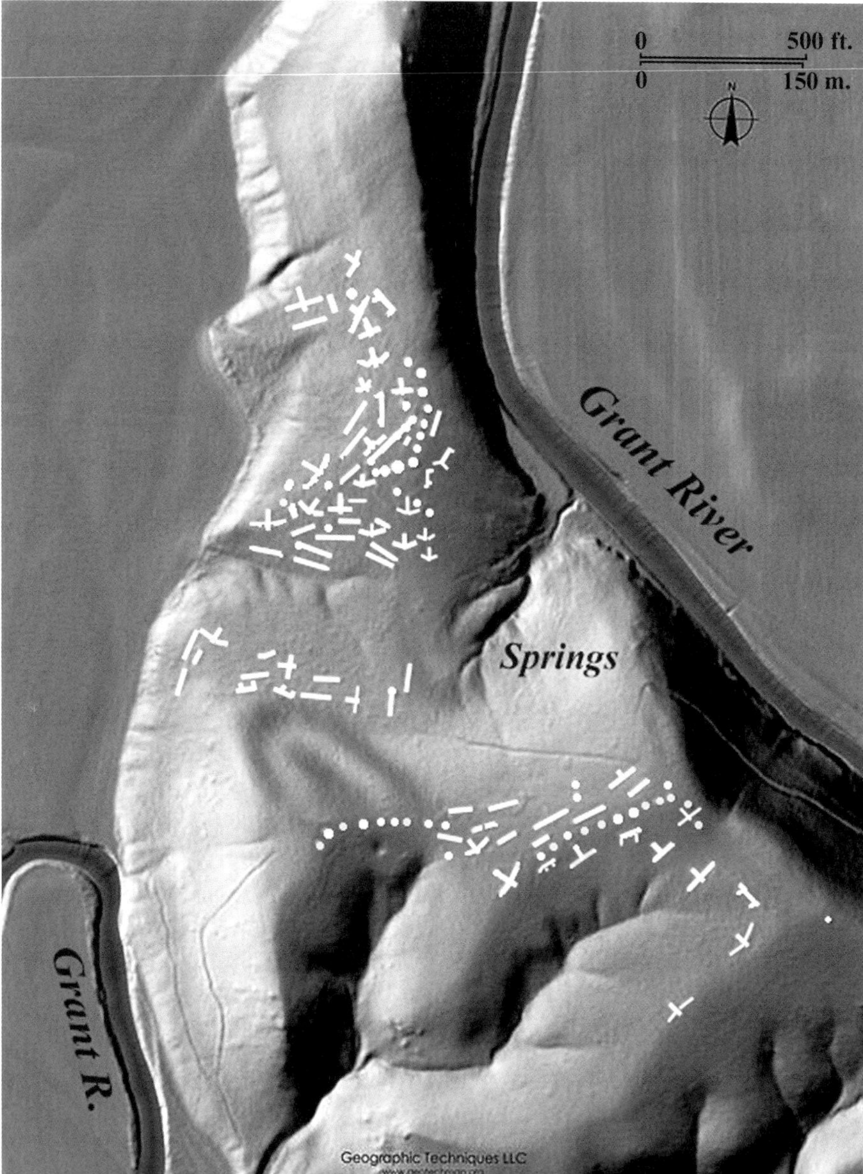

Fig. 1.13 LiDAR image of Raisbeck Mound Group in southwestern Wisconsin showing birds to be the dominant effigy form (© Geographic Technologies).

How these concepts were expressed varied in a mound grouping or landscape depending on the meaning the builders attached to local landscape features, but a very clear pattern exists in broader regional contexts correlated with major geographical differences. Bird mounds are most common in the central and western part of the effigy mound region, especially in the hill country called the Western Uplands or the Driftless Area that escaped flattening by the last glaciation (Birmingham and Eisenberg 2000; Figs 1.12 and 1.13). The association of birds with high places such as cliffs, bluffs, and ridges is obvious. Other earth animals, especially bears, are also concentrated in the central and western parts of the region, while long-tailed Water Spirits and water birds are most commonly

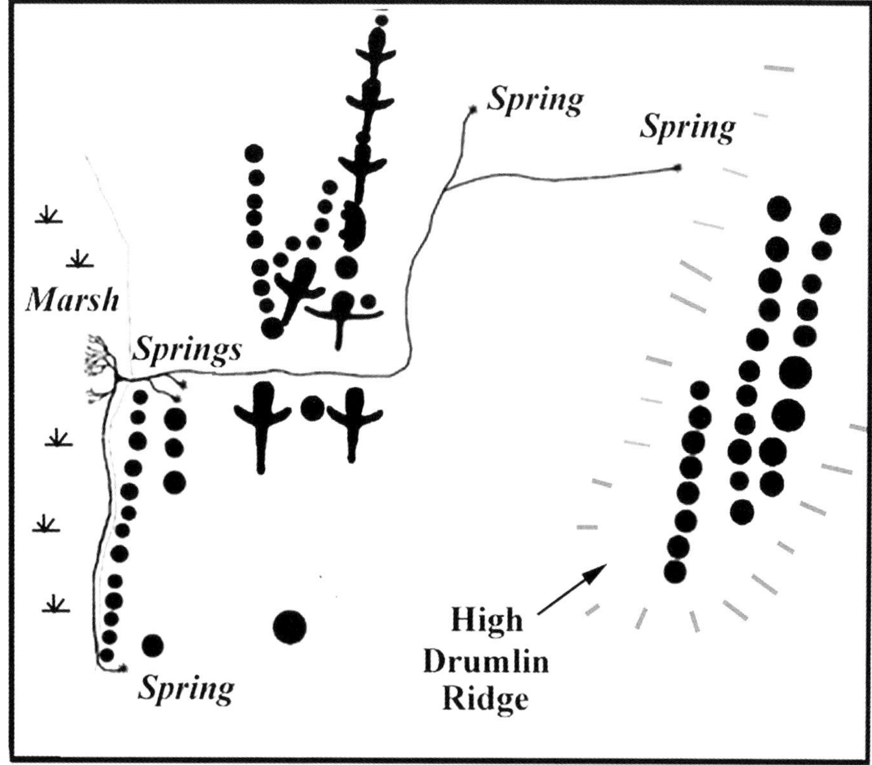

Fig. 1.14 A line of geese fly south at the Clark's Woods Mound Group along the Horicon Marsh in eastern Wisconsin (adapted from Bruder 1951).

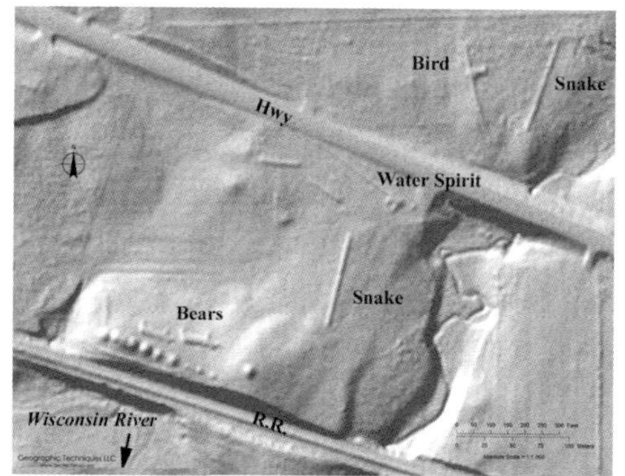

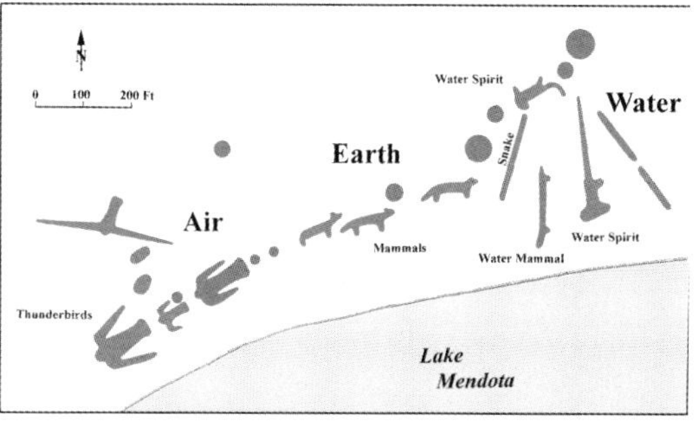

Fig. 1.15 Examples of the combination of mound forms in south-central Wisconsin. Above: the group on the Wisconsin River now owned and managed by the Ho-Chunk Nation; below: the Woodward Mound Group on Lake Mendota as mapped by T.H. Lewis, showing the underlying structure of effigy mound ceremonials with, starting at left, birds (Thunderbirds), earth mammals, and finally water-related forms that abruptly change direction to orient to the lake (see Chapter 5).

found in mound groups in the low lying eastern side of the region, now eastern Wisconsin, called the Eastern Ridges and Lowlands where lakes and wetlands abound (Birmingham and Eisenberg 2000; Rosebrough 2010; Fig. 1.14). The great marshes are today on the migration route of millions of ducks and geese (Volkert and Sampson 2023).

Within the eastern and western areas of the effigy mound region, the air–earth/water dualism observed by Hall (1993) is apparent in the types of mounds present in groupings although in different forms. Birds (often water birds) and Water Spirits appear many times together in the east, while birds and bears are the frequent representatives of the Upper and Lower Worlds in the western part of the effigy mound region.

In between these extremes, in south-central Wisconsin, mound groups containing a mixture of air, earth, and water forms - birds, bears, and other earth mammals, Water Spirits, water mammals, and snakes - are sometimes found together and sometimes spatially separated, providing idealized models for underlying and organizing belief structure of effigy mound ceremonial activity (Birmingham 2010; Fig. 1.15).

Celestial orientations

The curious and seemingly non-random arrangements and orientations have led some to conclude that, in some cases, mounds are aligned to closely track the movements of celestial bodies - the sun, moon, and even stars and planets. Such alignments have been established in ancient monument building throughout the world, most famously at Stonehenge and associated ceremonial structures in England and at New Grange in Ireland. Earthwork or other structural alignments to the movements of the sun and/or moon are strongly indicated in North America among the Hopewell ceremonial landscapes in Ohio and, a thousand years later, at the Mississippian city of Cahokia and other Mississippian sites, among other places (Pauketat 2012; Lynott 2014).

Only a comparatively few effigy mound groups have been studied for celestial alignments. A few mounds have been found to align to solstices that may or may not be purposeful but, overall, correlations are dubious, non-existent, or equivocal (Birmingham and Eisenberg 2000, 128–33; Romain 2013). One of the problems in detecting such patterns in effigy mound groups is that there are a myriad of possible sighting points and lines among the thousands of differently oriented mounds and their appendages, so that almost any alignment that one is looking for could be found. In addition, the presence of hills determines where the sun or the moon actually rises above the horizon, while the presence of tree cover would be a consideration in terms of interference with views and sightlines, so direct observation is necessary to link orientations to specific events, which has been done in only a few cases (Scherz 1991).

Celestial alignments have also been proposed at the Henschel Mound group on the Sheboygan Marsh where long-tailed Water Spirit effigy mounds and much earlier large, conical mounds are argued to orient to the solstices and equinoxes as well as lunar movements (Henschel 1996). An alternative explanation is that the Water Spirit mounds arc towards a former large spring, now a trout pond, as can be seen in Figure 1.16. Again, springs are abodes of the Water Spirits in Native traditions. Of course, the two types of orientations, celestial and earth feature related, are not mutually exclusive but the existence of an alternative explanation obscures proof of celestial arrangements.

Archaeologist William Romain, an expert on astro-archaeology, conducted a study of potential celestial alignments in the large mound landscape arranged along the high bluffs overlooking the Mississippi River at Effigy Mounds National Monument and found no correspondence (Romain 2013). Instead, he observed that the mounds closely followed the natural topography, often shifting directions with the flow of the land as can be easily seen in many of the illustrations in this book.

Astronomical alignments have been alleged for the Lizard Mound or the Hagner Group in eastern Wisconsin, now a Wisconsin State Park, that spreads across a low plateau in Sheboygan County (Fig. 1.17, top). The site was so named because early settlers thought that many of the mounds resembled lizards but these are actually long-tailed Water Spirits shown in the flattened or aerial perspective that is common to the watery eastern part of the effigy mound region. Some of these mounds are paired, as they are at a few other sites, but the meaning of these twins is presently unknown. Paring and a water association are also represented by two central water birds, geese, or cranes, flying away from each other. There are no 'terrestrial' effigy mounds but there are tapering linear mounds, one of which assumes a long, straight, snake-like form. The main theme of the group is a depiction of the Lower watery world.

An initial study of alignments by University of Wisconsin civil engineering professor James Scherz reported a variety of solar, lunar, and planetary alignments (Scherz 1991) but a review by a professional astronomer found that, while it is conceivable that a few linear mounds were used to observe or mark solar events such as the solstices, other conjectural alignments are arbitrary or, at best, not clear (Birmingham and Eisenberg 2000, 132–3).

The most recent investigation of alignments at Lizard Mound is by independent researcher Frederick Martin (2022), who used previous survey maps of the site produced by Scherz and an astronomy computer program to study the alignments and orientation of the group. He concluded that there are multiple orientations to movements of the sun, moon, the Milky Way, and a star called Rigel.

However, a close inspection of a LiDAR image of the Lizard Mound (Fig. 1.17, bottom) suggests that many of the mounds are simply arranged to follow the contours of the natural landscape: for example, running along low ridges and knolls. It is the contention in this book and other works by the authors that

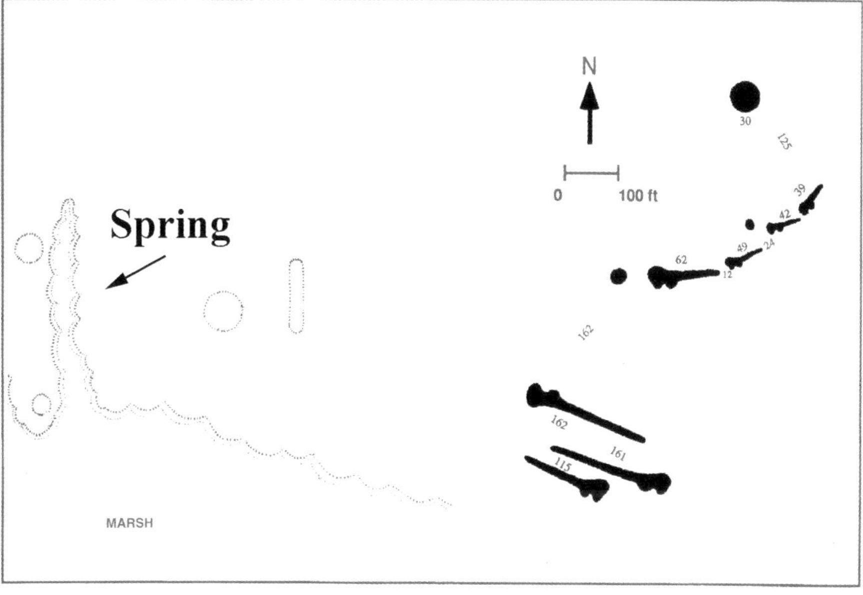

Fig. 1.16 The Water Spirit mounds at the Henschel Mound Group on the Sheboygan Marsh have been said to have astronomical alignments but probably the most significant direction was to a large spring, now a trout pond, that the Water Spirits are curving towards (map adapted from Gerend 1920).

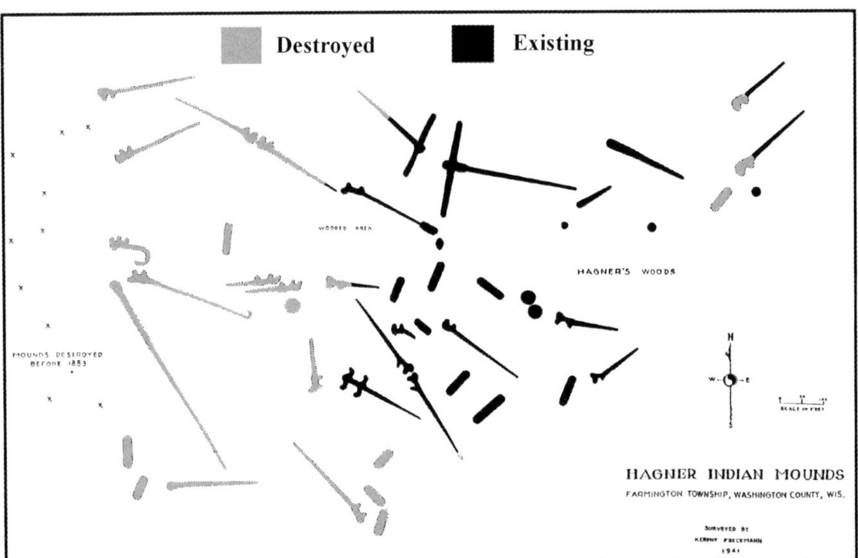

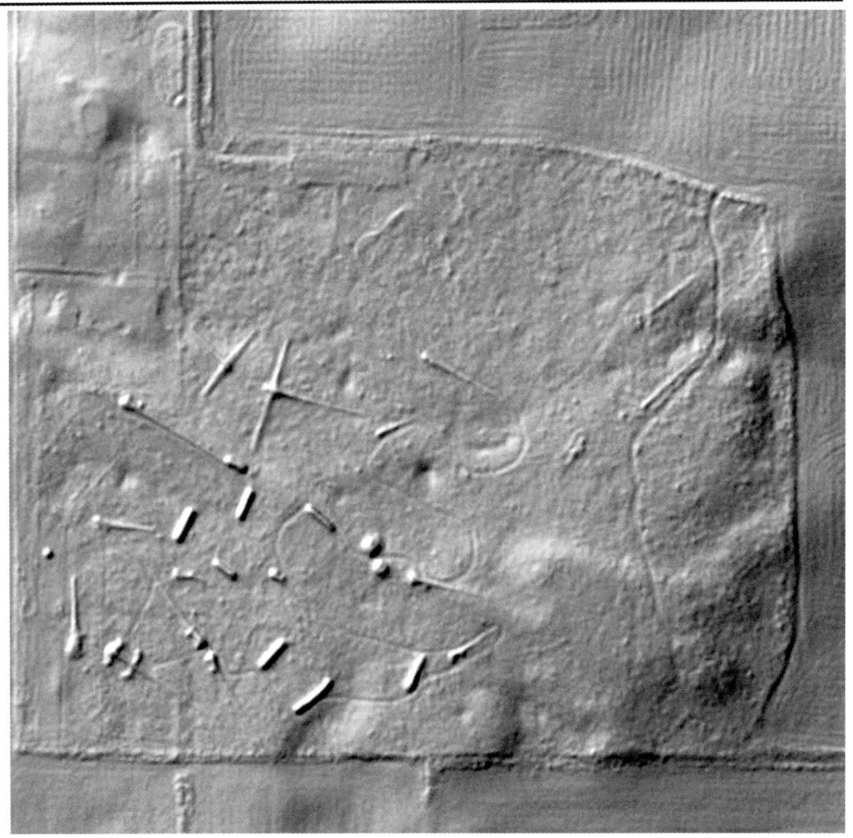

Fig. 1.17 Above: original map of Lizard Mound or the Hagner Group made by Kermit Freckmann in 1941 (Freckmann 1942, pl. 1); below: LiDAR image of Lizard Mound from the WisconsinView website.

it was the spiritual meaning that the effigy mound builders attributed to the natural landscape as being a reflection of their worldview that played the most important role in orientation and arrangement, rather than the actual tracking of the movements of celestial bodies in the heavens. Numerous other examples discussed throughout this book strongly support this model or paradigm. Obviously, it is certainly possible that mound orientations could be the result of both topography and celestial tracking but the hypotheses presented by Martin needs to be tested at other major sites where the same diverse orientations should be able to be replicated. Indeed, while celestial orientations for effigy mounds remains unproved or equivocal, it is important to note that such orientations have been established in North American cultures before and after the effigy mounds period, and that effigy mounds have very much to do with death and rebirth of the world that was observed by special ceremonies by peoples all over the world on such occasions as the summer and winter solstices. More professional research is needed among the numerous effigy mound landscapes to discover whether or not the Late Woodland builders were, at least occasionally, also ancient astronomers.

Native American traditions

Ancient Native people did not have a written language, so there is no record of knowledge concerning the meaning of mounds or their authorship that was shared by Native people who dwelt – and continue to live – in the Upper Midwest, except for oral history passed down through the generations. Such traditions may be considered sacred knowledge, not to be shared with the outside world. The Ho-Chunk Nation of Wisconsin, also referred to as the Winnebago, and their relatives who had been removed from Wisconsin to a Nebraska Reservation, most closely identify with the effigy mounds and generally believe their ancestors built them (cf. Radin 1923). Indeed, ancestors of the modern Ho-Chunk occupied large parts of the eastern effigy mound region far back into antiquity and mound forms resemble the named Ho-Chunk clan animals, although other Midwestern Native peoples also have similar clans. The apparent lack of specific oral history is undoubtedly due to the length of time involved and the great cultural and physical disruptions and dislocations created by European contact. Diseases like smallpox, for example, on their own would have killed a large number of Native people following European contacts, erasing much oral history. Some Ho-Chunk people say that the mounds provided spiritual protection for those interred or even that mounds were the result of spirit actions (Tigerman 2006, 47), ideas not too different from the archaeological interpretation derived from landscape analysis suggesting that the mounds were viewed by the builders as spirits animated or brought to life at places where they dwelt (Birmingham 2010).

The rise and demise of the effigy mound tradition

The appearance of the effigy mound phenomenon is rather abrupt in the archaeological record of the Upper Midwest but the underlying structure of beliefs represented by the forms had already been present for a long time before. Aside from great supernatural celestial birds and Water Spirits, long a part of cosmology of Native North Americans, the bear is a common mound form and its presence can be traced to the preceding Middle Woodland period associated with the spread of the Hopewell ceremonial movement from Ohio, in which the bear played a prominent ceremonial role (Lynott 2014). While rooted in a pre-existing belief structure, the stimulus for sculpting these beliefs from the ground in time consuming and labor intensive efforts remains a mystery, although some thoughts are provided in this book. After the collapse of Hopewell, with its vast trade networks, the Effigy Mound Ceremonial Complex grew from a Hopewell ideological base as a regional, unifying process as populations greatly increased in the Upper Midwest but without external trade networks.

The demise of the effigy mound tradition is correlated with a highly dynamic period of cultural and climatic events that help explain the end of this custom by *ca* AD 1200. Most notably, after AD 1000, the complex and agriculturally based Mississippian Tradition began expanding into the effigy mound region from the south, engendering profound changes to the Late Woodland people living there through cultural contact. Among current hypotheses is that Late Woodland people became 'Mississippianized', resulting in a new, third cultural entity broadly called Oneota, who were village based farmers that did not engage in mound building to any great extent (Stoltman 2000; Stoltman and Christiansen 2000). Some of the earlier Oneota ceramics, quite different from Late Woodland ceramics, even bear decorations similar to that found on Mississippian vessels. Another view is that the Mississippians displaced or even exterminated the Late Woodland people, and that Oneota developed independently in the Midwest after 1000 and become prominent in the region as the Mississippian culture collapsed (Overstreet *et al.* 2000).

Whatever the case, both the Late Woodland and Mississippian traditions disappear from the Midwest between 1200 and 1300 and this is further correlated with climate change. At the same time, many areas of the Southwest were becoming depopulated through the collapse of subsistence regimes and an increase in internecine warfare. The Medieval Warm Climate ended about 1200 in the Midwest and other parts of North America with a period of severe droughts that certainly would have greatly affected agriculture. This was followed by a phase of global cooling, called the Little Ice Age or Neo-Boreal, lasting to the 1500s (Bryson and Bryson 2000). Although other factors must certainly have been involved, the great Mississippian city of Cahokia was abandoned at this time and the Mississippian civilization in the northern part of what is now the United States disappeared. But Mississippian cultural traditions continued in the American southeast through to European contact. The only cultural tradition present through this time in the former effigy mound region was the Oneota, and their villages are concentrated only in a few areas (Overstreet *et al.* 1997), probably where agriculture was most practical during the cooler time with vast tracks of land in between vacant of major habitations. It is almost certain that some of the broadly defined Oneota groups survived into historic times as the various Indian tribes the Europeans encountered in the 1600s, such as the Ho-Chunk and their close relatives the Ioway, as well as several other tribes. In many cases direct connections have been difficult to make because of the social dynamics and population decimation stimulated by European contacts.

Reconstructing effigy mound landscapes

Most effigy mounds – an estimated 80% – have been destroyed by modern development and especially farming, but hundreds still remain due to preservation efforts throughout the 20th and 21st centuries. Further, nearly 150 years of research by both amateurs and professionals has left behind hundreds of maps of mound groupings long gone that, along with existing effigy mounds, provide important information from which large areas of the ceremonial landscapes can be reconstructed. Modern archaeological and broader anthropological research is contributing to the understanding of the effigy mound cultures and even providing insights into the meaning of mounds for those who made them. But, as the adage goes, 'much more is yet to be learned'.

2

The history of effigy mound research

Our knowledge of effigy mounds comes from over 150 years of archaeological research by explorers, antiquarians, amateurs, and professional archaeologists (Birmingham and Eisenberg 2000; Birmingham 2010; Birmingham and Rosebrough 2017). Ancient effigy mounds first came to the general public attention in the late 1830s as the Native people were formally removed from the region to western reservations on designated 'Indian land' in the Great Plains, opening up new lands for white settlement. The *Indian Removal Act* that was signed into law in 1830 by President Andrew Jackson sought to separate Native populations from increasing white settlement in the east, both because of the need for new lands and the conflict that settlement pressure was creating with and between the indigenous people. Explorers, land surveyors, and new settlers found a variety of complex earthworks that were perplexing because Native populations, who by then had been decimated by disease, conflict, and frequent relocations, were viewed as a primitive and inferior race, incapable of such sophistication that spoke of 'civilized' people.

From the start, four major and interrelated questions emerged concerning the huge numbers of effigy mounds encountered in the Upper Midwest: who made them? when were they made? what did the effigies represent? why were they built? Modern research has answered these questions in the broader level but more narrow issues concerning each have also been raised. In the beginning the questions were very basic, stemming from the facts that there was no way to date the mounds, the prehistory of the Americas was unknown, and many even believed that Indian people could not have been involved. Native traditions were largely unknown and generally were not examined for clues. There was also no concept of deep time and cultural changes involved in North American prehistory, or even the rest of the world for that matter, so all prehistory and history occurred in a short span of time. The concept of cultural change and even human physical evolution through time was part of a prominent worldview that was largely derived from a Christian reading of biblical sources which infamously, according to the calculations of Bishop James Ussher (1581–1656), saw the creation as occurring at 6 pm on 22 October 4004 BC (*Oxford Dictionary of National Biography*: doi:10.1093/ref:odnb/28034). If the Natives did not make elaborate earthworks during recent times, there was no reason to believe that they ever did. Science, and an empirical view of the world, was in its infancy and even notions of change through time in the natural and cultural worlds would have to await the acceptance of the observations and writings of Charles Darwin and a host of early anthropologists and archaeologists working in the Old World and America.

Lacking empirical information and reflecting ethnocentric views that precluded a connection between Native people and sophisticated monuments, the newcomers sometimes conjured up instead legends of a superior race lost to history, killed off by the more primitive Indians and the search for this 'lost race' continued throughout the 19th century. A few did entertain the obvious explanation that the earthworks had been made by indigenous people, but of a race of Natives that were far superior to those living in the area in more recent times.

Many looked elsewhere in the world for the identification of the mound builders. The first publication of the Smithsonian Institution, established in 1848, concluded that Native peoples were incapable of building the elaborate earthworks found throughout the Mississippi River catchment, such as the huge complexes in Ohio, and that the architects probably came from Mexico (Squier and Davis 1848). Other candidates for the lost race included the Hindus of India, Phoenicians, Vikings, Welsh, Aztecs, people from the mythical Atlantis, and the lost tribes of Israel.

Early descriptions and speculations

The earliest description of effigy mounds came from antiquarians, land surveyors, and other curious people many decades before American archaeology emerged as a field in the opening years of the 20th century. Increase Lapham, destined to become a famed American natural scientist, first drew public attention to the effigy mounds with an article he authored in 1836 in a newspaper in Milwaukee, then a tiny town on the shore of Lake Michigan. Originally from Ohio, Lapham was a trained land surveyor who had been hired to plat new roads in and around the growing community and later took on other surveying projects in the region. Already familiar with earthworks in Ohio, he observed the ancient mounds on lands he surveyed made in animal forms. One particular mound at the present-day city of Waukesha in southeastern Wisconsin caught his attention and his 1836 article described it as a large 'lizard-like' mound. This was subsequently reprinted in eastern newspapers for an audience curious about the American frontier (Fig. 2.1).

Several other explorers traveled to what is now Wisconsin territory to examine mounds they had heard of on the frontier, and wrote about the puzzling earthworks. One of these was Richard Taylor, who published an article called 'Notes Respecting Certain Indian Mounds and Earthworks in the Form of Animal Effigies, Chiefly in Wisconsin Territory' in 1838 that was accompanied by maps of the mounds (see Figs 2.2 and 2.4). He characterized the curious mounds he found as 'forming a species of *alto relievo* of gigantic proportions' (Taylor 1838, 90). Taylor seems to have recognized that the mounds were built by Native peoples, but of a different 'race' than contemporary Indian people who he viewed as 'degenerate' and 'slothful' and who only recently came to occupy the area in a series of population replacements. Nevertheless, he offered the first reasonable interpretation of the mound forms, noting their correspondence to animal totems and clans described for many Native tribes. Might not these shapes represent the 'respective tribes or branches of the people buried in the mounds?', he queried (Taylor 1838, 104).

John Locke, a physician from Ohio and a notable early American natural scientist, traveled west into the frontier on a scientific expedition and took time to study the effigy mounds, adding additional observations and drawings (Fig. 2.3). He had read Taylor's work and his interest in ancient earthworks had been piqued with the vast earthen constructions in his own state now attributed to the Hopewell culture. He was so struck by the mounds on what was, at the time, the western frontier that he published maps and descriptions in the Congressional Records of 1840 and 1944 under the title 'Ancient Antiquities in Wiskonsin [sic] Territory' (Locke 1840).

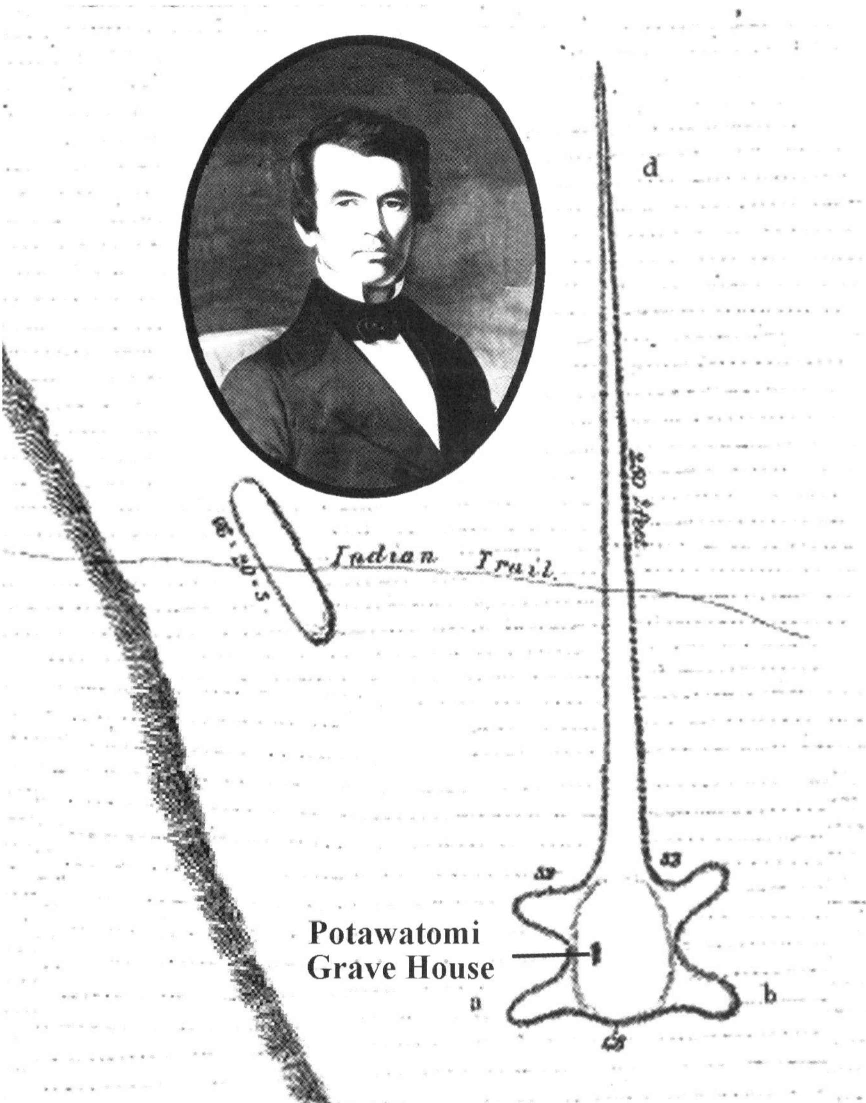

Fig. 2.1 Portrait of Increase Lapham from the Wisconsin Historical Society archives (Whi (W3) 17916) and the effigy mound he mapped at Waukesha in 1836 (from Lapham 1855).

Fig. 2.2 Location of sites mentioned in text (by Amy Rosebrough).

Another Taylor, named Stephen, a new settler to what is now Richland County, Wisconsin with antiquarian interests, visited effigy mounds in southwestern Wisconsin and published his maps and thoughts in 1843 in the *American Journal of Science and Arts.* Among the mounds he sketched were those now attributed to the vast effigy mound landscape called the Eagle Township cluster or locality on the north side of the Wisconsin River (Fig. 2.3). He also made inquiries about the mounds among Native people he occasional encountered and wrote that they mainly 'expressed total ignorance' about the origins. One, however, offered the opinion that the Great Manitou was responsible. He offered no personal opinion on who built the mounds and when they were built but surmised that the mound builders had vanished (Taylor 1943, 40).

Increase Lapham continued his interest in the mounds with the volume *Antiquities of Wisconsin* – a landmark in North American archaeology published by the Smithsonian Institute in 1855, dealing mainly with the subject of effigy mounds he visited and mapped in southern Wisconsin in the 1850s. His accurate maps of the mounds are valuable today because most, even the mound he described in 1836, have since been destroyed by farming and development.

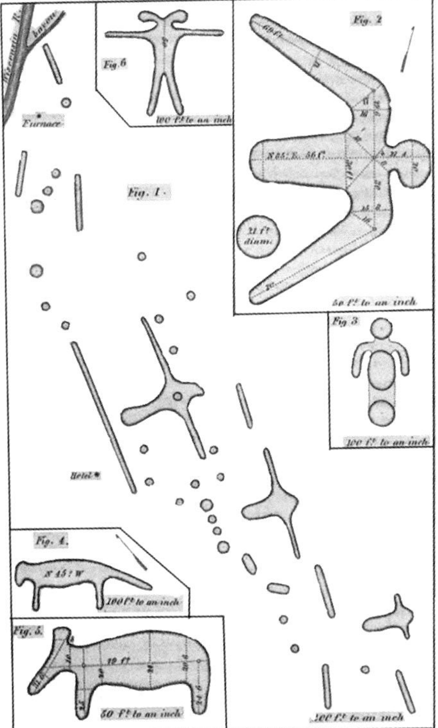

John Locke

Fig. 2.3 Above: Stephen Taylor mapped this mound group along the north bank of the Wisconsin River now known to be part of the vast Eagle Township Effigy Mound Landscape (from Taylor 1843); below: portrait of John Locke (courtesy of The Ohio Connection).

Based on what he observed, including information obtained by digging some mounds, Lapham was among the first who offered the idea, obvious to us now, that they were built by indigenous people, not a different race altogether. He considered the other lost race theories 'far fetched' (Lapham 1855, 89). Using the analogies of ancient Egypt, Greece, and Rome, he pointed out that dramatic changes could take place without replacement of indigenous peoples. At the same time, he also did not see a direct ancestral connection to the recent modern tribes who occupied the region who he viewed as 'little advanced in civilization'.

Lapham observed that Native peoples who had lost their land used the ancient mounds for burials and this pattern has been confirmed by modern research. On some effigy mounds, Lapham observed recently made graves covered by a log structure characteristic of the Potawatomi, who occupied southeastern Wisconsin until most were removed, along with the Ho-Chunk, to western reservations in the 1830s. Having lost their traditional villages and cemeteries these landless refugees would occasionally bury relatives in effigy and other mounds, which would certainly have been recognizable as principal spirit beings and clan totems (Birmingham and Eisenberg 2000, 173–9), probably with the thought that the remains of their relatives would be protected by ancestors and spirits.

Another land surveyor, William H. Canfield, settled in Baraboo along the Wisconsin River in south-central Wisconsin where numerous effigy mounds caught his interest. He noted that these interesting monuments were disappearing under the plow and needed to be documented. He used his surveying skills to make maps of mounds and mound groups in the area, still consulted today. Canfield was the first to map the famous horned Man Mound near Baraboo that is the last surviving human being effigy mound (Fig. 2.4). He also mapped another huge horned human found among other effigy mounds further to the northwest but this has disappeared under the plow, leaving his map as the only testament to its former existence.

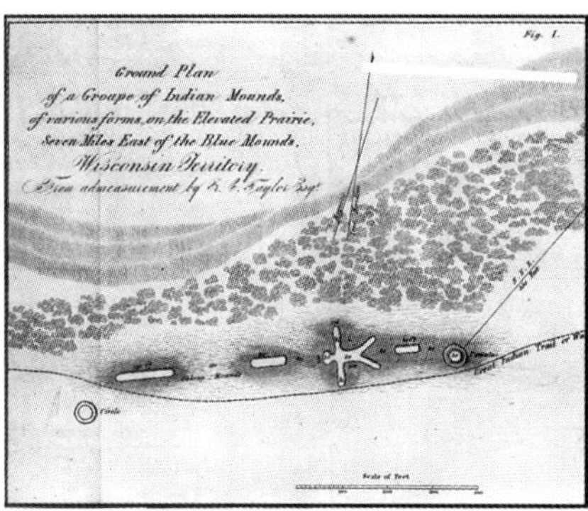

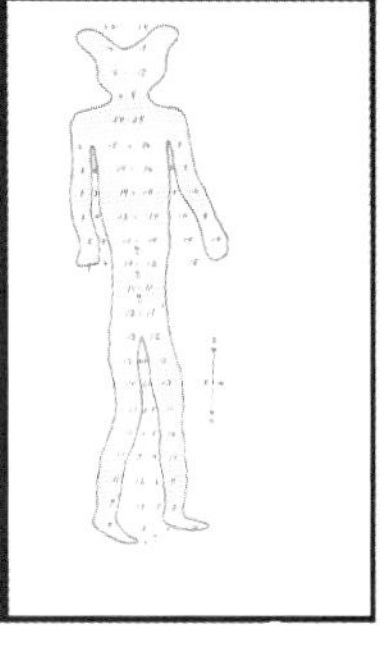

Fig. 2.4 Above: effigy mound group mapped by Richard C. Taylor on a high ridge in Dane County, west of Madison. The site has been destroyed by farming; below: Canfield's map of Man Mound (from Brown 1908).

One fantastical 19th century explanation for effigy mounds came from a 1853 book by William Pidgeon with the lengthy title common to the times *Traditions of De-coo-dah and Antiquarian Researches; Comparing the Extensive Explorations, Surveys, and Excavations of the Wonderful and Mysterious Earthen Remains of the Mound Builders of America; the Traditions of the Prophet of the Elk Nation Relative to their Origin and Use; and Evidence of an Ancient Population More Numerous Than the Present.* The book reflected the lost race explanation of the time, creating an epic, mythological, and often incoherent story whereby we learn that the mound builders descended from an indeterminate race, the 'Elk Nation', who intermarried with Native people and then vanished amid many calamities including a flood of biblical proportions.

Pidgeon wrote that he acquired his interest in ancient earth monuments in his native Virginia before he headed west to Ohio in 1829 to become a trader. He traveled further west in the later 1830s where he visited the new settlement of Muscoda on the Wisconsin River where he viewed large concentrations of effigy mounds. The mounds he observed are real, comprising a spectacular cluster of effigy mound groupings documented by later, less fanciful researchers in Eagle Township, Richland County, across the river from modern Muscoda, although his renditions of these were bizarre.

Pidgeon writes that he went to Prairie du Chien at the confluence of the Wisconsin and Mississippi Rivers where he met an old man named De-coo-dah who Pidgeon claimed to be the last member of the Elk Nation and who, as it happened, was descended from the very family entrusted with the sacred traditions of the nation. The old man revealed the secrets of the mounds and the dramatic history of the builders recorded in hieroglyphic form by the mounds. There are, he explained, mounds built during national festivals while others commemorate important events such as the union, extinction, and migrations of affiliated tribes. There are matrimonial mounds, battle mounds, and those that recorded the history of dynasties. Illustrations of oddly geometric mound patterns accompany the narrative (Fig. 2.5). Later mound researchers visited the very effigy mound groups that Pidgeon described and found little resemblance, broadly characterizing Pidgeon's writings as 'modern myths, which have never had any objective existence' (Lewis 1886a, 69). One modern writer on the history of Native American mound perceptions bluntly dismissed Pidgeon's narrative as a 'crazy piece of pseudo-science' (Silverberg 1986, 150).

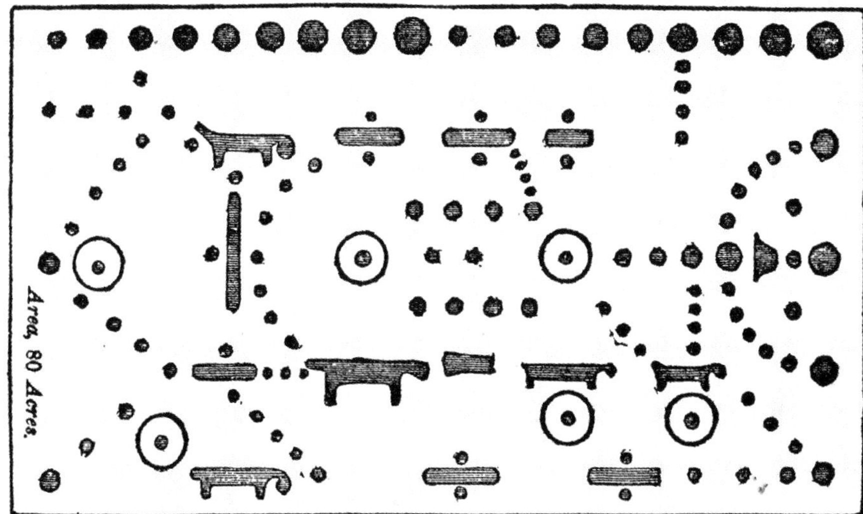

Fig. 2.5 Bizarrely patterned effigy mound group illustrated in *Traditions of De-coo-dah ...* by William Pidgeon (1853).

Stephen Peet, a minister from Beloit, Wisconsin had a passion for the study of American antiquities and founded a national archaeology journal, *American Antiquarian*, in 1878 as a 'medium of correspondence between Archaeologists, Ethnologists, and other Scientific Gentleman'. He later published the two volume *Prehistoric America* (Peet 1890). In these works, Peet contributed articles and accompanying maps of mound groups he sketched in south-central Wisconsin. As with earlier researchers, his work is helpful since he located effigy mound groups now gone but, despite his enthusiasm, his maps and descriptions are crude, impressionistic, and, in some cases, simply wrong when compared to surviving mounds and the works of later investigators. However, Peet can be recognized as the first to study the distribution of the different effigy mound forms that he logically attributed to different clans found among Native people of the Midwest. He identified 13 territories where he believed particular clans were predominant over others (Peet 1992).

While Peet and others were conducting research, the most extensive and valuable contribution to mound research in general was underway. This was the ambitious and unparalleled Northwestern Archaeological Survey conducted by Theodore H. Lewis (Fig. 2.6), another trained surveyor, who mapped thousands of mounds throughout the Midwest, the eastern Great Plains, and into Canada using survey equipment and techniques (Finney 2006). Lewis's work was funded by Alfred Hill, a wealthy Minnesota businessman. Hill and Lewis sought evidence about who made the mounds, continuing this line of research from early days. During the process, Lewis published a number of his observations in various antiquarian and natural history journals (eg, Lewis 1885; 1886b; 1889).

The Northwestern Archaeological Survey ended in 1895 but not before he had recorded and, in many cases, meticulously mapped over 13,000 mounds in 18 states and Canada, 900 of which were effigy mounds in the Upper Midwest. Most of these are now gone, making Lewis's work all the more valuable. The overall results were never published but his many maps and notebooks have been diligently curated by the Minnesota Historical Society (Lewis 1880–1895). The material was familiar to archaeologists in Minnesota where the records resided but remained largely unknown to others until the late 20th century. Since then, use of Lewis's maps and descriptions have led to the identification of many previously known effigy mounds and has provided details for hundreds of recorded mound sites for which there had been only vague descriptions.

The most important published archaeological study from the 19th century regarding the builders of mounds and earthworks came in 1895 with the *Report on the Mound Explorations by the Bureau of Ethnology* written by Cyrus Thomas.

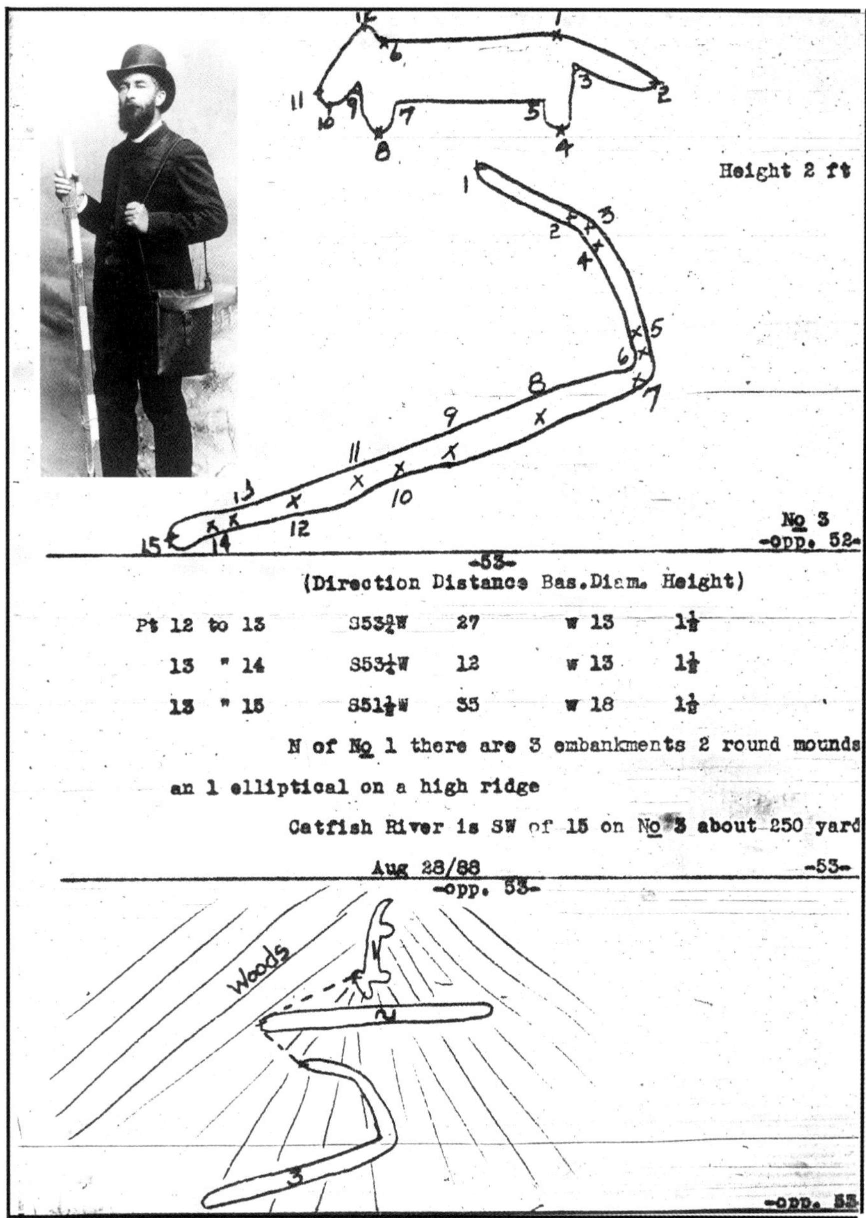

Fig. 2.6 Portrait of T.H. Lewis (courtesy of the Goodhue County Historical Society) and pages from his Notebook 24 of the Northwestern Archaeological Survey showing a canine, linear, and snake mound that are now a part of Indian Mound Park in McFarland, Wisconsin.

The Bureau of Ethnology was created in 1879 within the Smithsonian, headed by John Powell, a Civil War hero and western explorer, to document the traditions and languages of Native people that were rapidly disappearing. Powell had previously argued to the United States Department of the Interior that cultures of Native people were sufficiently rich to deserve such documentation. Paradoxically, it was the US Government, the very creator of the Bureau, that was responsible for the elimination of Native cultural traditions and decimation of the people themselves that now required such documentation for posterity.

The Bureau employed the first generation American ethnographers to undertake this work and, in 1881, Congress appropriated further funding to create the Division of Mound Exploration, largely to address the question of who among the peoples of the earth made the numerous mounds since this 'was not abstract scholarly debate, but had its roots in the great nineteenth century campaign of extermination waged against the American Indian' (Silverberg 1986, 159–60). Proof that the Native people were only the most recent occupants of the land who had killed off a far superior race with ties to the Old World would certainly help legitimize American usurpation of Native lands. Cyrus Thomas, an entomologist and botanist from Illinois, headed the division and started off as a lost race advocate. Thomas and division personnel sought evidence by opening mounds and collecting information from antiquarians from throughout eastern North America who had also dug into mounds in their regions to examine the contents. Although flawed in some of its reasoning and methods of data collection, the 1895 final report provided overwhelming evidence that indigenous Native people had made the mounds, not some mysterious lost race (Thomas 1885).

But despite this conclusion, work of the Bureau of Mound explorations would come back to haunt the US Government 90 years later. The bones of thousands of Native people had been disinterred as a direct result of the great debate over the lost race and these were stored on shelves by the Smithsonian and in many other museums and institutions, among many more thousands from excavations as the focus on burials to understand the past continued well into the 20th century. Native people had always decried this disrespect shown for them and this matter reached a crisis point in the late 20th century when Native people demanded return of their ancestors and successively lobbied the US Congress for a law that would do that. The *Native American Graves and Preservation Act* was passed in 1990 'which governs the return of Native American remains, funerary objects, sacred objects, and objects of cultural patrimony to lineal descendants, culturally-affiliated Indian Tribes, and Native Hawaiian organizations' (https://www.bia.gov/service/nagpra#:~:text=The%20Native%20American%20Graves%20Protection,affiliated%20Indian%20Tribes%2C%20and%20Native).

Twentieth century effigy mound research

Now that the general issue of who made the mysterious mounds was settled, there remained questions as to when and why they were built. Also, there remained the matter of who among the modern tribes had effigy mound building in their ancestry. Finding the answers to these questions would require another century of research by the new field of American archaeology and others engaged in the broader parent field of anthropology.

Early 20th century research took several intersecting directions and approaches. One approach sought information from Native people themselves and was short lived. For practically the first time, the new breed of American anthropologists and archaeologists examined Native beliefs, traditions, and insights regarding the mounds as provided by Native peoples themselves. A second approach was taken by Charles E. Brown, who became museum directer of the State Historical Society of Wisconsin in 1908, and by Wisconsin Archeological Society (WAS), founded in 1899 and headed by Brown, that was dedicated to 'advancing the study and preservation of Wisconsin Indian antiquities'. Reflecting a growing interest in Native antiquities, similar archaeological societies were formed in other states offering artifact collectors opportunities to report and discuss their finds. Drawing upon a large pool of amateur archaeologists and artifact collectors, members of the WAS ranged through Wisconsin and beyond locating archaeological sites and reporting the artifacts found in them, as well as mapping Indian mounds. The results were reported in the Society's journal, *The Wisconsin Archeologist*, edited by Brown, the first state archaeology journal of its kind. In the early 20th century the WAS also launched a campaign to preserve the ancient places, especially mounds, that were rapidly disappearing as a result or farming and urban development.

A third approach emerged with the new field of American archaeology early in the 20th century that emphasized scientific and empirical data. Beginning with major Upper Midwestern institutions like the Davenport (Iowa) Academy of Natural Science, later the Putnam Museum of History and Natural Science, and especially the Milwaukee Public Museum, controlled archaeological excavations of hundreds of mounds in the Upper Midwest were conducted including a considerable number of effigies. Lasting into the 1950s, this great wave of excavations would help define the different prehistoric cultures involved in mound building as well as revealing specific aspects of mound construction and contents.

Tribal connections

While the antiquity of mounds was surmised, it could not be established since techniques for dating, like radiocarbon, were still far in the future, Therefore, the next question to be addressed was tribal identity of the effigy mound builders. In the early 20th century the spotlight fell on the Winnebago, more properly known as their name for themselves, Ho-Chunk. The Ho-Chunk are one of the indigenous tribes of the Upper Midwest that had once been a populous and powerful nation according to early historic sources and tribal tradition. The connection between the Ho-Chunk and mounds had been asserted as early as the mid-19th century when the WAS reprinted a 1829 newspaper account supposedly acquired from a Ho-Chunk chief that identified certain Indian mounds as burials of Ho-Chunk chiefs who died in battle (Haskins 1903).

A series of articles in *The Wisconsin Archeologist* in the first two decades of the 20th century promoted this connection with information gleaned from Ho-Chunk culture and knowledgeable Ho-Chunk people. One writer was George West, a lawyer from Racine, who was much interested in Native American antiquities and history, and who published an article on the identity of the mound builders in 1907 in which he related that effigy mounds represented Ho-Chunk clan symbols. Among other evidence, he described a ceremony observed on the Winnebago reservation in Nebraska during which small ritual mounds were made. West predicted that the hypothesis linking effigy mounds to the Ho-Chunk would be eventually confirmed as 'undisputed fact' (West 1907).

Arlow Stout, who would later in his career become a highly respected naturalist, and Charles Brown of the WAS, also took up the Ho-Chunk connection. Stout published the results of his own mound surveys on Lake Koshkonong and the Four Lakes region in southern Wisconsin as a student at the University of Wisconsin in Madison (Fig. 2.7). In one article he told of a visit to a traditional camp near Wisconsin Dells occupied by a Ho-Chunk family, the descendants of those who refused to be removed to a western reservation in the 19th century, where he inquired about the effigy mounds (Stout 1911). He learned that the Native people could identify specific mounds as supernatural spirits. One type of tailed effigy mound, referred to as a panther or lizard at the time, was a supernatural or spirit creature, a spirit that lived in water and came out at night. From this, Stout made the inference that other effigy mounds may also be spirit animals, the interpretation used today.

Charles Brown also conferred with Native people about their traditions, beginning in 1908 with a visit to Ho-Chunk camp near his home in an area that was, at the time, at the very the fringes of the city of Madison, the Wisconsin state capital. He subsequently visited with several men from the Winnebago Reservation who had worked with pioneering ethnographer Paul Radin, who had been collecting information about traditional Ho-Chunk culture on the reservation. Brown took the men to effigy mounds in the Madison area who told him, as they did Radin, that they represented both spirit beings and clan symbols. In one case, the men identified a huge earthen cross that Lapham had mapped earlier as the symbol of Earthmaker, the creator of the world that did not have a human form. Brown, however, acknowledged that some information about the mounds appeared to

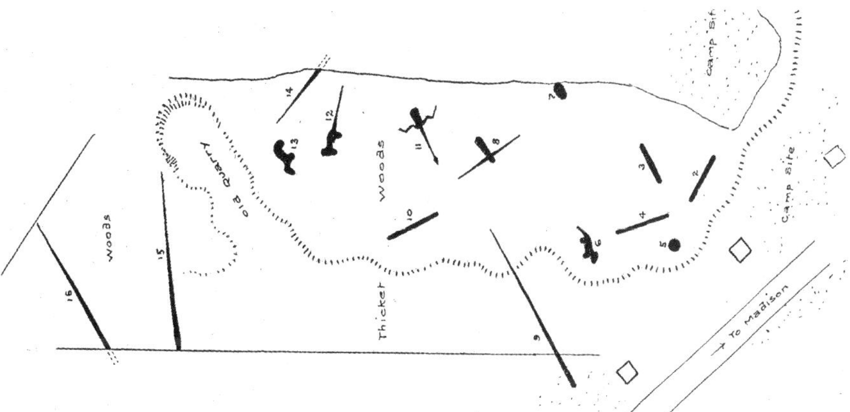

Fig. 2.7 Map of the Wingra Group (now gone) on Lake Wingra made by A.B. Stout in 1908 (from Brown 1915; see Chapter 5).

be simply opinions since they conflicted with what was archaeologically known about other mounds. Nevertheless, he became convinced that Native traditions and beliefs had the potential for providing key insights on the effigy mounds, writing that, at least, 'ethnological science may greatly assist in our archaeological history' (Brown 1911, 129).

It was ethnographer Paul Radin who most promoted the link between the Ho-Chunk and effigy mounds. Trained in the new field of ethnology in Europe and the United States, Radin was among the first of the American ethnographers to study Native cultures first hand. He joined the debate on the tribal origins of effigy mounds in 1911 with an article on the Ho-Chunk-effigy mound connection in *The Wisconsin Archeologist*, and subsequently in his monumental *Winnebago Tribe*, published as an annual report of the Bureau of American Ethnography (Radin 1923). Like Cyrus Thomas, Radin had worked under the auspices of the US Bureau of Ethnology and, along with other ethnographers, was charged with the responsibility of recording the traditional customs and languages of living Native people for posterity because these were disappearing. Radin did his work on the Winnebago Reservation in Nebraska to where most of this people had been removed from Wisconsin in the previous century. There he gained access to formally secret traditions maintained by the Grand Medicine Society, keepers of sacred knowledge and oral history not shared with other tribal members (Hall 1997, 64–78). Such knowledge, including that relating to world creation and the transformation of the Ho-Chunk people from animal spirits, was to be passed down verbatim, ostensibly without modification. Due to pressures of forced assimilation some former members had been converted to Christianity and abandoned traditional ways. As previously mentioned, the public airing of knowledge from those bound by secrecy is still a matter of great discomfort for some modern Ho-Chunk people.

Radin explored the relationship between tribal traditions and the effigy mounds found throughout the 19th century Ho-Chunk territory of Wisconsin and concluded that different types of effigy mounds were symbols of Ho-Chunk clans and this was affirmed by the Ho-Chunk themselves. He reasoned that the Ho-Chunk could only have been responsible since, to his knowledge, at the time of European contact there were only three indigenous tribes in Wisconsin: the Ho-Chunk, Dakota, and Menominee. Other tribes that later occupied the region, such as the Ojibwe, Sauk, and Fox, had migrated from the east in the early historic period. Since effigy mounds were not commonly found in Menominee and Dakota territories that left the Ho-Chunk as the mound builders. At the time, of course, Radin had no idea about the great antiquity of effigy mounds and huge cultural changes that had taken place in the Upper Midwest in the millennium since their construction.

A preservation movement

At the time that tribal authorship of the mounds was being debated, it was also becoming clear that the very objects of the debate, the effigy (and other) mounds, were vanishing from the landscape through farming, town and city development, and looting by curiosity seekers and artifact collectors. Modern studies indicate that about 80% of the estimated 15,000–20,000 mounds from all periods that once existed in Wisconsin alone had been destroyed before preservation laws were enacted in the late 20th century. This, of course, had the effect of eliminating monuments reflecting the rich ancient Native American history and revered as sacred places by Native people but also of limiting archaeological research.

Charles Brown and the Wisconsin Archeological Society aggressively responded to these threats by organizing a mound preservation movement, unparalleled for its time, and the legacy of these efforts are found in dozens of parks and other public, as well as private, lands where hundreds of mounds are preserved today. Brown, who served as secretary of the WAS and editor of *The Wisconsin Archeologist*, urged the Society to make mound preservation a priority. He developed and maintained a 'Record of Antiquities' – an inventory of archaeological sites periodically published in the journal that has since evolved into a sophisticated Geographic Information System database continually updated by the Office of State Archaeologist at the Wisconsin Historical Society. Brown communicated with hundreds of individuals to obtain information about the location of archaeological sites, especially mounds, and his voluminous records are curated by the WAS archives where they are much used by researchers (Brown 1872–1945, papers box 20).

In 1911, Brown led a WAS delegation that successfully lobbied the Wisconsin legislature for enactment of a state law protecting archaeological sites on public lands from vandalism and looting that remains in effect today. Remarkably for the time, Brown also convinced the legislature to make an appropriation of $1500 a year to the State Historical Society of Wisconsin, as it was then known, to have the WAS locate and map ancient places in the state, particularly mounds. The legislature also approved a small stipend for the publication of *The Wisconsin Archeologist* to report results. The WAS organized a special section, called the Wisconsin Archeological Survey, consisting of volunteers who fanned out across the state. The funding, used for travel expenses, lasted only two years but, during this time, hundreds of new mound groups were recorded and mapped. It would be another half century before public funding at both federal and state level would make this type of preservation work available again, although the small stipend for publication of the journal continues today.

Brown himself mapped mounds and recorded ancient village and camp sites in and around Madison with the help of talented and energetic volunteers such as Dr McLachlan of McFarland, who mapped and described a considerable number of mound groups (many now gone) during his vacations (Fig. 2.8). *The Wisconsin Archeologist* published lengthy reports on the mounds of Lakes Mendota, Monona, Waubesa, and Kegonsa mounds between the years 1912 and 1922, showing maps of many ancient earthworks for the first time. Brown and his colleagues were not trained surveyors and mappers so researchers use these with caution. Modem surveys and analyses of Brown's own maps show some discrepancies and errors in mound arrangements and directions.

The WAS established a permanent committee that worked to save mounds primarily by public education and acquisition. Collaborating with a variety of philanthropic public service organizations and local communities, the WAS placed historic markers and plaques at mounds on public lands as a means of

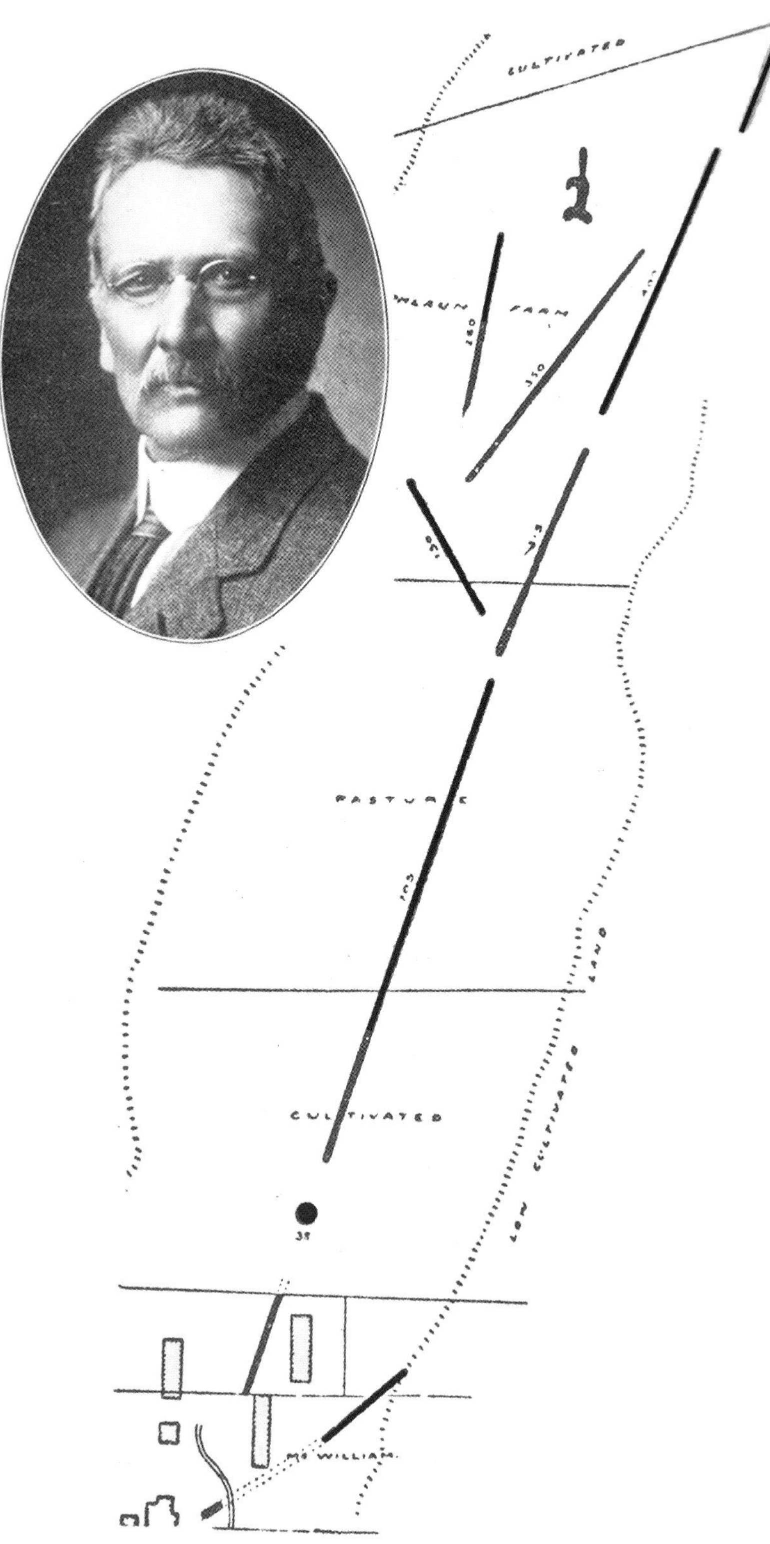

Fig. 2.8 W.G. McLachlan and mound group with extraordinarily long linear mounds he mapped near Lake Monona in southern Wisconsin (from McLachlan 1914).

Fig. 2.9 Left: Charles R. Brown and Albert Yellow Thunder who was the grandson of noted Ho-Chunk war chief Yellow Thunder and who frequently shared Ho-Chunk cultural perspectives and information during Brown's public mound tours; right: Brown (with cap) and volunteers excavate a mound in the Madison, Wisconsin area before it was destroyed by development in 1931 (Wisconsin Historical Society visual archives (Whi-38944)).

calling attention to the importance of these ancient earthworks. Many of these are still in place. By the early 1920s the WAS could boast that 500 mounds had been preserved in the state by its efforts. Among these were a few mound sites the Society purchased through special fundraising efforts. One of the earliest purchases, in 1906, was that of the famous, huge, horned Man Mound at Greenfield near Baraboo, documented by Canfield (1859; Figs 2.4, 3.17). The feet had been destroyed by county roadwork and this stimulated the purchase to preserve the rest of the earthwork. It is now a National Historic Landmark located in a county park and the last surviving human effigy of several that had been documented in the same region.

Brown recognized the need for public education regarding the uniqueness and importance of the mounds. He wrote articles, pamphlets, and brochures, and became a popular lecturer. He organized public tours soliciting the help and perspectives of Native people in educational and preservation work (Fig. 2.9, left). But as an archaeologist and student of ancient Indian cultures, Brown was naturally curious about the physical structure of the mounds themselves and how they fit into the archaeological scheme of things. Brown and volunteers excavated several mounds and accompanying burials in the Four Lakes, although mostly just before they were to be destroyed by development or to reconstruct mounds that had been mutilated (Fig. 2.9, right). Neither his training nor the state of knowledge of the time allowed Brown to gain great insights but his descriptions continue to inform present studies. At the very least, the bones of some of the ancient people have been preserved for anticipated reburial when they could have been ignobly pulverized by the bulldozer.

The great preservation efforts of the early 20th century largely came to an end by the 1940s as the Great Depression and World War II understandably diverted public attention, although Brown himself would engage in these efforts until his death in 1946. Systematic mound preservation efforts would not emerge again until the late 1970s. One major exception was the establishment of Effigy Mounds National Monument in 1949, stemming from a proposal discussed as early as 1917 to create a National Park along this exceptional scenic and wildlife rich stretch of the Mississippi River in Iowa that also had a large number of interesting effigy and other mound groups.

Mound excavation

Up through the end of the 19th century, the study of archaeology of the Americas was becoming more organized and scientific, leading to the professional field of North American archaeology. Earlier work determined that Native people made the mounds and other earthworks in past times and that the variations and differences observed in the archaeological record could be explained by the fact that the Americas had been occupied by different Native cultures. But no general or local sequences had been worked out except in rudimentary fashion and even the ages of the different cultures could only be guessed at, except for the American southwest where they could occasionally be dated using tree ring chronologies preserved in ancient wood timbers used in construction. Therefore, the establishment of chronologies of ancient cultures became the primary goal of archaeological research in the 20th century and a refinement of the sequences continues today.

In the Upper Midwest, the chronological sequence would eventually come from camps, villages, and especially caves and rock shelters where the ancient history of the region was arranged in neat layers but initial research by the new profession involved the unusually numerous mounds stemming from a traditional focus of archaeology on cemeteries, mortuary customs, and mounds. In Wisconsin, the heartland of the Effigy Mound Ceremonial Complex, professional archaeologists excavated many hundreds of mounds primarily between 1919 and the 1950s using increasingly controlled and careful methods and, similarly, mounds were explored in adjacent areas like Iowa.

Samuel Barrett of the Milwaukee Public Museum conducted the first professional excavations of mounds at the Kratz Creek Group on Buffalo Lake in south-central Wisconsin (Fig. 2.10). At Kratz, Barrett dug trenches into 36 of the 51 conical, linear, and animal effigy mounds, allowing for comparisons to be made between them (Barrett and Hawkes 1919). He broke from 19th century excavation methods by carefully observing and documenting the internal structuring and layering of mound soils. Although crude in comparison to modern archaeological procedures, Barrett was able to make some basic observations on the general nature of effigy mound groups:

1. mounds were arranged in a definite order and with reference to the nearest water courses and physiographic features;
2. mounds were not 'heaped' but built according to a pre-conceived plan;
3. all forms of mounds were used for burial purposes;
4. elaborate ceremonial procedures attended mound construction and burial of the dead; and
5. mounds were built by successive cultures over time.

Barrett's work also documented a local variation in mound building not found in the many mounds excavated later: some of the mounds at Kratz were built up with alternating layers of brightly colored sands. Samuel Barrett's research subsequently moved on to the ancient town of Aztalan in south-central Wisconsin, now recognized as representing a northern extension the great Mississippi Culture

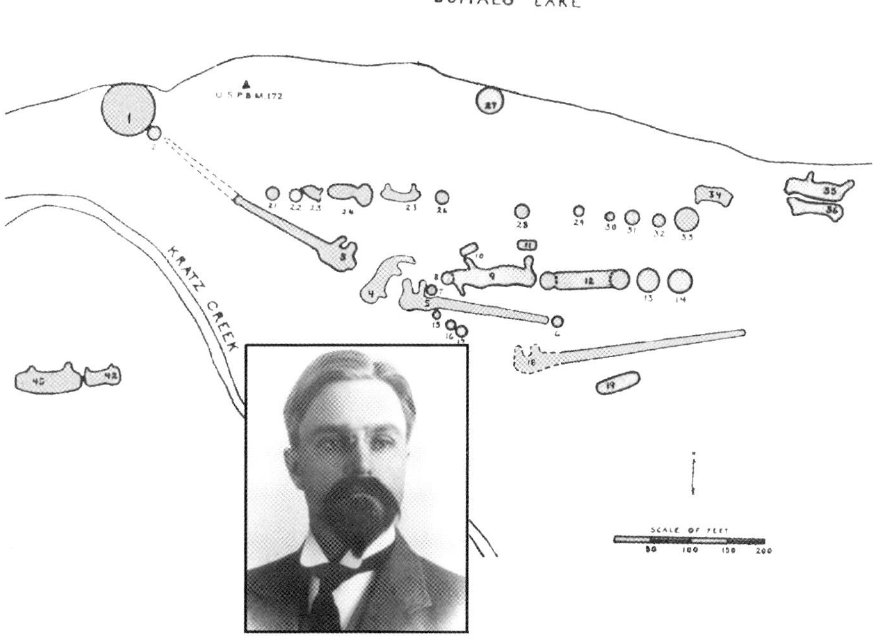

Fig. 2.10 Photograph of Samuel Barrett, and map of the Kratz Creek Mound Group (images courtesy of Milwaukee Public Museum).

Fig. 2.11 William McKern excavating at the McCaughry mound group that he mapped and excavated in 1925 (from McKern 1928).

in southern Illinois, very much due to Barrett's initial extensive excavations conducted in 1919, 1920, and 1932 (Barrett 1933).

The most prominent of the 20th century mound excavators was William McKern of the Milwaukee Public Museum. McKern joined the staff of the museum in 1926 and 'moved Wisconsin to the forefront of scientific archaeology' (Kehoe 1997, 13; Fig. 2.11). In order to acquire data on the ancient societies that once inhabited the region, he developed a strategy to excavate sites along an east-west line across the state, cutting across river systems and ecological zones, with mounds a particular, although not exclusive, focus. He subsequently excavated more than a dozen mound groups and several camps and villages from the late 1920s into the 1930s.

By the late 1930s McKern had acquired enough information to present the first classification and sequence of the ancient cultures of Wisconsin and the Upper Midwest based on similarities and differences in artifact types as well as burial customs: Old Copper, Hopewellian, Woodland, Middle Mississippian, and Upper Mississippian (McKern 1939). Pioneering professional archaeologists in Iowa, Ellision Orr and Charles Keyes, also formed similar classifications and sequences

(Alex 2000). However, these defined cultures could not be placed in calendrical time and, because only a few habitation sites had been examined, the lifestyles of the various peoples were unclear. These would be topics for new generations of archaeologists to come.

McKern challenged Radin's argument for a direct connection between the effigy mounds and Ho-Chunk, citing archaeological data that conflicted with what some Ho-Chunk had said regarding use of the mounds. He advanced a more objective, scientific approach that rejected the subjective information from ethnology and Native oral traditions, stating that 'When ethnological findings are in drastic conflict with known archaeological facts, I do not hesitate to insist that the ethnological data must give way' (McKern 1928, 463). McKern presented other archaeological evidence that, in his view, the Ho-Chunk *could not* be the effigy mound builders. Based on data excavated from mounds and a few habitation sites in areas that the Ho-Chunk once occupied, he defined two main classes of pottery. In the mounds he found 'Lake Michigan ware', eventually referred to as Woodland pottery, tempered by crushed rock and decorated by cordage that had been impressed in wet clay during manufacture. In the other sites he found smooth-surfaced pottery decorated with geometric symbols and tempered by crushed clam shell that he called Upper Mississippian, now referred to as Oneota. He connected the Upper Mississippian/Oneota to the Ho-Chunk, ironically based on information collected from the Ho-Chunk stating that they once made shell-tempered pottery! In his view the differences in pottery eliminated the Ho-Chunk as builders of the effigy mounds.

More recent research led to one hypothesis that would credit both Radin and McKern as being right in certain respects: the Ho-Chunk were indeed among several tribes that emerged from the Upper Mississippian Oneota cultures but they were, in turn, the descendants of the Woodland effigy mound people, who were culturally transformed by various types of contact with the Mississippian Culture of southern Illinois that spread into Wisconsin *ca* AD 1000–1200 (Stoltman 2000; Stoltman and Christiansen 2000).

In his 1956 book *The Effigy Mound Culture* Chandler Rower also eliminated the Ho-Chunk as descendants of the mound builders. The book, based on his dissertation research at the University of Wisconsin, synthesized the accumulated information on the effigy mounds obtained earlier by McKern and others as well as from his own mound excavations. The purpose of his research was to define the effigy mound culture by providing a list of cultural characteristics. As part of his study he examined the connection between the long asserted claim that animal mound forms represented Native clans by comparing mounds to lists of clans drawn from ethnographic accounts of various Native people who had occupied the Upper Midwest, such as the Menominee, Chippewa (Ojibwe) Sioux, Potawatomi, Fox, Sauk, and Winnebago (Ho-Chunk). Rowe could not find a good match between effigy mound forms and clans among these tribes and even dismissed the clan totem theory as an explanation.

Rowe was actually on the right track by examining social systems but his conclusions were limited by a lack of knowledge about beliefs systems that underlie Native social systems and he ignored the relationship between some mound forms

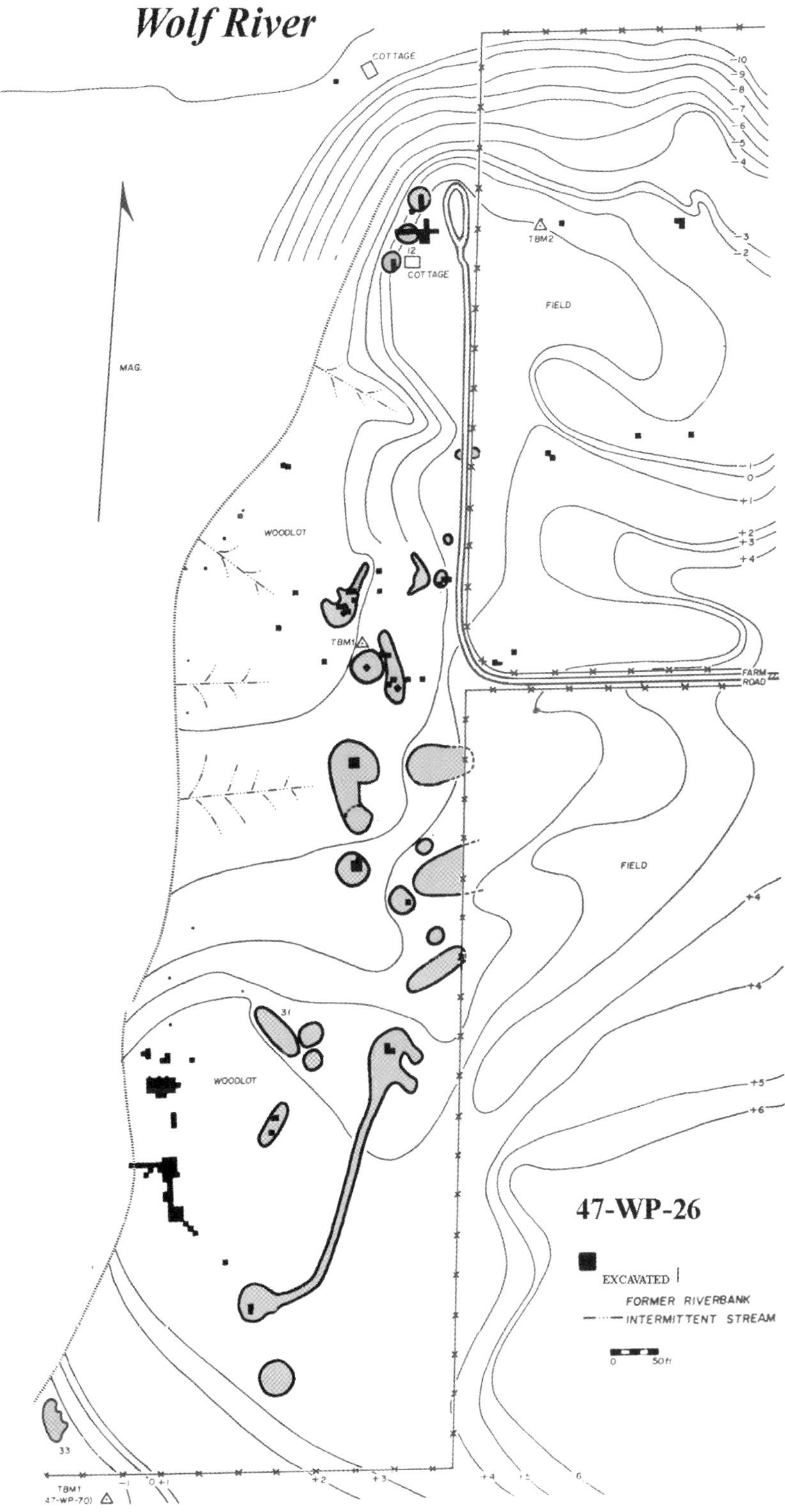

Fig. 2.12 Map of Sanders Mound Group on the Wisconsin River (from Hurley 1975).

and the principal spirits and clans of Native people, as established by Brown, Stout, Radin, and others in the early 20th century. On this basis Rowe's conclusions would later be challenged.

Placing ancient cultures in time

After World War II, returning veterans seeking college educations and supported by veteran benefits helped fuel the growth of American universities and these now became primary institutions for archaeological research. Departments focusing on archaeology and general anthropology expanded, from which a new generation of students arose that would pursue the past assisted by technological and methodological innovations.

Certainly, the most important scientific development was the use of radiocarbon dating, an outgrowth of wartime study and experiments with radioactive isotopes. Until the 1950s, the dating of archaeological sites in the Upper Midwest and many places of the world was educated guesswork largely based on artifact, especially pottery, typologies. Radiocarbon dating based on decay rates of the isotopes $Carbon^{14}$ in organic matter, often found on archaeological sites in the form of charred wood or seeds, as compared with $Carbon^{12}$ that remains constant as long as organic matter is preserved or until such point that $Carbon^{14}$ can no longer be measured.

William Hurley used the radiocarbon method in the 1960s to date the Sanders and Biegelow Mound Groups and adjacent camps in central Wisconsin (Hurley 1975; Fig. 2.12) from *ca* AD 300 to historic times. Apparently he wanted to avoid debate about tribal affiliation so he did not identify a historic period tribe he thought may be involved although he made broad hints at the Dakota Sioux who had occupied parts of northern Wisconsin at European contact. Subsequent study has demonstrated that Hurley defined the effigy mound complex too broadly. His evidence that it persisted into the historic period is not supported and actually his own dates from mounds themselves are between AD 600 and 1200, a time range that brackets the effigy mound tradition as currently known. Otherwise, Hurley contributed valuable information on the Effigy Mound Ceremonial Complex, including a detailed analysis of the pottery styles made by the effigy people, emphasizing the intricate and time consuming cord designs.

Camps, villages, and rock shelters

Even before Hurley's work, it had become clear that mound excavation and archaeology of the dead alone could not provide enough evidence to reconstruct the past, or provide the broader cultural context for mound building. In order to do this, research needed to delve into more places where people had actually lived to learn about the technological and socio-economic changes that had taken place over the millennia. And so eager archaeology students and their professors turned from mounds to camps and villages in the 1950s for clues about the past.

Table 1. Culture chronology of southern Wisconsin

Culture	*Date range*	*Characteristics*
Early Paleo-Indian	10,000–8000 BC	Big game hunting
Late Paleo-Indian	8000–6500 BC	
Early Archaic	8000–4000 BC	
Middle Archaic	600–1200 BC	Old Copper Ceremonial Complex
Late Archaic	1200–100 BC	Red Ochre Complex. First burial mounds, expansion of trade networks
Early Woodland	500 BC–AD 100	First use of pottery
Middle Woodland	AD 100–400	Hopewell Ceremonial Complex, extensive trade
Late Woodland	AD 400–1250	Transition from Hopewell, agriculture
Effigy Mound Ceremonial Complex	**AD 750–1100**	
Middle Mississippian	AD 1050–1250	Expansion of Mississippians from Cahokia/southern Illoinos, intensive farming, complex social and trade relations, monumental earthen mound construction
Oneota	AD 1000–1600s	Clan based agricultural villages along Upper Mississippi River, Upper Fox River/Lake Michigan, and Lake Koshkonong
Historic	AD 1600s–1800s	European fur trade, Native removals and/or resettlement, Euro-American settlement

Much of the new information on the cultural sequence for the Upper Midwest came from caves and rock overhangs called rock shelters in the deep valleys of the Driftless Area in Iowa and Wisconsin where glaciers had not flattened the natural landscape. Native people had long used these places as temporary seasonal shelters especially during winter deer hunts, as well as for rituals. Deer used the protected valleys themselves in winter to gather or yard in large herds and so the caves and rock shelters functioned as good hunting stations for humans. Use of these places over thousands of years left numerous superimposed layers that produced organic material like charcoal that could be now be dated using the radiocarbon method. Out of this archaeological era emerged a chronology of ancient Native cultures, that with some revisions is still used today (Table 1) and places the effigy mound tradition within the broader Late Woodland period *ca* AD 500–1200.

A new nationwide preservation movement

A nationwide concern that many important historic places and sites of all types, including buildings, battle grounds, and archaeological sites lacked any kind of protection led to the passage of the *National Historic Preservation Act* (*NHPA*) of 1966, amended in 1972. The concern for historic preservation paralleled that about pollution and destruction of the natural environment as a whole, resulting in legislation such as the *National Environmental Policy Act* of 1970 and the *Clean Water Act* of 1972. The *NHPA* required federal agencies to take into account and protect significant historic and archaeological places in their actions, such as federal projects, funding, and licenses. The measure of significance is whether or not a particular place or site would be eligible for listing on the National Register of Historic Places maintained by the Department of the Interior, according to certain criteria. A total of 45 Upper Midwestern effigy mound sites are currently listed on the National Register from Iowa, Illinois, and especially Wisconsin.

NHPA set up historic preservation offices in states with federal funds, matched by state funding, that are charged with the responsibly of establishing inventories of significant historic and archaeological places and providing nominations to the National Register. This was primarily done by sub-grants to communities, universities, and historic preservation organizations, and, in Wisconsin, Native nations. Some states, like Wisconsin, subsequently passed and enacted parallel legislation and regulations concerning state and other publicly regulated projects that modified the landscape.

It is impossible to underestimate the impact these preservation programs, broadly referred to as Cultural Resource Management, had on the understanding of the rich prehistory of the Upper Midwest. Thousands of projects, from the construction of roads to laying of sewers and pipelines, have been studied for their effects on archaeological sites. If impacts could not be avoided, as often occurred in the construction of roads and highways, significant archaeological sites in the zones of potential destruction were first carefully excavated to preserve information that otherwise would be lost. As a result of Cultural Resource Management, more archaeological work has been conducted since the 1970s than in the proceeding 150 years, resulting in complete rewriting of the ancient history of the Upper Midwest.

In the 1990s, the Office of the State Archaeologist at the Wisconsin Historical Society added to preservation efforts and the rapidly growing archaeological knowledge by developing a state-funded regional archaeology program in partnership with universities as well as the Lac du Flambeau Ojibwe nation in northern Wisconsin. Cutbacks in state funding for the Society eventually eliminated the program, but not before the regions developed specific chronologies for their areas and reported hundreds of new archaeological sites, including many mounds.

Growing recognition for Native concerns and sensibility, often ignored in the past, had led to the 'in place' preservation of mounds and burial grounds in many cases but important legislation also addressed the long standing claims that the remains of tens of thousands of Native people that resided in museums and universities and had been excavated from burial mounds and cemeteries must be returned for proper reburial. Congress passed the *Native American Graves and Protection and Repatriation Act* (*NAGPRA*) in 1990 that required federal and federally funded institutions to inventory their collections and return human remains and sacred items to the appropriate Native tribes and nations. It also required that the treatment of graves and human remains found on federal lands be directed by consultation with the appropriate Native people. Since this Act was passed, over tens of thousands of human remains have been returned for reburial.

NAGPRA, for the most part developed a new, positive relationship between Natives, institutions, and archaeologists as all worked together to implement the law. There have been exceptions though. The 1996 discovery of a 9000 year old skeleton, called the Kennewick Man, on federal land in Washington State created much controversy. Local Indian tribes claimed the skeleton under *NAGPRA* but archaeologists challenged the claim on the basis that the skeleton was far too old to assign a specific tribal association and, in any case, the rare skeleton representing the earliest people in the Americas was so important that it must be studied. The case went to court and, much to the distress of local Native people, the courts sided with the scholars. Subsequent analyses revealed much about early New World populations, sparking even more controversy about the concept of 'race' since the skull features of Kennewick Man are different from later Indian people of the Americas (Chatters 2001). Following analysis, the remains were eventually returned to a coalition of Columbia Basin tribes for reburial at an undisclosed location. *NAGPRA* regulations have now discarded the 'culturally unidentifiable' category, so that the Kennewick Man situation cannot be repeated – concerns of Indigenous Nations and their oral histories take precedence.

Many American states passed their own versions of burial preservation laws, noting that there had long been a difference between the treatment of Indian graves and the more respectful treatment of non-Indian cemeteries and burial places. In Wisconsin, heartland of the effigy mound builders, legislation created a new law that protected all burial places, even on private lands, including all Indian mounds. To compensate for loss of land for other purposes, a waver of state property taxes is provided for lands covered by burial grounds and mounds. This has also produced a close working relationship between state officials, scholars, and Indian Nations in a common preservation endeavor. Occasionally, challenges to the law have been made by commercial and other landowners on the grounds that protection of ancient Native mounds preclude other economic uses; these claims are settled in court and defended by state attorneys.

But, for the most part, the general public has gained a deep appreciation of Native history and culture and a new respect for ancient sites and monuments like the effigy mounds. Many private landowners take pride in having mounds on their properties and even make inquiries about the best ways to maintain them. Many communities own and maintain effigy mound groups that can be visited, thereby helping to emphasize their importance in the history of the land. The Ho-Chunk Nation has acquired important mound sites such as the Kingsley Bend Mound Group near Wisconsin Dells that is also open to the public. There are now books, brochures, and websites describing places that can be visited by the public. A selection of publicly accessible sites that best illustrate the Effigy Mound Complex appears as an appendix to this book.

An ideological approach to the effigy mounds

In frustration with the inability of archaeology to explain the meaning of effigy mounds, William Hurley (1986) wrote that knowledge in these regards had not progressed since the work of Increase Lapham over 100 years earlier. But even as Hurley wrote this, a change in the study of the effigy mounds was underway.

The late, eminent Midwestern archaeologist Robert Hall helped spark the change in 1976 by publishing an article in *American Antiquity*, the professional North American archaeological journal, in which he observed that archaeology had itself become a 'soulless artifact of a dehumanized science' (Hall 1976). He observed that the profession had focused primary on artifacts and other aspects of material culture as well as subsistence and economic systems to explain the past but had left out a critical element – the beliefs or ideology of the people behind the physical remains. He argued that, if archaeologists were to understand ancient people and cultures, they had to try to view the world as they did and not through the lens of modern European-American culture. He urged archaeologists to 'think in Native categories and to proceed deductively in this frame of reference' and that such frames of reference, or what might also be called worldviews, are accessible through the form of more recent rituals, ceremonies, and cosmologies of more recent Native people, recalling Brown's (1911) comment that ethnology could inform archaeological research. Hall gave examples of ancient earthworks that he linked to more recent Native beliefs about the supernatural (Hall 1976; 1979) and continued his lessons in subsequent publications (Hall 1993; 1997).

Hall defended his approach by noting that the general cultural processes that molded Native societies in the ancient past would be expected to be the same as in more recent times and, further, pointed out that the long and dramatic period of mound building could not have come and gone without leaving some clues in Native traditions that can help archaeologists reconstruct ancient ideologies (Hall 1993).

He also re-opened the debate about the Ho-Chunk connection to the effigy mounds. He challenged Rowe's rejection of the relationship between effigy mounds and clans by pointing out that Rowe had ignored vital information presented earlier in the century by Stout, Brown, and Radin, in that among the most common effigy forms was a long-tailed panther (Brown 1936) equivalent to the Water Spirits and Underground Water Panthers found in the cosmology and clan systems of the Ho-Chunk and other tribes. Rowe had also failed to see the rather obvious connections between Thunderer clans, found in many tribes, and the especially powerful, invisible spirits called Thunderbirds because they make thunder by flapping their giant wings. Hall did not assert that the Ho-Chunk had made effigy mounds but argued that Rowe had failed to prove that they did not. Whether or not effigy mounds represent social systems, Hall's analysis that there are spirits of the air, earth, and water in Native traditions led to the important conclusion that effigy mound groupings are 'monumental constructions of the cosmology of their builders and represent the division of the world into earth/water divisions' (Hall 1993, 51).

Other archaeologists have increasingly come to the conclusion that the many types of traditional analyses failed to explain cultural processes completely and thus were getting old, so to speak. Many have adopted an ideological approach to explain monument building in the Americas and other places in the world, as well as the meaning of other symbols such as the long inscrutable ancient paintings and carvings found on many rock faces and in caves, referred to as rock art. From this comes the important insight that, in many cases, an understanding about what ancient people built or made requires an understanding of what they believed about the supernatural world. In some cases this approach has been called cognitive archaeology because it attempts to delve into the very minds of ancient people. One recent study by Lewis-Williams (Lewis-Williams and Pearce 2009) entitled *Inside the Neolithic Mind* takes us back tens of thousands of years in Europe and the first evidence of systematic religious practices that the author relates to evolutionary changes in the workings of the human brain itself.

The approach of cognitive archaeology has been advanced by other Midwestern archaeologists in the study of effigy mounds, emphasizing the symbolism involved and the function of effigy mound building in maintaining balance and harmony in the world through periodic recreation, including the air, earth, and water resources upon which humans depend, through spiritual and ceremonial means that connect humans with supernatural forces (Mallam 1976; 1982; 1984; Benn 1979). In one (1982) study appropriately titled 'Ideology from the Earth', R. Clark Mallam proposed that the effigy mounds were built by small groups of mobile hunters who seasonally came together in earth renewal ceremonies that reinforced a broader group identity.

As pointed out by critics, the ideological approach is subjective. It relies on ethnography and oral Native traditions that cannot be corroborated or tested (Mason 2006). Certainly, archaeologists must always be cautious and critical in using such information but, in defense, connections between phenomena like the effigy mounds and long held worldviews and belief systems of Indian people are logical and compelling and, as pointed out by Robert Hall, the more we understand the structure of ancient belief systems and worldviews, the clearer the past will become.

Building on the insights provided by Hall, Mallam, and others, as well as the 'map' metaphor introduced by Goldstein (1995, 118) in regard to effigy mound arrangements, Birmingham and Eisenberg (2000) opened a new century of effigy mound research in the book *Indian Mounds of Wisconsin* with the assessment that the arrangement of different effigy mound forms on various places of natural landscapes created maps of ancient belief systems that divided the universe into into Upper and Lower Worlds, and sub-divided the Lower World into earth and water. Further, how this cosmology was expressed varied throughout the region in relation to topography and geography. Water related forms, specifically Water Spirits, dominate the low lying and watery world of the eastern part of the effigy mound region while, in the western hilly part, birds, sometimes huge in scale, are most common. In between is south-central Wisconsin where virtually all forms of effigy mounds are found and these are sometimes arranged horizontally and vertically on the natural landscape so as to provide, *in three dimensions*, the very models of the underlying structure of effigy mound ceremonialism.

New research

The 21st century has produced a surge in effigy mound research as a result of increasing recognition of the importance of this unique phenomenon, as well as increasingly sophisticated types of analysis not available in the past. Much new research has involved re-analysis of data acquired in years past with modern insights

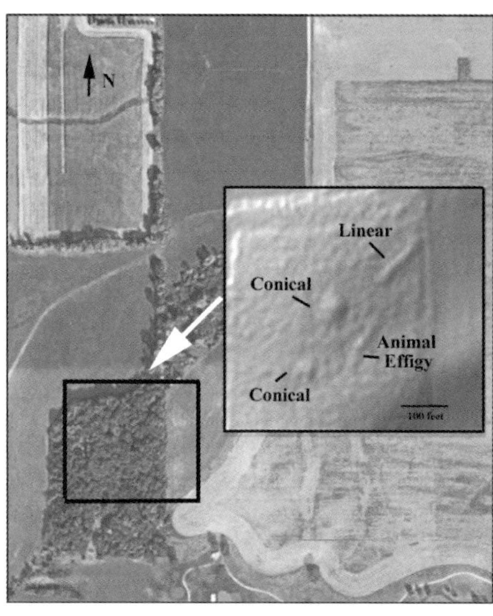

Fig. 2.13 A new mound group was discovered in 2017 in a rural wooded lot near Madison, Wisconsin using LiDAR imagery from Dane County Land Information. The discovery was surprising since mound groups in the area had been well documented over a century of research (see Chapter 5).

and techniques, as well as the use of non-destructive remote sensing technologies. The most promising of new technologies to emerge for the study of effigy mound landscapes is LiDAR or Light Detection and Ranging imagery that is much used in this book. LiDAR uses satellite or airplane mounted lasers to scan the surface of earth, eliminating obscuring foliage. It is being used the world over by archaeologists to study remains of archaeological sites and has led to identification of patterns not visible on the ground as well as whole new ancient places. The increasing availability of LiDAR imagery is, in itself, an archaeological revolution particularly suited for effigy mound landscape research. New mounds and whole new mound groups are continually being discovered and then verified by field research (Fig. 2.13). The imagery shows ceremonial landscapes in three dimensions rather than as flat maps of the past and a three-dimensional perspective was much in the minds of the effigy mound people as they made particular forms and mound arrangements, reflecting the vertical and horizon dimensions of the underlying cosmology and belief structure. The use of LiDAR has also been useful in easily and quickly checking existing mound groups represented by older surveys for discrepancies in such things as arrangements and orientations.

Furthering an ideological approach, Birmingham and Rosebrough (2003) addressed the meaning of effigy mounds by following Hall and others in relating effigy mound arrangements to belief systems and cosmologies of Native people and providing many more examples of this throughout the effigy mound region. In *Spirits of Earth: Effigy Mound Landscape of Madison and the Four Lakes*, Birmingham (2010) took a closer at the effigy mounds along the shores of lakes around modern-day Madison, Wisconsin, as a case study – a region referred to as the 'Four Lakes' (Fig. 2.14). This area is one of the largest and best documented landscapes in the effigy mound region and in its very center. It also contains virtually all the zoomorphic or animal forms built during the effigy mound era. Information from that work appears here as Chapter 5.

At least 1100 mounds of various kinds in 100 groupings, small and large, have been recorded along the shores of the lakes and up along associated creeks and streams. Numerous habitation sites have also been identified and examined dating to the Late Woodland period. Birmingham (2010) proposed that the Four Lakes' people comprised a single social group with its major ceremonial center on the north shore of the largest lake, Mendota, with a village that may have been home to the leaders who associated themselves with powerful Thunderbirds. Giant eagle-like birds, hundreds of feet long, interpreted as Thunderbirds, are neatly arranged around the village area (see Chapter 5).

The mound groupings in the Four Lakes mound district or locality had been treated as separate sites but many bleed into one another forming a larger landscape. The study empathized the use of word 'landscapes' to describe great clusters of mounds and mound grouping as it had been used by other earlier scholars to describe effigy mound and other related cultural features (Goldstein 1995; Gartner 1999). The Four Lakes study called these 'ceremonial landscapes' not simply because of the inter-relationship of mounds to the natural environment but also in recognition that differences in mound groupings, probably representing different rituals and ceremonies that nevertheless sprang from the same underlying belief structure and worldview. A ceremonial landscape is actually a

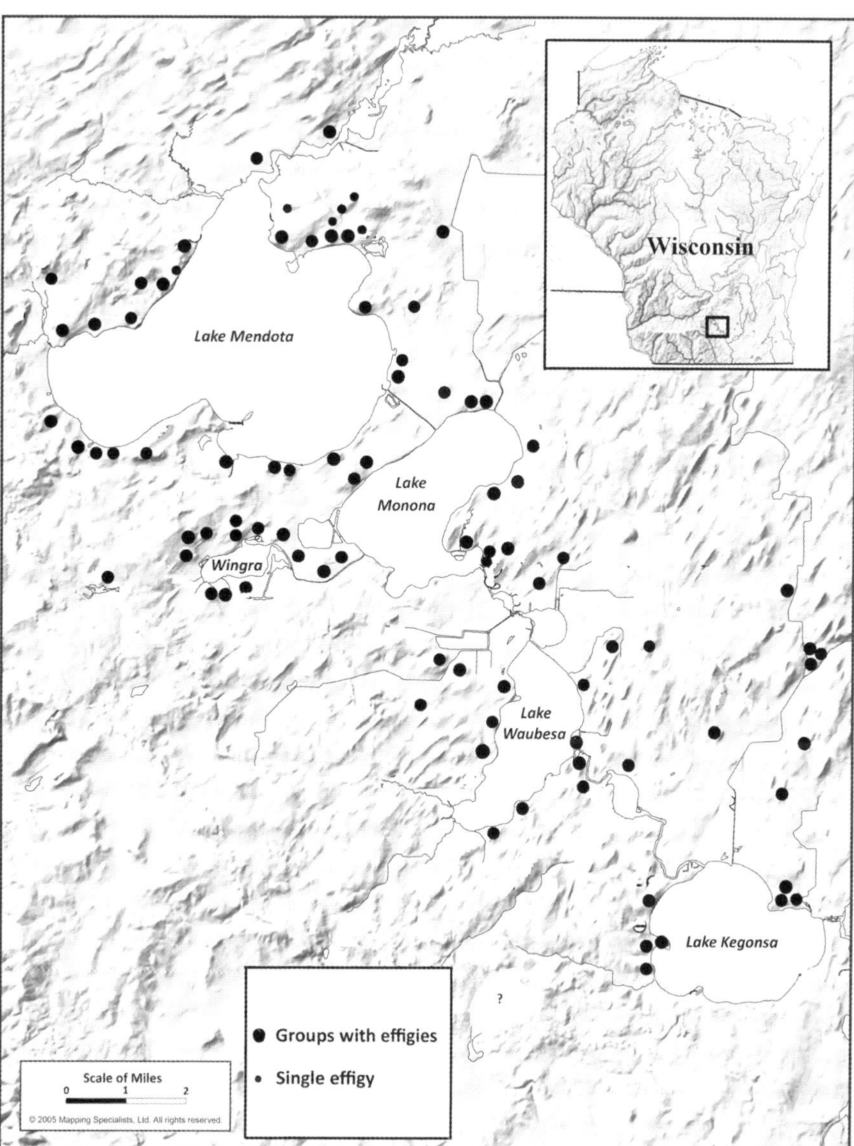

Fig. 2.14 Map of the Four Lakes district showing the density of effigy mounds and selected effigy mound groups (see Chapter 5).

type of ideological landscape, as defined by Snead and Pruecel (1999) and found in many parts of the world, as where places (ie, features of the natural landscape) and spaces (ie, monuments) are combined to produce special meaning. These have been variously called cultural, ritual, symbolic, sacred, or ceremonial, as well as ideological. Examples are the megalithic landscapes of Europe, England, and Ireland; the long lines and giant geoglyphs depicting supernatural beings in the deserts of Peru, Chile, and Bolivia; the giant earthworks and related sites in Ohio as most recently described by the late Mark Lynott (2014), and related settlements, shrines, petroglpyhs, and geographic features held sacred by the Pueblo people in the American southwest (Snead 2008).

Spirits of Earth noted that the Four Lakes effigy mound landscape recapitulated the pattern found throughout the effigy mound regions in that there is a close correspondence between topography and geography and effigy mound forms representing the spirits of the air, earth, and water. This further supports the view that communication with the spirit world and its powers linked to features of the natural landscape was more of an influence than a clan based social structure, although it might be that clans were responsible for the building of spirits that they believed were their ancestors. The study further proposed that the effigy mounds were not static symbols on vacant land, as one might paint religious representations on a blank canvas, but were built to be alive, bringing together the natural and supernatural worlds (Birmingham 2010, xx–xxi). With examples from the Four Lakes, the study also pointed out that effigy mound landscapes had their origins in prominent places that had long been used by earlier mound building cultures and the effigy mound people incorporated these into their more expansive mound arrangements.

In the same year, 2010, a University of Wisconsin PhD dissertation by Amy Rosebrough brought matters back to an objective world by closely examining many assumptions that had been present in previous research and providing fresh new data and insights drawn from modern statistical techniques, including the relationships between major effigy mound building areas throughout the effigy mound region. Analyzing all known mound groups for differences in mound forms as well as other cultural attributes, she defined 25 localities or large clusters of effigy mound groups that she characterized as reflecting separate social groups, rather than one large homogenous culture (Rosebrough 2010; 2014). She also advanced the idea that effigy mounds reflected social ranking, as opposed to the more egalitarian tribal type of society that had been assumed, despite the absence of prestige items in the burials. She proposed that it was the living, powerful leaders that gained status by directing construction of the effigy mounds, applying their arcane religious knowledge to do so.

John Broihahn and Rosebrough (2014) provided a highly detailed re-analysis of the Clarence Raisbeck Mound Group in southwestern Wisconsin that applied modern knowledge and techniques to the results of the excavations conducted in 1928 by McKern and the Milwaukee Public Museum, summarized by Chandler Rowe (1956). The huge effigy mound complex occupies a series of large ridges overlooking a great loop in Grant River, a tributary of the Mississippi. Eighty-two mounds were identified – effigy, conical, and linear – and 31 of these had been

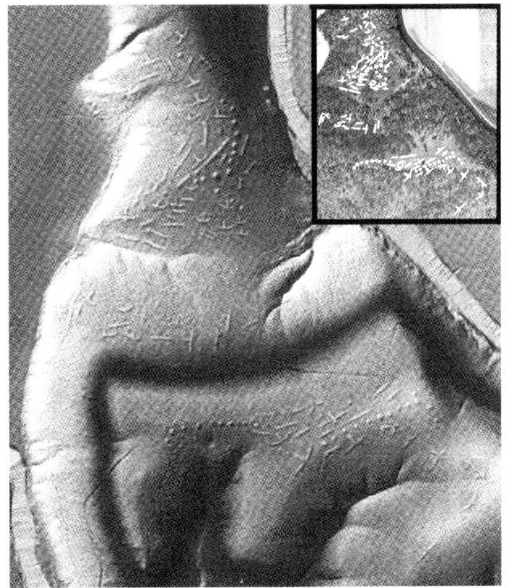

Fig. 2.15 LiDAR image from the Raisbeck Mound Group in southwestern Wisconsin (from Broihahn and Rosebrough 2014).

excavated by the Milwaukee Public Museum. The mound group remains virtually intact today so the modern investigators used LiDAR imaging to gain an overview as well as to study the relationship of the mounds to the natural environment. Field survey and use of LiDAR led to the astonishing discovery of an additional 41 mounds adding to those previously documented, making this one of the largest effigy mound groupings on record (Fig. 2.15).

There have been other major contributions in the new century dealing with different aspects of the Effigy Mound Ceremonial Complex. Among these are updates to the nature and dating of Late Woodland cultures (Stoltman and Christensen 2000), the reasons for the demise of effigy mound tradition and appearance of the subsequent Oneota (Stoltman and Christensen 2000; Theler and Boszhardt 2006), analysis of ceramics types (Boszhardt 1996; Clauter 2011), examinations of areas around effigy mounds for evidence of habitations, burials, and ritual use (Egan and Wier 1992; Rosebrough 2021), including the use of remote sensing techniques on and around the mounds (Kaufman 2005; Whitaker and Story 2008); group identity (Cornelison 2013); and the biological relationship between effigy mound populations (Lakey-Cornelison 2012). Birmingham and Rosebrough (2017) put effigy mounds in context in the history of burial mound building in Wisconsin.

As a requirement of *NAGPRA*, federal or federally funded institutions such as museums and universities must inventory collections of skeletal human remains recovered by past archaeological excavations that have contributed much new biological information. These inventories entail basic non-destructive analyses conducted by forensic anthropologists, such as determination of sex and age, as well as other information that might help determine cultural affiliation necessary to the return of remains to the appropriate descendant Native American nation. In their analysis, the specialists also make routine observations on instances of trauma and general health issues that can be detected in the bones.

One particularly relevant study, by William Green, former Iowa State Archaeologist and director of the Beloit College (Wisconsin) Museum, reprised the old question of connections between effigy mounds and modern Native people in 2000 but for a very important legal reason. Green's study, updated in 2014, took on the task of determining the descendants of the effigy mound people whose remains had been excavated from Effigy Mounds National Monument in Iowa, operated by United States Park Service (Green 2014). Objectively examining all available evidence from archaeology, ethnography, ethnohistory, and known tribal traditions, the study concluded that, because of enormous cultural changes that have taken place over 1000 years, it was not possible to draw a straight line from the effigy builders of the ancient past to any one tribe for the purposes of *NAGPRA*. The report emphasized that expansion from the south of the great Mississippian civilization had led to the demise of the Late Woodland effigy mound ceremonial and the mixing of populations and customs leading to a third cultural entity called Oneota by archaeologists.

The excitement and new insights that all these studies have generated are expected to continue in the future, not only contributing new information on the Upper Midwestern Effigy Mound Complex itself but also more broadly, to the role that monument building as related to the supernatural played in human societies throughout the world as they grew in complexity. Just how cultural complexity evolved in the Upper Midwest, leading to the extraordinary effigy mound landscapes, will be reviewed in Chapter 3 after we first take a closer look at the belief systems that underlay effigy mound ceremonial itself.

3

Cosmology, geography, and the underlying structure of effigy mound landscapes

As proposed by Robert Hall and followed here, effigy mound landscapes constitute 'monumental constructions of the cosmology of the builders' (Hall 1993, 51). Cosmology here refers to how people explain the origin and structure of the universe or world and their place in it. It is the basis of a distinctive worldview. As elaborated in more recent works, the effigy mounds are maps of an ancient worldview and belief system in the form of three-dimensional landscapes (Birmingham 2010; Birmingham and Rosebrough 2017). The underlying structure of this monumental ceremonialism is a dualistic view whereby the world or universe is divided into Upper and Lower Worlds with the sub-division of the Lower World into earth and water realms. Appropriate animals and key supernatural beings or spirits embody the powers of each of these realms.

This concept of dualism is hardly unique in the scheme of human affairs. the concept of opposite, yet necessarily complementary, Upper and Lower Worlds and their forces is a theme found throughout the cultures of the world, drawn from the contrasts in nature such as day/night, life/death, left/right, male/female, and deeply embedded in human consciousness, sensory perceptions, and probably the binary workings of the brain itself (Levi-Stauss 1969; Newberg *et al.* 2001). It is no accident that modern-day computers operate using binary codes.

Throughout the Americas, dualistic concepts of the world are interwoven with animism, the belief that there is no separation between the physical and supernatural and that animals and other features of the natural world have spirits, even those that most would describe as inanimate. Because of this, the powers or blessings of particular spirits can be obtained where such spirits dwell. In the Upper Midwest, for example, great heights are perceived to be associated with the spirits of the Upper World, especially birds such as the Thunderbirds, while watery places such as lakes, streams, springs, and wetlands are habitats of the powerful watery Underworld spirits (Fig. 3.1).

Native people expressed the opposing dualistic forces as a struggle of great supernatural celestial birds with Lower World serpents and similar creatures. The Mexican national flag captures this essential tension with an ancient Aztec emblem that depicts an eagle struggling with a serpent. Near the heart of the

Fig. 3.1 Early 20th century photo of Thunderbirds carved into face of a high bluff in central Wisconsin (Wisconsin Historical Society Archives. ID 34556).

Upper Midwestern effigy mound region is Devil's Lake (discussed further below), so called by early white settlers, that occupies a rock-strewn basin in the Baraboo Hills in south-central Wisconsin. In one legend, the lake resulted from a battle between Thunderbirds and Water Spirits during which the rocks were thrown at one another (Cole 1920; Brown 1936, 14; Saunders 1947). In some stories the lake itself is the residence of a powerful Water Spirit that lives in the center of the earth. The lake is sacred to the Ho-Chunk people who call it *Te Wakacak*, or Spirit Lake.

Thunderbirds, also known as Thunderers, are among the great celestial bird deities found throughout the Americas. They are invisible but thunder is produced by the flapping of their giant wings and lightning flashes from their eyes. They are 'capable of bestowing great blessings on man' (Radin 1923, 239–40) and in traditions of people of the Eastern Woodlands and Great Plains, including the Ho-Chunk, they are envisioned as huge eagles and depicted with wings outstretched or folded alongside the body, with a fan tail, or standing on two stout feathered legs. Figure 3.2 shows the standard ways that Thunderbirds are depicted in more recent times in various forms of art and iconography. In some cases, like a story told on a Menominee birch bark scroll, the Thunderbird is imaged as having a fork-tail much like the hawk-like shallow tailed kite, an occasional visitor to the area, or even the more common barn swallow (Sibley 2000, 110, 370). Among other ancient Midwestern cultures, like the Oneota and Mississippians, the Thunderbird apparently assumed the form of a peregrine falcon. Given that the Thunderbird is supernatural and not seen, there is variation beyond depiction of a raptor.

The powerful supernatural Water Spirits or *Wakcéxi,* in the Ho-Chunk language, are denizens of the watery world and perceived by the Ho-Chunk and other Midwestern peoples as horned panther-like animals, often with long curved tails

Fig. 3.2 Thunderbird iconography: a) red painted humans communing with or gaining power from a Thunderbird on a bluff face at Roche-a-Cri State Park, central Wisconsin; b) pictograph at La Moille cave, Minnesota (from Lewis 1890b); c) Thunderbird on a Menominee birch scroll (from Skinner 1913); d) painted falcon at Gottschall Rockshelter, southwestern Wisconsin (from Salzer and Rajnovich 2000).

(Fig. 3.3). The Menominee called them Underground Water Panthers. The Ojibwe have the equivalent *Mishebushu*, a horned monster that lived in lakes. Such creatures are commonly found in Native beliefs but in different forms, with or without horns (Lankford 2007, 109–13). The Underwater Manitou controlled access to the Great Lakes copper sources (see Clark and Martin 2005). They can have ominous connotations and are generally associated with disorder but are also viewed as great medicine beings whose powers can be accessed through offerings and rituals. Many forms of Native art illustrate Upper World/Lower World dualism including woven bags where renditions of Thunderbirds occupy one side and Water Spirits or earth mammals the opposite side.

People of the Americas in general perceived a tiered universe with animal and supernatural referents associated with each tier, some of whom had roles in the creation of the world and are important in its continued existence. But no matter how many the tiers, writes Jeffrey Quilter in his eloquent introduction to *The Pre-Columbian World*, there is also recognized air, earth, and watery underworlds that are:

> ruled by a master animal: a snake, a crocodile, fish, in the lower waters; a jaguar, a bear in land of the people; a powerful bird in the heights. One major link between the worlds is the sun, perceived as a living being that occupies the upper world during the day and sinks into the underworld at night. (Quilter 2006, 9)

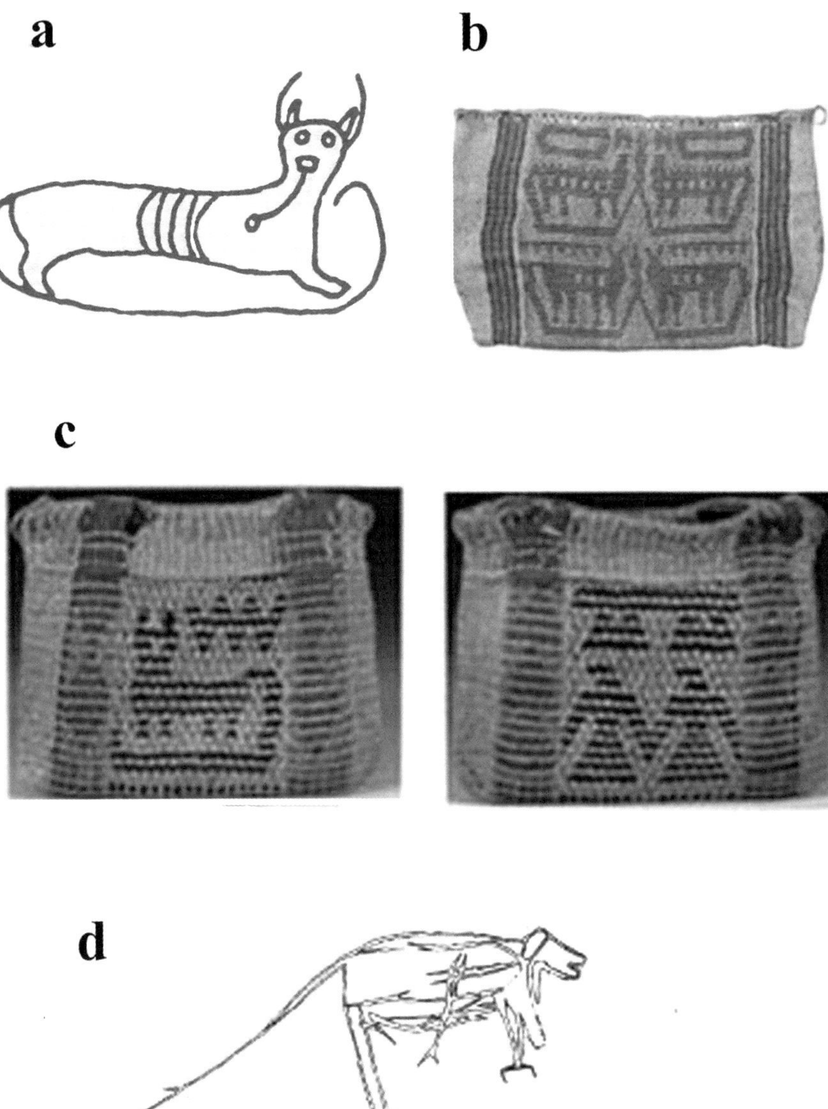

Fig. 3.3 Water Spirit (underground water panther) iconography: a) 'Medicine animal of the Winnebagos'; b) Potawatomi textile bag from Wisconsin (from the collections of the National Museum of the American Indian, Washington DC); c) Ho-Chunk basket from a private collection with Water Spirits on one side and Thunderbirds on the opposite side; d) probable carved water spirit with clawed feet from the back of Samuel's Cave, Wisconsin (from Loubser and Bozhardt 2004).

This concept is reflected in monument building and ritual art but also in social relations where it is often expressed in dualistic kinship patterns, called moieties, that divide people into those associated with the earth and Underworld comprising the lower realm, and sky, the Upper World.

> No matter how varying the physical surroundings, the social arrangements of people through the land are quite similar. Who are wife-givers, who are husband givers, and how large a group is considered true family may vary. But no matter how the particulars are arranged the underlying principal of dualism is operation. Communities are partitioned in two – Big Brother and Little Brother, the Reds and the Whites, the Upper and the Lower. (Quilter 2006, 9)

The moieties have reciprocal relationships to one another and are exogamous – one must marry into the opposite division – and both of these principles ensure the full integration of the broader society.

> Among the Osage of Missouri, two moiety arrangements of clans reflect cosmic dualism: just as the cosmos is divided into earth and sky one represents the sky and the other the earth and water and the clans in villages were organized as mirror images of the cosmos with an east–west road – the path of the sun dividing the two groupings of clans. (Bailey 1995, 40–1)

The clan arrangement of the Ho-Chunk provides another example of dualism. The Ho-Chunk/Winnebago are frequently mentioned in this book to illustrate certain concepts because their culture is one of the best studied of Upper Midwest Native people, they are indigenous to the region, and are almost certainly among the descendants of the ancient effigy mound people. One caveat here in relation of the mounds is that it is unlikely that various effigy mound forms only represent clan totems since the same beings played multiple roles – animal and spirit ancestor beings.

The clans of the Ho-Chunk are named for both animal and supernatural beings and are divided into two moieties: 'those who are above' (*wanegi*) and 'those who are below' (*mangeregi*) (Radin 1923, 137–45). Clan membership came through the male line (patrilineal descent) but Radin found evidence in older stories that in former times one belonged to the clan of the mother (matrilineal descent).

The upper moiety consists of Thunderbird, Eagle, Warrior or Hawk, and Pigeon clans. Thunderbird is the head of this division and, even today, the traditional chief (not to be confused with the elected president of the Ho-Chunk Nation) comes from the Thunderbird clan. The Warrior clan is closely linked to the Hawk clan and, in more recent times, Hawk was the name of the clan (Radin 1923, 144). The lower moiety is further sub-divided into two phratries, or related clans, of the earth and the water. Bear heads the earth clans that include Deer, Elk, Wolf, and Buffalo. Several members of the Winnebago Reservation told Radin that in former days the Water Spirit clan once ruled over the entire tribe but this role had been taken over by the Thunderbird clan (Radin 1923, 193).

The Bear, head of the earth phratry among the Ho-Chunk, is associated with earthly order in the traditions of many North American peoples and among the Ho-Chunk Bear clan members are called upon to keep order at gatherings but also have responsibilities to the earth itself. During the land cession treaties of the 19th century, Bear clan members were the only ones authorized to conduct land negotiations with the US Government (Lurie 2002, 21). As having responsibly of dealing with earthly matters, the Bear clan members may have had responsibility for burying the dead. Some Ho-Chunk people told Paul Radin that, in former days, interment of the dead was done by those of lower division clans because they are of the earth and 'have the right to dig into the ground and bury people' (Radin 1923, 98). Whether or not this was a custom practiced in ancient times, as with mortuary rituals attending the effigy mounds, is not certain, but excavations of the Kratz Creek Mound Group by the Milwaukee Public Museum (see Chapter 2), found a large Water Spirit burial mound covered a deep excavation (intaglio) in the form of a bear (Barrett and Hawkes 1919). It is possible that the bear intaglio had been made first by people associated with the bear spirit to obtain blessings for digging the graves accompanying the mound.

Radin's analysis of Ho-Chunk culture also identified a constant theme of the renewal of order in a chaotic world, accomplished by many rituals, and the maintenance of social power between the Upper and Lower Worlds as represented by the Thunderbird and Bear clans (Radin 1945, 54–5). The Water Spirit clan heads the water phratry that includes Fish and Snake. Ho-Chunk villages mirrored the clan arrangement, with Upper World clans living to the southwest and Lower World clans to the northeast, according to some people interviewed by Radin (1923, 140) (Fig. 3.4).

Ho-Chunk clans have different responsibilities for the good of the whole community and in the recent past this reflected an egalitarian social system. However, Radin's analysis of certain Ho-Chunk myths passed down in oral tradition had led him to conclude that, long ago, certain lineages with clans were considered more important than others and that social structure as a whole had been hierarchical (Radin 1923; 1948, 49), although some modern scholars are dubious (Green 2014, 60). The use of the word 'myth' here and throughout this book follows an anthropological definition referring to sacred stories involving supernatural, super-human, and heroic characters, set in primordial times and believed to be true (Bascom 1965), rather than the more common meaning of something that is dubious folklore or made-up. Myths often explain world creation and origins of important elements of a culture like rituals, medicine, and food.

The key animals and spirits found in the clan system of the Ho-Chunk, along with some others like Earthmaker, Hare, and various culture heroes, actually have multiple roles in the broader cosmology. They mirror cosmic order, confer supernatural powers and blessings through the right kind of ceremonials and rituals, played major roles in the creation of the world, and are the very ancestors of humans themselves in the form of clans, transformed into human form after the world was created.

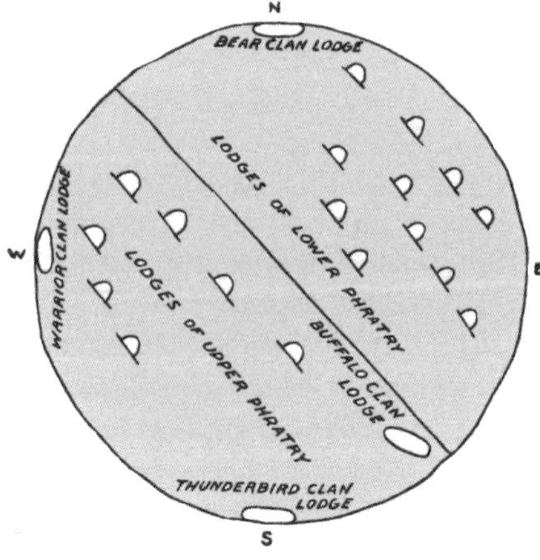

Fig. 3.4 Layout of Ho-Chunk village (from Radin 1923, 140).

There are several versions of the creation of the earth and people found among the Ho-Chunk, as recounted in oral history by different clans and the ritual organization, the Grand Medicine Society. A common creation myth recounts that, after Earthmaker made the world, it continued spinning so Earthmaker first sent down rocks and dirt. This did not work so Earthmaker sent down either Water Spirits (according to the Medicine Society rites), or bears (Bear clan) to anchor the four corners of the world, or snakes that pieced the corners much like tent pegs (Thunderbird clan; Funmaker 1974; see also Radin 1923, 64, 302).

Versions of this same creation story seem to be represented in the art of Mississippian cultures of Oklahoma and Tennessee, heirs of the great Mississippian

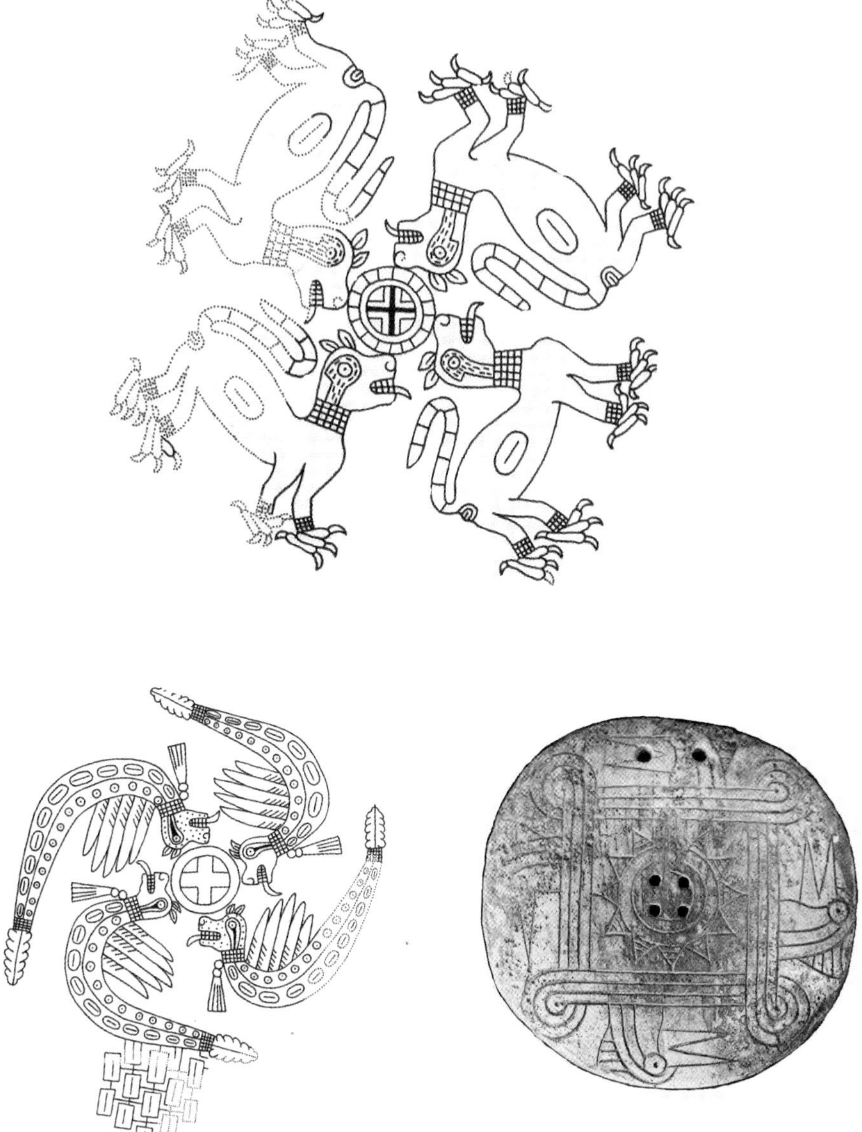

Fig. 3.5 Upper: incised motifs on whelk shells from the Spiro site in Oklahoma; lower: incised motif on a shell disc from Tennessee (from Brain and Philips 1996).

civilization that first formed in southern Illinois and eventually expanded into the Upper Midwest effigy mound region (see papers in Diaz-Granados 2023 for recent discussion). Two carved whelk marine shells from the great mortuary of Craig Mound at the Spiro site in Oklahoma show a central circle and earth symbol – the cross also being the symbol for Earthmaker for the Midwestern Ho-Chunk – surrounded by four creatures: clawed, panther like creatures with curved tails on one, and winged serpents on the other (Phillips and Brown 1984, pl. 228) (Fig. 3.5). On an engraved shell disk found in Tennessee, four crested, long beaked woodpeckers surround the circle and cross, conflated with the image of the sun (Brain and Philips 1996, 9). Although these motifs have been interpreted differently, they can be viewed as versions of what constitute earth anchors among Mississippian clans or ritual societies, much like the Ho-Chunk.

Another important story obtained by Radin from the Ho-Chunk Water Spirit clan people recounts how the Ho-Chunk tribe was formed from spirit beings and animals. First, a Thunderbird alighted on a tree and became human, thus becoming the progenitor of the Thunderbird clan. After some wait and anticipation, a white, horned Water Spirit emerged from a small nearby lake and 'became human and walked', giving birth to the Water Spirit clan (Radin 1923, 194). Other animals became human at other places but all joined together to form the Ho-Chunk nation. The Menominee, neighbors to the Ho-Chunk in the Upper Midwest, have a similar clan structure and believe that the first human among them transformed from a copper-tailed bear underneath the earth forming the Bear clan, and this clan was later joined by a Thunderbird who dropped to earth on a rock ledge, becoming the Thunderer or Thunderbird clan (Spindler 1978).

Effigy mounds are burial places and associated ceremonialism obviously incorporated humans into the cycle of death and rebirth of the world. The concept of the rebirth of humans along with the world is an important one in the worldviews of many Native people. Reincarnation and re-animation of the dead, for example, are recurrent themes in Ho-Chunk sacred stories (Radin 1923; Lurie 1978, 696). Paul Radin witnessed and recorded a Bear clan burial ceremony during which an oration told how the soul of the deceased would become a spirit bear and would 'walk just as original Bear clansman walked when they originated and approached the earth' (Radin 1923, 101). Applying these concepts to mound building, effigy mound ceremonials can be viewed as simultaneously and periodically recreating or reincarnating the World and joining the dead with spirit ancestors in another kind of rebirth.

Roots of effigy mounds ceremonialism

A worldview as described above was already present in the Eastern Woodlands long before the emergence of the Effigy Mound Ceremonial Complex. Based on the rich and diverse array of Hopewell art and iconography, David Penny (1985) described the cosmology of the Ohio Hopewell culture (*ca* 200 BC–AD 500) as a vertically layered universe with bird imagery representing the Upper World and serpent, the Lower. The bear, representing the Earth plane of the Lower World in

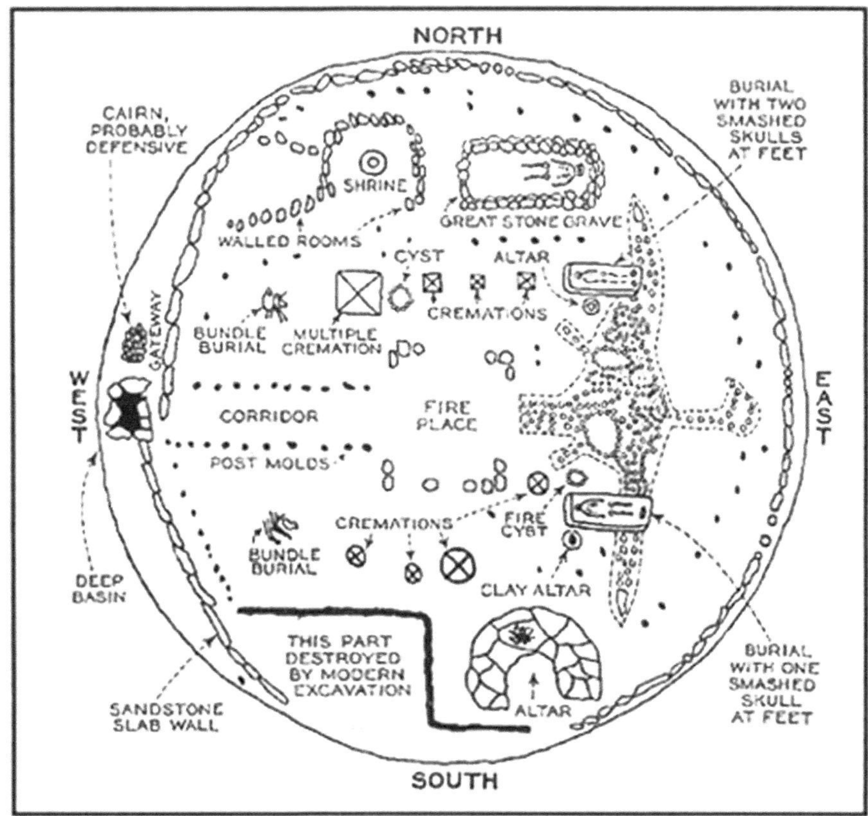

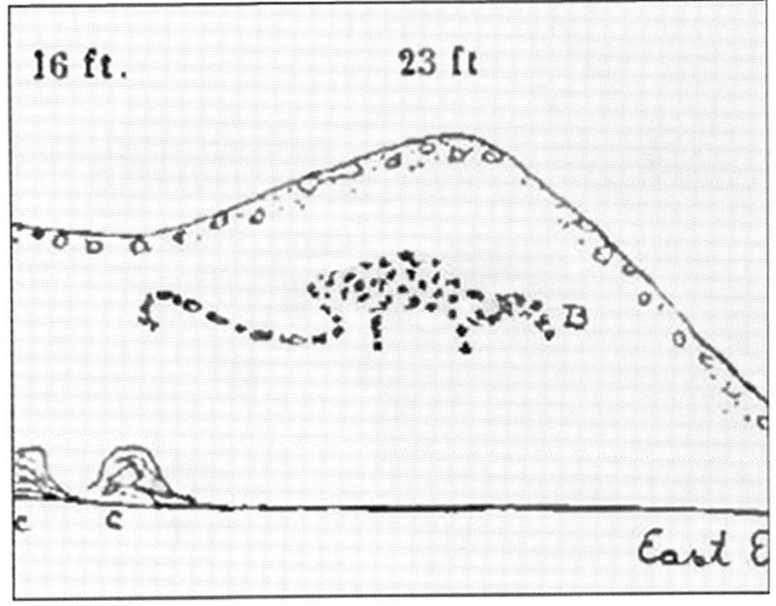

Fig. 3.6 Upper: the Benton Mound in Ohio (from McGrath 1945); lower: unpublished sketch by Warren Moorehead from an Ohio Hopewell mound (courtesy of Brad Lepper, Ohio History Connection).

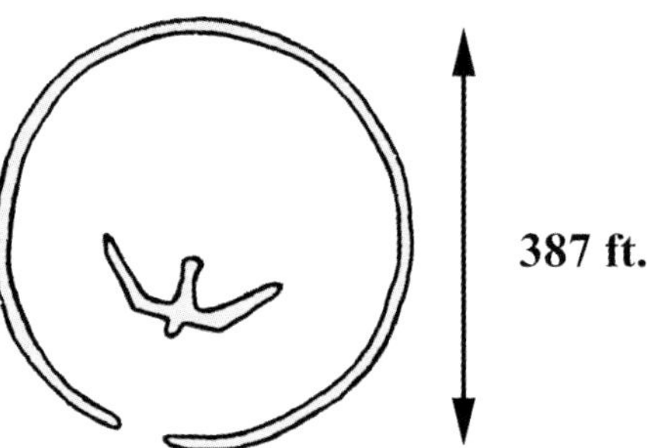

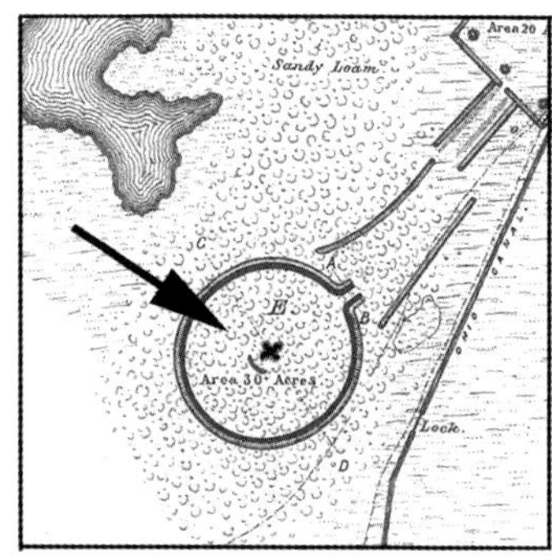

Fig. 3.7 Upper: smaller bird enclosure near the Kickapoo River in southwestern Wisconsin (Lewis n.d. a); below: bird enclosure at the Hopewell site in Ohio (from Squier and Davis 1848).

later Native cultures of the Midwest, was also a particular focus of veneration, evidently considered a great medicine animal. One carved stone figurine from Ohio is of a medicine man wearing a bearskin complete with its head (Dragoo and Wray 1964). Dualism is apparent in the gigantic enclosures that often feature circular and square structures linked together (Lepper 2004). The same creatures representing the different worlds found among the effigy mounds are present in Hopewell iconography and were also incorporated in monument building. Early excavations by Magrath (1945) of the North Benton Mound in Ohio unearthed a boulder outline of a great bird amid other rock ritual constructions within a circular rock enclosure and a central fireplace (Fig. 3.6). In the early 20th century, pioneering archaeologist Warren Moorehead found another large boulder creature in a Hopewell mound that looks very much like an Underworld Water Spirit, but only a sketch survives from his excavations (Fig. 3.6). Further west, a Hopewell mound at Utica, Illinois covered burials and a boulder effigy of either a snake or a long-necked bird, and a Hopewell style pottery vessel associated with burials is decorated with a similar motif (Henriksen 1965).

Moreover, there are several earthen effigies in Ohio that may reflect the actual roots of effigy mounds in the Upper Midwest although dating problems and controversies complicate the picture. Archaeologists believed that most famous of these, the great Serpent Mound, dated about 1000 years after the Hopewell culture, but recent redating using new experimental radiocarbon techniques, places its construction prior to the rise of Hopewell (Herman *et al.* 2014), although this also has been further challenged by additional radiocarbon dating (Lepper *et al.* 2018). The so-called Alligator Mound at Granville, Ohio has been interpreted as an underwater panther (as viewed from above; Lepper and Frolking 2003). It had also been thought to post-date Hopewell, but Squier and Davis (1848) originally mapped several effigy mounds lying within Hopewell enclosures. One is a bird at the center of the circular earthwork enclosure within the spectacular Hopewell era Newark earthworks (Fig. 3.7). The identification of this mound as a bird has been challenged by modern archaeological research (Lepper 2004, 78), but Theodore Lewis mapped a similar bird enclosure near the Kickapoo River, a tributary of the Wisconsin River in southwestern Wisconsin (Lewis 1886c, 36). The latter is now gone and the area has not been archaeologically investigated.

Although there is evidence that the effigy mounds had roots in prior Hopewell culture, it must be noted that there is a time gap between the collapse of the Hopewell along with its widespread influence about AD 400 and when the Effigy Mound Ceremonial Complex swept the Upper Midwest, beginning after AD 700, based on current radiocarbon dating. It may be that key effigy mounds were created in the interim, as discussed below, but the spread of the Complex needs to be explained by factors other than the simple, direct outgrowth of Hopewell ceremonial activity. Potential factors are explored in the next chapter as we look at the evolution of effigy mound landscapes.

Mound forms

As discussed in Chapter 1 (see Fig. 1.9), through the years there have been a number of attempts to classify effigy mound forms, often using comparisons to animals in the natural world instead of Native traditions that clearly describe some as supernatural beings. Peet (1890), for example, identified a class of curved-tailed effigy mounds as squirrels when, in fact, these can be easily related to how the great underwater panthers or Water Spirits are many times depicted with curved tails in other media, even in modern times. As well, until fairly recently, it was not commonly recognized that certain effigy mound animals and supernatural beings are depicted in two perspectives, leading to the conclusions that these were actually different types of animals altogether. A confirmation that the two perspective views existed even prior to the construction of effigy mounds comes from a broken stone smoking pipe found by an artifact collector in southwestern Minnesota and documented by archaeologist Robert Boszhardt (2006) (Fig. 3.8). The pipe is of the so-called Monitor style used by the earlier Middle Woodland people. Depictions of long tailed, horned creatures with zig-zag 'power lines' emanating from the eyes or face were carved on both sides and the top of the pipe. The creatures on the sides are 'panther' forms while creatures on the top look like horned lizards. However, decoration details and positioning indicate that the same creature is being shown, but in both aerial and profile perspectives, thus matching the two forms of mounds.

Finally, various mound surveyors and mappers had their own ways of depicting mounds and the researchers mapped what they expected to see based on their own worldview. Some are sketches, more-or-less, with some key measurements, while others used more precise survey methods. Unfamiliar with Native iconography and traditions, early investigators would, for example not even look for horns on animals perceived to be naturalistic panthers and would see any head protrusions simply as ears. Longer, horn-like projections or appendages would not even be obvious, since the edges gently blend into the natural topography. Unfortunately, most effigy mounds are now gone so many depictions cannot be corroborated and we must rely on those that have survived (still numbering in many hundreds) and even these, in many cases, have not been closely re-examined and compared with earlier maps.

Nevertheless, modern analysis reveals that the most common zoomorphic mounds are straight- and curved-winged raptors resembling eagles, hawks/falcons,

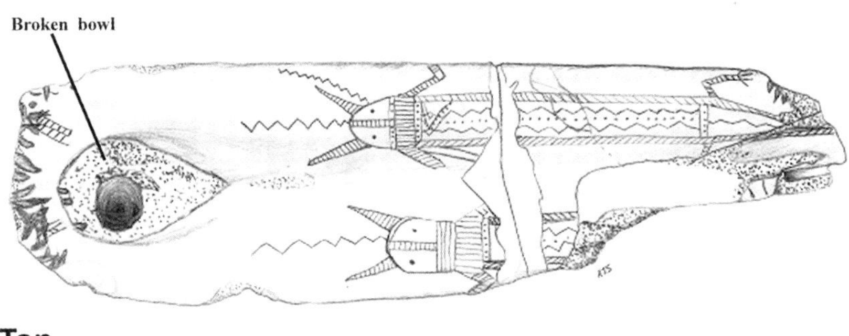

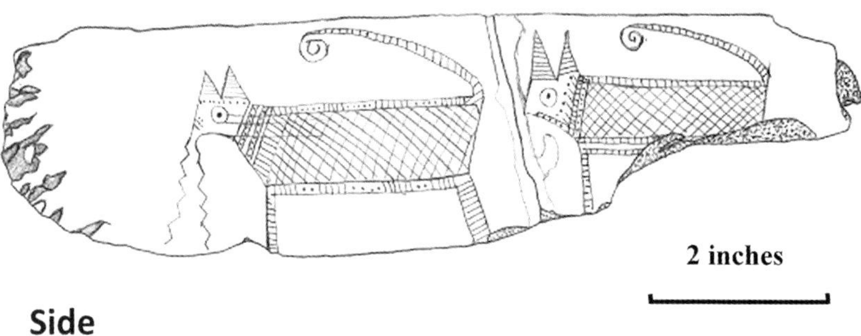

Fig. 3.8 Stone pipe from Minnesota with carved Water Spirit in aerial and profiled perspectives (from Boszhardt 2006).

bears, and long-tailed panther-like creatures or Water Spirits, with or without horns (Birmingham 2010; Rosebrough 2010; Birmingham and Rosebrough 2017). Others resemble canines (wolf or fox), water birds such as geese and possibly cranes or herons, deer, and water mammals such as otter, muskrat, weasel, or mink. Some spectacular mounds are in the form of humans. Other shapes, however, have eluded identification, but the meaning of even these can be inferred from ethnographic sources, arrangement within the groups, and their physical relationship to key natural landscape features.

For example, some very long, linear mounds with bulbous heads, which can be many hundreds of feet long, are most likely snake effigies and some of these have a recognizably serpentine form (Birmingham 2010). Lewis (1887) mapped a giant rattlesnake mound in Minnesota, complete with rattle, that was over 500 ft (152+ m) long and 5 ft (*ca* 1.5 m) high, and snake forms accompany other great spirit beings found in rock art of the region (Fig. 3.9). Ancient snake imagery is most obviously present in the form of the great Serpent Mound in Ohio and snakes are depicted many times on Hopewell pottery. Throughout the Americas, snakes or serpents inhabit the watery Underworld and are frequently associated with fertility (see papers in Diaz-Granados 2023 for recent discussion). A stone figurine found at the Mississippian city of Cahokia in Illinois depicts a woman hoeing the back of a great snake-like serpent that sprouts gourds from its back (Emerson 1989). Snakes also symbolize rebirth in that they shed their skins. Among the Ho-Chunk, people who are believed to have been reincarnated into the living through adoption ceremonies

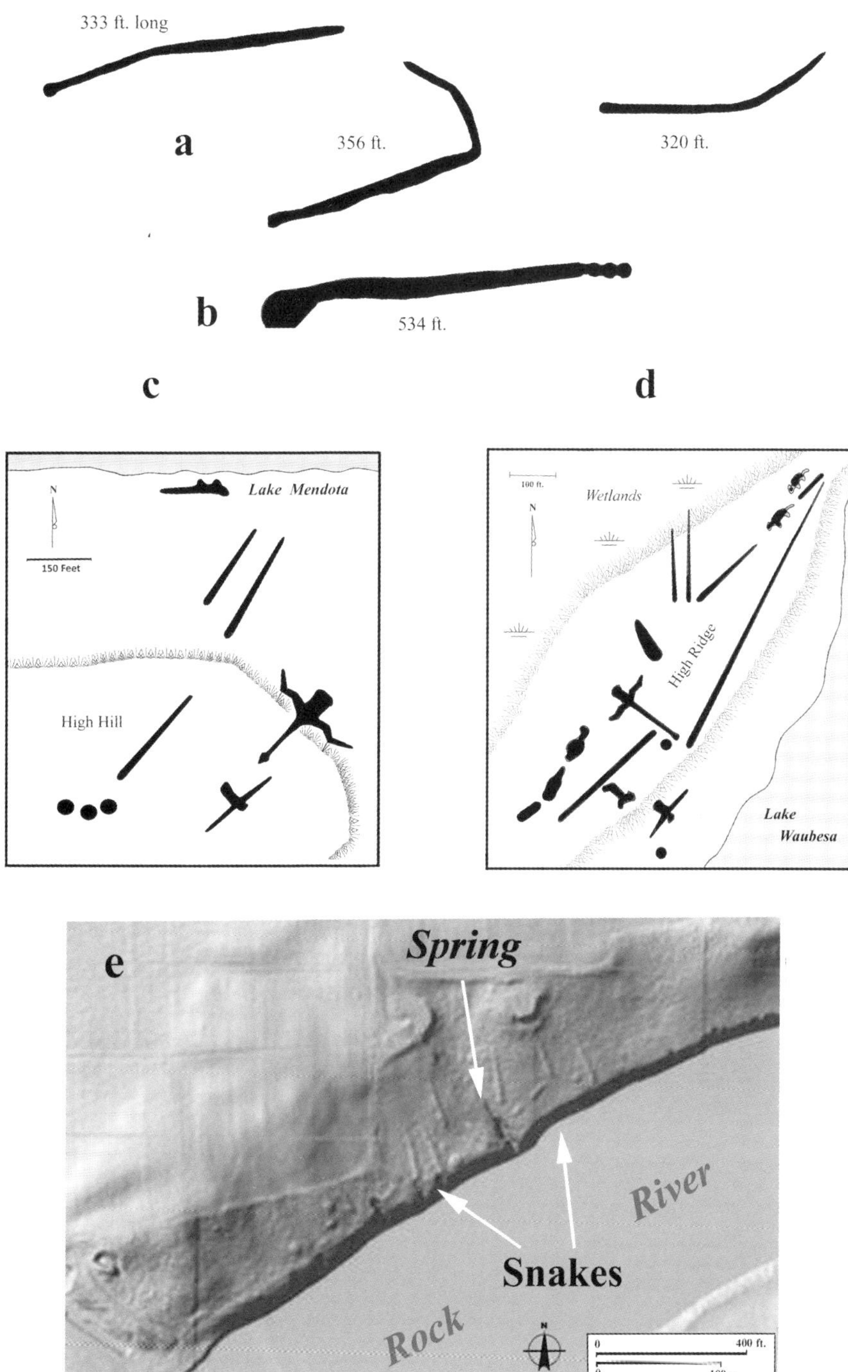

Fig. 3.9 Snake effigy forms: a) serpentine effigies on Lake Waubesa in south-central Wisconsin (from Birmingham 2010, 178); b) rattlesnake effigy in Minnesota (Lewis 1887); c) long and straight snake-like forms (tapering linear) at the Blackhawk Country Club on Lake Mendota (from Birmingham 2010, 180); d) the McConnell site on Lake Waubesa (from Birmingham 2010, 136); e) LiDAR image from the WisconsinView website showing snake-like forms surrounding a spring on a steep bluff face at the Indian Hills site on the Rock River in central Wisconsin.

are said to have 'shed their skins'. Also, according to Ho-Chunk versions of World creation, snakes were sent down by Earthmaker to stake down the corners of the earth. While some of the long mounds interpreted as snakes are serpentine in form, most are arrow-straight as an anchoring stake would be.

Fig. 3.10 (*opposite*) Major effigy and other mound forms from the vast Four Lakes Effigy Mound Landscape in south-central Wisconsin (see Chapter 5).

One of the authors (AR) has made a comprehensive study of effigy mound forms (Rosebrough 2010). A major focus of this research deals with the distribution of basic mound forms and their stylistic variation. It identifies over two dozen mound forms including those that appear to be the same animals and supernatural beings shown in different perspectives, as well as rare or anomalous types. Despite the great numbers of forms and variations, tabulation and analysis confirmed that the most common forms are birds, bears, and the long-tailed animals synonymous with Water Spirits (when two perspectives are combined) and these represent the three worlds of air, earth, and water in Native cosmologies.

Recent analyses also suggest that the differences in distribution reflect general differences in the natural landscape and therefore cosmological emphasis (Birmingham and Rosebrough 2017). Rosebrough acknowledges that cosmological principles could have been a guide, but close analysis of the distribution of key mound forms and other variables led to the conclusion that effigy mounds primarily communicated social segments in the form of clans, as long suspected, but also ritual societies and sodalities or other social sub-groups (Rosebrough 2010, 421). Some archaeologists believe there is material evidence for both formal clans and medicine or shamanistic ritual organizations in the earlier Hopewell culture (Thomas *et al.* 2005; Byers 2011; Romain 2011) and there is no reason to doubt that such institutions existed among the effigy mound societies.

Analysis of forms in the Four Lakes effigy mound locality in Wisconsin, where most of the zoomorphic mound forms appear to be present, led one of the present authors (RB) to define 13 different animals and supernatural beings, sometimes just shown in different perspectives (Birmingham 2010; Fig. 3.10). These are, as stated above, several types of birds: Thunderbirds, eagles, hawks and geese; bears; deer; canines (wolf or fox); water mammals (eg, otter, mink, muskrat, etc.); Water Spirits; and snakes. Most forms can be accommodated in the clan structures of the Ho-Chunk and/or other Midwestern peoples, although water birds or water mammals were not a part of the Ho-Chunk clan structure in modern times. As is true of the effigy mound region in general, birds, bears, and Water Spirits are most frequent in the Four Lakes effigy mound landscape. Analysis also broadly linked the uneven distribution of mound forms throughout the Four Lakes to geographical and topographic factors as has also been observed for the effigy mound region as a whole (see Chapter 5 for a detailed discussion).

As we have seen, among the Upper World forms, bird effigies are raptors such as eagles and hawk-like forms with swept back wings as though diving to prey. Some of the latter could feasibly be peregrine falcons. Falcon imagery was already present in the Middle Woodland culture that preceded the Late Woodland effigy mounds and falcon imagery continued to be of particular significance to the Mississippians and the Oneota cultures that followed the Late Woodland in the Upper Midwest, no doubt because of its fabled hunting prowess. Middle Mississippian warriors painted their faces with a forked eye decoration like that found around the eyes of a falcon and Oneota people even decorated some pottery with stylized and explicit falcon imagery (Fig. 3.11). The *ca* AD 1000 Mississippian paintings at the Gottschall Rockshelter in southwestern Wisconsin include a falcon that is interpreted as representing the Thunderbird in the story that was still recounted in Ho-Chunk oral history in the early 20th century and interpreted

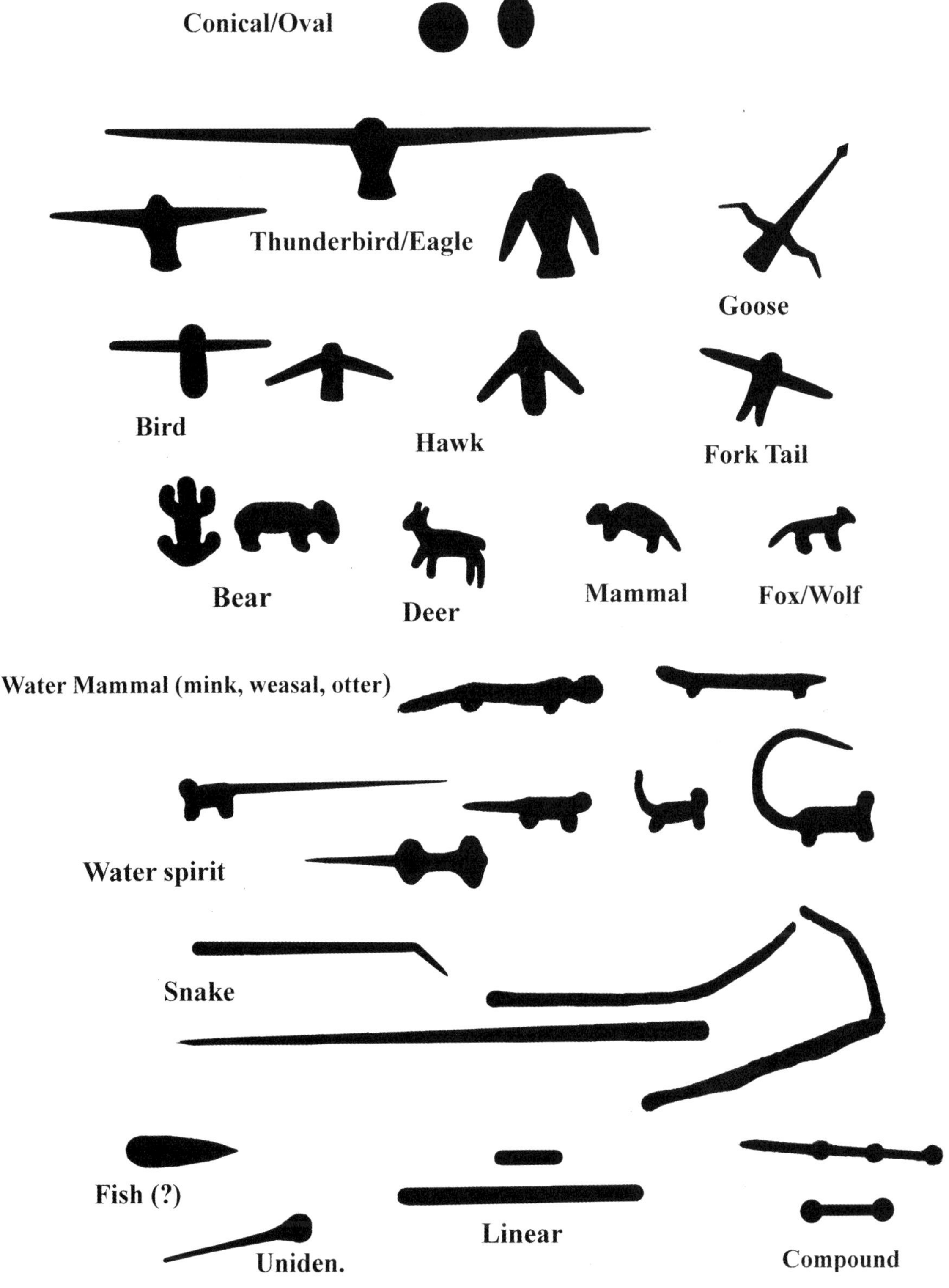
Conical/Oval
Thunderbird/Eagle
Goose
Bird
Hawk
Fork Tail
Bear
Deer
Mammal
Fox/Wolf
Water Mammal (mink, weasal, otter)
Water spirit
Snake
Fish (?)
Uniden.
Linear
Compound

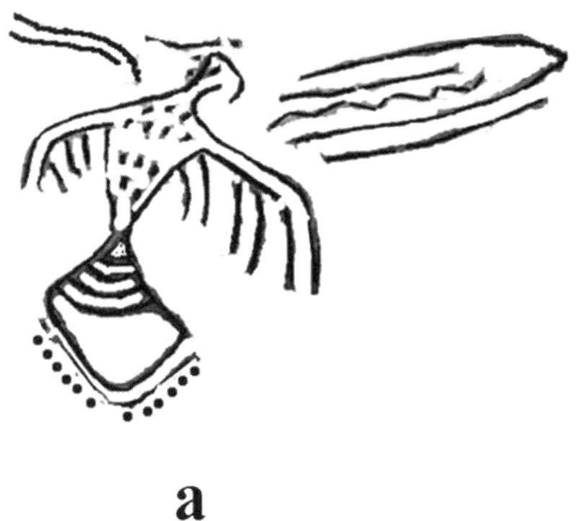

Fig. 3.11 Oneota pottery with stylized peregrine falcon imagery: a) falcon with power lines on a pot from the Bryan site in Minnesota; b) stylized falcon symbolism on some types of Oneota pots with the dots representing the speckled breast of the falcon; c) falcon tail on miniature pot from the Crabapple Point site, Wisconsin (photos: author).

by Robert Hall (1997) and Salzer and Rajnovich (2000), although there have been other interpretations.

Almost certainly the huge eagle-like forms such as those found in the Eagle Township mound cluster beside the Wisconsin River are Thunderbirds in Woodland traditions of the time: one huge example at the center of the mound landscape had a wingspan of one quarter of a mile (0.4 km). It can be argued that some other birds with folded wings are also Thunderbird but shown in a profile as though standing, with a flared tail or on stout feathered legs, because mound forms are nearly identical to more recent Native depictions of Thunderbirds in these different poses. Thunderbirds in Native traditions are sometimes also shown as having forked tails, as on the Menominee scroll mentioned above but some of these could also be 'bird men' showing the transformation of birds into human form.

All these types of bird forms most commonly occur in the central part of the effigy mound region and especially in the western hill country along the bluffs and terraces of the Wisconsin and Mississippi River valleys (Rosebrough 2010; 2014; Birmingham and Rosebough 2017). Similar birds are also found in the east where they are often found on high, or other otherwise prominent, places along with Lower World forms. In contrast, water birds such as geese and cranes or herons are rarely found in the west and are concentrated in the central and eastern parts of the effigy mound region; here they are associated with vast marshes as for example along great Horicon Marsh (Volkert and Sampson 2023) that covers 60 square miles (155 km^2) and today draws millions of geese and other water birds (Fig. 3.12). Geese have obvious fertility related symbolism since their seasonal migrations signal the onset of death of the world in fall, and its rebirth and abundance in the spring. In this connection, the once earth-lodge dwelling Mandan and closely related Hidatsa of the eastern Great Plains in modern-day North Dakota have fertility-oriented Goose Dance ritual societies whose members are older women; these tribes have many links to the Upper Midwest (Bowers 1950; 1992). Archaeologists specializing in Great Plains cultures point out that oral traditions of the tribes state that they originated in the Midwest but migrated to the Great Plains in ancient times (Ahler *et al.* 1991). Archaeological excavations of sites in the region produced cord impressed ceramics very similar to those made by Late Woodland people in the effigy mound region between AD 700 and 1200, who, incidentally, also lived in earth-lodges late in their history, albeit in smaller versions. Similar pottery is also found in southwestern Minnesota suggesting a scenario where a group of Late Woodland people living in the effigy mound region fled the turmoil caused by expansion of the Mississippians after AD 1000, moving through southwestern Minnesota to North Dakota where the people coalesced with Great Plains tribes (Green 2014). Besides pottery, it would be likely that the migrants took rituals and beliefs of their homeland including those that associated geese with fertility, but not in the form of effigy mound building.

As described above, earth effigy mound forms include bears, deer (or other antlered animals such as elk), canines (fox, wolf), with bears being the most frequent, although bear mounds, like birds, are most commonly found in the western half of the effigy mound region. As noted earlier, the bear head was prominent in the previous Hopewell culture and,

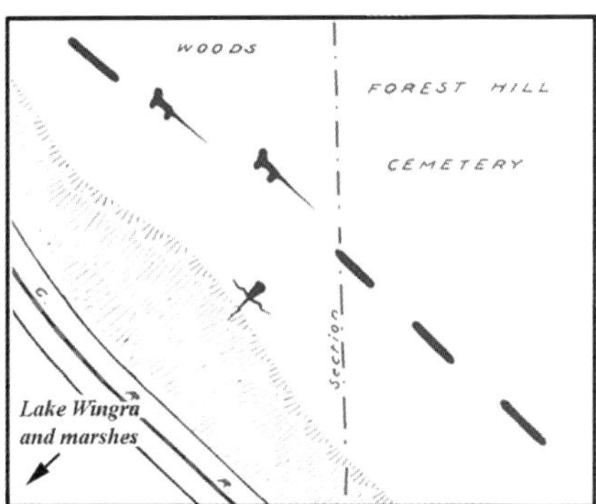

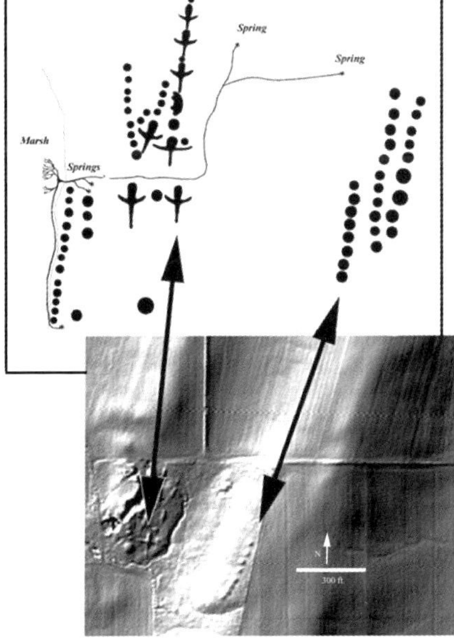

Fig. 3.12 Upper: a goose flies down slope towards Lake Wingra at the Forest Hill Cemetery in Madison, Wisconsin (from Brown 1915); lower: sketch by Bruder (1951) of the Clark's Wood Mound Group with six geese associated with a network of springs on the east side of Horicon Marsh; LiDAR of the same site from the WisconsinView website.

among the Ho-Chunk, the bear is the head of the earth clans. The association of bears with the west may well be ultimately derived from early Hopewell ceremonial activity that was the most intense along the Mississippi. The largest bear mound in existence, 138 ft in length and 5 ft high (*ca* 42 × 1.5 m), is now part of Effigy Mounds National Monument in Iowa near the Mississippi River. Some mounds have been identified as buffalo because of humped backs, but they lack horns, the defining characteristic of buffalo in Native traditions. It is probable that most of these are bears.

Water-oriented beings are Water Spirits, snakes, water animals, and probable fish. Water Spirits are by far the most frequent and are mostly found in the eastern half of the effigy mound region and in the far eastern lowlands, where they often dominate effigy mound groupings. These all have very long tails that are sometimes curved, shown in aerial and profiled perspectives, and sometimes clearly horned (Fig. 3.12). In recorded cases, Water Spirits appear in the form of intaglios among groups of effigy mounds, confirming the ceremonial association with the Underworld. Water Spirit forms are rarer in the far west but do occur, even in some numbers at specific sites, again supporting the view that the same overall cosmological structure is involved here. Snakes, also common to the eastern half of the effigy mound region, are associated with Lower World forms and/or depicted as crawling up slopes to or from bodies of water.

Short, tapering, linear, tear-drop shaped, so-called 'tadpole' and 'catfish' mounds could indeed be fish as though looking down on them in their watery habitat. These also are most common in the watery world of the east but rare in the western hill county. Barrett and Skinner (1932) of the Milwaukee Public Museum recorded small and isolated clusters of what they called 'catfish mounds' covering burials near the Wolf River on the present-day Menominee Reservation in northeast Wisconsin, far to the north of the main concentration of effigy mounds (Fig. 3.13). The reservation was established within a larger area bordered on the east by Lake Michigan, that was the original homeland of the Menominee. The Menominee share the Algonkian language family with other northern Great Lakes peoples like the Ojibwe with whom they also share beliefs and cultural institutions such as the Grand Medicine Society or *Midewiwin.*

Fish was important to the Menominee subsistence, especially the giant sturgeon. The Menominee have a Sturgeon clan and sturgeon fishing remains an important subsistence and cultural practice. However, with some exceptions, most shorter 'catfish' mounds are small and do not capture the essences or proportions of the long giant sturgeon, so other fish may be involved – if these are indeed fish. The relationship of these remote forms to broader effigy mound ceremonials is unknown but Barrett and Skinner (1932) also noted one isolated bird effigy in the region. However, it is quite possible that this mound and other curved mounds in this northern region derive from a different cultural tradition that may or may not have been directly influenced by the Effigy Mound Ceremonial Complex building to the south. Excavations by the Milwaukee Public Museum into two of the 'catfish' mounds, at two different locations, found a bear mandible interred with human burials in one and an entire bear skull with a severed human skull at the other (Barrett and Hawkes 1932). The investigators speculated that the mandible may have been part of a sacred medicine bundle. Among northern peoples,

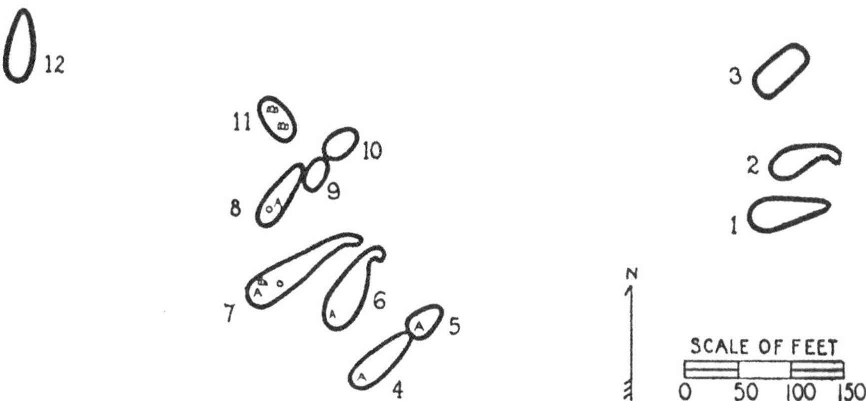

Fig. 3.13 'Catfish' mounds mapped by Barrett and Skinner (1932) on the Menominee Reservation.

the bear played an important role in the rituals of the Grand Medicine Society or *Midewiwin* as it is known by Ojibwe. Recounting of the origin of the *Midewiwin* is an important element of the *Mide* ritual and, in one Ojibwe version, it was the bear that carried the message of this great mystery from a higher spirit to the people. Hole in the Sky, an Ojibwe chief, drew a diagram tracing the path of the messenger bear for an anthropologist – showing two circles representing two worlds with bear paw tracks in between. Archaeologists have related the story and diagram to two 900-year-old bermed and ditched enclosures in southwest Michigan that are miles apart but with facing entranceways suggesting that society had ancient roots (Howey and O'Shea 2006). Analyzed in this context, one hypothesis is that the curved mounds in northern Wisconsin were meant to represent bear claws, not fish, and are connected to the doings of an ancient form of the *Midewiwin*. Additional evidence that the mounds belong to an unrelated cultural tradition is presence of the severed human head, an object not found in the more southerly effigy mounds.

Although the same animals and supernatural beings can be found throughout, there is much variation in style, as would be expected since different social groups and individuals were involved. Rosebrough (2014, 21) notes a tendency for some forms to become much more stylized and abstract as one moves east across the region. One possible explanation for this is that the effigy mounds complex became more abstracted as it diffused eastward from its postulated original source along the Mississippi River. Unfortunately there are too few radiocarbon dates to confirm that far eastern mounds might be somewhat later in time.

Human being mounds

By far, most identifiable effigy mounds are zoomorphic but in at least 10 instances human beings are depicted, several of which are horned or wearing horned head-dresses and animated in motion (Fig. 3.14). Along with key zoomorphic forms such as Thunderbirds, bears, and Water Spirits that relate to the realms of air, earth, and water, these certainly are a major clue to overall meaning of the effigy mounds ceremonialism, as is their limited distribution along the Wisconsin River and its tributaries in the modern-day counties of Sauk, Richland, and Dane in south-central

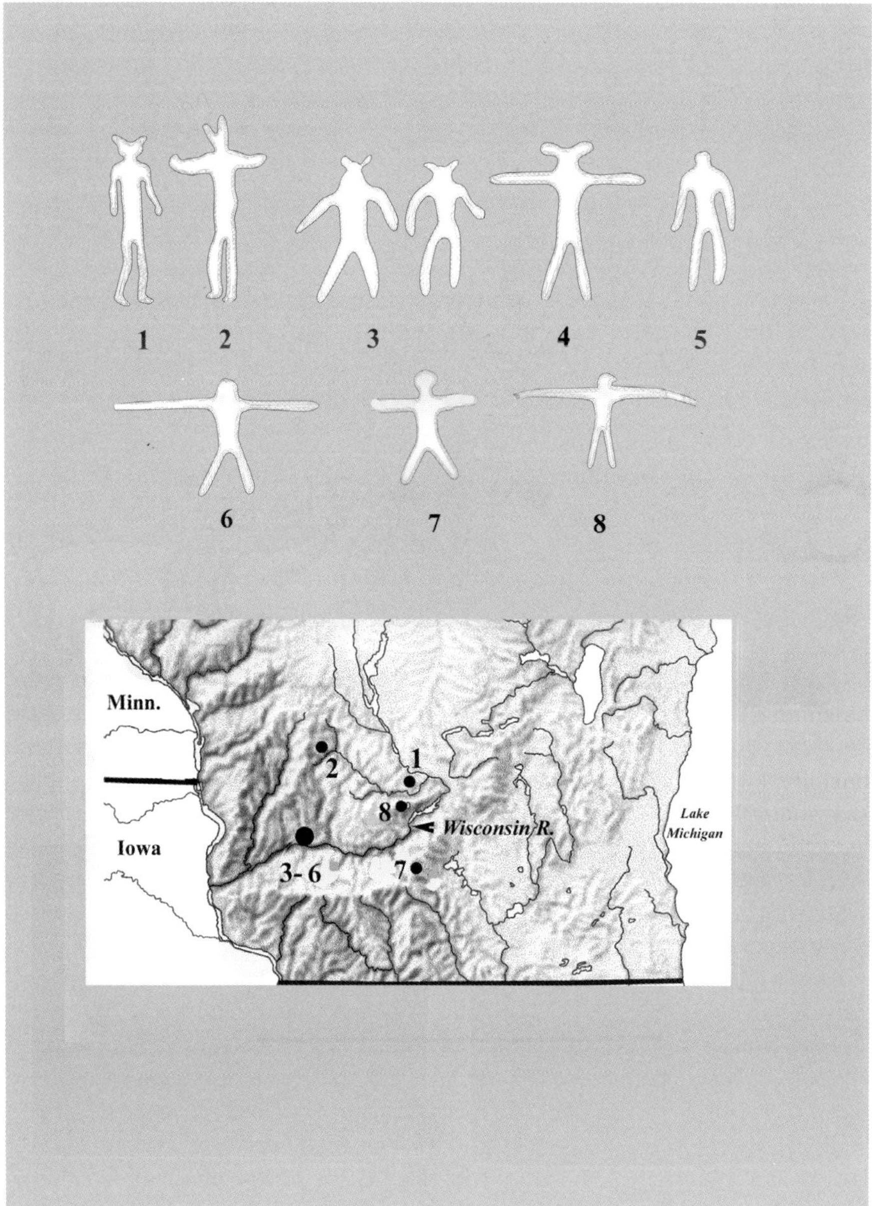

Fig. 3.14 Human and bird-man mounds: 1) Greenfield Man Mound, Sauk County; 2) LaValle Man Mound, Sauk County; 3–6) Human mounds from Eagle Township, Richland County; 7) Mt. Horeb, Dane County; 8) Devil's Lake State Park, Sauk County.

Wisconsin. These may provide a crucial link to oral traditions that describe the formation of the modern Ho-Chunk people placing this tribe, along with other, closely related tribes, in the context of the effigy mound era.

Monumental depictions of human beings in North America are not confined to the Upper Midwestern effigy mound region and apparently have a long temporal span. Elsewhere, images were produced by stones, boulder outlines, rock cobbles, or desert clearings (Fig. 3.15) and seem to be singular expressions of ritual activity rather than part of extensive, wide patterns or dense landscapes like the

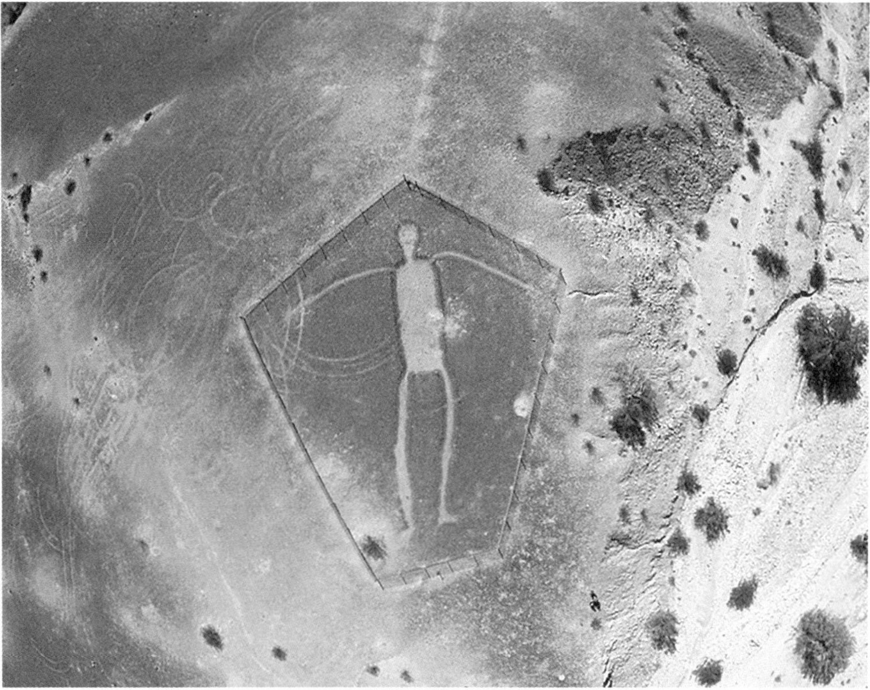

Fig. 3.15 Intaglio man geoglyph in California (image from Google Earth 2017).

effigy mounds. Most also date later in time than the human earthen mounds of the Upper Midwest. Undated horned or antlered human beings occasionally appear among other symbols in carvings and paintings in caves and rockshelters in the Upper Midwest that have a parallel to the human effigy mounds. Two of these, at the Samuel's Cave and Gullickson's Glen sites in western Wisconsin, show figures with arms raised and mouths wide open as though chanting and singing and one is horned or wearing an antlered headdress (Fig. 3.16).

The most famous of the horned human mounds, and the only one preserved today, is the giant Greenfield Man Mound near the city of Baraboo, Wisconsin, first identified and mapped by Canfield in 1842 (Fig. 3.17). It is located on a valley floor at the base of a high bluff or low mountain that is part of the Baraboo Range and just south of a small stream with prominent springs that drains to the Baraboo River, a major tributary of the Wisconsin River. Road construction amputated the feet prior to its preservation in a county park, but it originally extended 214 ft (*ca* 65 m) in length. The head features two prominent horns or a horned headdress and the figure is depicted as walking to the west. This horned man differs from the known others in that it is solitary and well away from other major effigy mound groupings, although some records suggest that there had been some conical and linear mounds somewhere on the bluff above. One linear mound is still present here today.

Fig. 3.16 Human figure at Gullickson's Glen rock art site with raised arms and a heartline. A heartline indicates a life force in Native traditions (adapted from Stiles-Hanson 1987, fig. 61).

Canfield mapped another large horned human in 1872 near LaValle, Wisconsin about 20 miles (32 km) northwest of the Greenfield Man but this was part of a cluster of zoomorphic mounds that included a bird, a horned Water Spirit and several linear mounds (Fig. 3.18). This 230 ft (70 m) long figure is animated, like the Greenfield Man, with its arms raised and feet in motion. Another human mound has been reported just south of Baraboo but a review of the sources makes its identification questionable (Rosebrough 2014).

Fig. 3.17 Modern aerial photo of the Greenfield Man Mound with former legs shown (from the Sauk County Historical Society).

The largest concentration of human mounds occurred further down the Wisconsin River within the giant Eagle Township Effigy Mound Landscape on a terrace and surrounding hills along the north side of the river, that functioned as a major ceremonial center. Radiocarbon dates from associated habitation sites show use of the area between AD 900 and 1000 (Birmingham 1994; Christiansen 2002). Spreading over several square miles, the landscape once contained several hundred mounds in various sub-groupings, mostly effigies dominated by birds, as well as habitation areas, ridged agricultural fields, and a circular, earthen bermed ceremonial enclosure. Most of the mounds have disappeared but much of this landscape had been documented in the past, especially through the efforts of Theodore Lewis. The Eagle Township landscape is highlighted in Chapter 5.

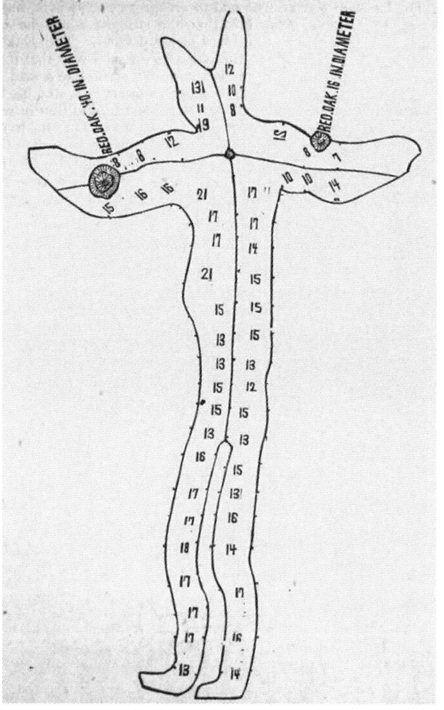

Fig. 3.18 LaValle Man Mound, as mapped by Canfield in 1872.

Among the many mounds were five human mounds, three of which wore horns or horned headdresses. Lewis mapped three clear human forms, two of which are paired in a sub-grouping along with effigies of birds, and a bear on the west side of the complex (Fig. 3.19, A–B; Lewis 1886c), but he noted that other mounds were in the vicinity that he did not map. Over 100 ft (*ca* 30.5 m) in

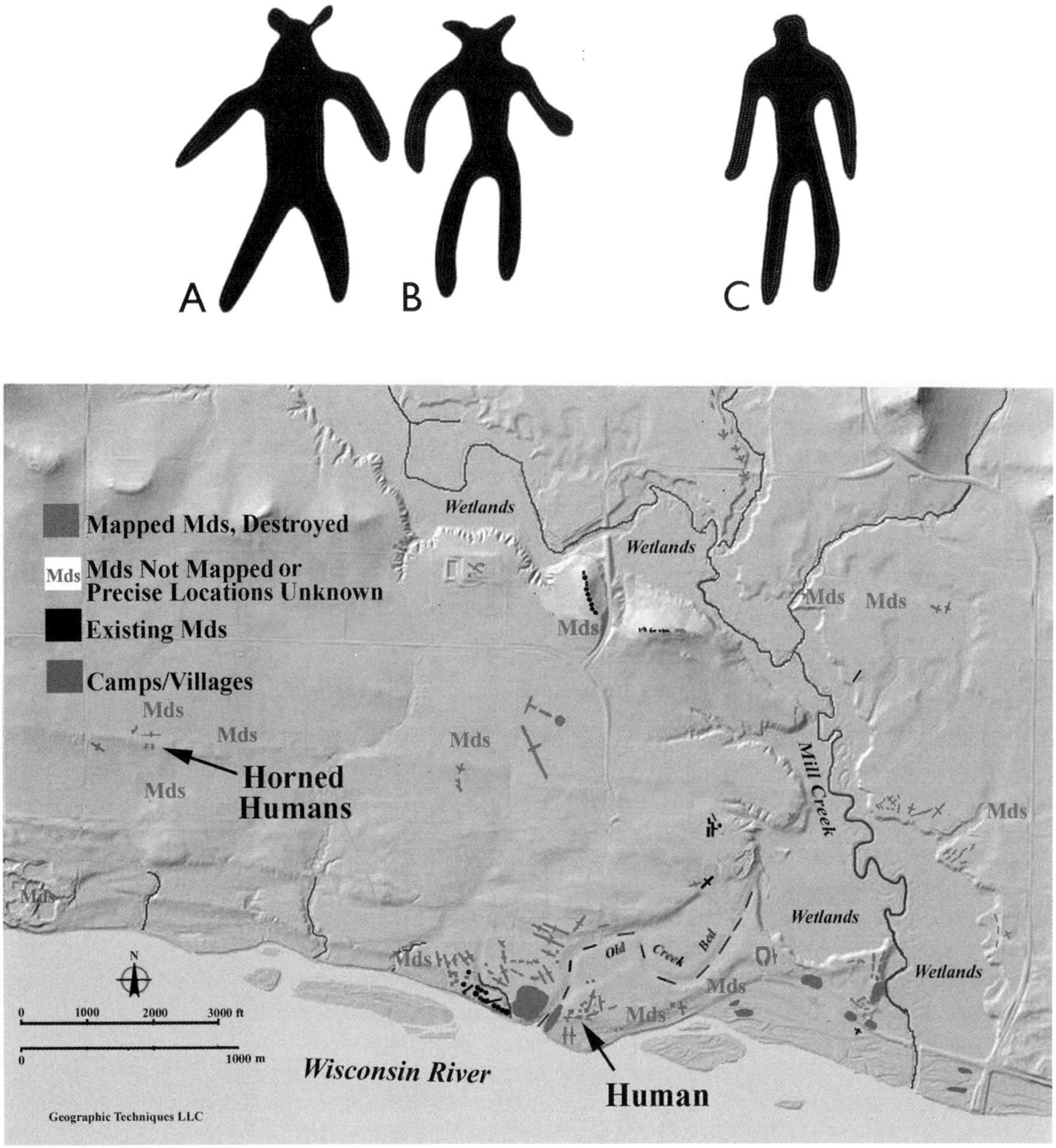

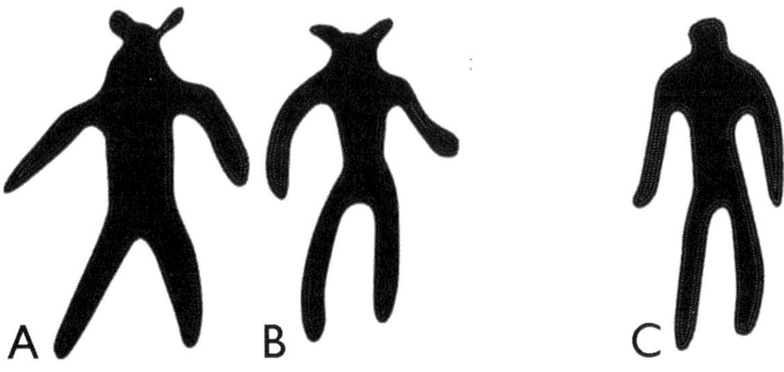

Fig. 3.19 Above: A–B, pair of horned humans and C, single human without horns near the Wisconsin River that were part of the Eagle Township Effigy Mound Landscape (lower) (drawing from Lewis 1880–1895, notebook 25).

length and 50–60 ft (*ca* 15–18 m) in maximum width, the humans were horned and in obvious motion. Interestingly, and no doubt symbolically significant, the orientation contrasts with those of the bird and bear effigies in the grouping in that the heads of the humans lie in an opposite direction and towards the Wisconsin River. They seem to have been created as to face or oppose the other mounds representing the Upper World (bird) and Earth (bear), and one gets the definite impression that a story is being told here.

To the east of the twins sub-grouping, Lewis (1886d, 42–48) mapped another human mound amid the main Eagle Township grouping in an area containing a dense concentration of effigy mounds, dominated by birds (Fig. 3.19 C and Fig. 3.20). It was 106 ft (*ca* 42 m) long with a rounded head and no horns, arms to the side and oriented with head to the west. Towards the eastern side of the Eagle Township landscape, along the river, Lewis also described and mapped a fork-tailed bird next to the enclosure that may or may not be a bird-man. At an unreported location somewhere further to the northeast, early mound researcher Steven Taylor located another probable horned human in 1843 but described it having a bilobed head, quite unlike the other effigy mounds he had encountered but 'the most perfect I have seen' (Taylor 1843, 34; Fig. 3.21). Like the mound twins, it headed south.

Finally, a human-like form at the center of the Eagle Township Effigy Mound Landscape was part of a grouping that contained a conical mound 200 ft (*ca* 61 m) in diameter, probably of Middle Woodland origin, a short linear, and the largest effigy mound ever recorded: an eagle-like mound, no doubt meant to be a Thunderbird, which had a wingspan of over 900 ft (274+ m). All of these had been plowed down by years of farming but still appeared as 'soil shadows', resulting from soil differences with the surrounding land, on an aerial photograph brought to light by James Scherz of the University of Wisconsin. The human form has outstretched arms but the head region cannot be clearly made out on the photograph.

Elsewhere, but in the same general area of Wisconsin, Richard Taylor (1838) found a 125 ft (38 m) long anthropomorphic figure within a long chain of effigy mounds running along an old Indian trail on a high ridge called the Military Ridge (Fig. 3.22). The effigy had long outstretched arms that were much longer the body (140 ft/42.7 m) with a round head without horns, leading Rosebrough (2014) to

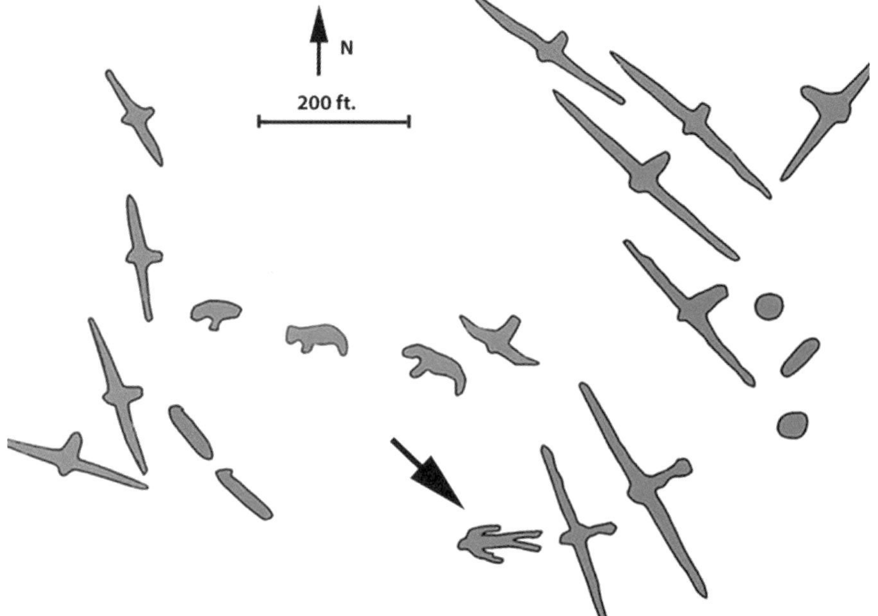

Fig. 3.20 Human being mound mapped by T.H. Lewis (1886d, 4–7, 10–12, 34–51) amid a dense cluster of bird and other mounds of the Eagle Township Effigy Mound Landscape.

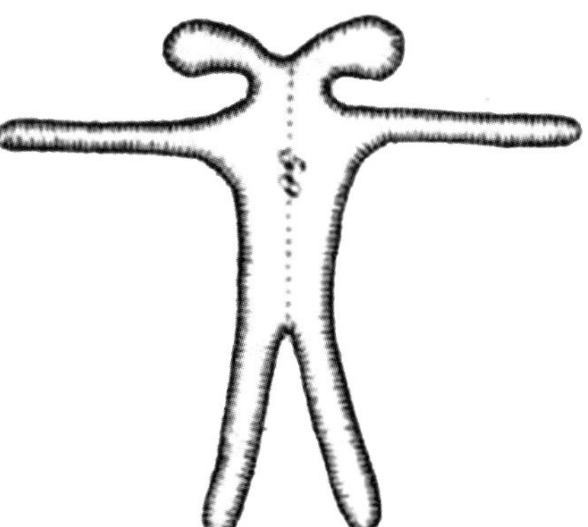

Fig. 3.21 Drawing of bilobed man mound (from Taylor 1843, pl. vii).

suggest it was a bird-man showing the bird/human transformation. There have been other scattered reports of human mounds but Rosebrough found these reports to be dubious. For example, a single, very large human-like mound was reported along a small creek in Black Earth, Wisconsin (Brown 1872–1945, papers box 20; 1906) but further research indicates that it was probably a smaller, fork-tailed bird.

The horns on the human effigy mounds provide clues to their identification but different interpretations emerge based on ethnographic sources and analogies. Paul Radin asked people living on Winnebago Reservation about the human mounds and most had no knowledge of them. A few elders said that they represented the Warrior or Hawk clan (Radin 1923, 33). Indeed, warriors among Great Plains peoples often donned buffalo or bison horns that provided them with spirit powers, and some spirits themselves had horns. Radin told of another clan story that could feasibly explain the presence of horned humans in this region. Near the center of the distribution of horned humans is the body of water called Devil's Lake, that is said to be the ultimate origin place of the

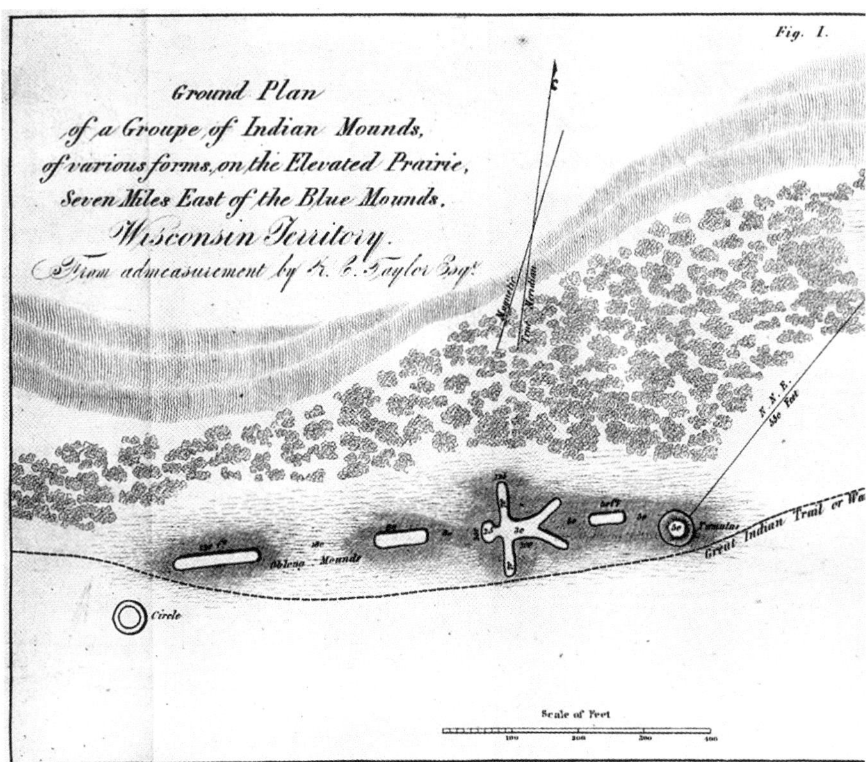

Fig. 3.22 Man mound in Dane County, west of Madison, south-central Wisconsin as mapped by Richard C. Taylor in 1838.

Buffalo clan people (Radin 1923, 197) and therefore humans with buffalo horns could reflect this origin story (see below).

In the Eastern Woodlands bison horn or deer/elk antlered headdresses are more commonly associated with Medicine people, frequently referred to as shamans, also representing great supernatural powers (Fig. 3.23). Such religious practitioners are in direct touch with the spirit world through dreams and visions. In many Native societies, including those of the Upper Midwest, Medicine people belonged to societies that cross-cut community boundaries and provided years of training in holistic healing, both spiritual and practical, and were invested as keepers of sacred knowledge, including of creation, not shared with other community members. Medicine Society members would be the most likely to oversee effigy mound ceremonies that required such connections, arcane knowledge, and contacts with the supernatural. The depiction of motion with arms raised would be consistent with Medicine people rituals and similar figures can be found in rock art of the region, amid other ritual paintings and carvings. Medicine Man figures with upraised arms are also common among rock art sites in Canada north of Lake Superior as described by Grace Rajnovich (1994, 75–80) and ethnographic accounts suggest that upraised arms indicate the dispensing or receiving of spirit powers.

With this information, the restricted distribution of the horned humans could be explained as indicating that this area was the very center of Medicine Society ritual and even its place of origin. The geographic association of origins of such societies is not unusual. One Ojibwe tradition places the origin of their Medicine Society, the *Midewiwin*, on Madeline Island near the south shore of Lake Superior where Medicine Society ceremonials were conducted into the 19th century (Dewdney 1975).

A third interpretation derives from the general theme of effigy mound ceremonial activity related to on-going recreation of the world and its people. The Ho-Chunk story cited above relates that Thunderbird and Water Spirit transformed themselves into humans and that other animals likewise underwent transformation, establishing the various clans from spirit ancestors. The Greenfield Man Mound especially recalls the Ho-Chunk tradition recorded by Radin that the horned Water Spirit became human 'and walked' (Radin 1923, 194). It may very well be that the horned human mounds represent the very transformation from the horned Water Spirit. Likewise, a least some bird-man like mounds of the area could record the transformation of the Thunderbird into human form.

The Ho-Chunk and related Ioway, who split from the Ho-Chunk sometime in late prehistory, place their origin along Green Bay of Lake Michigan where the Ho-Chunk were living in the 17th century (Radin 1923; Skinner 1926; Green 2014). The Ho-Chunk specifically identify the site as Red Banks on the Door County Peninsula of Lake Michigan near to an interior body of water called *Within Lake* in the Ho-Chunk language, meaning that it lies within some specific geographic area or feature (Radin 1923, 165, 168, 194, 201). *Within Lake* is where the great Water Spirit dramatically emerged to form the Water Spirit clan. In some controversial interpretations, codified even by a historical marker, this Red Banks is where the French, in the form of Jean Nicolet, first met the Ho-Chunk in 1634. This has long been the view of the imminent anthropologist Nancy Luire, an expert on Ho-Chunk

Fig. 3.23 Historical photograph of Winnebago (Ho-Chunk) and Fox (Mesquake) medicine men wearing bison horn headdresses (Wisconsin Historical Society archives image WHi [x3] 52437).

history (Luire and Yung 2014) but is disputed by other scholars who place Nicolet's first contact at various other places from eastern Lake Superior to northern Illinois (Hall 1993; 1997; Mason 2014). Prior to European contact, the Ho-Chunk had been a widespread and populous people so their territory could have been very large.

The Green Bay Red Banks region has no effigy mounds, which would seem to disconnect the Ho-Chunk with the effigy people on the basis of geography, as well as in time. However, Robert Hall (1993) pointed out that the Ho-Chunk population concentration along Green Bay documented in the late 1600s was the result of reconstitution of the tribe after it had been greatly decimated and nearly wiped out by earlier calamities such as disease and warfare with the Illinois, who may have been their southern neighbors (Lurie 1978). Hall once proposed that the original Red Banks had been the cliffs of the Niagara Escarpment immediately east of Lake Winnebago and that *Within Lake* was Lake Winnebago itself, but that the Ho-Chunk adapted the Green Bay location as their origin place only after the tribal re-organization, 'naturalizing' their origin to their late 17th century home (Hall 1993). There are, indeed, both many major villages on Lake Winnebago that are assigned to the Oneota that many archaeologists believe had their origins partly at least in historically known tribes including the Ho-Chunk (Overstreet 1993), and a large concentration of earlier effigy mound groups. Many Midwestern archaeologists are convinced that the Oneota culture had formed from interaction and intermarriage between the indigenous Late Woodland people and the

Mississippians who expanded into southern Wisconsin after AD 1000 (Stoltman 2000; Stoltman and Christiansen 2000). Even if Hall was correct about relocation of the Red Banks as the Ho-Chunk origin place, there is much earlier evidence of Red Banks and *Within Lake* that could take Ho-Chunk origins much further into the past and back into the time of effigy mound builders.

The center of the World?

Within the limited distribution of human and human-like forms lie unusual and visually stunning geological features, in Sauk County, Wisconsin. One of these, already mentioned above, is provocatively called Devil's Lake. It is a small, spring fed, lake surrounded by high bluffs of reddish rock called Baraboo Quartzite, with large talus slopes made of quartzite blocks and boulders and is now a popular Wisconsin State Park (Fig. 3.24). The Ho-Chunk name is *Tamahcunchukdah*, or Sacred or Holy Lake, which was given an evil connotation by white settlers, no doubt because of the association of the horned Water Spirit that recalls the devil in Euro-American tradition. In legend, the rock blocks resulted from a battle between the Thunderbirds and Water Spirits during which the rocks were thrown (Cole 1920; Brown 1947, 14). The lake itself is said to have been the abode of a powerful Water Spirit at the very center of the World, who had been put in charge of the Earth by Earthmaker, who arose at one time to defeat Thunderbirds at Lake Winnebago (Radin 1954, 47–8).

The nearby Wisconsin Dells, deep and scenic gorges that cut through thick layers of sandstone, were said to have been created by a green Water Spirit and an oral tradition passed on by Albert Yellow Thunder, grandson of a warrior chief, recounts how Devil's Lake itself formed when the Water Spirit leaped and plunged down in the Lower World of the Earth (Saunders 1947). As discussed above, Paul Radin also linked Devil's Lake to one of the Ho-Chunk origin stories: the area of lake is said to be where the Buffalo people lived in spirit form prior to their transformation into the Buffalo Clan, along with others, to form the Ho-Chunk nation at the Green Bay Red Banks location (Radin 1923, 197 n. 23).

Fig. 3.24 Wisconsin Department of Natural Resources photo showing rock-enclosed Devil's Lake.

Effigy mounds along its shores reflect the prominence that Devil's Lake has in Ho-Chunk stories in that it had been long been associated with supernatural beings from the Upper and Lower Worlds (Figs 3.24 and 3.25). On the south shore of the lake is a 150 ft (45.7 m) long effigy with a beak, long wings, and long human-like legs. It looks very much like a bird-man or perhaps a bird becoming human. In Native traditions, the south direction is associated with Upper World – air, light, summer, and life – and in some traditions Upper World clans occupied this direction in the layout of Ho-Chunk villages in ancient times. Effigy mounds at

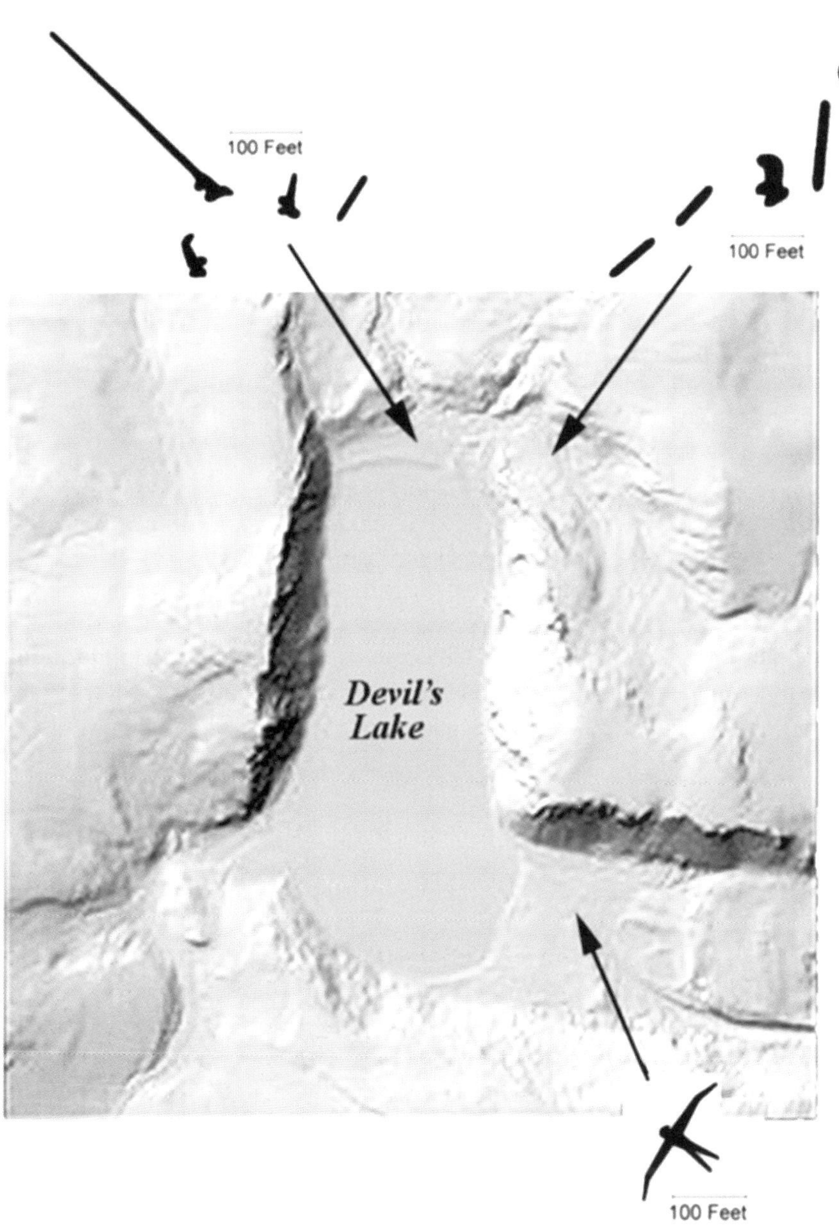

Fig. 3.25 LiDAR image of Devil's Lake from the WisconsinView website with location of mounds added, some of which have been destroyed since recording (Stout 1906, based on Lewis 1880–1895, notebook 25).

the northern end of the lake are from the opposing Lower World (earth/water) consisting of a bear, an unidentified animal, a large Water Spirit, and several long snake-like mounds. North is generally perceived as symbolizing darkness, winter, and death and Lower World clans of the Ho-Chunk were said to have lived in the northern part of former villages.

It is certainly possible that effigy mounds already present on the lake and in the surrounding area inspired legends and stories among the Ho-Chunk when they expanded into the region in the late 18th or early 19th century. Various spirits represented by the mounds would certainly have been recognized as related to their cosmology and clan, but there is evidence that Native people had long associated the geological features of the area to the supernatural, even before the time of the effigy mounds. The Minnesota Middle Woodland pipe decorated with Water Spirit symbolism, discussed above, was made from a purplish Baraboo Pipestone found only in the Baraboo Range around Devil's Lake, and archaeologists have discovered ancient quarries for the stone within 2 miles (3.2 km) of the lake itself (Broihahn 2003). The pipestone obviously had special meaning for Native people and the Middle Woodland pipe suggests that it symbolized the powers of the Underworld. This stone also had special meaning for later and different Native people. Ear spools worn by people of the Mississippian site of Aztalan in southern Wisconsin, 60 miles (*ca* 96 km) from the quarries, were also made from Baraboo Pipestone.

The evidence presented above is admittedly circumstantial but leads to a hypothesis that the original Red Banks in Ho-Chunk tradition are the red piles of rock and cliffs that enclose Devil's Lake and the lake itself is the *Within Lake* from which the great Water Spirit emerged and, in later traditions, in which a Water Spirit continued to live in the center of earth. It is not being proposed that the Devil's Lake area was the origin place of effigy mound ceremonials but rather that the origin story about the formation of Ho-Chunk clans crystallized around the lake during effigy mound times and then transferred to a series of different locations due to population relocations and through cultural changes into more recent times.

Mound twins and pairs, crossed mounds

The paired, horned human beings at the vast Eagle Township Effigy Mound Landscape along the Wisconsin River mentioned above are an example of another kind of dualism commonly found throughout the effigy mound region – that of mound twins. These are virtually identical effigy mounds found next to one another in broader groupings, and sometimes even joined together (Figs 3.26–3.28). Most appear to be Water Spirit forms but other forms, such as birds and bears, have been recorded. Figure 3.26 shows several examples at the Lizard Mound group; Water Spirits and a pair of long-necked geese or cranes flying away from each other. Pairs of crossed long, linear mounds, probably snakes, have been recorded at several different sites in the Four Lakes area and south-central Wisconsin (Figs 3.27 and 3.28).

The presence of mound twins and pairs are among the many mysteries of effigy mound arrangement. There is no single pattern of arrangement or orientation:

some are parallel to one another and others point in different directions that vary, suggesting that as a whole the phenomenon is not related to the movements of sun, moon, planets, and stars, as has been asserted for other monument building in the Americas, including the effigy mounds. Perhaps they simply represent an artistic symmetry derived from a general ritualistic worldview. It is also feasible that at least some orientations, especially the long, crossed linear mound, may also be snakes and, therefore, the joining could also represent skin shedding, an action symbolic of renewal and rebirth as discussed by Hall (1997).

Another, quite feasible, explanation is that at least some of the pairs are related to traditions of mythological Hero Twins found among indigenous people through the Americas and elsewhere in the world (Lankford 1987; Hall 1997, 161–2; Duncan and Diaz-Granados 2023). These are brothers with magical or supernatural powers often likened to stars or animal spirits, although they play various roles in different cultures. Twins, named Ghost or Stump and Flesh, occupy a cycle of sacred stories among the Ho-Chunk, as recorded in detail by Paul Radin (1948). As offspring of the sun and moon they first appear as spirits but become transformed into humans. Raised separately, one is wild, and one is part of a traditional household (i.e., civilized). Eventually reunited, the twins roam the world engaging in numerous adventures and their stories are interwoven with other spirits and supernatural beings such as the Earthmaker, Thunderers, and different types of Water Spirits with which they sometimes do battle. In one version, Ghost dies after childbirth and is buried next to a tree stump, hence the name Stump. He is reincarnated and lives with a Water Spirit until reunion with his father and brother. Together the boys reincarnate their uncle, Blue Horn, a Water Spirit, who had been killed by Thunderbirds. The twins are also connected in stories to the planet Venus whose human name becomes Red Horn and He-Who-Wears-Human-Heads-As-Earrings and will be further mentioned in other contexts in this book, most notably associated with a story told in Mississippian rock art at the Gottschall Rockshelter in

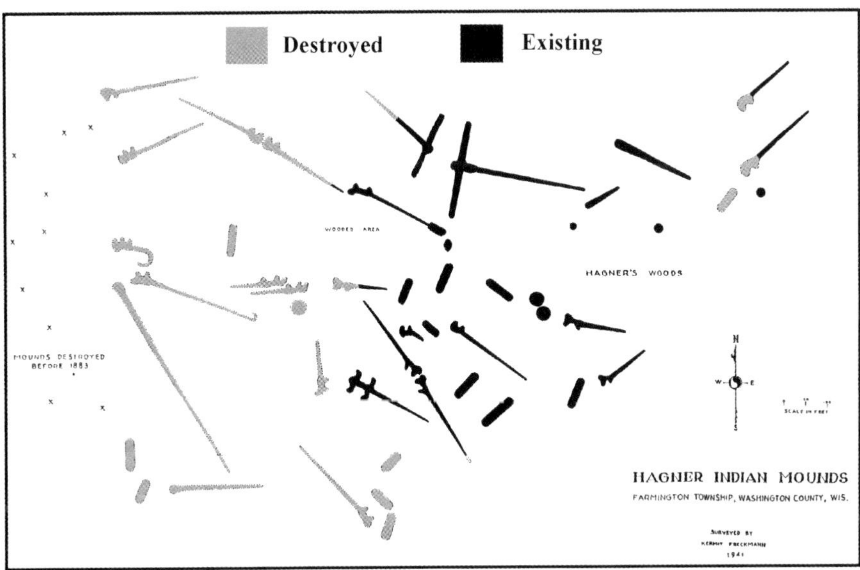

Fig. 3.26 Map of Lizard Mound by Kermit Freckmann (1942) with mound pairing highlighted.

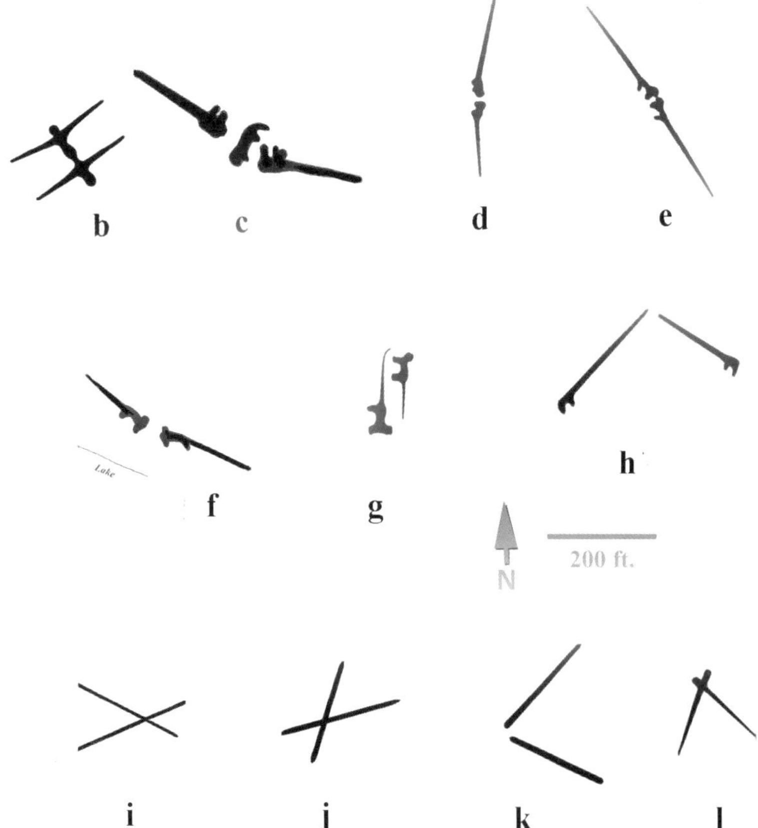

Fig. 3.27 Mound pairs and crossed mounds in Wisconsin mound groups: a) 1915 photo of joined Water Spirit mounds at the Gaasch or Ridge site on the east side of Lake Winnebago; b) joined birds at the Siamese Birds site on the Wisconsin River (from Lewis 1880–1895, notebook 25); Water Spirit mound pairs at c) Hammersly site in south-central Wisconsin (from Brown 1911); d) Eli Johnson site overlooking the Yahara River in south-central Wisconsin (from McLachlan 1914); e) Lizard Mound State Park, Wisconsin (Freckman 1941); f) Lake Ripley (Lapham 1855, pl. XXIX); g) Fairhaven on Lake Monona (Brown 1922); h) Ward//Schlitz at Milwaukee, Wisconsin (Lapham 1855, pl. IV); i) Eli Johnson on the Yahara River, McFarland, Wisconsin (McLachlan 1914); j) Big Cross at Madison, Wisconsin (Brown 1927); k) Kennedy Pond at Madison, Wisconsin (Brown 1912); l) North Shore Resort site in central Wisconsin (from Brown and Drexel 1921).

southwestern Wisconsin. Duncan and Diaz-Granados (2000) identified another Mississippian ritual cave in Missouri that appears to show Red Horn himself as a severed head.

The twins here are culture heroes that, as with other similar myths in the world, seem to represent multiple and layered dualistic themes such as order/chaos,

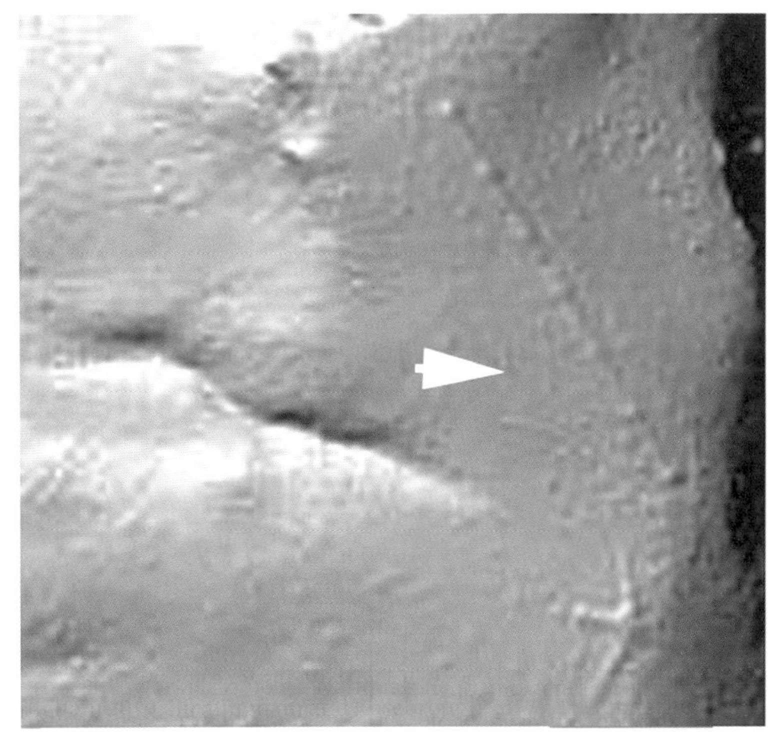

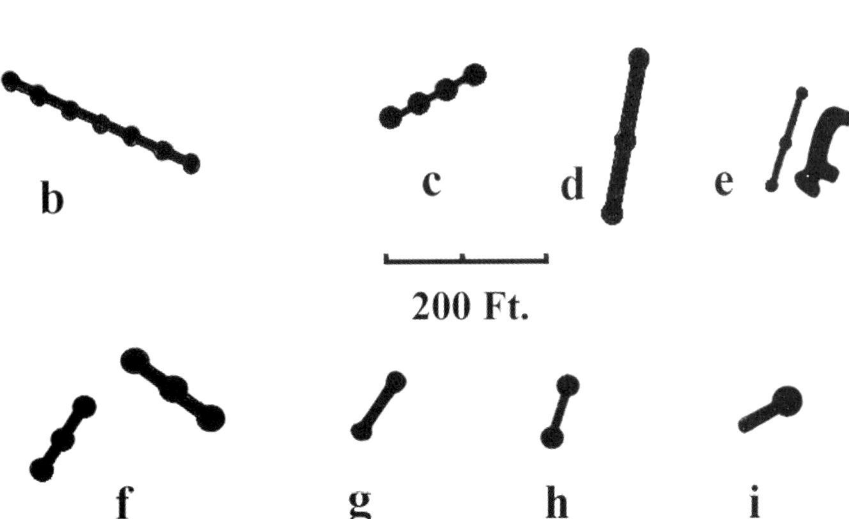

Fig. 3.28 Examples of compound mounds from: a) Effigy Mounds National Monument, LIDAR courtesy of William Romain; b) Turkey River site on the Mississippi in Iowa (from Green 1988, 195, fig. 6.2); c) Hogback site, Iowa (from Lewis 1885, 30); d) Merrill Springs site on Lake Mendota in south-central Wisconsin (from Lewis 1886f); e) McGregor Pikes Peak 4 site at Pikes Peak State Park, Iowa (from Kidder n.d); f) Spook Hill site at Wyalusing State Park near the Mississippi River in southwestern Wisconsin (from Brown 1911); g) Pleasant Springs site in south-central Wisconsin (Salzer and Johns 1992); h) Gee's Slough site on the Wisconsin River in central Wisconsin (from Buell 1918); i) Keller site, Iowa (from Benn *et al.* 1978).

death/rebirth, bereavement and mourning, and the differences between the soul (Ghost) and corporal body (Flesh). As such, twins would have a place in the general dualistic underlying structure of effigy mound ceremonials. But, aside from the existence of the paired mounds, there is thus far no other evidence that might support the interpretation as the mythological twins, so this also remains a matter of conjecture. Other interpretations for the paired mounds are certainly possible in addition to the ones mentioned, and this should be a topic for future research since, like the human being mounds, the widespread and recurring pattern offers a major clue to the overall meaning of the effigy mound ceremonial landscapes.

Conical, short linear, and compound mounds

Conical and short linear mounds are common in effigy mound landscapes and, in the case of conical mounds, are even more numerous than zoomorphic effigies. Both types also contain interments but conical mounds often have multiple burials. In many cases the conical mounds are arranged in long lines and in others groups of conicals are spatially segregated from effigy mounds. Robert Hall (1993, 44) observed that a considerable number of mound groups in the Upper Midwest have round or oval and short linear mounds and thought that these symbolized moeities in which societies were divided into Upper World (conical/oval) and Lower World people (linears) in an abstract form, but the picture seems more complicated than that. The numerous conicals found among the effigy mound groups provide important additional clues to the Late Woodland mound building chronology, mortuary customs, social structure, as well as broader cosmology.

Many effigy mound landscapes developed around large conical mounds built during previous mound building traditions, dating as far back as 1000 years before the emergence of the Effigy Mound Ceremonial Complex and such places reflect the long continuity of sacred places. As Late Woodland landscapes developed, lines of conical mounds accompanied construction of effigy mounds but are often found on the highest or more prominent parts of the landscape or are otherwise segregated from the effigies. Further, there is evidence that some conical mound associations may be unrelated to social status but, rather, to frequent communal earth renewal rituals independent of those rituals involved in the effigy mounds.

The Late Woodland people expanded into some new areas not previously used for mound building, consecrating new sacred grounds starting with moving the bones of people from former burial grounds and reburying the cleaned bones *en masse* in bundles or as disarticulated bones *covered by conical mounds.* Excavations conducted by the Milwaukee Public Museum at the Raisbeck mound group along the Grant River in southwest Wisconsin identified one mound in a long line of conicals that covered the mass reburial of 65 individuals (Figs 3.29 and 3.30). Likewise, Kratz Creek mound group on Buffalo Lake was arranged around one large conical mound that occupies the highest part of the area along the lake and is also central to the effigy mound landscape (Fig. 2.10, above). Excavation conducted by Barrett and Hawkes (1919) found evidence quite different from the other mounds sampled at the site. Stratified layers of charcoal and colored sand covered a mass grave of bundled reburials representing 45 people. A projectile point found embedded in the pelvis of one individual is characteristic of the late Middle Woodland period *ca* AD 400–600 – the time when mound building was expanding in the Upper Midwest. The Nitschke Mound Group is located in a remote area not previously used by mound builders and may have been part of one of the last effigy mound groups constructed. Here also one mound, larger than the others, in a line of conical mounds, contained the interment of a number of individuals more than the many other mounds excavated (Fig. 3.31). This too likely symbolized the sanctification of place by virtue of the presence of ancestors.

In the western part of the effigy mound region, especially along the bluffs of the Mississippi River, linear and conical mounds are joined creating chains or what have been called compound mounds that appear to represent the symbolic joining of the Upper and Lower Worlds. Based on mound landscape analysis, it has been further proposed that these arrangements immediately pre-date the more explicit zoomorphic forms during the early part of the Late Woodland with the effigies built later.

Insights into the evolution of effigy mounds have come from examination of the key mound landscape of the Four Lakes, discussed in detail in Chapter 5, where one of the authors (RB) has traced the evolution from a few earlier conical burial mounds to smaller conical and short linear mounds, possibly accompanied by the first effigies, to the great expansion of effigy mound building across the natural landscape after AD 700 (Birmingham 2010). The building of conical mounds continued though the effigy mound era and even dominated construction in the last throes of that era and earliest part of the next cultural tradition, Oneota, signaling a cultural change and a probable separation of the mortuary sphere from broader ceremonials that had integrated Late Woodland peoples. Hall (1993, 51–2) proposed that the long period of effigy mound construction, with an emphasis on earth renewal, shifted to a new agricultural emphasis on fertility that became separated from the death ritual. The Oneota developed social mechanisms such as large, permanent villages and other types of non-monument building ceremonials that replaced the social, spiritual, and mortuary functions embedded in mound building. Eventually burial mound building in the form of small conical mounds disappears among the Oneota, with individual interments made in unmarked and below ground cemeteries.

Where there is topographic relief, the effigy mound era conical mounds often occupy lines or clusters on the highest places of effigy mound landscape. At the Nitschke Mound Group, arranged on a glacial drumlin, for example, a line of conical mounds runs along the highest part of the ridge amid a variety of zoomorphic forms, and five of the conical mounds are superimposed on an aerial perspective or flattened Water Spirit, emphasizing the relationship of the two forms in a vertically tiered cosmos (Fig. 3.31).

Long lines of conical mounds, ranging from 14–41 ft in diameter and 3–5 ft (4.3–12.7 × 0.9–1.5 m) in height, occupy the highest elevations of the vast Raisbeck mound group as noted by Broihahn and Rosebrough (2014) in a re-analysis of data excavated by William McKern in 1931 and later described by Rowe (1956) (Figs 3.29 and 3.30) and all except one contained burials of 1–5 individuals, mostly as bone bundles but also one extended 'in the flesh'. Several of these were surrounded by clusters of rocks and other features and the burials and rocks covered some of the burials themselves. Whether or not these mounds are contemporaneous with effigy mound construction at the site is unknown but they point to the possibility that mound building began here just prior to the expansion of effigy mound construction after AD 700. The mounds included some extended burials that are rare in effigy mounds and more common to earlier mounds.

In a multi-tiered mound landscape that reflects a multi-tiered cosmology, the interpretation that these circular mounds represent celestial bodies is logical, and most obvious of these heavenly bodies is the sun, the giver of all life that occupies the highest cosmological level among American Native people and other well-known ancient cultures of the world where it is viewed as a deity. Radin, in fact, found evidence in the Ho-Chunk mythology that the sun had once been a deity but this role had subsequently been taken by Earthmaker (Radin 1923, 238) whose great symbol, the cross of the four directions, was discovered in giant mound form by Increase Lapham in eastern Wisconsin (Lapham 1855, 52). Perhaps the two eventually merged into one creator concept, but it also appeared to Radin that some of the functions and powers of the former Sun deity were transferred to Thunderbird, the most powerful of spirits for humans in more recent times. After creation of earth, Earthmaker pretty much stays out of human affairs, unlike Thunderbird, but remains the great symbol of creation and of the world itself.

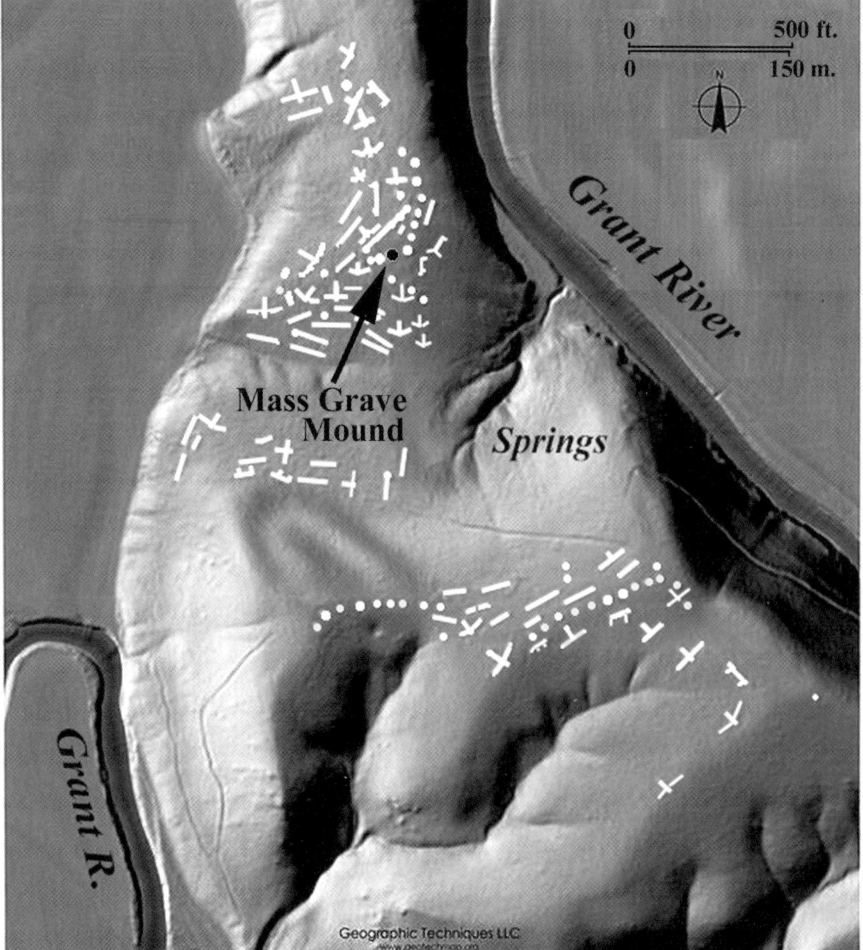

Fig. 3.29 Modern LiDAR from the WisconsinView website of the Raisbeck site in southwestern Wisconsin showing lines of conical mounds among effigy mounds along the top of the site.

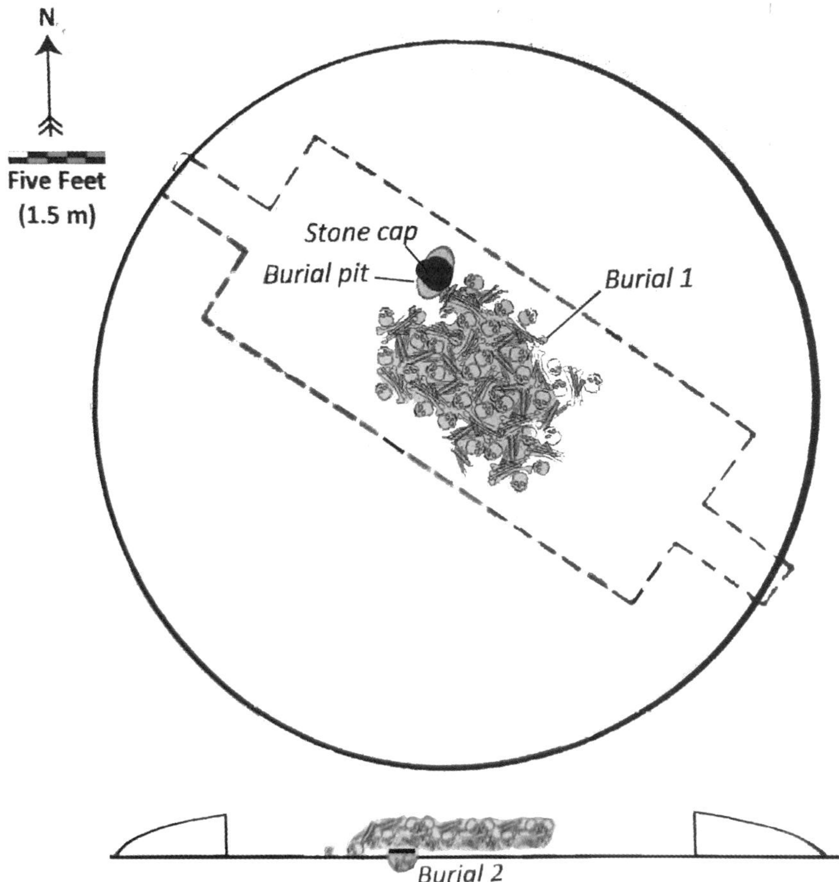

Fig. 3.30 Above: Mound 42 of the Raisbeck mound group (MPM image #182565); below: plan of Mound 42 ossuary (from Broihahn and Rosebrough 2014, 143).

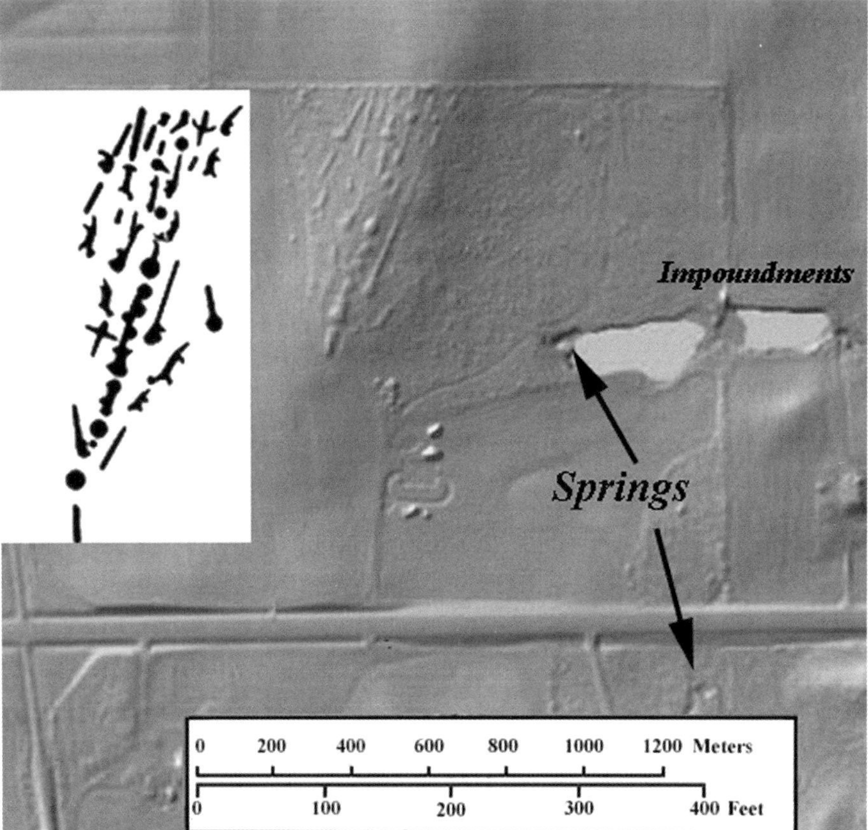

Fig. 3.31 Map and LiDAR from the WisconsinView website of the Nitschke mound group showing line of conical mounds on the summit of the site.

The clusters of rocks that surround the burials at Raisbeck may indeed be world creation symbolism while the effigy mounds represent the concept in other more specific ways. The clusters of rocks are reminiscent of earth anchors described in the creation of the world by Earthmaker as in some Ho-Chunk stories, but Robert Hall (1997, 17–23) suggested similar arrangements found in earlier Upper Midwest mounds, in the form of piles of muck, could be from a related or much older creation story called the Earth Diver Myth, that may be the oldest known creation story since it is shared by many peoples of the Earth. In these stories, animals of various types dive into a primordial sea and retrieve earth from the bottom from which the Earth is created. Whatever the interpretation, arrangements of rocks, muck, or upturned sods have been found around central burials in mounds dating to Early and Middle Woodland in the Midwest, indicating great antiquity for the overall symbolism (Van Langden and Kehoe 1971; Hall 1997, 17–18).

The individuals interred in the conical mounds at Raisbeck would seem to be associated with highest level of cosmology and have some intimate connection to the sun, Earthmaker, and/or general concepts of world creation, and therefore occupied the highest social ranks in effigy mound society. Among the Mississippians, the principal deity appears to have been the Sun, the giver of all life, as clearly indicated by iconography, and among the socially ranked Natchez, historic period Mississippians of the lower Mississippi River valley, the highest ranking social group came from the Sun clan.

Recent analyses of the bones from the Raisbeck ossuary, comparing to those found in other mounds at the site, revealed further provocative evidence of possible status differences. Angela Zamecnik, of the University of Wisconsin-Milwaukee, found that the people of the ossuary, men, women, and juveniles, suffered more pathologies reflected in the bones, such as osteo-arthritis, than others interred at the site (Zamecnik 2009). On the other hand, the other remains had a greater number of dental problems, such as cavities and hypoplasia, than those of the mound ossuary. This is probably the result of diet containing more corn since corn contains sucrose that causes tooth decay. Archaeologists have traced a dramatic increase in tooth decay in prehistoric populations of the world that accompanied the shift to farming and domestication of plants that contain sucrose (Lanfranco and Eggars 2012, 1–33). Corn horticulture was introduced into the diet of Upper Midwestern people and the culture of the effigy mound builders about AD 900. These analyses suggest that the people of the mound ossuary had a harder life and the others had better access to food, at least corn. Such differences would be expected in a hierarchical society where there would be different life roles and access to resources. However, if the people interred in the ossuary are ancestors reburied from somewhere else, the differences may also reflect the different lifestyles and diets of the ancestors and their descendants.

After reviewing the plots and characters in 'innumerable myths', Paul Radin (1948) came to the conclusion that Ho-Chunk society had been 'stratified', meaning socially ranked, where some clans and family lineages within clans had more prestige than others, particularly in the case of the Thunderbird and Bear clans. For example, he found evidence in the stories that chiefs occupied a position of unusual authority and where they and their children were essentially considered nobles. Again, the Ho-Chunk are among the possible descendants of the effigy mound people via the Oneota tradition.

Perhaps those few buried in some conical mounds at Raisbeck represent more important family lineages within a kinship or some other social group while the lower lineages of the same social or kin group were accorded only periodic mass burials. If so, this model could be extended to those interred in the effigy mounds, also found in few numbers – in many cases only a single individual – whereby only people from the most important lineages were accorded a mound burial associated with a particular revered spirit.

A problem with this model is the lack of evidence for where the less important lineages were interred. Perhaps these graves were not marked by a mound. In 1995, James Stoltman made the surprise find of large underground crypt that was not marked by a prominent mound and dated to the earlier Middle Woodland period, at the Tillmont Site, on a low island in the Mississippi River. It contained the skeletons of over 30 individuals put here not long after each death, with few grave goods (Stoltman 2005). It had long been known that people of obvious importance had been placed in pit graves with a rich variety of precious and exotic objects on higher ground and these had been covered by large conical mounds. The two mortuary patterns clearly represent social distinctions. There are over 3000 effigy mounds recorded, not including many long linear mounds that may be effigies of snakes. There are one or two burials per effigy and these generally lack high status grave goods. This suggests that most effigy mounds were not reserved for only a small elite group.

Here it should be noted that early major excavations of effigy mound sites focused on the mounds themselves or obvious habitation areas and not on areas around or between the mounds. In recent decades, the existence of burials of individuals or small groups of individuals outside of mounds has been confirmed by an increasing number of limited archaeological surveys and accidental discoveries during various forms of construction (e.g. Egan and Weir 1992). Modern remote sensing at mound groupings had also identified features yet to be defined (Kaufman 2005).

While the matter of ranked social groups awaits further research, Rosebrough (2021, 568–9), as mentioned earlier, proposed another possible indicator of social status among effigy mound people, although not one that would *necessarily* be indicative of a ranked and hierarchical social structure based on inherited kinship lineages. She proposes the presence of 'masked' status that is not *directly* observable in the archaeological record because items signaling prestige would not have been present. Instead, leaders demonstrate power and gain status by employing arcane and sacred ritual knowledge not accessible to others in ceremonial monument building. It is possible that such knowledge could have been passed down in leadership lineages but most likely it would have been gained by years of training in secret Medicine Societies. In these cases, sacred knowledge and the status it conferred would not be inherited through family lines.

Enclosures

Earth enclosures defining some sort of sacred space go back several thousand years in North America, as illustrated by the immense Hopewell circular, square, and octagonal structures in Ohio. Whittaker and Green (2010) also describe smaller earthen bermed enclosures dating to the Early and Middle Woodland periods prior to the Late Woodland appearance of effigy mounds. A few enclosures are part of effigy mound groups, such as the circular enclosure around the bird near the Kickapoo River, mentioned above, and a roughly circular enclosure at the Eagle Township complex on the Wisconsin River (Fig. 3.32, lower), both identified by Lewis (1880–1895, notebook 20, 36). Lewis also mapped hexagonal and rectangular enclosures among bird and Water Spirit mounds on top of a terrace overlooking the Black River, a major tributary of the Mississippi (Fig. 3.32, upper). These look much like some of the Ohio Hopewell enclosures but are very much smaller. The two forms here may represent different ceremonial activities associated with the Upper (circular) and Lower (rectangular) Worlds, as also represented by the birds and Water Spirits at the site. At several effigy mound group sites low, semicircular earthen enclosures abut riverbanks and may have been made for other ceremonial purposes.

These enclosures obviously marked sacred places but the ceremonial or ritual functions are unknown since none has been excavated and most have been destroyed. They could be places for special ceremonies or where the dead were kept in buildings or on scaffolds until the appropriate time for burial in a mound. As noted, a considerable number of effigy mound burials are in the form of bone bundles gathered long after the bodies had decomposed. During the late 19th and 20th centuries, Upper Midwestern Native peoples, such as the Ojibwe, Potawatomi, and Menominee, constructed circular, earthen, bermed, and wooden fenced circles for ceremonial dances of the Dream Dance or Big Drum ceremonial societies, providing one model for a type of activity conducted within the prehistoric enclosures (Birmingham 2015).

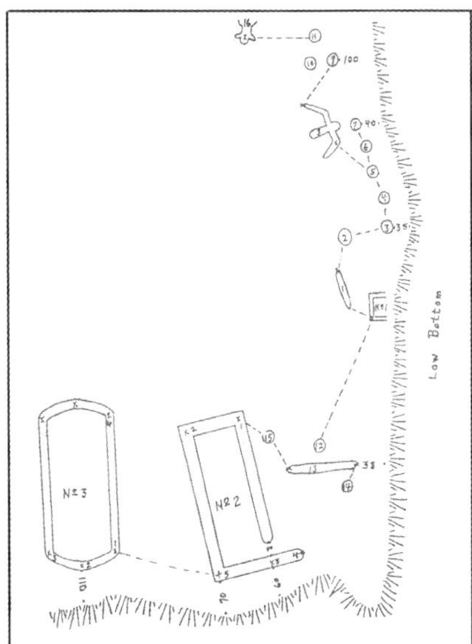

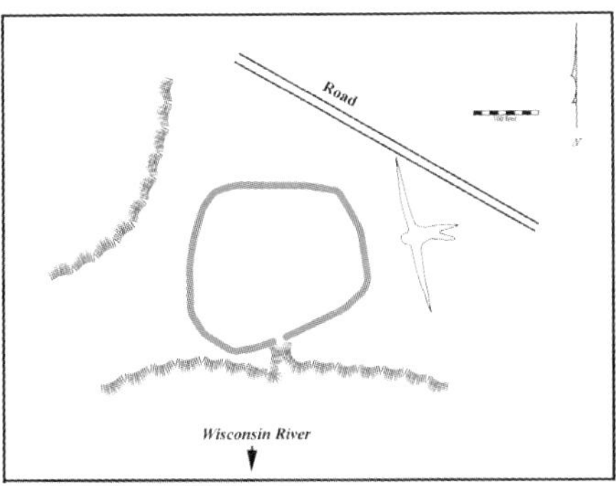

Fig. 3.32 Above: hexagonal and rectangular enclosures among bird and Water Spirit mounds on top of a terrace overlooking the Black River, a major tributary of the Mississippi; below: roughly circular enclosure at the Eagle Township cluster on the Wisconsin River identified by Lewis (1880–1895, notebook 27, 7).

Effigy mound groupings and landscapes

As we have seen, effigy mound groups are typically found along major bodies of water such as rivers, streams, and lakes. There are exceptions but these also provide important insights into the belief structures of the builders. The Nitschke and Lizard Mound groups, for instance, are associated with springs rather than larger bodies of water. In Native traditions, springs provide life giving water and are dwelling places or portals to the Underworld for Underworld spirits and are therefore places on the natural landscape of great spiritual importance.

Mound groups vary greatly in size from a few to several hundred. Many single effigy mounds occur but these appear to be a part of larger widespread ceremonial landscapes. As discussed earlier, the largest effigy mound group reported is the Harpers Ferry mound group along a terrace of the Mississippi River in Iowa. Here, Theodore Lewis claimed that there had been over 900 mounds, including hundreds of effigies, although he only mapped a few (Lewis 1880–1895, notebook 32(1)). However, modern scholars point to several inconsistencies in Lewis's information and suggest that he relied on exaggerated accounts by local informants and mistook low natural rises as mounds (Finney 2006). Only six mounds survive today. As we have seen, the largest number of effigies in a single group is the Raisbeck mound group on the Grant River in southwestern Wisconsin. Arranged along high ridges overlooking the river, a tributary of the Wisconsin, the 123 mounds included 38 effigies – primarily birds and canine forms – along with conical, oval, linear, and other forms. The birds are hawk-like, possibly peregrine falcons as discussed above. Identical bird forms with falcon silhouettes are found at Effigy Mounds National Monument in Iowa where they are swooping up and down the high bluffs to the Mississippi River as though hunting. Falcons had commonly nested along the high bluff edges into modern times. Native people would certainly have perceived the bluffs at the Monument as the place of the falcon spirits.

To recap, Raisbeck is characteristic of groupings of the western part of the effigy mound regions that have both air and earth themes, usually birds with bears, but occasionally birds with other earth animals, as at Raisbeck. Groups in the east tend to be heavily water themed with many Water Spirits and water birds but also with occasional celestial birds representing the Upper World. The greatest diversity of mounds occurs in south-central Wisconsin, the heart of the effigy mound region (Birmingham 2010; Rosebrough 2014) where air, earth, and water themes combine with several types of birds, a variety of earth animals, particularly bears, Water Spirits, snakes, water birds, and water mammals.

Landscapes

As proposed here and elsewhere, effigy mound groups are ceremonial landscapes that combined place and space to create special meaning. The concept of landscape has long been applied to effigy mounds (for instance, Goldstein 1995; Gartner 1999) but more recent analyses of ritual or ceremonial landscapes have achieved much due to the increasing recognition by archaeologists of the all-pervasive role that 'religion' or a general worldview pertaining to the supernatural, played in ancient societies of the world. It has become recognized that ritual practices linking the supernatural to human activity may be spread out over vast areas where ancient people gave meaning to different features of the natural landscape. Even the famous Stonehenge is now viewed as only one part of a vast and long-lived ceremonial landscape on Salisbury Plain, in Wiltshire, southern England, that also contains massive earthwork sites, wooden henges, burial mounds, long embanked enclosures called cursus monuments, habitation areas for people coming to the place for periodic ceremonies in great numbers, processional roads, and even a segment of the River Avon that provided a connection between ceremonial henges (see, for instance, Parker Pearson 2013; Parker Pearson *et al.* 2022). In a similar fashion, ceremonial landscapes of the Hopewell in North America consisted of huge enclosures, burial mounds, wide ceremonial roads, ditches, post-circles, pavements, and probably less permanent shrines (Lynott 2014, 224–5).

Another pertinent and recent example of such a landscape comes from the American southwestern world of the Pueblo peoples, ancestors of Hopi and others. Using a landscape archaeology approach that incorporated much relevant ethnography, James Snead (2008) described ritual landscapes covering thousands of square miles around pre-European contact Pueblo communities, which served as ritual centers themselves including elaborate, stone community shrines, local shines, places where ritual paintings were made on rock faces, and roads or trails connecting ritual places. He also noted that topographic features such as certain lakes, hills, and mountains were and remain places of veneration and communication with the supernatural for Native people (Snead 2008, 84–5). The different rituals and symbolism connected people to the land and to the supernatural through ancestors – as is proposed for the effigy mounds of the Upper Midwest.

In the case of the effigy ceremonial landscapes, the building of earthen monuments in the form of revered spirits included other associated elements such as intaglios, occasional earthen enclosures, habitation areas, gardens, and burials outside of the mound themselves. But the concept of a ceremonial landscape can also extend to other special ritual sites not directly associated with mounds, such as those found in caves, rockshelters, and rock outcroppings where there are carvings and paintings with iconography similar to effigy mound themes. These were often long used by Native people before and after the Late Woodland period for specialized ritual activity.

These sites are especially found among the cliffs, bluffs, and valleys of the western 'driftless' part of the effigy mound region and three are believed to be contemporary with them. One is the aforementioned Gotschall Rockshelter, one of the most important archaeological sites in Wisconsin, which site investigator Robert Salzer identifies as a ritual cave or shrine (Salzer and Rajnovich 2000; Fig. 3.33). The paintings found on the back rock wall were executed in Mississippian artistic style but excavations found no obvious Mississippian artifacts. Instead, Salzer linked the paintings, by evidence of paint droppings, to a layer with Late Woodland style pottery, dated between AD 900 and 1000. Excavations at the site also produced a unique painted sandstone head, also associated with the type of pottery made by the effigy mound people.

Although this association and date have been challenged (Boszhardt 1998, 210–11), Robert Hall (1997, 147–50) recognized the story being told by the paintings because it was still recounted by the Ho-Chunk and the related Ioway in the early 20th century, as recorded by Skinner (1926) and Radin (1948). It relates to a mythological cycle of stories involving a culture hero named Red Horn or He-Who-Wears-Human-Heads-As-Earrings. In various versions of these stories Red Horn has contests and battles with a race of giants and is eventually killed. His sons also fight with the giants and they eventually retrieve the severed head of Red Horn who is subsequently reincarnated. Hall (1997, 148–51) specifically relates the Gottschall figures to a story involving one of the sons and, in this context, the stone head could well be a representation of Red Horn's severed head. Duncan and Diaz-Granados (2000) identified a painting at Picture Cave in Missouri that they also propose to be the son who is holding a severed head of Red Horn before he is reincarnated. Hall, Salzer, and Duncan and Diaz-Granados believe that the Red Horn mythology figured is important in the ritual adoption ceremonies of outsiders into Mississippian societies. Duncan and Diaz-Granados (2000, 21–2; 2023) suggest that these would be war captives and, moreover, show that Red Horn mythology is interconnected with that of the Celestial Twins, discussed above.

Since the paintings at Gottschall are in Mississippian style, it could seem that they were the adopters, possibly seeking an alliance with the Late Woodland people through a fictive kinship, and it has been assumed that the Red Horn cycle, which turns up many centuries later in Ho-Chunk sacred stories,

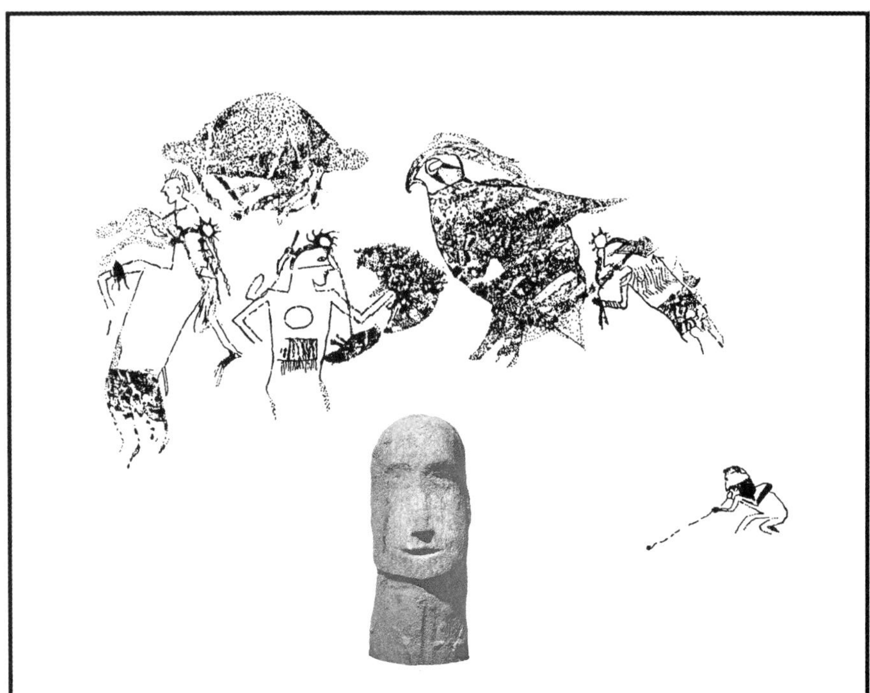

Fig. 3.33 Above: drawing of Gottschall rockshelter paintings with sandstone head found in excavations (from Salzer and Rajnovich 2000); below: drawing of painted pictograph panel at Tainter Cave (from Boszhart 2003).

originated with the Mississippians from the south (Green 2014). However, this has not been confirmed, and the only thing that can be said is that iconography relating to the Red Horn stories has not yet been identified as prior to the Mississippian period.

Gottschall is located at the base of a deep stream valley near its head, that drains down from the uplands to the Wisconsin River, 8 miles (*ca* 13 km) away. The original mouth of the stream joined the river directly across from the spectacular Eagle Township cluster that included twin human effigy mounds described above. The Gottschall Rockshelter could well have been a place used by religious specialists by both Mississippian visitors and the local creators of the effigy landscape for ritual activities more appropriately carried out in private and underground. It is likely that the Mississippians and effigy mound builders had a generally similar worldview since many aspects of these have great antiquity and were widespread in North America. This may have ultimately allowed for incorporation and merging of mythologies through the processes of culture contact that survived among the Ho-Chunk and Ioway. Archaeologists with the Mississippi Valley Archaeology Center discovered a second underground ritual site also believed to date to the time of the effigy mounds building called Tainter Cave, in the Kickapoo Valley not far from effigy mound groups (Boszhardt 2003). In one dark chamber of a cave, the archaeologists found a large, extraordinary panel of charcoal drawings that show a herd of deer being hunted by humans with bow and arrows, above which, and separated by a natural crack in the cave wall, are faded remnants of birds, no doubt thunderbirds (Fig. 3.33). A telling aspect of the panel is that the arrows of the hunters are connected with lines to foetal deer within the bodies of the adult deer. The symbolism seems obvious: the rituals involved are a form of hunting magic whereby a plea was made to the supernatural for productivity of *future* deer herds and not simply for the success of one particular hunt. A faded but apparent human figure was found in another part of the cave and appears to be a Medicine Man with arms raised, although it is not clear that it is contemporary with the deer paintings.

The extensive rock carvings within another rockshelter/cave, Gullickson's Glen, may well have been created by Late Woodland people although the art, again, has not been directly dated, and the rockshelter had been long occupied by various people through time, as determined by various test excavations (Stiles-Hanson 1987). Located along a creek in a remote part of Jackson County, Wisconsin, the art was carved into sandstone, now heavily eroded and marred by graffiti, and includes naturalistic renditions of animals with parallels to effigy mounds such as deer, geese, a wolf, and a catfish as well as several human figures, among which is a possible Medicine Man or Shaman, again with arms raised (also see Fig. 3.17). A major clue for the purpose of the art comes from a series of geese, sitting with necks bent over towards their feet as though tending eggs or young. These nesting geese along with the depiction of other animals and of a shaman-like figure provide the theme of the rock art: renewal of the world and its bounty through the ritual actions of medicine men.

Summary

Key and very common effigy mounds correspond to spirit beings and animals long important in the cosmologies and social structures of Native peoples in the Americas and the eastern Woodlands of North America. The dualistic Upper World/ Lower World underlying structure of effigy mound ceremonialism was already formalized and reflected in art and monument building of the Middle Woodland Hopewell culture that exerted much ideological influence over the Midwest prior to the extensive Late Woodland effigy mound building, and the Hopewell people may even have been effigy mound builders themselves to a limited degree.

The distributions and arrangements of effigy mounds are closely linked to geography and topographic features that had spiritual meaning for the builders and the mounds themselves are interpreted as key spirits re-animated and joined with the dead and metaphorically re-animated in the cycles of death and rebirth. Prior interpretations linked mound shapes to clans, but Rosebrough's re-analysis stresses an emblematic function of several kinds including, but not exclusively, totem symbols (Rosebrough 2010). Given the fact that social arrangements mirror cosmology in the Americas, there is good reason to believe that the effigy mounds reflected a clan based social organization, but effigy mounds were quite clearly neither earthen statues of deities nor elaborate grave markers. Many are in motion and the natural landscape further animates the mounds as they follow changes in the topography and are oriented as coming to, or from, landscape features that had special meaning. Creation or re-creation seems to be the major theme in the zoomorphic mounds, so the bringing back to life of great spirits at the places that they dwell seems to be the primary ceremonial function.

The evoking of such spirits and their powers could be done for various reasons designed to bring blessings on human kind as, for example, as part of major seasonal ceremonies to renew the fertility of the earth, as great protectors of humans, as clan ancestors in the context of clan ceremonials attending burials, as shrines, or as the work of special ritual or Medicine Societies connected to specific spirits. William Romain (2009) identifies what he believes to be as many as six types of 'Shamans' and shamanistic societies that operated in the Ohio Hopewell culture.

In this broader context, effigy mound landscapes can most easily be viewed as well-organized out-door temples or churches exquisitely sculptured from earth and, as with temples and churches in more recent times, these served as centers for a variety of rituals and ceremonies stemming from a specific worldview or 'religion', including the burial of the dead. A major difference with this analogy is that the effigy mounds were not mere symbols or representations of the supernatural – they were perceived to be alive and the effigy mound landscapes to be populated by a variety of living ancestors and viable supernatural beings summoned from the dead or their respective spirit worlds through ritual action by humans. Effigy mound ceremonialism reflects the work of socially complex societies, as clearly indicated by the mound themselves that are sometimes huge and that, overall, required great investments of time in labor, scheduling, and co-ordination above and beyond basic subsistence activities. The various mound forms – effigy, conical, short linear, etc. – obviously imply different statuses for those interred in the mounds during the course of ceremonials, but whether or not this represents a hierarchical rather than egalitarian social arrangement will require more research, for example at habitation areas. The existence of a hierarchical arrangement in at least some effigy mound societies would hardly be surprising because the prior trajectory in Upper Midwestern prehistory had been towards increasing complexity and hierarchical social arrangements beginning even before the period of monument building in the form of burial mounds about 500 BC. The next chapter describes this trajectory based on current but rapidly accumulating archaeological evidence, takes a closer look at Late Woodland society at the time of the Effigy Mound Ceremonial Complex, and examines its eventual demise.

4

The evolution of effigy mound landscapes

The spread of the Effigy Mound Ceremonial Complex in the Upper Midwest after AD 700 seems sudden but the phenomenon derives from earlier customs of mound building, burial practices, and pre-existing belief systems and worldviews, indicating both change and continuity. It is analogous to widespread monument building found in other parts of the world where the growth of populations accompanied the shift from predominantly hunting and gathering to food production in the form of agriculture and domestication and the development of more complex societies.

Taking a broad view, the prehistory of mid-continental North America can be viewed as social evolution to increasingly larger and more complex societies from tiny bands to the formation of America's first city, Cahokia, on the banks of the Mississippi River in what is now southern Illinois, that was supported by intensive agriculture. No similar urban area formed further north in the Upper Midwest but societies here, as in many areas, were dramatically affected and re-oriented by the brief expansion of the Mississippian civilization and their histories can therefore be viewed as intertwined.

Monument building in the form of large burial mounds appeared in the mid-continent and Upper Midwest about 2500 years ago and mound and earthwork building became more elaborate as populations increased and social systems became more complex. Since a march to complexity and monument building is not inevitable in human social evolution in general, the specific circumstances promoting such a process are of great interest to archaeologists. Effigy mounds comprise a particularly informative case study, since the meaning of the various earthen forms can be related to belief systems still present in native cultures.

The first people

Present evidence suggests that the Americas were first occupied from Asia sometime prior to 14,000 years ago, with people adapting to the various environments of the continent as they spread. The ancestors of modern Native people came to the Upper Midwest about 13,000 years ago when it was a harsh, cold, place during the last vestiges of the great Ice Age that had covered much of the land with mountainous glaciers. One glacial lobe had covered the eastern and northern parts of what would become the effigy mound region and to the southwest of this lies the Western Uplands, or Driftless Area, a rugged, much older landscape not leveled by the last glaciation (Fig. 4.1). Both these natural landscapes would become meaningful to much later effigy mound builders. For example, the northeast–southwest trending drumlins (large, oblong hills of sand and gravel deposited by one glacial lobe) were important to the effigy mound people who many times filled the tops of these land forms with their earthen monuments, using the natural topography to orient the mounds.

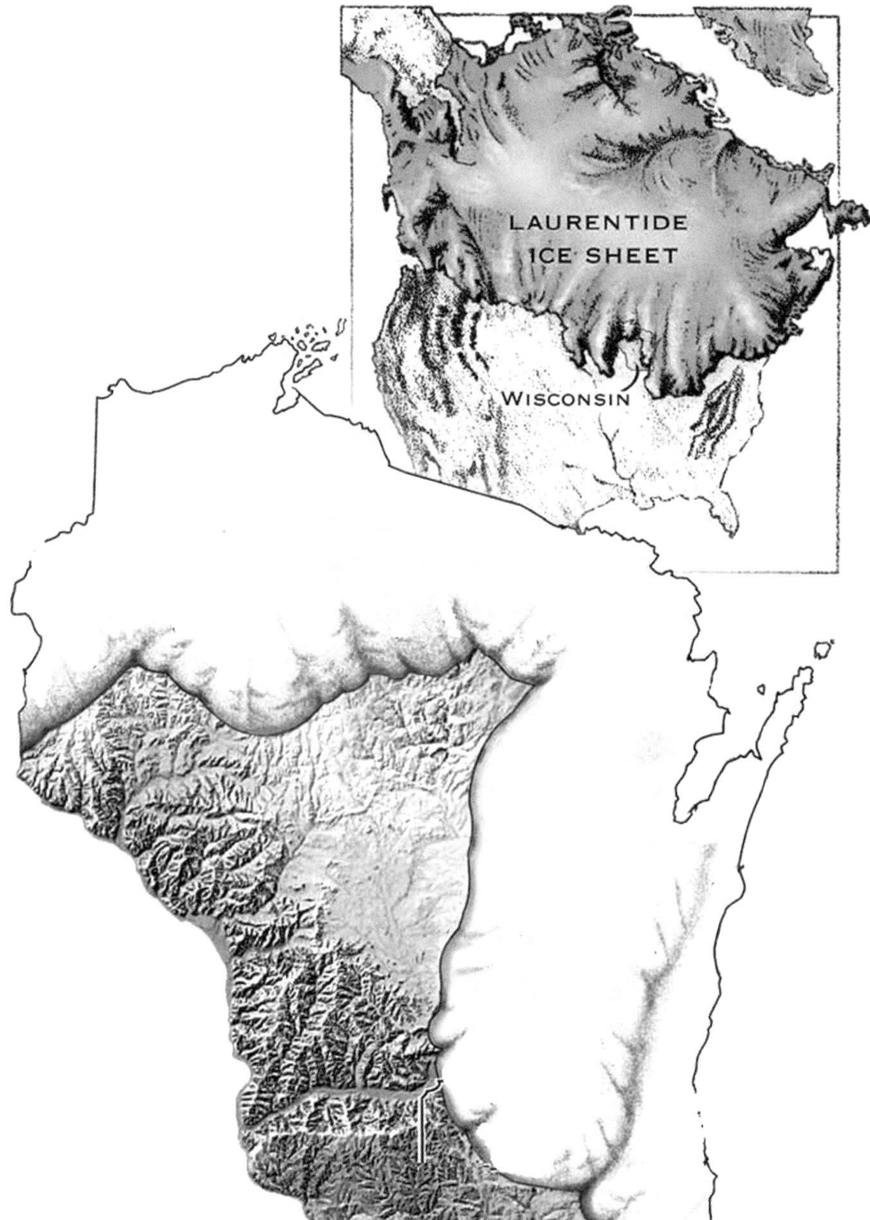

Fig. 4.1 Map showing extent of the glaciation to affect North America (from the Wisconsin Geological and Natural History Survey).

Small bands of hunters followed game into the region as the Ice Age ended. These first people, referred to as *Paleo-Indians* by archaeologists, moved into a cold and snowy environment with short cool summers. Spruce and fir boreal forest and tundra covered the land, resembling the environment found today in parts of Canada and Alaska. Early people shared this environment with mega-fauna such as mammoth and mastodon and other animals that disappeared at the end of the Ice Age. In Kenosha county, in southeastern Wisconsin, archaeologists unearthed entire, although disarticulated, skeletons of mammoths preserved in former wetlands. Cuts and other marks on the bones have convinced scholars the animals had been butchered for meat (Overstreet *et al.* 1993; Joyce 2006; Johnson *et al.* 2007).

The later Paleo-Indians probably hunted caribou herds and perhaps large bison – ancestors of modern bison or buffalo – as well as more familiar game such as moose, elk, and deer. Specialized hunters in the western Great Plains focused on now extinct forms of bison. These animals inhabited parts of the Upper Midwest in some numbers but, as yet, no kill sites have been identified. The early people sought a variety of smaller game (Meinholz and Kuehn 1997).

Little is known about their lifeways and beliefs given the small size of the bands, a highly mobile lifestyle, and the great time that has elapsed. Habitation and burial sites are rare. Evidence of their existence is most often attested by distinctive spear points found across the region, similar to those found at the

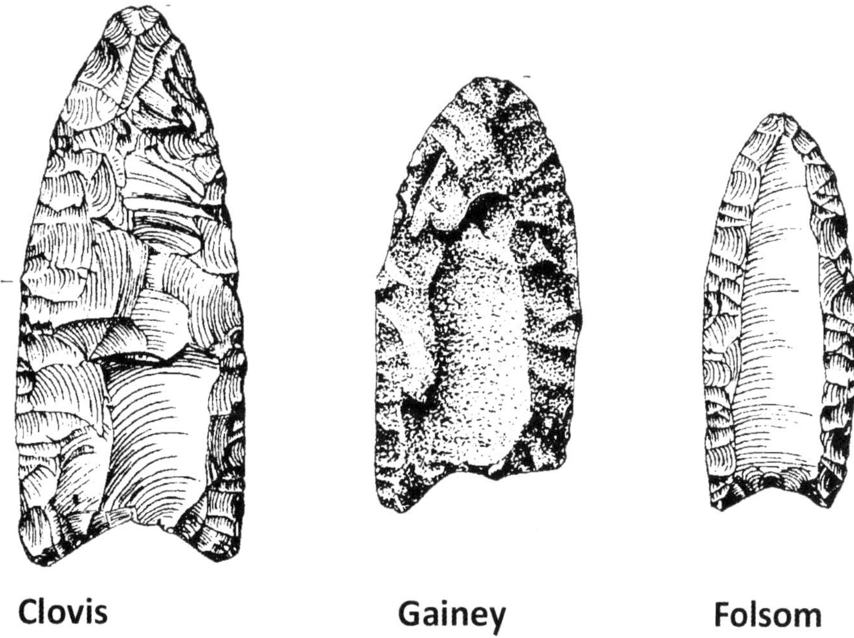

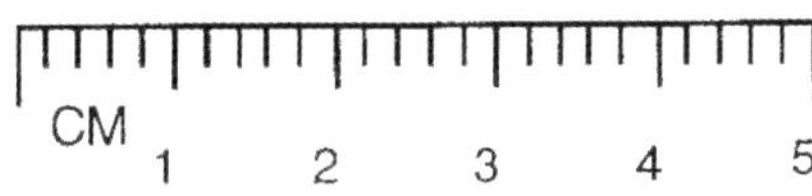

Fig. 4.2 Types of Paleo-Indian fluted points (from Mason 1997, 84).

time throughout North America. Earlier types, called Clovis, are easily identified because of distinctive grooves or flutes for secure attachment to shafts (Fig. 4.2). Long, thin, and beautifully made spear points later replaced the fluted types. Other types of artifacts found on Paleo-Indian sites include stone gravers for working bone or wood and hide scrapers. Bone, wood, and other organic materials are not generally preserved in the Upper Midwest.

Paleo-Indians valued distinctively colored stone for spear points and other implements, with sources often far away from the find locations, indicating that the people covered huge territories and/or participated in exchange or trade with other small bands of similarly roaming people. Paleo-Indians obviously ascribed special meaning to these types of stone, perhaps perceiving them as the sources of magical power in hunting. One rock especially important to these early people in the Upper Midwest is a type of ortho-quartzite called Hixton Silicified Sandstone. Deposits of this stone are found in west-central Wisconsin along with related orthro-quartzites also found in the area. Spear points and other tools made from these stones have been found throughout the Upper Midwest but are especially common in Wisconsin. A study of several hundred early Paleo-Indian fluted points from Wisconsin and northern Illinois shows that nearly 40% were made from Hixton (Loebel 2007).

The colors of Hixton range from light sugar to golds and reds: the shades of the sun. The source of Hixton Silicified Sandstone is a geological formation called Silver Mound in west central Wisconsin, where there are dense workshop areas while the surrounding land has produced artifacts from many cultural periods, including Paleo-Indian. Images carved and painted by later Indian people in rock

Fig. 4.3 Fork-tailed Thunderbird petroglyph at the Table Rock site a quarter mile from Silver Mound, near Hixton, Wisconsin (courtesy of Robert Boszhardt).

caves and outcrops of Hixton Sandstone at Silver Mound and in the near vicinity include birds and Thunderbirds, suggesting a logical association with the powers of the Upper World (Fig. 4.3).

In contrast, another common stone used by Paleo-Indians, especially in north-eastern Illinois and Wisconsin, is dark blue and often banded and is called Moline

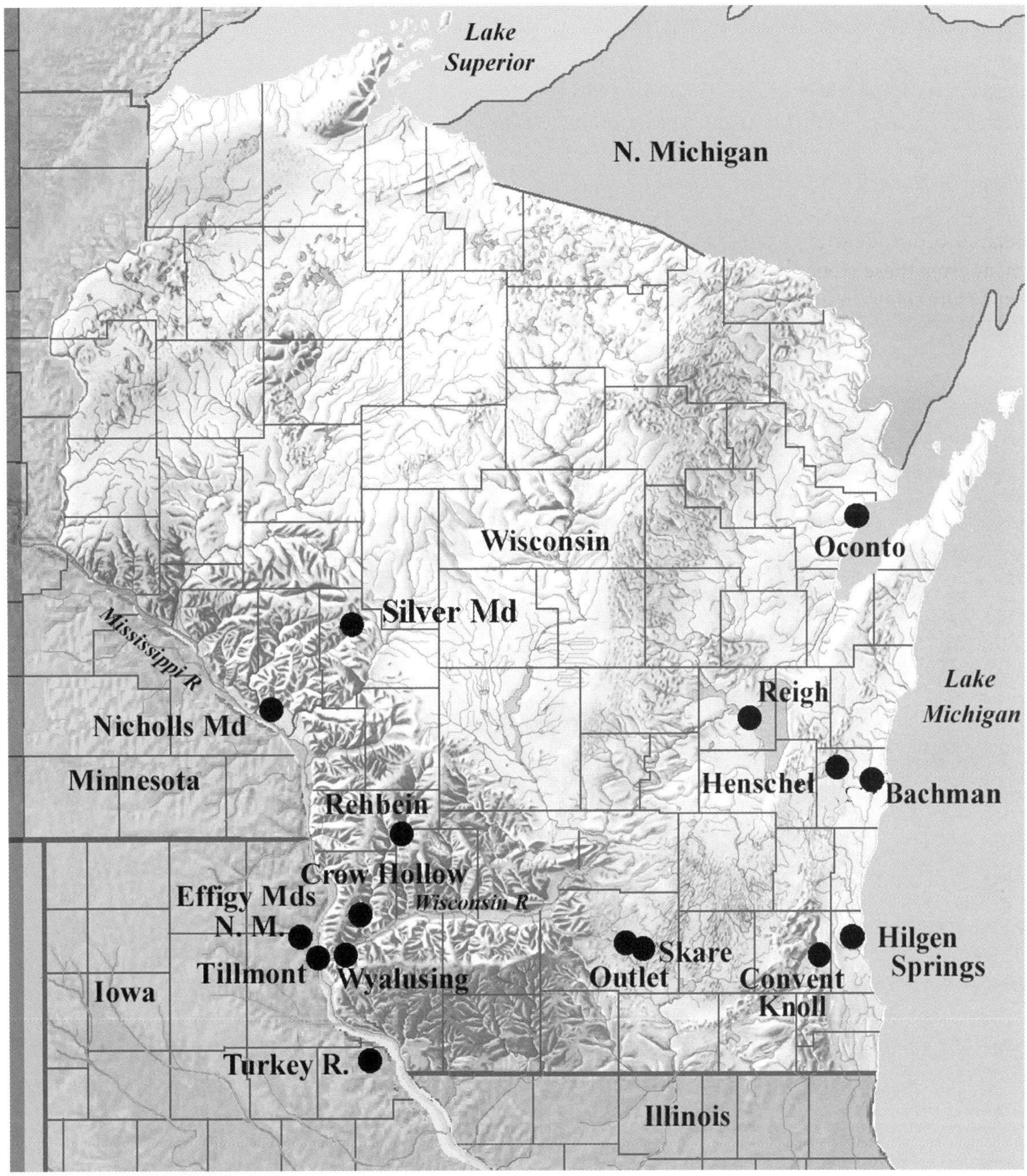

Fig. 4.4 Map showing location of sites mentioned in text (by Amy Rosebrough).

Fig. 4.5 Projectile points from the Skare site: above: early Paleo-Indian fluted points; below: Late Paleo-Indian lancelate points (photos: David Burton).

chert after its source at Moline, Illinois, near the confluence of the Rock and Mississippi Rivers (Birmingham and Van Dyke 1981). Here, long used extraction sites have also been identified in narrow stream valleys where erosion of softer rock has left the harder chert exposed in shelves. On adjacent hills people worked the stone into rough forms that could be easily transported and later formed into appropriate implements, or traded as raw material. Fluted points of Moline chert are much more numerous in Wisconsin than in Illinois where the chert originates, indicating that the significance of the stone increased with distance. Since the sources of this dark colored rock are in low watery places, its use may have been perceived as drawing upon the powers of the Lower World.

Occasionally, perhaps on an annual basis, scattered family bands gathered together for communal hunts and social activities. The Skare site in the heartland of the later effigy mound region along the Yahara River near modern-day Madison, Wisconsin, is one such place (Fig. 4.4). During Paleo-Indian times it occupied a point or peninsula in a huge glacial lake. Artifact collectors and archaeologists have discovered large numbers of smaller fluted Folsom points through the years, as well as many other distinctive Paleo-Indian tools for processing game for food and tools, such as gravers for working bone and scrapers for working hides (Fig. 4.5). Both points and tools suggest that this site functioned as a communal base camp for hunting herd animals but, as yet, no animal remains have been identified. One possible prey species is woodland caribou. These ancient hunters probably followed the herds in small bands during their annual, lengthy, north–south migrations and the Skare site, located on a point in the glacial lake, may have been a particularly good place to intercept herds for communal hunting. Modern migrations of caribou in Canada are known to take them across bodies of water instead of around them, during which the swimming animals are easily dispatched. Points and other artifacts of Hixton and Moline occur in some quantity suggesting that exchange of the material took place at the large gathering.

The Archaic tradition

As the climate warmed, the boreal environment gave way first to thick conifer forests, followed by hardwood forests, and then the spread of grasslands corresponding to climatic changes that, in turn, stimulated subsistence and cultural changes. Archaeologists define a long, gradual period of change as the Archaic tradition between 8000 and 500 BC (e.g., Stoltman and Pleger 2009). By the end of the Archaic the environment of the later effigy mound region consisted of a mosaic of hardwood forests, oak savannas, and grasslands that, along with many wetlands, lakes, and rivers, provided a rich habitat for animals and plants. Deer had become especially plentiful along with a variety of edible plants and other animals. Streams and rivers offered abundant fish and freshwater clams. The many lakes and wetlands left in the wake of the glaciers also provided habitats for fish, waterfowl, and aquatic mammals.

Over time the Archaic people developed new technologies to take advantage of increased food and other resources. These included the use of the wooden spear thrower, large stone axes, milling stones for grinding plants, and many other specialized tools and weapons. The spear thrower, also referred to as an atlatl was a powerful weapon that consisted of a wooden shaft with a hooked end. It could propel a spear with much greater velocity and force than the arm alone (Fig. 4.6a). Some of the most most beautiful artifacts of the Archaic tradition are colored stone weights attached to the wooden shaft of the throwers that were carved into the shapes of birds and other animals, attesting to the cultural and symbolic importance of the spear as a weapon (Fig. 4.6b).

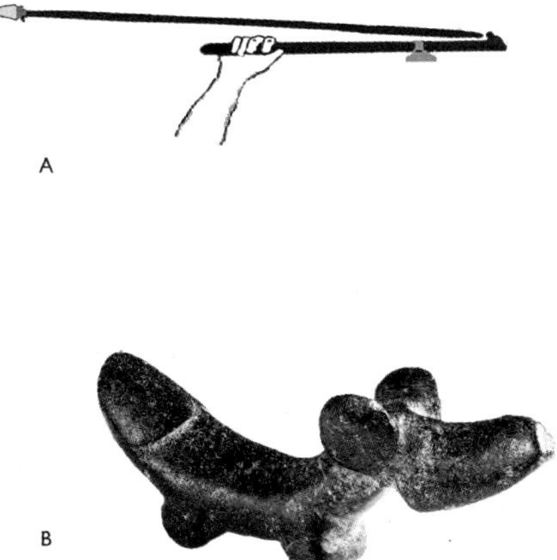

Fig. 4.6 A: spear thrower; B: Archaic period 'Bird Stone' found in Dane County, Wisconsin (from Beer 2016).

Evidence of the earliest burial practices in the region appear in the form of a cremated individual found in a grave pit near Green Bay, Wisconsin, accompanied by burned and heat-shattered stone spear points (Mason and Irwin 1960). Small pits containing burned stone artifacts of the same period occur elsewhere but with no human bone, perhaps because it was not preserved in the prevailing soil conditions. Cremation was one of the many mortuary customs used by Native people of North America as by ancient and modern people through the world through time, although the role and meaning no doubt differed from time to time and culture to culture. In this early context of a highly mobile lifeway it may well be imagined that reduction of a corpse to burned bone fragments offered a way of transporting the dead until the most appropriate conditions or places of permanent burial could be attained. The inclusion of burned spear points nonetheless indicates that the grave offerings were part of the mortuary ritual, either out of respect for the individual or as necessary implements to accompany them to an afterworld.

Middle Archaic

Several significant developments during the middle part of the Archaic had implications for much later Native cultures such as the Late Woodland effigy mound builders. First, the climate became very warm and this, along with geological events, greatly altered the environment. Secondly, we see the emergence of societies in eastern Wisconsin that are more complex than small bands of hunters and gatherers and who participated in extensive trade, both internal and external, and who made large cemeteries staking long claims to territories by the presence of ancestors.

Mid-Holocene warm climate

Beginning about 6500 years ago, annual temperatures rose to levels much warmer than today, accompanied by a significant drop in moisture, resulting in an extensive and long drought that climatologists call the Altithermal or Mid-Holocene Dry Period that has been documented for large areas of North America and the world. In the Upper Midwest, the dry period is dated between 4500 and 1500 BC. During the drought, water tables would have dropped, streams dried up, and inland lakes and marshes shrunk. Grassland prairies spread over former forested areas that would have been sustained by frequent grass fires that raged over the parched land, killing herbaceous species not resistant to fire. Upland areas were virtually abandoned by people (Harris 2002) and studies of animal remains elsewhere in the Midwest show that deer underwent nutritional stress and that climate affected the availability of other animals.

Excavations of a few identified camp sites occupied between 4000 and 3000 BC in south-central and southwestern Wisconsin show that these were located near wooded areas in wetter areas (Hamilton *et al.* 1995; Meinhotlz and Kolb 1997, 76–9; Kuehn 2007). At the Crow Hollow site near the Kickapoo River in southwestern Wisconsin, archaeologists found charred fragments of hickory and walnuts in shallow pits. A few projectile points and scrapers used for hide preparation were also found, providing evidence that some hunting of large mammals also took place.

The long dry period limited the size of human populations in some areas but had the long term effect of establishing oak savanna and prairies as the major vegetation type in the region that continued to develop with the addition of forest and greater wetland areas as the climate became moister, surviving over much of the southern parts of the Upper Midwest into the time of the first white settlers in the 1830s (Elarson 1949; Winkler *et al.* 1986). Oak savannas are prairie grasses mixed with forest herbs and scattered oak trees, giving them a 'parkland' appearance. They are frequently called 'oak openings'. Such open woodlands along forest edges are rich habitats for deer and elk. Deer would eventually emerge as the single most important animal, providing not only meat but also hides for clothing and bones for a variety of tools. Oak savannas are naturally maintained by frequent prairie fires but there is historical evidence that Native people, in more recent times, intentionally set grass fires to maintain oak savannas as game habitat (Lake *et al.* 2017) but the oral traditions of modern Native people also describe smaller scale burning to create openings and foster berry growth.

A completely different environment developed along and near to the shores of Lake Michigan due to a dramatic rise in lake level. This was not the result of increased rainfall here but rather the effects of geological events associated with the end of the Ice Age. As glaciers retreated northward the land, depressed by the great burden of their weight, rebounded, sending water in Lake Superior southward, expanding Lake Michigan, and raising the water level until it was 20 ft (*ca* 6 m) higher than today (Larsen 1985; Hansel and Mickelson 1988), creating an environment much moister than the dry conditions elsewhere. The expanded lake would have moderated inland climates, as Lake Michigan does today, making it moister and providing a richer variety of plant and animal foods. This, in turn, attracted an enormous human population. The expansion of the lake over shallower areas provided easy access to fish, stimulating a fishing complex. Among the fish species sought would have been the huge, bottom dwelling sturgeon that would have come to shallow areas and rivers and could have been easily speared or harpooned in great quantity. The long-lived sturgeon can attain lengths of over 6 ft (2 m) with weights up to 200 lb (90+ kg). Sturgeon fishing played a major role in the traditional economy of the Menominee who have long occupied northwestern Wisconsin bordered on Lake Michigan and continues to be a practice of ceremonial and economic importance today. Sturgeon is also one of the Menominee clans.

As populations grew along the lake and adjacent areas, an extraordinary material culture developed that included trade of vast numbers of copper implements, which were exchanged mostly as finished items. Some of these related to fishing, but also included many different objects: axes, adzes, gouges, many types of spear points, knives, and ornaments (Fig. 4.7). There are no copper deposits in the bedrock of the region, although chunks of copper, small and large, are still occasionally found in eastern Wisconsin that had been ripped up from northerly sources and redeposited by glaciers. Copper was mined mainly in northern Michigan and Isle Royale in Lake Superior, where thousands of quarry pits can still be seen. After extraction from veins, copper was worked into implements by hammering with hard stones, followed by heating and cooling in water – a process called annealing. This process was repeated until completion of the desired implement.

The use of copper dates as early as 5500 BC, making it among the earliest metallurgies in the world (Plegar and Stoltman 2009; Reardon 2014). Copper, like rock, cannot be dated directly but occasionally remnants of wooden shafts and other organic material adhering to copper implements are preserved by copper salts that are toxic to the bacteria that would normally cause decay of the wood, allowing use of radiocarbon dating. During the years 4000–1500 BC, exchange and trade in copper became so common that archaeologists once referred to the phenomenon as the Old Copper Culture. Because the use and trade of copper probably involved people of different cultural backgrounds, it is now known as the Old Copper Complex, referring to a shared custom.

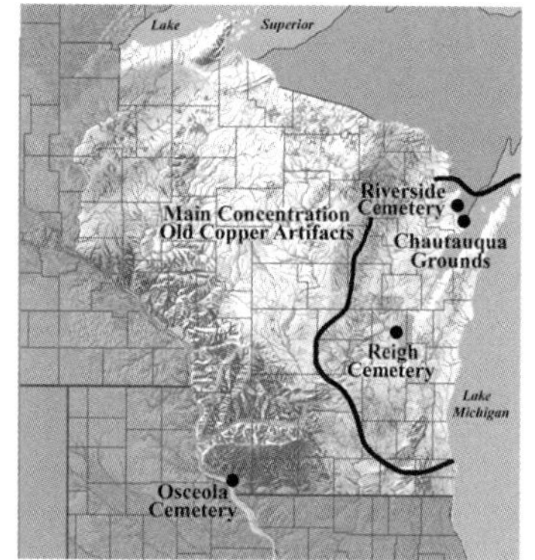

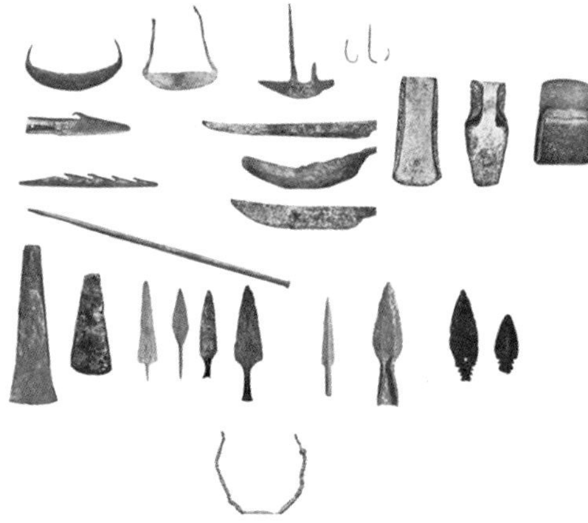

Fig. 4.7 A sample of copper artifacts from the Old Copper Ceremonial Complex in the collections of the Milwaukee Public Museum, with site locations.

Most of this trade and exchange occurred between local population of the region but similar copper artifacts have been found in more distant places such as the eastern Great Plains, Canada, and the eastern seaboard, indicating development of vast trade networks among Archaic peoples. Copper objects have been found at a series of sites in Wisconsin along the Mississippi and lower Wisconsin rivers, well away from the main Old Copper region; perhaps this area, with its strategic location on North America's main transportation route for people, goods, and ideas, served an early external trade center. Among the sites here is the earliest cemetery known from Wisconsin called the Osceola site.

Tens of thousands of copper artifacts have been found over the years, many as surface finds, by artifact collectors, but now by collectors using metal detectors who, unfortunately, have damaged many potentially important sites by digging out the copper artifacts. Some Old Copper implements directly relate to fishing, reflecting the growth of this enterprise, including socketed harpoons for catching large fish such as sturgeon and even fishhooks. Some long heavy bars with wear at the ends may have been used to make holes in the lake ice for winter fishing. Woodworking tools like adzes and gouges would have been useful in making dugout log canoes. Preserved dugout canoes have been dated back several thousand years in the western Great Lake areas and were used by people along with birch bark canoes into the 19th century. The Kenosha Public Museum in Wisconsin displays a dugout radiocarbon dated to 2000 years ago and Wisconsin Historical Society divers recently discovered several dugout canoes in Lake Mendota at Madison: one dated to the Late Woodland effigy mound period.

Some Old Copper artifacts are almost identical to slate or metal ulus with curved blades used by the much later Arctic-dwelling Inuit for slicing fish and other meat. One of the few excavated Old Copper settlements or camps, the Chautauqua Grounds site, is located at the mouth of the Menominee River and produced a variety of fishing related copper artifacts (Plegar 1992).

The mystery of the Old Copper Complex is why copper was so important for the people in this particular region so far from its major sources. At first glance it would seem that use of metal would have a technological advantage over stone and bone generally used for the production of implements. Certainly it is true that working of the soft metal made the forming of some objects possible that could not be done with stone, such as gouges used for woodworking, socketed harpoons for fishing, and some ornamental objects. However, copper is much less durable than stone and the crafting of copper into implements is much more labor intensive, as described above. Moreover, stone tools with parallels to many copper implements continued to be made at the same time, such as spears, knives, and axes. Similarly, an overall technological advantage does not explain the demise in the use of copper even as societies in the area actually became more complex. After about 1200 BC the use of copper in the region becomes largely restricted to ornaments, objects of ritual importance, and sharp pointed awls useful in fabricating hides into clothing.

If copper offered no real technological and economic advantages over more easily obtained and worked stone and bone then why was it so important to the people at this time? This question is similar in some respects as to why people of the Paleo-Indian made their spear points from certain exotic lithic materials when other easily chipped stone would have been abundantly available. Because of this, archaeologists have focused on the symbolic qualities of the metal in traditional Native beliefs that point to the association of copper with supernatural forces indicating that the metal would have had 'wonderful power' in the words of archaeologist Susan Martin (1999).

Martin observed that northerly peoples such as the Ojibwe and Menominee associate copper with the powers of the watery Underworld and in particular a great horned monster called *Mishipeshu*, *Mishipizheu*, or *Gitche-anah-bezhe*, alternately translated as the Great Lynx, the Great Underground, or Underwater Wildcat and often described as having a long copper tail (Rajnovich 1994, 102–3; see Fig. 4.8). The related Ottawa made sacrifices to *Mishipeshu* in order to calm lake waters and bring sturgeon, and carried power-laden copper nuggets in their medicine bags (Rajnovich 1994, 104). Painted images of *Mishipeshu* can be found in ancient art panels that adorn rock ledges overlooking the waters of lakes across the north. The Menominee of northeastern Wisconsin also trace their ancestral roots to an underground bear with a copper tail.

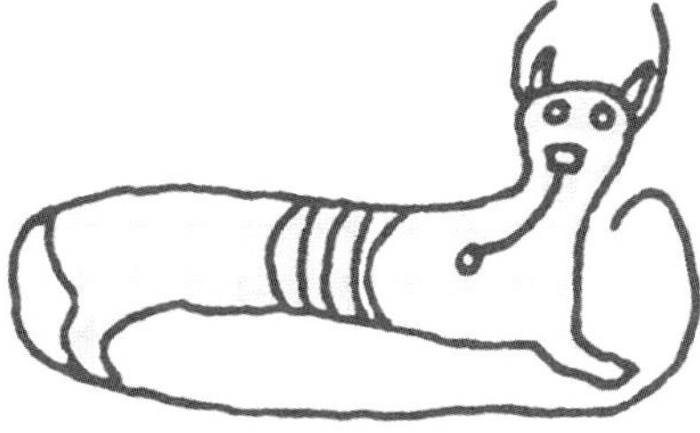

Fig. 4.8 Drawing of *Mishipeshu* on an Obijwe birch bark song scroll (from Tanner 1830, 377).

The exchange of copper, therefore, was not so much focused on exchange of useful items – often identical types of implements appear to have been involved – but rather on social and ideological considerations: the offering and receiving of gifts of supernatural power. But the exchange of such power-charged objects secured friendly relations among different groups in an area so packed with people that violent conflict over resources would otherwise seem inevitable (Birmingham and Rosebrough 2017). This same cultural process may very well explain the much later appearance of the Effigy Mound Ceremonial Complex, where large populations of individual Late Woodland societies shared ceremonies and rituals, most notably the continuation of effigy mounds, that functioned to avoid friction and conflict over several hundred years. Until the end of the Late Woodland phase there is no evidence of warfare and violence. After *ca* AD 1000, fortified villages appear but these are correlated with the expansion of Mississippian people from southern Illinois into the territory of the effigy mound builders.

First cemeteries

The earliest cemeteries recorded in the Upper Midwest appear between 4000 and 1500 BC and are linked to the Old Copper Complex. Two large Old Copper period cemeteries are located within the main area of copper use and exchange in eastern Wisconsin and contain copper objects as grave offerings as well as other symbolic items from other regions of North America. These are the Reigh site on Lake Winnebago near Oshkosh and the Oconto site near Lake Michigan, both in Wisconsin. These cemeteries comprise multiple ossuaries containing the remains of several individuals and the main mode of burial was fully articulated and extended 'in the flesh' indicating burial soon after death, although there were also some bone bundles and cremations. The extended burials indicate that most people were buried right after they died so suggests that settlements were nearby. Grave goods, including numerous copper objects, accompanied specific

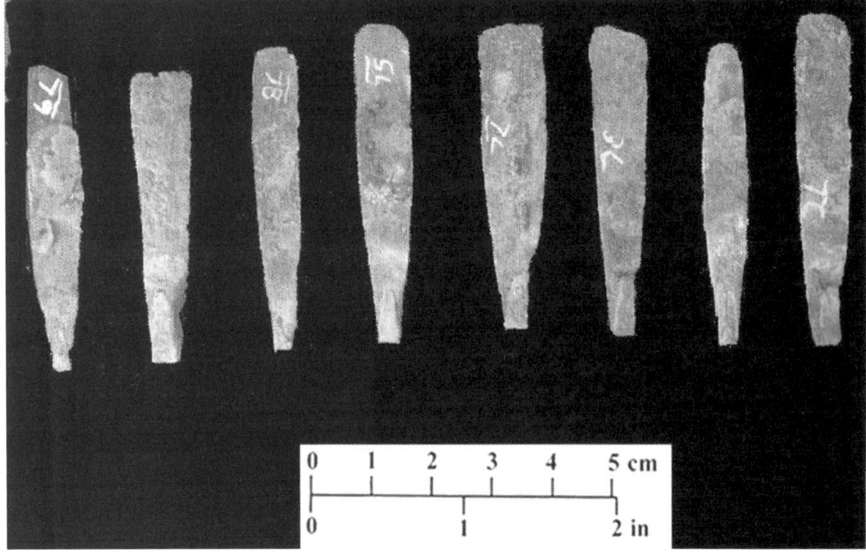

Fig. 4.9 Copper feathers from headdress (from Stoltman 1997, 132).

individuals and also suggest the rise of differences in social status. One individual at Reigh had been interred with a sandal-shaped ornament called a gorget, made from seashell, and another was accompanied by a feathered headdress like those worn by 'chiefs' in later societies, but entirely made of copper (Fig. 4.9).

Red Ochre Complex and the first burial mounds

The Mid-Holocene Warm Climate ended by 1200 BC and another global climate shift brought generally cooler and much moister conditions throughout the Midwest. Although punctuated by short dry periods, the climatic shift greatly extended richer habitats for game such as deer and fish, and plants including nuts throughout the Upper Midwest. By the end of the Archaic, people throughout the region were using all major environmental zones for camps, from the shores of the lakes, streams, and wetlands to upland areas, reflecting a substantial increase in population throughout the region not just in certain places as with the Old Copper Complex. Native Americans adapted to resource-rich environments by scheduling hunting and collecting activities in tune with the maximum availability of the food – in this way and bands of people could efficiently use much smaller territories.

Much broader trade networks developed for exotic and symbolic items that would eventually link much of northeastern North America in one vast trade network. Cemeteries contained 'in the flesh' burials and, for the first time, there is clear evidence of violence and conflict. The first burial mounds and related earthworks appear in small numbers. Interment immediately after death reflected the fact that people were using smaller territories and that exotic and beautiful grave offerings obtained through long distance trade accompanied the burials of only certain people. Among the objects were ceremonial stone knives, seashell, and, in one case, a block of obsidian from Wyoming. The use of copper now became largely restricted to the manufacture of ornaments and a few types of tools. However, the fact that men, women, and even children were buried with these exotic items indicates that social status extended to family or kinship groups, not just to individuals.

A red, powdery pigment was used to cover many burials, leading archaeologists to define a new cultural expression: Red Ochre Complex, a ceremonial complex that spread into the Upper Midwest from the east between 1200 and 500 BC (Pleger 2000). Red Ochre is a deep red powder made by grinding iron oxide derived from rock. With the addition of water, Native peoples also used the powder to make red paint.

Violence and warfare erupted during this time as is apparent from a grave complex with red ochre and distinctive Red Ochre Complex artifacts discovered during building construction at the Convent Knoll site in Elm Grove, Wisconsin (Overstreet 1980). One of the burials was of a young girl who had been interred with prestige items: a large ceremonial knife and string of shell beads. However, nearby were the haphazardly arranged skeletons of eight adult men, all of whom had probably been killed in a single battle or attack. Spear points were embedded in the bones and some bodies were partially dismembered and scalped. (Contrary to some sources of information, scalping was not first introduced by Europeans and modern Americans but goes back thousands of years, along with the taking of whole heads as war trophies or for other purposes.) It is possible that the burial of these men was an offering that accompanied the high status girl but this remains speculation.

The first burial mounds and other earthworks associated with Red Ochre include one rather spectacular site, the Turkey River Mound Group, located on a high bluff overlooking the confluence of the Turkey and Mississippi rivers in Iowa (Green and Schermer 1988; Fig. 4.10). Mound building began at the site with the Red Ochre Complex but expanded over several centuries as cultures and customs changed. Several of the early conical mounds are located within and around a roughly circular ditch enclosure. Bone bundle burials and a cremation within the mounds were found in circular limestone enclosures, one capped by limestone slabs and accompanied by exotic ceremonial items typical of the period: chert 'turkey tail' blades of Indiana hornstone chert and marine shell beads (Fig. 4.11).

The human remains show the widespread violence that spread at the time, as evident at the previously mentioned Convent Knoll site. These included one individual who had apparently been stabbed with a copper awl and another who had a spear point lodged in the rib cage or sternum. Four others were headless, possibly decapitated, and one of these had a 'turkey tail' ceremonial blade in place of the head. Later Woodland peoples added burials and earth to the tops of the Red Ochre mounds and expanded mound building along the bluff edge to the northwest. These included a short Late Woodland linear, compound, and several effigy mounds (Rosebrough 2010, 952).

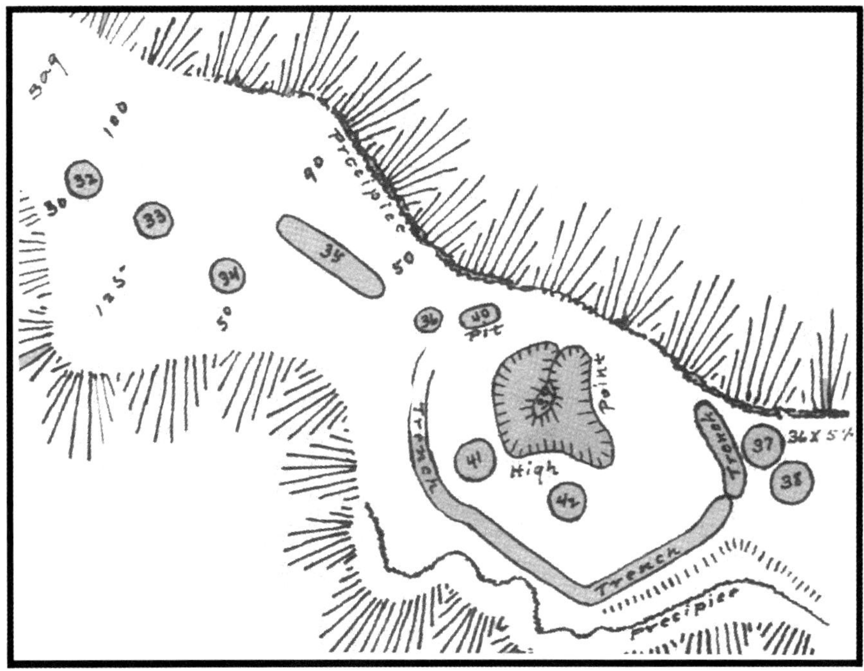

Fig. 4.10 Turkey River earthworks in Iowa (from Orr 1938, 94).

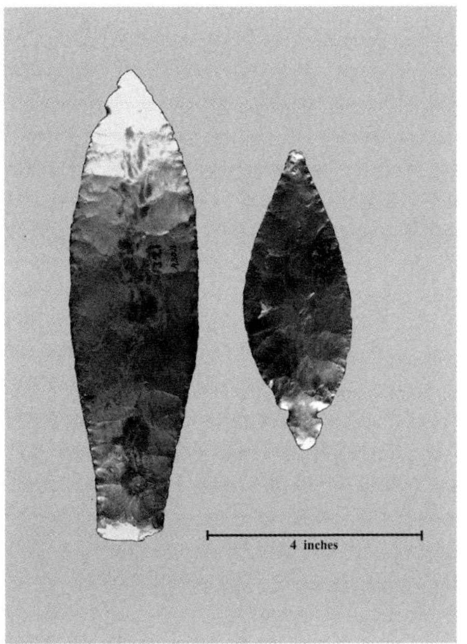

Fig. 4.11 Chert 'turkey tail' blades of Indiana hornstone chert from the Turkey River Mound Group.

Red Ochre mound building has also been reported for the Henschel site on a hill overlooking the huge Sheboygan Marsh in Sheboygan County, Wisconsin, that was also used for later mound building during the time of the effigy mounds. The Sheboygan Marsh provided an extraordinary abundance of food resources – waterfowl, fish, mammals, and a wide variety of edible plants – to the people who used the mounds. It must have been a place where people gathered frequently and thus was a logical location for periodic ceremonial activities. Three large conical mounds are arranged around a spring, which is significant because springs issue life-giving water and are the sources of special earth, fine sands, and muck, all of which are associated with concepts of rebirth and fertility in many Native American belief systems. As we have seen, springs are believed to be entrances to the watery Underworld, the residence of the great and powerful Water Spirits. For all these reasons, many types of mound groups were constructed on or near 'sacred' springs throughout the entire period of mound building. Three later Water Spirit effigy mounds arc in a curved line towards the same spring (see Fig. 1.16).

The Red Ochre mounds also provide more evidence that mounds were reserved for high status people. Like those of many others, the above ground portions of the three conical mounds at the Henschel site were leveled by farming. However, a map made in 1920 by Alphonse Gerend, a Sheboygan dentist, preserved a record of their locations (Gerend 1920). The largest of the three, which was about 8 ft (2.5 m) high, reportedly had been excavated in the 1870s by a local mound digger. In a probably inaccurate or exaggerated report the digger had found a large boulder vault or enclosure within which many skeletons were arranged around a large conch shell. This startling discovery made the local newspapers and a version of the story found its way into Cyrus Thomas's report for the Bureau of Ethnology (Thomas 1885). More than a century later, in the 1990s, heavy machinery inadvertently exposed part of a burial pit that had been beneath another of the leveled mounds (Overstreet *et al.* 1996). This portion of the chamber also contained a concentration of large rocks, possibly a cairn or vault, and an unknown number of burials covered with red ochre. Grave offerings included copper and conch-shell beads as well as knifes or spear points similar to previous forms but made of hornstone chert from Indiana typical of the Red Ochre Complex, This part of the chamber was covered by a layer of black soil. Radiocarbon dates from charcoal from the pit places the funerary activities to about 600 BC, a date consistent with the last phases of the Red Ochre Complex.

The Woodland tradition

Archaeologists separate the Woodland tradition (*ca* 500 BC–AD 1200) from the Archaic by characteristics such as the expansion of burial mound building and horticulture and, for the first time, the appearance of pottery vessels used for cooking and storage. In many other aspects the people during the short Early Woodland stage (*ca* 500 BC–AD 100) lived much like their ancestors during the Late Archaic. Long distance trade networks flourished and items acquired through trade accompanied the burials of important people. Bands of hunting and gathering people continued to occupy defined territories, occasionally shifting locations, but people now stayed longer in warm weather camps or villages supported by a wide variety of foods and other resources found within short travel distances. Excavations at the Beach site, a large warm weather habitation on the shores of Lake Waubesa in south-central Wisconsin, yielded fish, mammals, waterfowl, and plant seeds and nuts (Salkin 1986). The charred remains of nuts and acorns found at the site indicate that people continued to live here through the fall. A large amount of broken pottery indicated either a degree of sedentism or frequent use of the site. Elsewhere Early Woodland communities cultivated small amounts of sumpweed, the first signs of a domesticated plant. At the late summer/early fall Mill Pond site, Early Woodland people gathered clams, fished, and hunted riverside mammals (Theler 1986). As in the Paleo-Indian and Archaic, no evidence of Early Woodland housing has been found, probably because they were small, temporary, wigwam-like structures that left little surviving evidence.

Pottery

The first ceramic containers appeared about 800 BC, no doubt reflecting decreased mobility that made such breakable containers now practical for storage and cooking. Before that, easily transportable hide, bark, and basket containers served for such purposes. Over the next 1200 years Woodland potters used local clays mixed with crushed rock as a temper and decorated the pots with variety of designs and symbols. Through time the pots would become thinner, sturdier, and more elaborately decorated. Woodland people first roughened or marked the surfaces of the pots with cords or fabrics pressed into the wet clay. Decorations were then stamped, impressed, incised, or trailed on this surface (Fig. 4.12, left). Although there is much individual variation, the decorative motifs found on pottery were not based on the fanciful whim of the potters or selected for purely aesthetic reasons. The very first pots were plain but quickly designs and symbols were added that seem to reflect the basic Upper/Lower World cosmology explicit in art and monument building and, perhaps, even reflect kinship divisions to which the potter belonged. Chevrons found on Woodland pots are interpreted as bird symbols that denote the Upper World in Native American cosmology, while other designs, such as some arrangements of parallel lines, may represent the Earth (Benn 1995). Long tail-like designs on the bottom of some Early Woodland pots seem to symbolize the tails of Water Spirits or snakes (Fig. 4.12, right). Variations on these themes appear in decorations on many types of pottery made through to

Fig. 4.12 Two Early Woodland pots (Prairie Phase) from Southwestern Wisconsin (from Stevenson *et al.* 1997, 152, fig. 7.6).

the time of European contact when imported metal containers largely eliminated the pottery making craft.

Burial mounds

Early Woodland burial mounds are few but occur in small groupings of high (6–8 ft/*ca* 2–2.5 m) round mounds built over pit graves typically containing several individuals as extended 'in the flesh' burials or as bone bundle reburials. Several of the mounds excavated in the past at various places feature pieces of limestone and brightly colored field stone surrounding a central burial pit. There were four such concentrations of stones at at the Hilgen Spring Mound Group in the City of Cedarburg placed in the cardinal directions (Van Langen and Kehoe 1971) (Fig. 4.13). Similar arrangements consisting of sod or mounds of dirt in other mounds in the Midwest have been related to the widespread Earth creation stories as discussed previously, with the four concentrations of sod or dirt representing the four corners of the Earth (Hall 1997, 17–23). Remnants of grave preparations and burial rituals suggest, like the later effigy mounds, that the concepts of creation and renewal of the Earth were a main theme of the ceremonies.

Middle Woodland Hopewell

After 1000 BC the custom of building burial mounds was also practiced by people living in the Ohio River valley, where it marks the beginning of the Early Woodland stage of that area, called the Adena Complex (Fagan 1995, 403–10). Like the Old Copper and Red Ochre Complexes in the Upper Midwest, Adena was not one culture but indicates a related cluster of rituals shared by a number of different peoples. One ritual was the erection of large conical mounds over burial pits or chambers

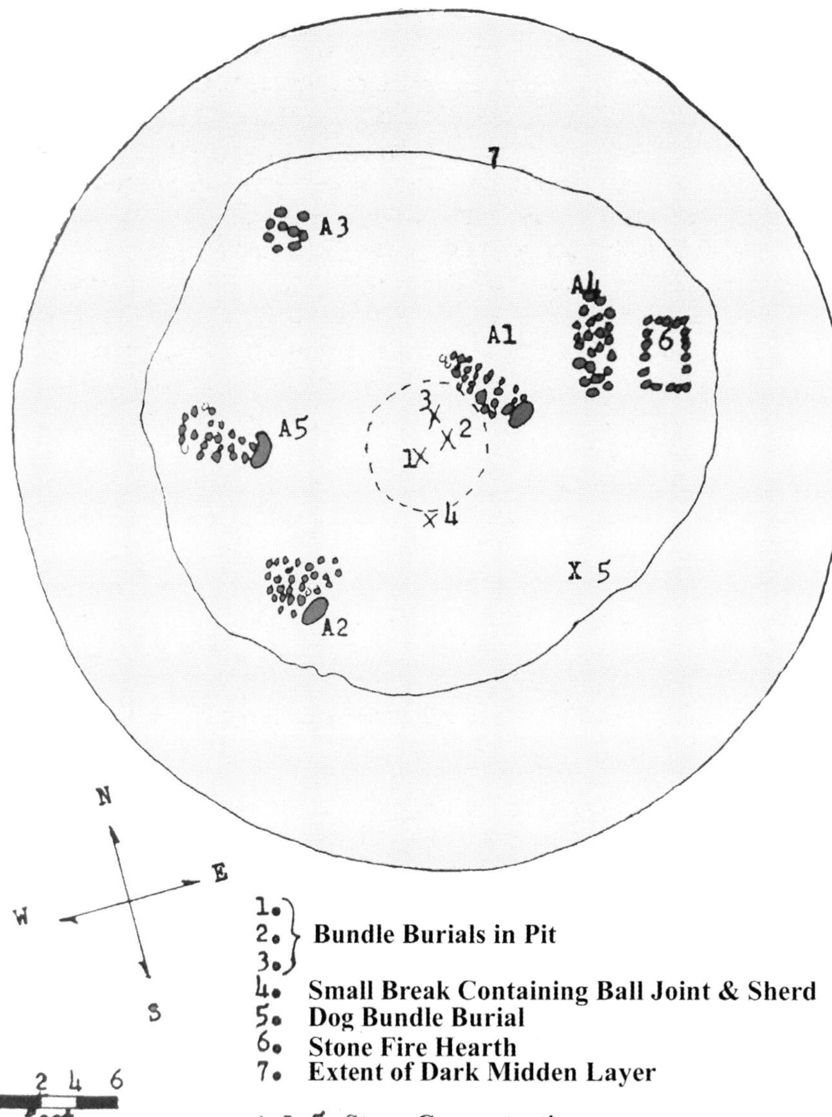

Fig. 4.13 Drawing of an excavated mound at Hilgen Springs in southeastern Wisconsin (from Van Langedon and Kehoe 1971).

dug into the ground and sometimes these elaborate chambers were lined with logs and lay beneath the floors of pole-and-thatch grave shelters that were burned to the ground before the mounds were constructed. Mounds grew in size through time by the addition of more burials and earth. One Adena mound in Moundsville, West Virginia, was more than 67 ft (*ca* 20.5 m) high. The Adena people also built large earthen enclosures close to the mounds that possibly served as sacred spaces for conducting ceremonies related to the burials.

The burial of relatively few people in pits below mounds reflects the growing complexity of Native societies in eastern North America, in which differences in social status were becoming even more evident. Simultaneously, long distance trade networks grew even more elaborate, and important people buried in the mounds were often accompanied by more symbolic items of great prestige value acquired from distant places, such as seashells, sheets of mica from North Carolina, pipestone from Minnesota, blue-gray hornstone chert from Indiana, lead (for white pigment) from southwestern Wisconsin or northern Illinois, and copper from around Lake Superior. Adena, and the following Hopewell, were artistic communities who provide substantial insights into the worldview and supernatural beliefs of the time in the form of statuettes, images on pottery, and other art that features animals and supernatural beings.

The Hopewell civilization grew from Adena during the Middle Woodland *ca* 100 BC–AD 400, greatly expanding on ideological themes and earthwork building. Facilitated by vast trade networks, the construction of earthworks in Ohio reached awe-inspiring dimensions. Huge geometric earthworks – squares, circles, and octagons – covered vast tracts of land, sometimes hundreds of acres (Lynott 2014; see Squier and Davis 1848 for comprehensive illustration of Hopewell earthworks; Fig. 4.14). It has also been proposed that large, wide 'sacred roads' connected some of these ceremonial areas. Considerable engineering, mathematical, and architectural skills were involved and attest to great social complexity.

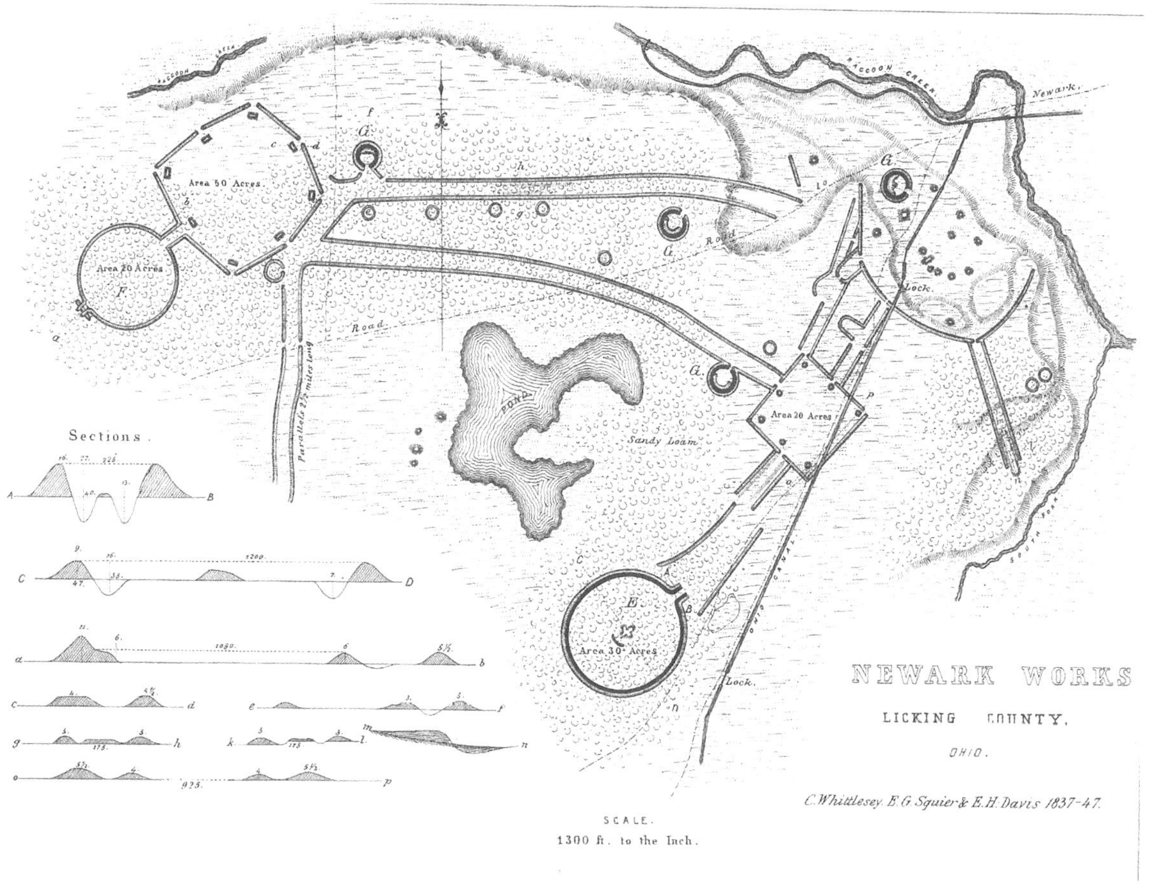

Fig. 4.14 The Hopewell earthwork complex at Newark (from Squier and Davies 1848).

The Hopewell observed the movements of the moon from the enclosures adding astronomical knowledge to Hopewell ideology and engineering (Romain 2000; 2015; Lepper 2004; Lynott 2014).

Studies of these monuments have suggested that Hopewell societies were equivalent to chiefdoms with social groups ranked in importance, although subsistence patterns continued to be based on hunting and gathering. Archaeologists originally referred to the phenomena as the Hopewell Interaction Sphere but now also as the Hopewell Ceremonial Complex.

Dualism is apparent in the layout of many Hopewell ceremonial centers with large pairs of both square and circular or octagonal enclosures, although sometimes there are three (Lepper 2004; Lynott 2014). These logically have been interpreted as representing ritual places for different segments of Hopewell society. The dual arrangements could well reflect the existence of a two-part or moiety social structure representing clans of the Upper and Lower Worlds. Martin Byers (2011) alternatively proposes that ceremonial activities of both clans and cults, specialized internal organizations devoted to world renewal ceremonies, took place at the ceremonial centers. Clan ceremonies transformed the deceased into ancestors but, for the cults, their deceased members were considered to be offerings intended to enhance the sacred powers of nature.

Hopewell period mounds are often found within enclosures and frequently cover an elaborate, log-lined pit, as with the earlier Adena where burial chambers appear to have functioned as repositories for the dead for some time before being covered by mounds. Offerings of great prestige accompanied people buried beneath the mounds indicating high status. Beautifully crafted ornaments and objects of copper, mica, slate, fine chert, obsidian, and silver were placed with these special burials, as were beautifully crafted pottery vessels with intricate designs. Also included were stone smoking pipes, sometimes carved in the form of beautiful animal effigies. Unlike modern habits, tobacco smoking was, and still is, an important part of ritual life for Native people. Tobacco, a plant originally domesticated in Mexico, was grown only for ceremonial purposes for Native people and such reverence for the substance continued after the appearance of the Europeans who took it back to Europe – and then brought it back to the New World as a recreational drug!

As a result of vast trade networks, Hopewell ideology and rituals spread in many directions including to the west where Hopewell centers grew up in Indiana, southern Iowa, and Illinois where it is known as Havana Hopewell. While these places have burial mounds, the giant earthworks characteristic of Ohio Hopewell are lacking. Nevertheless, the western Hopewell sometimes built smaller earthen enclosures and there is unmistakable evidence of Hopewell religious and social influence in the form of art, pottery, trade goods from distant places, and Hopewell-related burial mound building customs. In the later effigy mound region there is ample evidence that the Effigy Mound Ceremonial Complex had roots in major Hopewell landscapes, albeit without the vast trade networks.

Hopewell ceremonials adopted by Woodland people are most clear in the western part of the later effigy mound region and especially along and near to the Mississippi River. Grave offerings accompanying burials under the mounds along the

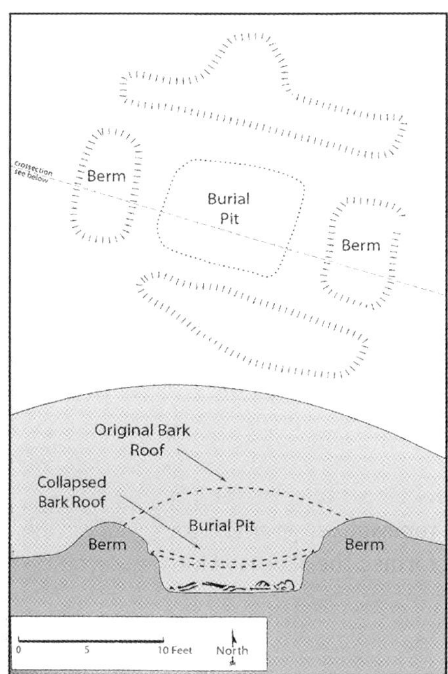

Fig. 4.15 Upper: plan and profile of the Nicholls Mound showing central burial pit, berms, and original bark roof (drawings: University of Wisconsin-Madison Cartography Lab after McKern 1931); lower: exotic Hopewell artifacts found in the Nicholls Mound (from the collections of the Milwaukee Public Museum).

river attest to both the participation in the Hopewell complex and the high status of those interred. Below the large Nicholls Mound, near the river town of Trempealeau, Wisconsin, a central burial pit excavated by the Milwaukee Public Museum revealed the remains of 46 individuals laid out in an extended fashion and bone bundles, one of which was accompanied by silver-covered wooden beads (McKern 1931; Fig. 4.15).

However, interment below high mounds was only one part of dual Middle Woodland mortuary customs. Many more people were interred in even larger burial pits in lower lying areas, unmarked by high conical mounds and lacking elaborate grave offerings. Further to the south, a larger, unmounded grave pit was found by James Stoltman of the University of Wisconsin on an island in the Mississippi River at Prairie du Chien, Wisconsin (Stoltman 2005). The Tillmont Site contains the remains of up to 30 individuals and appears to have been long used as a below-ground crypt, probably originally with some sort of covering. People were placed in the grave pit as they died since most skeletons are extended in natural form with bones articulated. The excavation terminated upon discovery and documentation of the burials, which were not removed. Since grave goods with prestige value did not accompany these interments it is likely that they represent either less important social groups in Middle Woodland society and/or, considering the low-lying watery location of the site, people associated with a Lower World social division in Middle Woodland societies.

Similar Hopewellian burial practices were found in the very center of the later effigy mound region at the Yahara outlet of Lake Monona in the modern city of Monona. In 1948 road builders exposed dramatic evidence of a classic Hopewell era tomb just south of the largest mound at the Outlet site (Bakken 1950). This was a 12 × 9 ft (*ca* 3.7 × 2.7 m) pit containing the skeletal remains of

13 people ranging in age from infants to adults (Fig. 4.16). Most of the people lay on their backs in an extended position but several bundles of bones were also present. No mound had been mapped here by previous researchers so it is likely that the feature is an unmounded crypt of Lower World moiety people, like the Tillmont mass grave. Also, like Tillmont, there are no characteristic Hopewell grave offerings but white clay, probably marl, covered the faces of two of the skeletons and may represent the decayed remains of, or served a similar purpose to, clay masks such as that found covering a cremation deposit

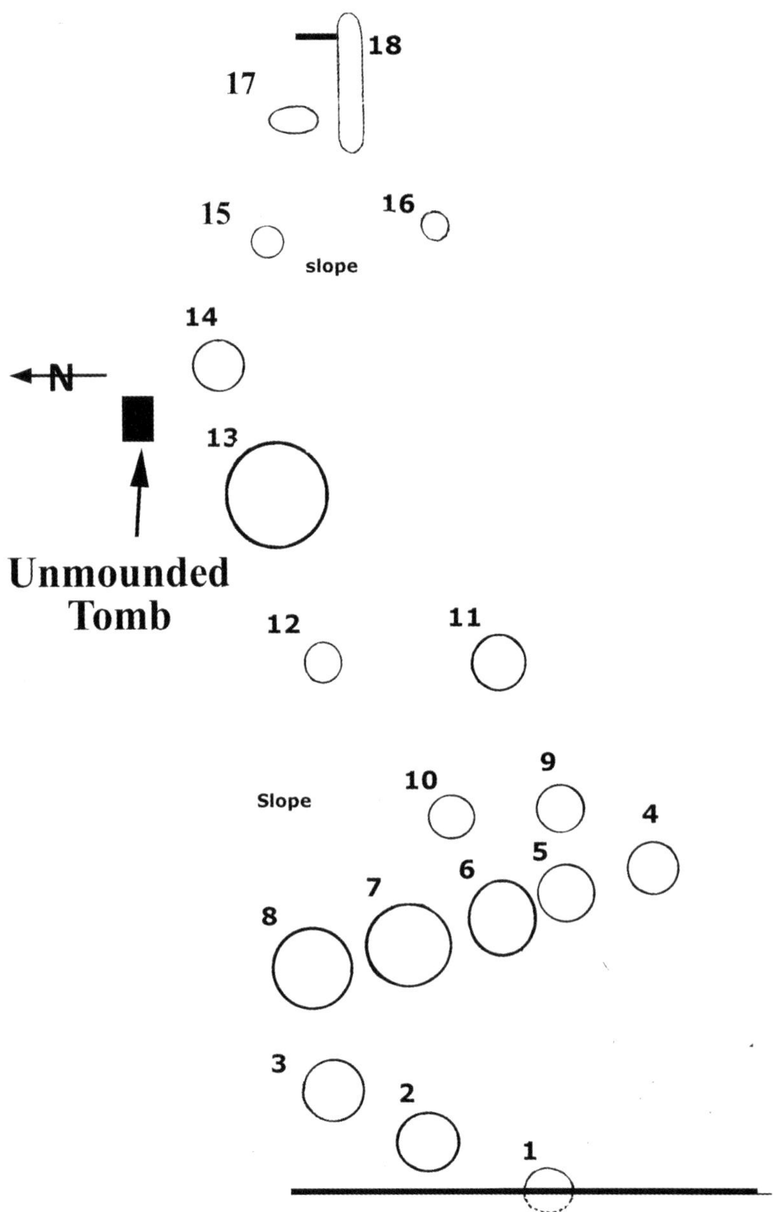

Fig. 4.16 Map of the Outlet site showing location of unmounded mass tomb.

Fig. 4.17 A Woodland clay death mask (reconstructed) that covered a cremation at the Wakanda Park site in northwestern Wisconsin (from Wittry 1959).

at Wakanda Park, northwestern Wisconsin (Fig. 4.17). Marl is a calcium deposit composed mainly of shell found on the bottom of some lakes in the area and its use by Native Americans has been connected to concepts of rebirth and to the watery and marl covered dens of the Water Spirits. An interesting legend collected by Charles Brown from the local Ho-Chunk in the early 20th century told that people drowned by the Water Spirits would have marl in their mouths (Brown 1927a). Subsequent excavation of a nearby Hopewell burial mound by the University of Wisconsin uncovered the remains of several individuals accompanied by a 9 in (22.9 cm) long Hopewell-style knife made of Hixton Silicified Sandstone (Bender *et al.* 1982), presumably reflecting a higher, Upper World, status.

Middle Woodland Hopewell people in the Upper Midwest did not build ceremonial centers with immense earthen enclosures like those in Ohio but may have used smaller rectangular, octagonal, and circular embankments as sacred places. Earthen enclosures and circular ditches do go back as early the Late Archaic in Iowa so it is certainly a possibility that the custom continued into later times but influenced by Hopewell ritual. However, the few known examples at mound groups in Wisconsin are, at least in some instances, associated with effigy mounds classified as belonging to the later Late Woodland tradition, suggesting that the custom continued into later times. The enclosures were built prior to the effigy mounds at these sites, or it is even possible that effigy mounds began to appear in small numbers already in the Middle Woodland, growing directly out of Hopewell influence (Fig. 4.18). One example of the later case may be a circular earthen berm mapped in the late 19th century by T.H. Lewis near the Kickapoo River in southwestern Wisconsin that enclosed a central bird effigy that is remarkably similar to a bird enclosure documented for the Hopewell Newark Earthworks in Ohio mapped in the 1840s by Squier and Davis (1848) (Fig. 4.19). While tantalizing, a connection between the two cannot be established: the Kickapoo River site is now gone and modern archaeologists are uncertain that there had been a bird in the Ohio enclosure. Excavations in the 1920s revealed that the area of the supposed bird covered a large ceremonial structure (Brad Leper, Ohio connection, pers. comm.).

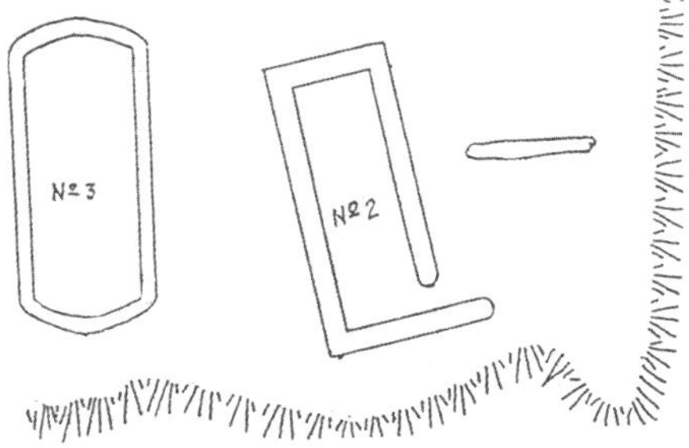

Fig. 4.18 Octagonal and rectangular enclosures reminiscent of Ohio Hopewell enclosures at an effigy mound site in Trempealeau County, Wisconsin as mapped by T.H. Lewis in the late 19th century.

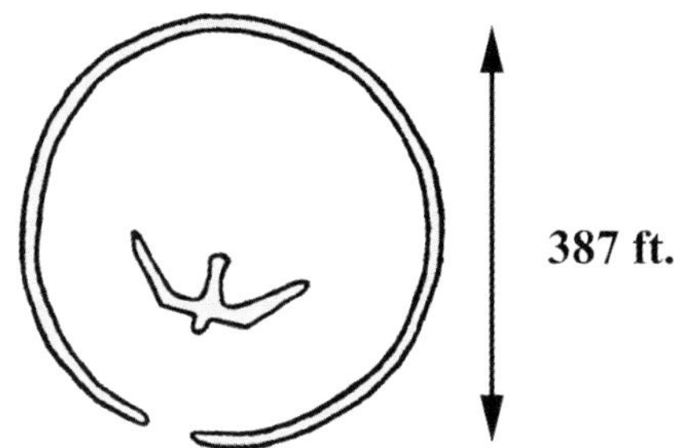

Fig. 4.19 Upper: enclosure with bird in the center on the Kickapoo River in Wisconsin, mapped by T.H. Lewis (1880–1895, notebook 20, 36–7); below: similar enclosure with bird at the Newark Hopewell site in Ohio (from Squier and Davies 1848).

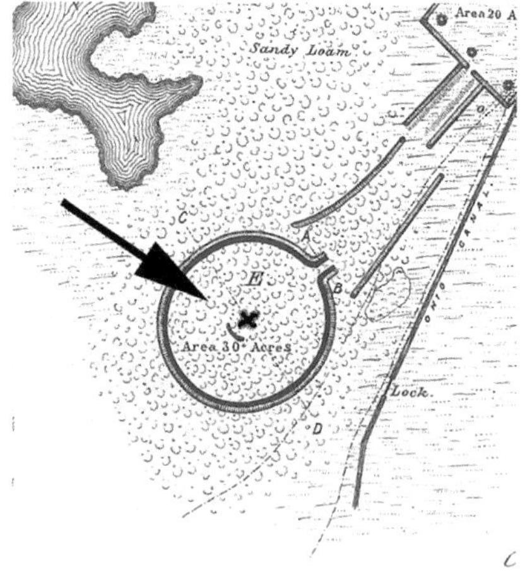

Middle Woodland effigy mounds

There is other, more substantial, evidence that the building of effigies of supernatural beings or spirits had roots in Hopewell ceremonial customs, if not before, and that these customs could have disseminated into the Hopewell centers in the Wisconsin area, leading to the later explosion of effigy mound building found here. Early excavations of the Hopewell North Benton Mound in Ohio uncovered a boulder outline of a great bird amid other rock ritual constructions within a circular rock enclosure and a central fireplace (McGrath 1945; Fig. 4.20). In the early 20th century, pioneering archaeologist Warren Moorehead found another large boulder creature in an Ohio Hopewell mound that looks very much like a long-tailed Underworld Water Spirit in Native traditions. Unfortunately, only a sketch survives from his excavation (Lepper, pers. comm; Fig. 4.21). Much further west, a Hopewell mound at Utica, Illinois, covered burials and a boulder effigy of either a snake or long-necked bird (Henriksen 1965). It seems that it is only one step from these boulder effigies to above-ground earthen effigies of the same types of creatures that were obviously important in the supernatural beliefs of the time.

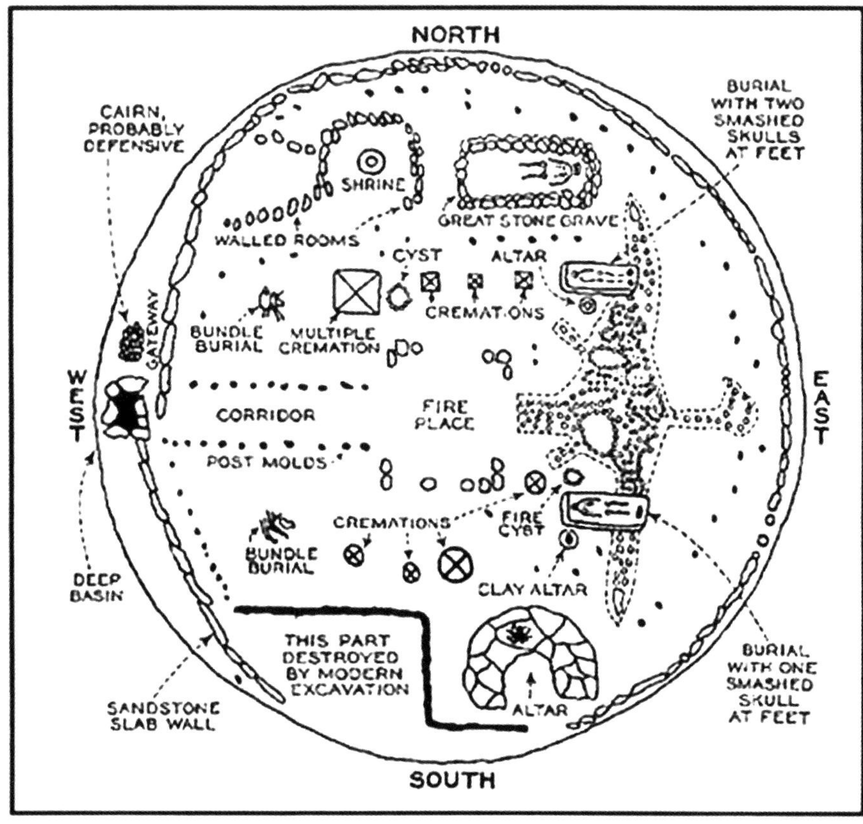

Fig. 4.20 The Ohio Hopewell North Benton Mound showing a large stone bird effigy (from McGrath 1945).

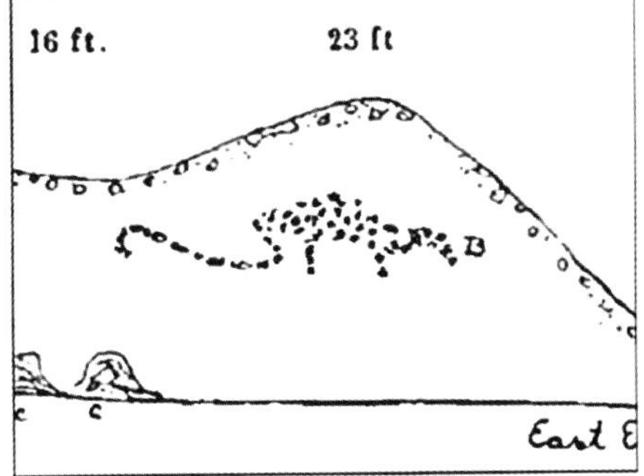

Fig. 4.21 Ohio Hopewell mound with stone Water Spirit effigy from the records of Moorehead (courtesy of Brad Lepper, The Ohio Connection).

Two of the most famous earthen effigy mounds are in Ohio: the great Serpent Mound and the so-called Alligator Mound (Fig. 4.22), but both have been attributed to cultural developments long after Hopewell by radiocarbon dating. However, redating of the Serpent Mound using new experimental radiocarbon techniques places its initial construction much earlier – back to Adena times (Lepper *et al.* 2018). The earlier date (on charcoal) remains controversial since an even more recent radiocarbon date taken from Serpent Mound places construction much later, as originally believed (Lepper *et al.* 2023).

The Alligator Mound, described by Lepper and Frolking (2003), is unlikely to be an alligator and instead appears to be a long-tailed 'Underground Water Panther' or Water Spirit commonly found in Native tradition and cosmology, but it is flattened as though viewed from above. It has not been redated but is interesting because the form is very similar to a long-tailed creature with horns etched on a Middle Woodland stone pipe found in southeastern Minnesota by an artifact collector (see Fig. 3.8, above). The creature is shown in two perspectives like many of the later effigy mounds. On the side of the pipe it is shown in profile as a horned panther-like animal with a long, looped tail. The same animal is shown on top as indicated by the same interior decoration, but as viewed from above, much like the Alligator Mound. At the very least it can be said that the concept expressed by Alligator Mound in monumental form was already present during the Middle Woodland Hopewell in another type of ceremonial representational art. Interestingly, the pipe was made of purplish Baraboo pipestone and came from near Devil Lake, Wisconsin, a later major effigy mound building center (Boszhard 2006; see Chapter 3).

The great Middle Woodland Hopewell civilization with its vast trade networks collapsed between AD 200 and 400 for reasons that are still unclear although climate change is believed to be involved. However, the legacy of Hopewell continued on during the Late Woodland and the beginnings of the Effigy Mound Ceremonial Complex in the Upper Midwest, as did the long-held worldview of ancient Native peoples that divided the world into the Upper and Lower realms with supernatural powers and animal spirit beings associated with each.

Unfortunately, comparatively few effigy mounds have been dated because most archaeological excavations into the mounds themselves had taken place before the advent of radiocarbon dating. Those that have been dated, along with many more dates from related habitation sites, mostly show a time span between AD 700 and 1100, or well after Middle Woodland. The earliest radiocarbon date for an effigy mound in the Upper Midwest was obtained in the 1960s from a bear mound at Effigy Mounds National Monument on the Mississippi River in Iowa that placed construction prior to the effigy mound era centered on AD 375 (this was very early in the use of radiocarbon dating and the error margin is ±100 years; Stoltman and Christiansen 2000), which would place it well before the effigy mound era. The bear was an animal held in great reverence by Hopewell people and probably considered a provider of great medicine, as indicated by an Ohio Hopewell stone figure showing a medicine man wearing a bear skin cape (Dragoo and Wray 1964). Bear mounds are unusually common at the Monument and surrounding Mississippi Valley area and there is much evidence of substantial Hopewell-related activity in the form of conical mounds with Hopewell period burial and artifacts. Taken at face value, the early date would seem to provide evidence of effigy mound building during Middle Woodland and perhaps with roots in Hopewell, but there is an issue. The same mound produced a second date that was 250 years later, greatly confusing the matter, and no artifacts were found in the mound excavation to clarify the situation. As it stands, archaeologists are understandably reluctant to accept the early date for the bear mound.

Middle Woodland to Late Woodland effigy mounds

Despite such issues and problems, it remains likely (and an interesting matter for continuing future research) that Late Woodland effigy mound construction had its roots in the Hopewell Ceremonial Complex that eventually sparked development

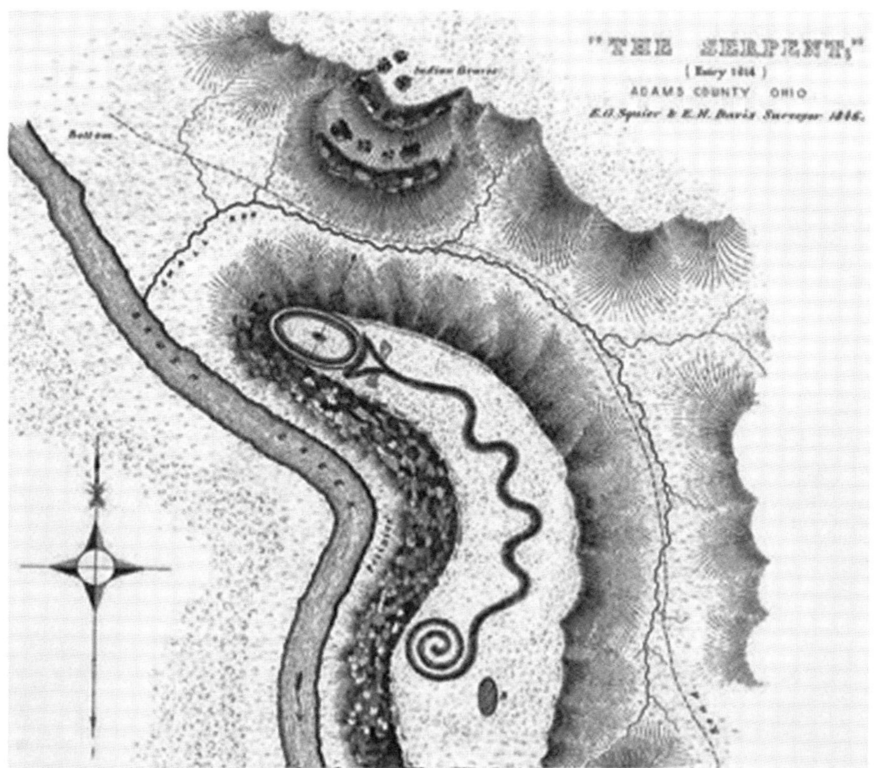

Fig. 4.22 Drawings of the Great Serpent and 'Alligator' mounds in Ohio (from Squier and Davis 1848).

of a new, spectacular ceremonial movement: the Effigy Mound Ceremonial Complex. One site that traces the poorly understood transition from Middle to Late Woodland mound building, Rehbein I, is located along a bluff top near the Kickapoo River, a tributary of the Mississippi in southwestern Wisconsin (Mead 1979) (Fig. 4.23). In what was the last major burial mound excavation in Wisconsin

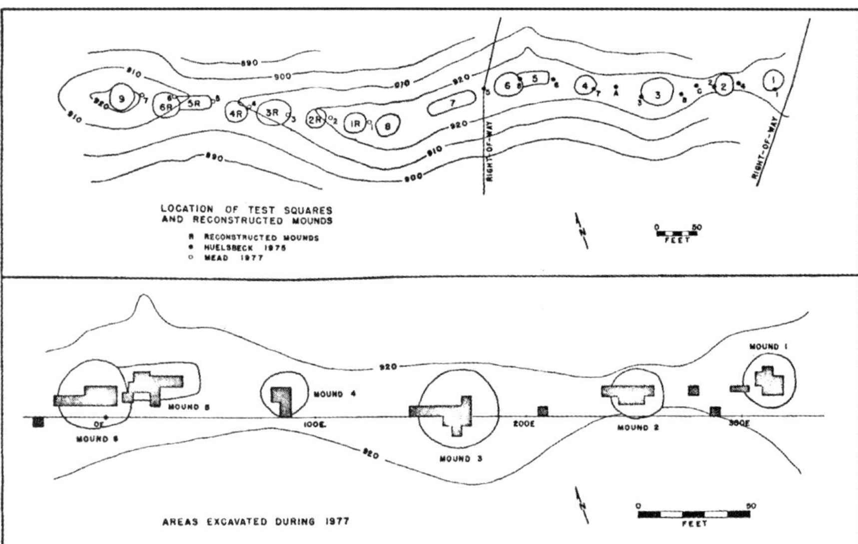

Fig. 4.23 Map of the Rebbein site near the Kickapoo River in Wisconsin (from Mead 1979).

to date, archaeologists from the Wisconsin Historical Society excavated the six mounds at the site along the planned route of a new highway. The demolished mounds were reconstructed nearby and the recovered human remains re-interred in the new mounds at the request of the Great Lakes Intertribal Council.

The earliest mounds date to the later part of Middle Woodland and lacked the prestige grave offerings characteristic of earlier Hopewell. One mound covered burial pit had been lined with logs and roofed with bark, much like Hopewell tombs. The tomb had been burned, no doubt as a part of formal closure ceremonies. At about AD 700, a short, linear mound, typical of Late Woodland, was added and another conical mound appears to have been added to the group.

The first effigy mounds in the Upper Midwest appear to have been created on bluffs along or near the Mississippi where Hopewell influence had been the strongest. In several instances bird, bear, and/or canine mounds are found at the ends or adjacent to long lines of mounds, called 'processions' composed of small conical mounds, short linear mounds, and sometimes compound mounds arranged along bluff tops and adjacent spurs. One example is the Eagle Valley Mound Group on a bluff edge overlooking the Mississippi near Glen Haven, Wisconsin. Here a single hawk-like bird effigy is found at the north end of a line of conicals, short linears, and compound mounds (Fig. 4.24).

Effigy Mounds National Monument

Other similar lines of mounds are found on the bluffs at the confluence of the Mississippi, Wisconsin, and Yellow rivers. The longest is at the Effigy Mounds National Monument in Iowa and others lie directly across the river at Wyalusing State Park in Wisconsin. The Effigy Mounds National Monument is the most famous mound landscape in the Upper Midwest and traces the evolution of mound building from Middle Woodland Hopewell through the Late Woodland into at least the

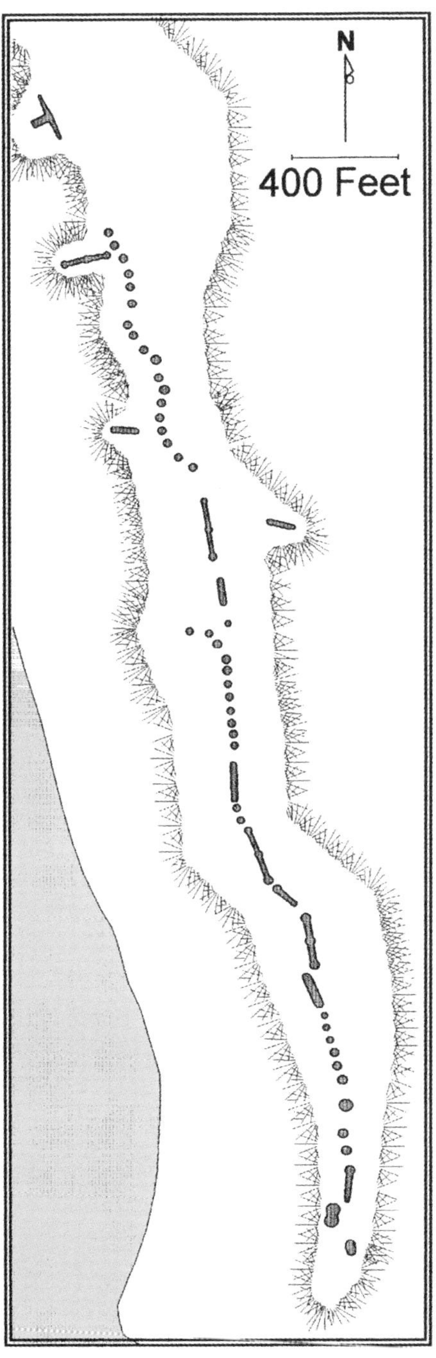

Fig. 4.24 Map of Eagle Valley Mound Group on top of a bluff overlooking the Mississippi River, showing mainly small conical and short linear mounds with an effigy mound at the north end.

beginnings of the formation of the Effigy Mound Ceremonial Complex that later spread widely in the Upper Midwest as Late Woodland populations greatly expanded after AD 750.

Mounds have been subject to various types of research since T.H. Lewis first made maps in the late 19th century. Archaeologists conducted limited mound excavations throughout the 20th century but no mound had been completely excavated. The earliest mounds are dated to Hopewell influenced Middle Woodland and other substantial evidence of Hopewell habitations and burial sites has been found along the Mississippi River in this area (Stoltman 2005). The development of a Hopewell trade center here makes sense since it is where the Yellow and Wisconsin rivers converge with the Mississippi, providing water transportation access for vast areas of the Hopewell trading networks. These trading networks disappeared as Hopewell collapsed and this region seems to have lost its role as a major ceremonial center, although effigy and other mounds continued to be built in small numbers until about AD 1000. After that the confluence area appears to have been abandoned until it re-emerged as a fur trade center during the historic period. Only a few mounds have been radiocarbon dated, but none with modern and more accurate testing. However, other types of evidence trace the origins of the Monument mound landscape to the Middle Woodland Hopewell *ca* 100 BC–AD 400 with mounds continuing to be created into the early part of the Late Woodland, perhaps in the AD 600s and 700s.

Isolated conical mounds are found on the hills throughout the highly dissected lands of the Monument while others were destroyed by land use prior to its establishment. Most of the 98 mounds occupy the bluff edges and spurs overlooking the Mississippian, extending on both sides of the Yellow River and Mississippi. The mound landscape along the bluff top is virtually continuous but six main groupings have been defined (Fig. 4.25). One exception to this pattern is the Nazekaw Terrace Mound Group, a concentration of conical, linear, and club-shaped mounds originally located on a lower Yellow River terrace but mostly destroyed by early farming.

The mounds include conical, short linear, 'club', and compound mounds and the effigies are of 18 bears and four birds. One bear mound, appropriately called the Great Bear, is the largest and most massive bear mound in the effigy mound record. It is 137 ft long, 70 ft wide, and 5 ft high (41.8 × 31.4 × 1.5 m). The birds are raptors, apparently falcons, as at the Raisbeck site further south along the Grant River. Falcon imagery continued to be of particular significance to the later Mississippians and the Oneota cultures that followed the Late Woodland elsewhere in the Upper Midwest, no doubt because of its fabled hunting prowess. The bluffs along the Mississippi had long been nesting areas for peregrine falcons and the ancient and Native peoples would have perceived the bluffs as the place of the falcon spirits. Over the years the native falcon population has dwindled but the National Park Service has been introducing breeding pairs to restore numbers. In general, the high frequencies of bear and bird effigies is typical of mound groups around the confluence, in the Prairie du Chien locality, covering both sides of the Mississippi in Iowa and Wisconsin (Rosebrough 2010; 2014).

Figure 4.26 provides LiDAR examples created by William Romain, of the bluff top groupings. The arrangements clearly illustrate the correspondence between mound orientations and topography. The orientations of mounds follow the ridge tops and spurs and the birds are found on slopes, animated in flight.

The evolution of the Monument landscape appears to have begun north of the Yellow River with the Hanging Rock Group arranged on a bluff spur, which consists of 19 conical mounds that are rather larger than most other conical mounds at the Monument, as well as a compound mound near the west end. The large size of the mounds suggests early mound building and a narrow trench placed through a conical revealed

Fig. 4.26 (*opposite*) LiDAR images of selected mound groups at Effigy Mounds National Monument: a) Hanging Rock; b) Red House Landing; c) Wild Cat/ Big Bear; d) Compound; e) Fire Point/Little Bear; f) Marching Bear (courtesy of Willam Romain).

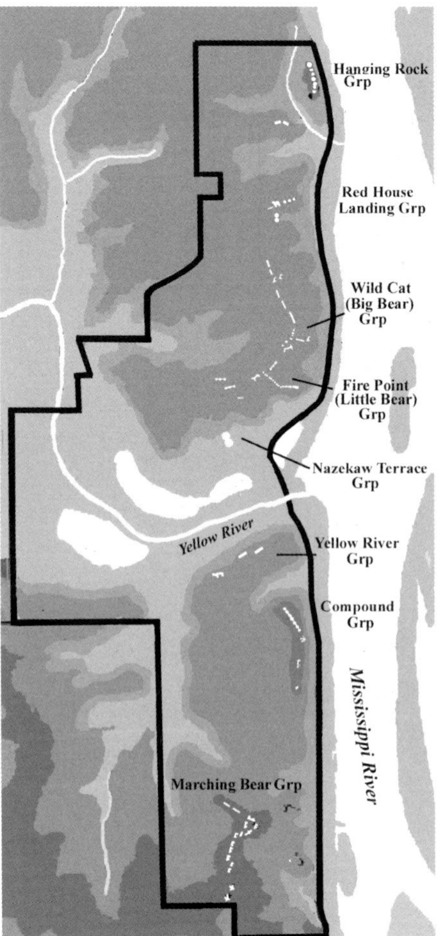

Fig. 4.25 Relief map of the Effigy Mounds National Monument showing locations of major mound groupings.

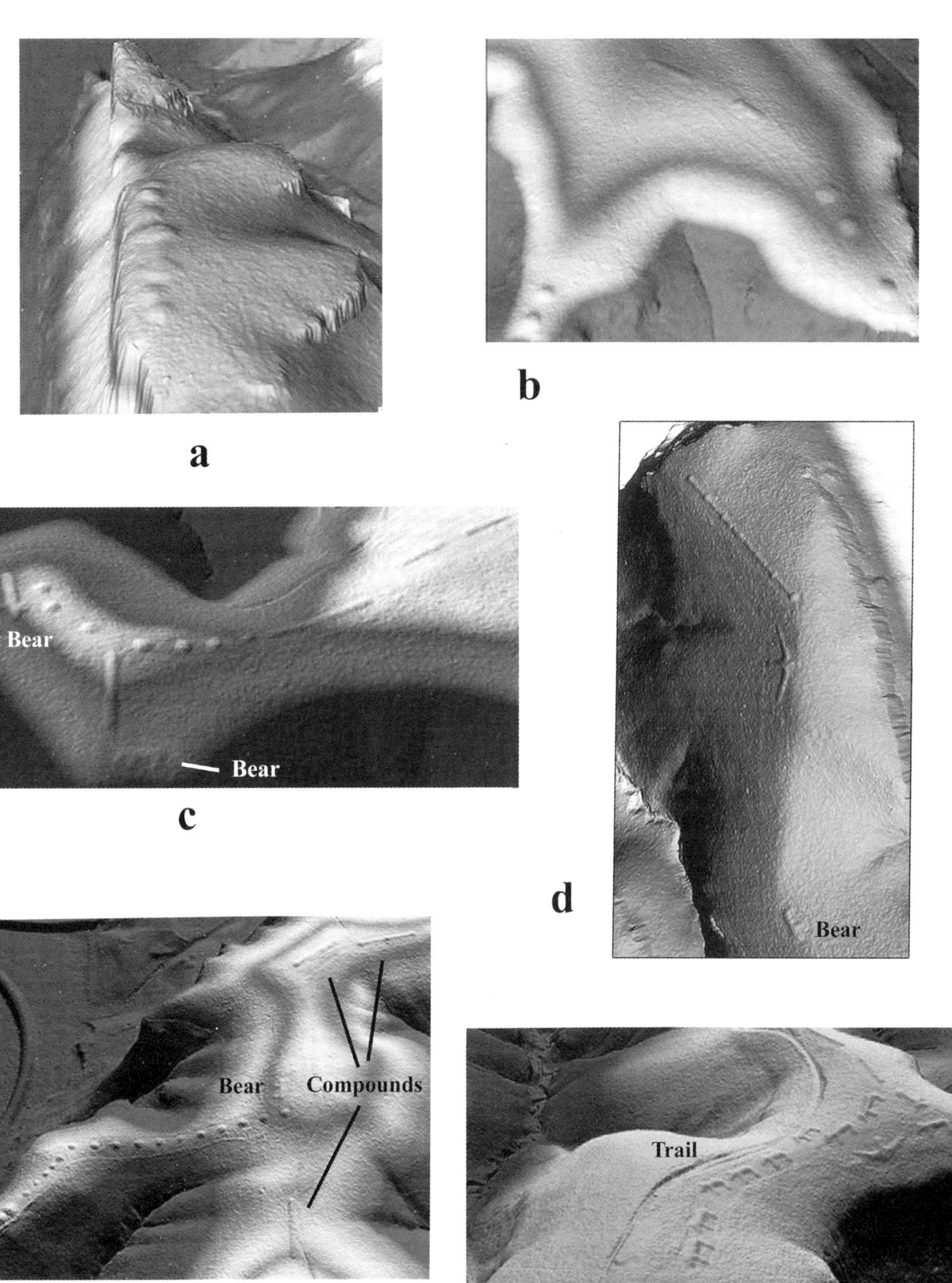
a
b
Great Bear
Bear
c
d
Bear
Bear
Compounds
Trail
e
f

burials and a stone platform or crypt for which a Middle Woodland affiliation is surmised (Green *et al.* 2001, 23).

The Red House Landing Group is arranged in a line of seven mounds, while the Wild Cat Group is also a line, with five effigies. The Fire Point Group, on the bluff nearest to the Yellow River, also produced definite evidence of origins in Middle Woodland. It is a line of 19 conical mounds with a bear effigy near the western end. Early excavations of the first mound at eastern end of line, Mound 33, unearthed Middle Woodland Hopewell artifacts: a copper breast plate, copper beads, a sheet of mica, and a pearl bead associated with 6–8 burials of adults and children (Logan 1971), including both extended and bundle burials, and cremations.

Three groups lie south of the Yellow River. The first is the small Yellow River Group composed of two short linear mounds and a bear effigy. Next is the Compound Group named for its compound mounds, composed of seven conical mounds joined by linear ridges, unlike the other three conical compounds found at the Monument. The meaning of compound mounds remains a mystery. The compound is accompanied by a bear and a falcon-like raptor on the slope heading to the Mississippi River.

The southernmost grouping, the Marching Bear Mound Group, is fully an effigy mound era grouping dominated by effigies: 10 bears, three birds, but also two linear mounds. The bears and linear mounds follow the curve of the ridge top and the falcon-like birds swoop down the steep slopes towards the Mississippi as though hunting.

Four of the mounds were sampled by trenching in the 1960s, unearthing bundles of bones and, beneath one bear mound, there was evidence that an intaglio of the form had been first excavated into the earth prior to construction of the mound. Testing of another produced conflicting radiocarbon dates of AD 375±100 and AD 625±100 (Tiffany 1981, 61). On the face of it, both dates would indicate effigy mound construction along the Mississippi earlier than expected, leading some archaeologists to reject the dates as unreliable, especially given the very large error margins.

The broader cultural landscape includes habitation areas and other evidence of ritual and mortuary activity. Excavation of a rockshelter occupying a crevice in the bluff face found refuse with pottery dating to both the initial and later Late Woodland and, possibly a little earlier, rock art, and remains of burials of at least 15 individuals along with other scattered bone. The children included infants and one that was 10–12 years old at the time of death. The cranium of the latter was partially burned and bore many cut marks suggesting defleshing (Green *et al.* 2001, 32–3), perhaps to prepare the corpse for cremation or bone bundling. One habitation site, called FTD, is located along the Yellow River, where archaeological testing discovered cultural material from both Middle Woodland Hopewell and Late Woodland people (Benn and Thompson 1976).

Fig. 4.27 (*opposite*) Above: LiDAR from the WisconsinView website showing major mound groups in Wyalusing; below: drawing of the Spook Hill and South Point Groups in the southwest part of what is now the state park. Spook Hill was mapped by Cyrus Thomas in 1894. He said previous digging recovered artifacts now recognized as typical Middle Woodland Hopewell (Thomas 1885, 90).

Wyalusing State Park

Across the Mississippi River from Effigy Mounds National Monument, near the city of Prairie du Chien, ancient mound building people also used the high bluffs and dissected terrain of what is now Wyalusing State Park. The park is mainly

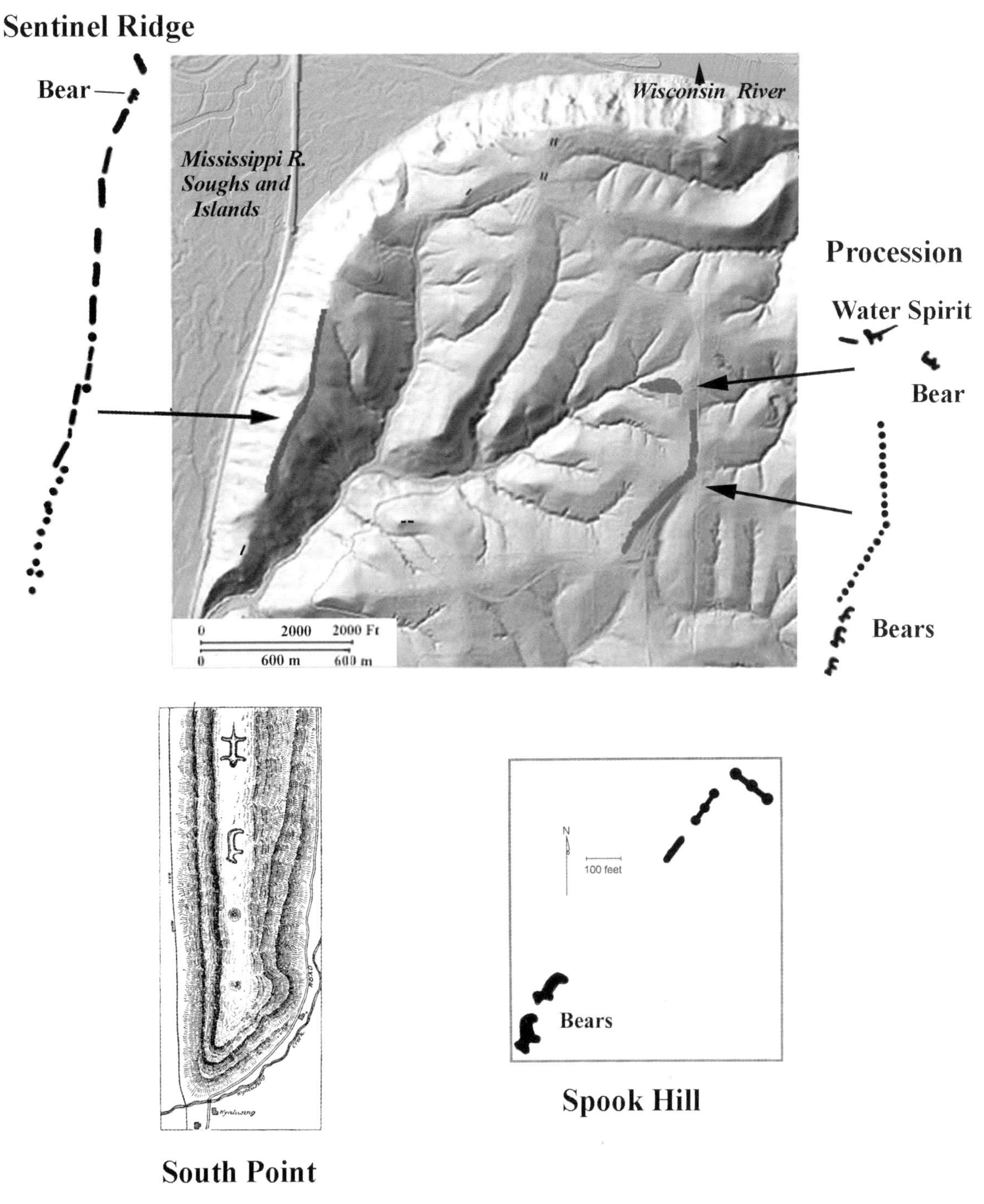

Sentinel Ridge

Bear

Mississippi R. Soughs and Islands

Wisconsin River

Procession

Water Spirit

Bear

Bears

0 2000 2000 Ft

0 600 m 600 m

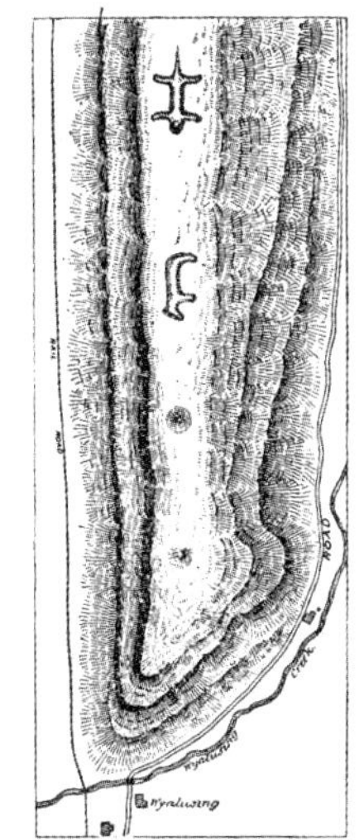

South Point

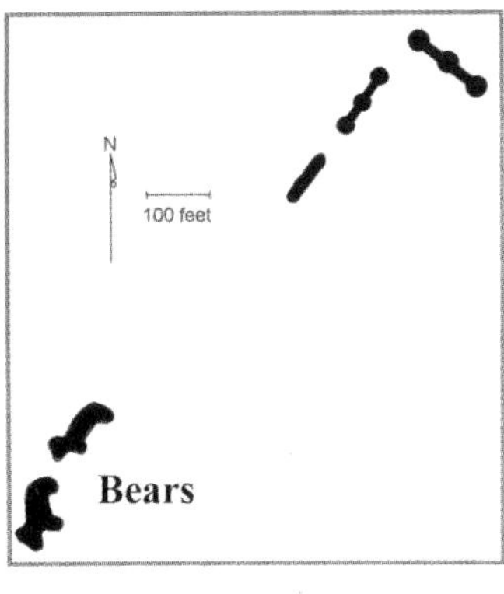

Spook Hill

composed of soil covered limestone buffs overlooking the confluence of the Mississippi and the broad floodplain of the Wisconsin River. Several mound location sites have been recorded in the park, once totaling more than 130 mounds but many mounds had been obliterated by agricultural activities and stone quarrying before establishment of the park. The mound landscape shares similarities with that of Effigy Mounds National Monument and could be the work of the same social group. Here, the earliest mound building also began during the Middle Woodland Hopewell and, judging by mound forms and arrangements, continued into the initial and early years of the Late Woodland Effigy Mound Ceremonial Complex development. Effigy mounds, mostly bears, are present but lacking are the large effigy groupings which characterize the later stages of the complex, suggesting that ceremonial use shifted elsewhere, for example, further up the Wisconsin River where enormous effigy mound landscapes are also found.

Sixty mounds remain, including the well-preserved Sentinel Group set on a high, north–south trending ridge overlooking the Mississippi (Fig. 4.27). This comprises a single line of conical and short linear mounds with a lone bear effigy at the north end (Fig. 4.28). Further inland, but also on top of a long ridge, the Procession Group once consisted of a similar line of conical and short linear mounds with a bear and Water Spirit at the north end and three bears at the south end. Curiously, and in contrast to other mound groups in this area, no birds have been found on the bluffs here.

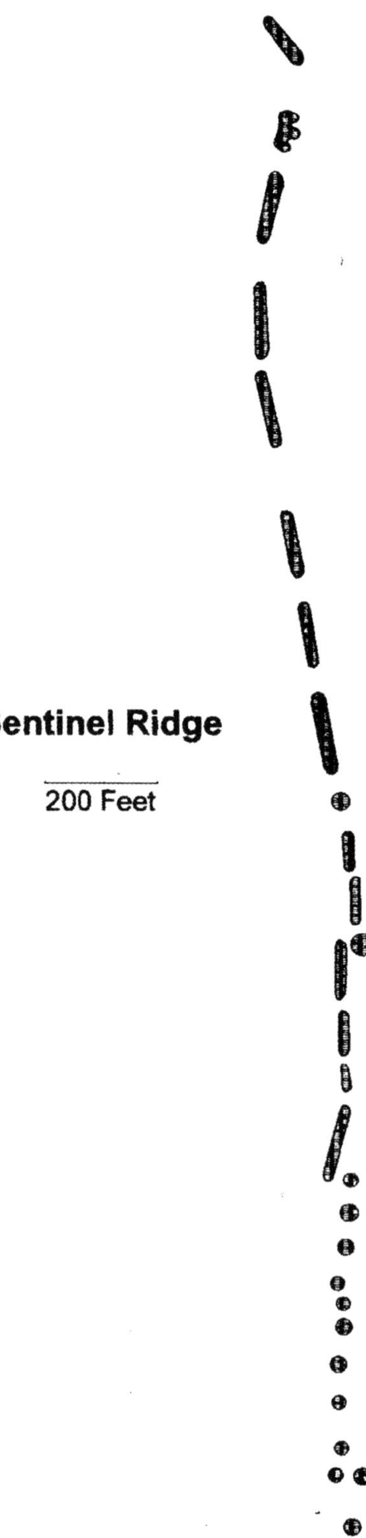

Fig. 4.28 Map of Sentinel Ridge or Signal Hill Group mapped by Brown (Brown and Drexel 1909).

None of the mounds has been professionally excavated but Cyrus Thomas identified numerous mounds arranged along a bluff edge and adjacent spurs in his late 19th century search for the identity of the mound builders (Thomas 1885, 87–91). Thomas reported one 19th century mound excavation of a conical at the Spook Group that produced evidence of what is now recognized as mortuary activities of the Middle Woodland Hopewell. The mound is located at the end of a spur and covered a circular stone tomb with human remains associated with typical Hopewell artifacts such as a platform pipe, shell beads, and a copper celt (Thomas 1885, 90). Two effigy mounds, a bear and a flattened canine, are found further along the spur, suggesting that Late Woodland effigy mound building quickly succeeded Middle Woodland or, perhaps, they were created at the same time, as with the Effigy Mounds National Monument.

5

The Four Lakes: a key example of an effigy mound landscape

Located at the very center of the effigy region is a key example of a large effigy mound ceremonial landscape and its evolution, the Four Lakes Effigy Mound Landscape (Fig. 5.1). Spreading across a chain of lakes around and near Madison, Wisconsin, it is one of the best archaeologically studied areas in the effigy mound region, owing to the presence of the University of Wisconsin-Madison and Wisconsin Historical Society. It also received the attention of early mound researchers. Much information of Four Lakes mounds, including those that have been since destroyed, had already been gathered in the 19th and early 20th centuries and research is continuing. A wealth of information was contributed by pioneering archaeologist Charles Brown, director of the Wisconsin Historical Society in the early 20th century. Brown was also a founding member of the Wisconsin Archeological Society, the mission of which was the documenting and preserving of Indian Mounds in the state. In the Four Lakes, Brown was assisted by local volunteers from the Archeological Society, such as A.B. Stout and W.B. McLachlan, who conducted surveys and produced maps. Mound research by Brown, Stout, and McLachlan was published in the journal *The Wisconsin Archeologist*, edited by Brown during the first half of the 20th century (eg, Brown 1910; 1912; 1922; McLachlan 1914; 1925; see also Birmingham 1996; 2004; 2010). Much of the following is summarized from the latter work with updates and new analyses supported by recently available LiDAR imagery.

The Four Lakes was known as *Taychepera* by the Ho-Chunk, who once lived on the shores, after the four principle bodies of water that came to be known as lakes Mendota, Monona, Waubesa, and Kegonsa. The lakes are widenings of the Yahara River that flows to the Rock River, a long tributary of the Mississippi. Habitation sites have been documented that date to various times during the period of effigy mound building and include both small and substantial villages.

There is a fifth lake, Wingra, that is actually more of a large shallow pond and is not an expansion of the river but a spring fed body connected to Lake Monona by a small stream. This lake obviously also had great significance among the greatest density of effigy and other mounds per square mile in the effigy mound region. The significance is no doubt derived from the presence of major sacred springs surrounding the lake that were used for ritual purposes by the Ho-Chunk into the 20th century.

Over 1200 individual mounds had once been on or near the shores of the lakes in at least 100 different groups or locations. Prior to Euro-American settlement and destruction of many Native American sites, pioneering mound researcher

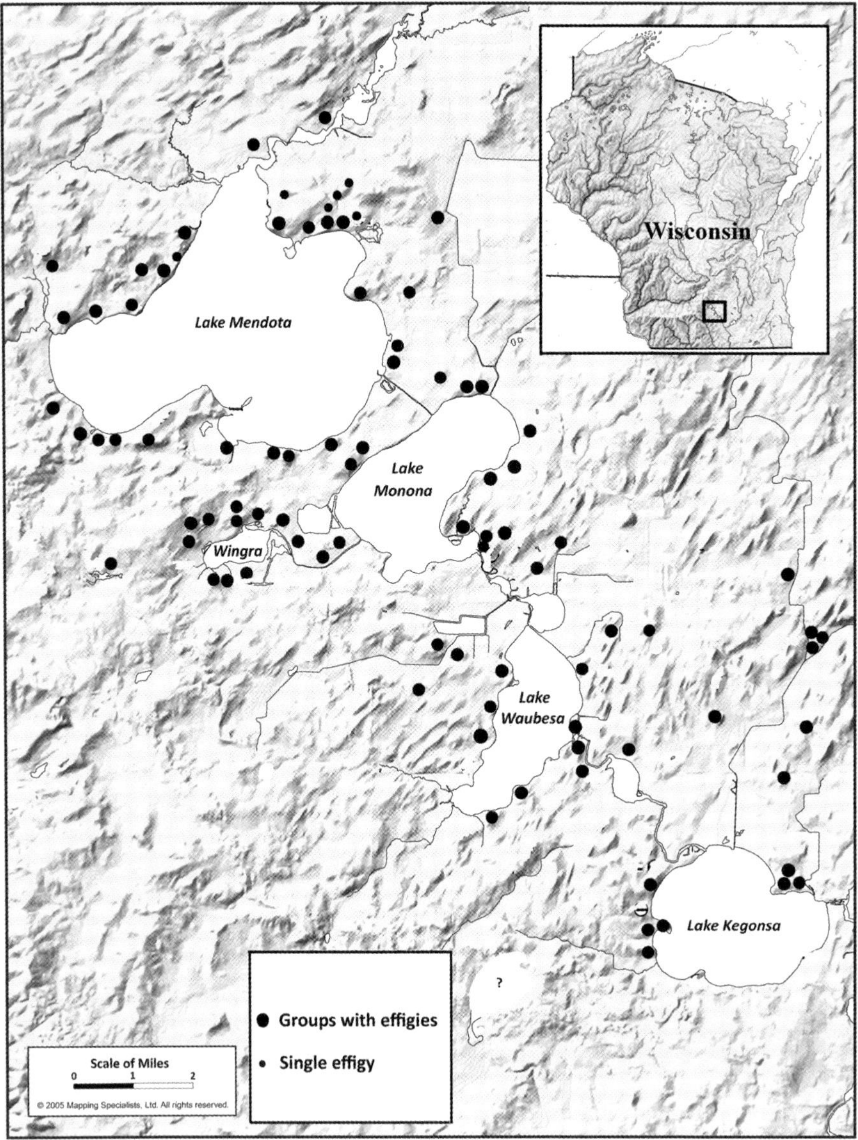

Fig. 5.1 Map of Four Lakes mound landscape.

Richard C. Taylor characterized the mounds of Four Lakes, which were mainly built during the effigy mound period, as 'forming a species of *alto relievo* of gigantic proportions' (Taylor 1838, 90). Mounds had once covered every elevation around the lakes, sometimes merging into one another and creating a vast cultural landscape, probably made by a single Late Woodland society. Camps and small villages have been documented that date to various times during the period of effigy mound building and have provided much more information on the lifeways of the ancient people. The people of the Four Lakes seem to have followed a pattern of congregating during warm weather and then dispersing into smaller groups. Population estimates are hard to make, but settlers found about 600 Indian people living along the lakes in the early 1800s and this is the low end of an educated guess for the ancient population. The large number of camps and villages found throughout the Four Lakes indicate a large population.

Being at the very center of the effigy mound region, all major zoomorphic effigy forms are present and thus is formed a microcosm of broader effigy mound symbolism. As previously noted, avian effigy forms, along with bears, are most commonly found in the western, unglaciated, part of the effigy mound region, while water related forms, such as Water Spirits and water birds dominate the lower and more eastern and watery lowlands.

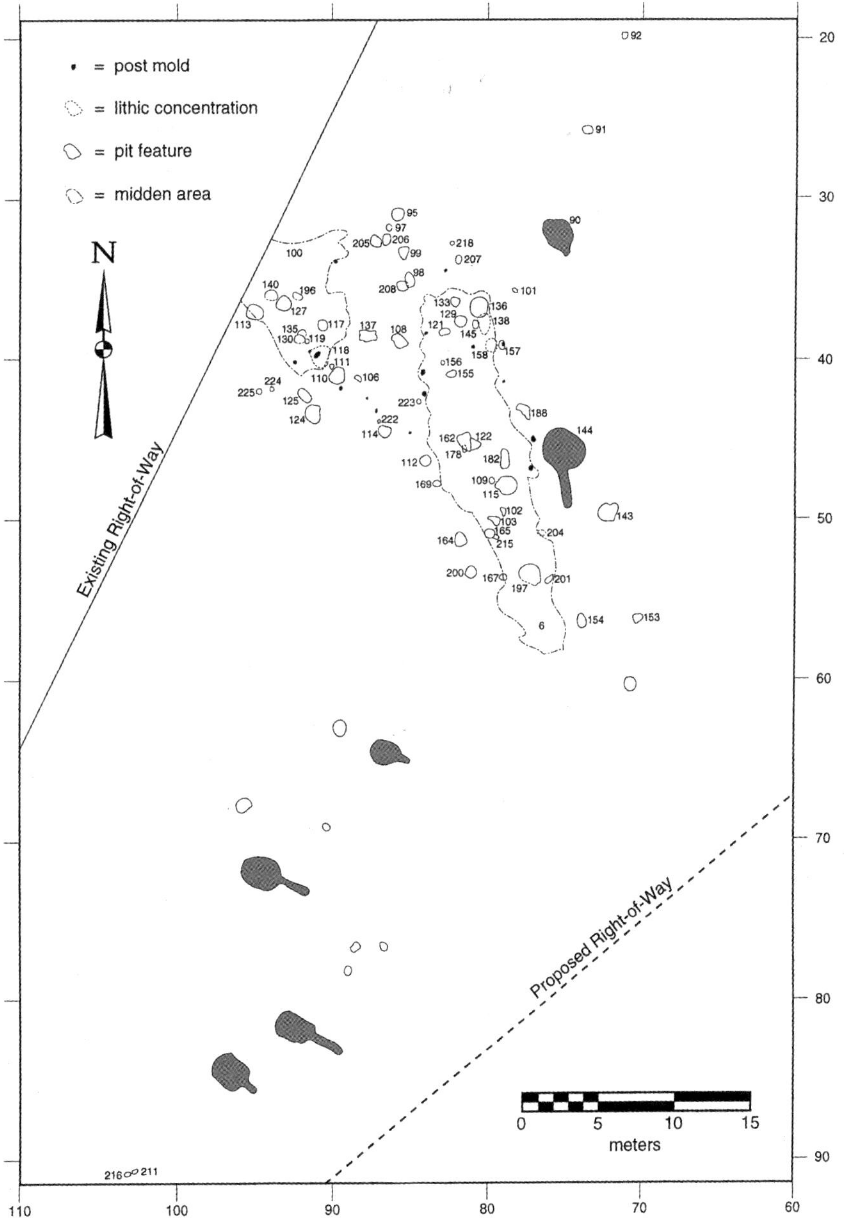

Fig. 5.2 Small 'keyhole'-shaped pit houses at the Statz site (from Meinholz and Kolb 1997).

A tour of the Four Lakes ceremonial landscape

Lake Mendota

Yahara River, from which the major lakes are formed, has its headwaters several miles north of Lake Mendota, the largest lake. It widens into Lake Mendota at a point near where Late Woodland people built some of the largest and most spectacular mounds in the effigy mound region. Late Woodland people used the marshy headwaters stream, Six Mile Creek, for a small seasonal hamlet called the Statz site, living in several small 'keyhole' shaped pit houses (Meinholz and Kolb 1997; Fig. 5.2). The creek once flowed to the Yahara River at its original inlet at Lake Mendota. This inlet is now underwater since modern installation of a lock and dam at the outlet of the lake has raised the water level, which is now 5 ft higher then it was earlier in the 19th century. Lake Mendota now covers nearly 10,000 acres (4470 ha).

The Wisconsin state capital building overlooks an isthmus dividing Lakes Mendota and Monona. Lake Mendota was originally referred to as the 'Fourth Lake' by early settlers. The Ho-Chunk called it *Wonk-sheek-ho-mik-la* or 'where the man lies', derived from a legend concerning the love of a young man for a female spirit that lived in the lake. The legend recounts how the man obtained a vision from the spirit and magically turned himself into a catfish to pursue her. Traveling from lake to lake, he arrived at Lake Mendota where he found his spirit love and lives with her today beneath its waters.

The Ho-Chunk have other legends concerning the lake that were collected by Charles Brown and his wife Dorothy in the early 20th century (C. Brown 1927a; D. Brown 1947). The Ho-Chunk lived on Lake Mendota in the early 19th century and some of them continued to use the lake long after their formal removal west in the 1830s. These people passed down stories about the lake's supernatural inhabitants, possibly inspired by the visible presence of these very beings in the form of ancient effigy mounds. The long-tailed Water Spirits dwell in deep water dens off Governor's Island on the north shore. Here one must exercise caution lest the Water Spirits should rise, capsizing canoes and drowning the occupants. The Ho-Chunk made tobacco offerings to gain the goodwill of the Water Spirits. The Thunderbirds once roosted on the west shore at Fox Bluff (Fig. 5.3), presently occupied by a housing sub-division. According to a Ho-Chunk account, the Thunderbirds could be seen flying high in the air in the early days during stormy weather, thunder rolling from their wings and lightning flashing from their eyes. This bluff was also the focus of long-time mound ceremonialism with one mound enclosing a circular and nest-like stone tomb, discovered by Charles Brown.

The Ho-Chunk went to *Sho-hetka-ka* (Horse Hill) on the south shore of Lake Mendota to gain power from the Spirit Horse through fasting and dreaming. It is now a part of the University of Wisconsin campus, called Eagle Heights (Fig. 5.1). According to the original Native residents, a horse could be seen on the hill on misty days and heard neighing and stamping. Since a horse is featured, the legend must necessarily post-date the appearance of Europeans who brought the animal to the New World but the story reinforces the long-time sacred nature of this natural feature. It too was used by the ancient mound builders who constructed linear and conical mounds on the hill, including one linear with a curious bend.

Mounds occupied virtually every elevation and bit of dry land around Lake Mendota. Current state records count at least 370 individual mounds at over 50 locations, most of which appear to date to the effigy mound era between AD 700 and 1200. Particularly dense concentrations were at the Yahara River inlet to Lake Mendota, extending on a large high rock bluff overlooking the northeast shore, north of the formerly marshy outlet of the lake. Mounds on the lake include some of the best and largest examples of effigy mound forms and, in several instances, provide models for the ideological structure of effigy mound landscapes. Most major types can be found in the vicinity of Lake Mendota although, as elsewhere in the Four Lakes, conical and linear mounds dominated the landscape. Of the zoomorphic mounds, birds, long-tailed Water Spirits, and bears were the most common. Snake forms were plentiful, if we can include tapering linear mounds in that category, as has been proposed.

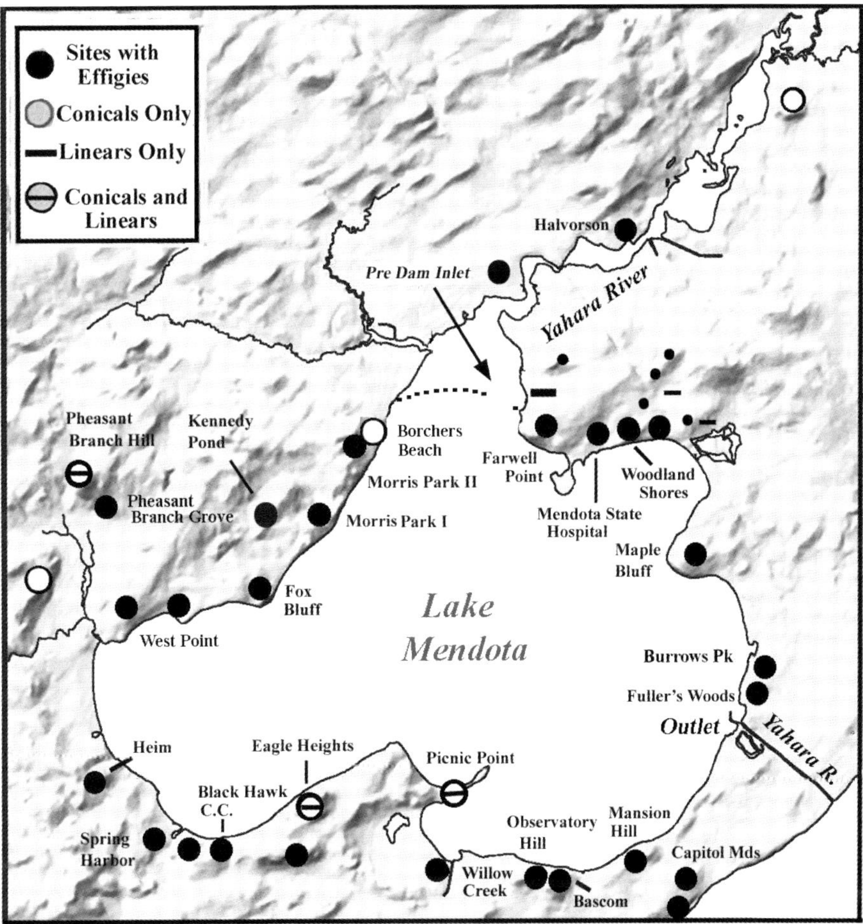

Fig. 5.3 Mounds of Lake Mendota. Those mentioned in text are identified.

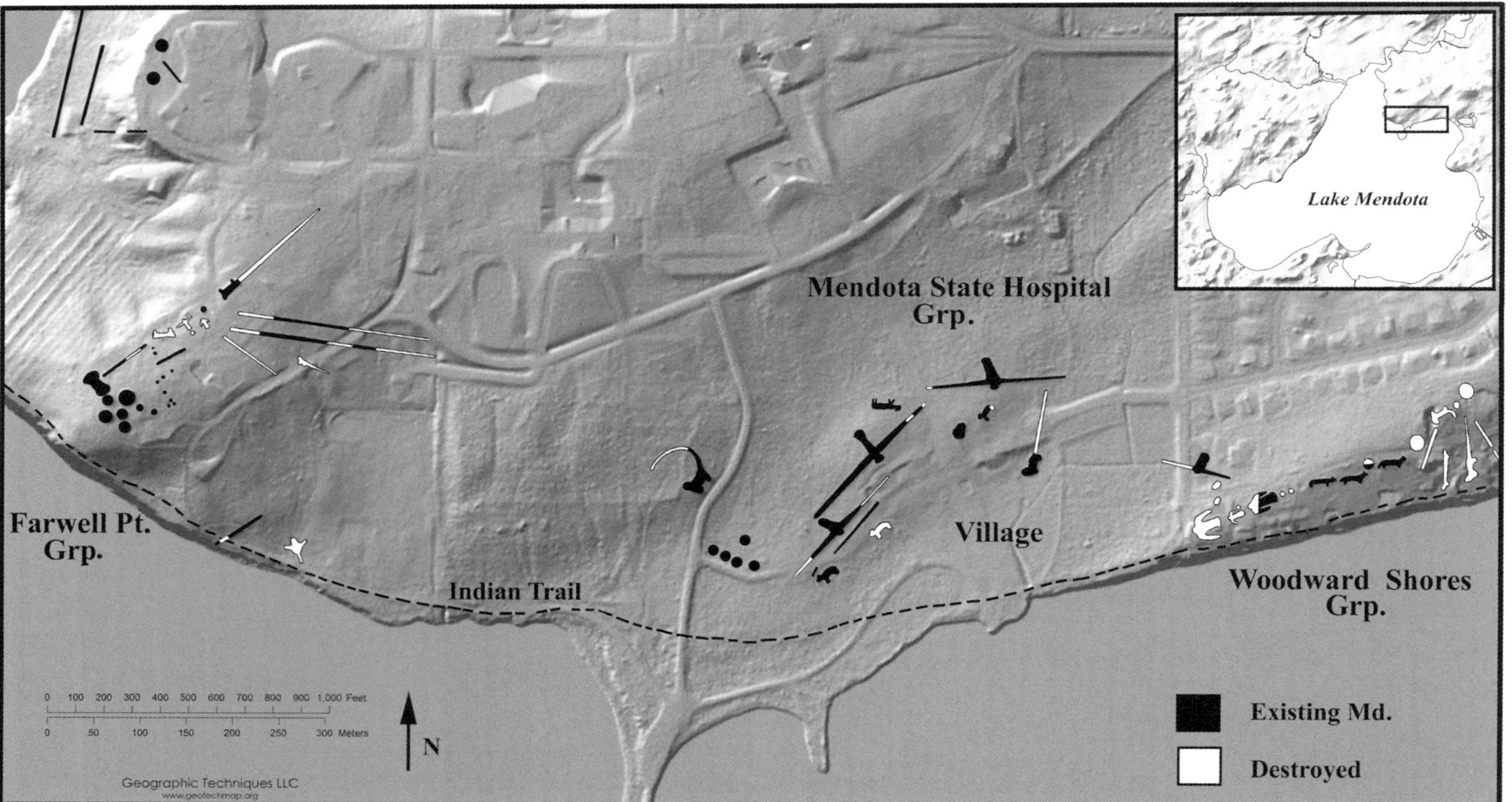

Fig. 5.4 LiDAR image of mound groups on the grounds of the Mendota Mental Health Institute and vicinity (image: Geographic Technologies LLC).

Here too are major Late Woodland, lake shore settlements, including the fortified Camp Indianola village and another partly encircled by effigy mounds on the other side of the inlet at the Mendota Mental Health Institute. Everything about this large lake suggests it was the center of the Four Lakes effigy mound society and its most important ceremonial area. Given the number, size, diversity of mound forms, and degree of modern preservation, one could rightly consider Lake Mendota the symbolic capital of the whole effigy mound region.

Yahara River and north shore mounds

Just north of the present Yahara River inlet, a large Water Spirit and a bear mound can be found in Yahara Heights County Park and these serve as an appropriate introduction to the mound landscape of the Four Lakes. Measuring 228 ft (68.8 m) in length and shown in profile (panther shape), the Water Spirit mound is part of a larger grouping of effigy mounds called the Halvorson group that once contained two Water Spirits, a bear, an oval, and a linear mound. Only the Water Spirit, oriented to the river and marsh, and the bear survived early farming and erosion. Another effigy mound grouping of large birds had been on higher ground to the southwest but disappeared before the mounds could be mapped.

Across a small bay and former inlet, the effigy mound landscape originally spread over the north shore of Lake Mendota to the marshy outlet of the Yahara River. The most spectacular and well preserved of the Four Lakes mound groupings along the western shore across the present grounds of the Wisconsin State Mendota Mental Health Institute, comprising three large effigy mound groupings apparently made for different purposes: Farwell Point, Mendota State Hospital, and Woodward Shores (Fig. 5.4). The groups trace the evolution of effigy mound building, protect and identify a large village, and provide the very structure of effigy mound symbolism.

Farwell Point Mound Group covers a high ridge, beginning above the former Lake Mendota inlet of the Yahara River on the grounds of Mendota Mental Health Institute (Fig. 5.5). The mounds trace mound building over about a 1000 year period from probable Middle Woodland origins into the Late Woodland effigy mounds. Several large conical mounds are preserved on the highest elevation along with an unusually massive effigy mound. Nineteenth century digging revealed that one of the conicals covered a stone burial vault with human remains, built on the former ground surface: the marks of this excavation are still visible

The massive mound shares the same knoll as the conical. It is of a flattened or aerial perspective effigy without a tail. It is 85 ft long and stands over 5 ft (1.5 m) high, much higher than other effigy mounds. Although referred to as a 'turtle' it is most likely a bear. The proximity of the large effigy to the earlier conical mounds suggests that it may have been among the first effigies built on Farwell Point; bears are a common form in the Four Lakes but earlier, Middle Woodland Hopewell people also venerated the bear, as indicated by much surviving art and the common use of bear tooth necklaces (see Lynott 2014). Given this, and the massive nature of the mound – more similar in height to Middle Woodland mounds than to Late Woodland earthworks, it is feasible that it actually was built during the Middle Woodland period or the transition to the Late Woodland effigy burial mound rituals.

If so, this would offer a physical earthwork link between Middle Woodland beliefs and later effigy mounds (see Chapter 4). Whatever the case, the presence of the massive effigy further identifies the Lake Mendota/Yahara River outlet area as an important part of the Four Lakes Effigy Mound Landscape.

Linear, smaller conical, and zoomorphic effigy mounds surround this high, early mound at Farwell Point and extend along the ridge to the northeast. One of these, now gone, was the largest Water Spirit mound recorded in the Four Lakes with a length of over 500 ft (152+ m). Three very long, linear mounds, one tapered like a body of a snake, radiate downslope from conical mounds and bird effigies. The longest of these extended over 600 ft (183 m). A linear mound of similar length was once part of a grouping lower in the landscape near the Yahara River inlet.

T.H. Lewis mapped two bird mounds in the late 19th century on lower ground, south of Farwell Point. One is a bent-wing goose mound that once flew downslope to the lake. This is one of about a dozen geese recorded for the Four Lakes mound district found on or near all the lakes. The other was a possible long-necked water bird, possibly a crane, eroding into the lake with wings that had a mysterious depression down the middle.

Both are gone, but further to the east at the western end of the Mendota State Hospital Mound Group remains what is perhaps the most beautiful mound of its type found in the effigy mound region – a huge, curved tailed Water Spirit, shown in profile, on a steep slope above

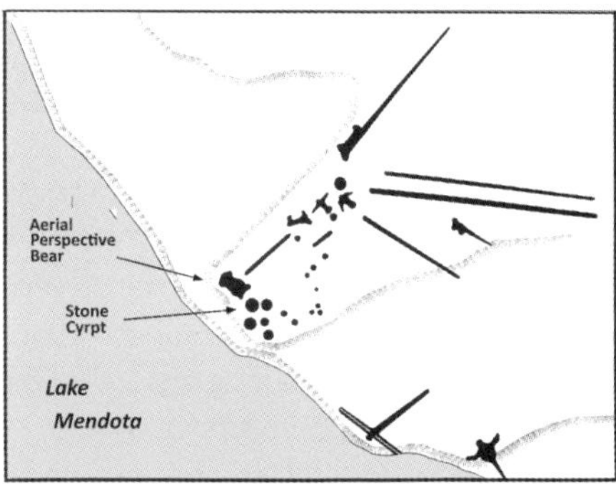

Fig. 5.5 The Farwell Point Mound Group.

Fig. 5.6 Aerial photo of curved-tail Water Spirit mound. The mound was outlined with chalk (photo: James Stoltman, University of Wisconsin-Madison).

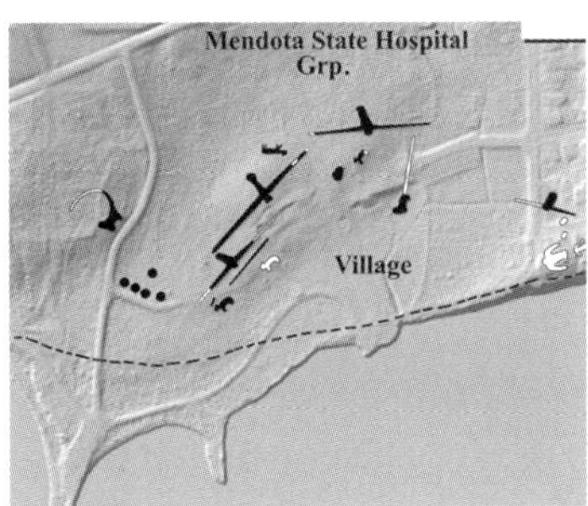

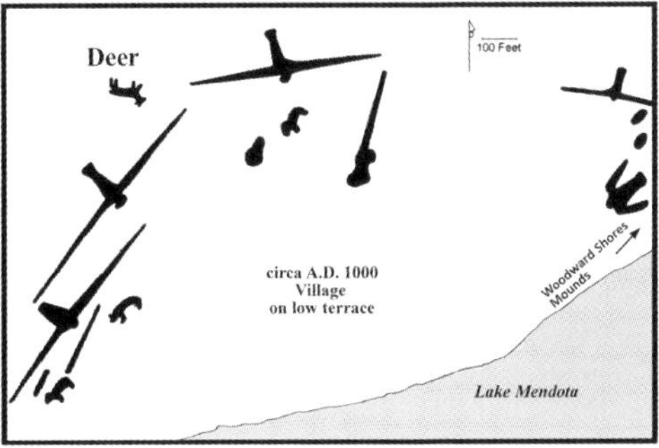

Fig. 5.7 The Mendota State Hospital Mound Group.

a wetland (Fig. 5.6). It is one of three similar effigies documented in the Four Lakes and the only one that survives. The curved tail form is part of an extraordinary and comparatively well preserved arrangement of effigy mounds located on a low terrace above the lake shore. The Mendota State Hospital Group contains the largest surviving effigy mound in the effigy mound region, an eagle-like form, perhaps a great Thunderbird that has a wingspan of 624 ft (*ca* 190 m; Fig. 5.7). Adjacent are other eagle forms, bears, Water Spirits, conical and linear mounds, and a unique four-legged walking deer that has been carefully preserved. Like those at Farwell Point, the Wisconsin state-run Mendota Mental Health Institute maintains the mounds with great pride and uses the large Thunderbird mound as its logo.

These mounds, along with two large birds overlapping the Woodward Shores Group to the east, partly encircle a Late Woodland village of unknown size discovered lower down along the lake shore by archaeologist Philip Salkin (1988). Salkin sampled part of a village in an area where a proposed playground was built and found domestic features, food remains including fish and deer, and pottery attributed to the effigy mound builders and named Madison Ware, along with a larger amount of later, collared pottery. Madison pottery has also been reported for Governor's Island, a large point of land that extends into the lake adjacent to the village area. This seems to be one of the main settlements, if not *the* main settlement, of the Four Lakes Late Woodland people. It is possible that the large eagles or Thunderbird-like mounds and their arrangement identifies the village of the civil chiefs of the Four Lakes effigy mound builders, and the spirit mounds built to protect the important village. Significantly the traditional chiefs of the Ho-Chunk, who lived in this same area in more recent times, come from the Thunderbird clan.

The model of effigy mound symbolism

Effigy mounds extend continuously along the north shore to the Woodward Shores Mound Group, currently occupied by private homes and lots. As we have seen, this grouping best illustrates the principles of effigy mound landscapes and has been coincidentally used for an artistically rendered symbol for ancient people in the Madison area in the public installation *Forum of Origins* created by Brower L. Hatcher in 1993. Many of the mounds have been destroyed or damaged by residential development but maps made by T.H. Lewis in 1888 show a classic effigy mound group neatly segregated into birds, mammals, and Water Spirits, with

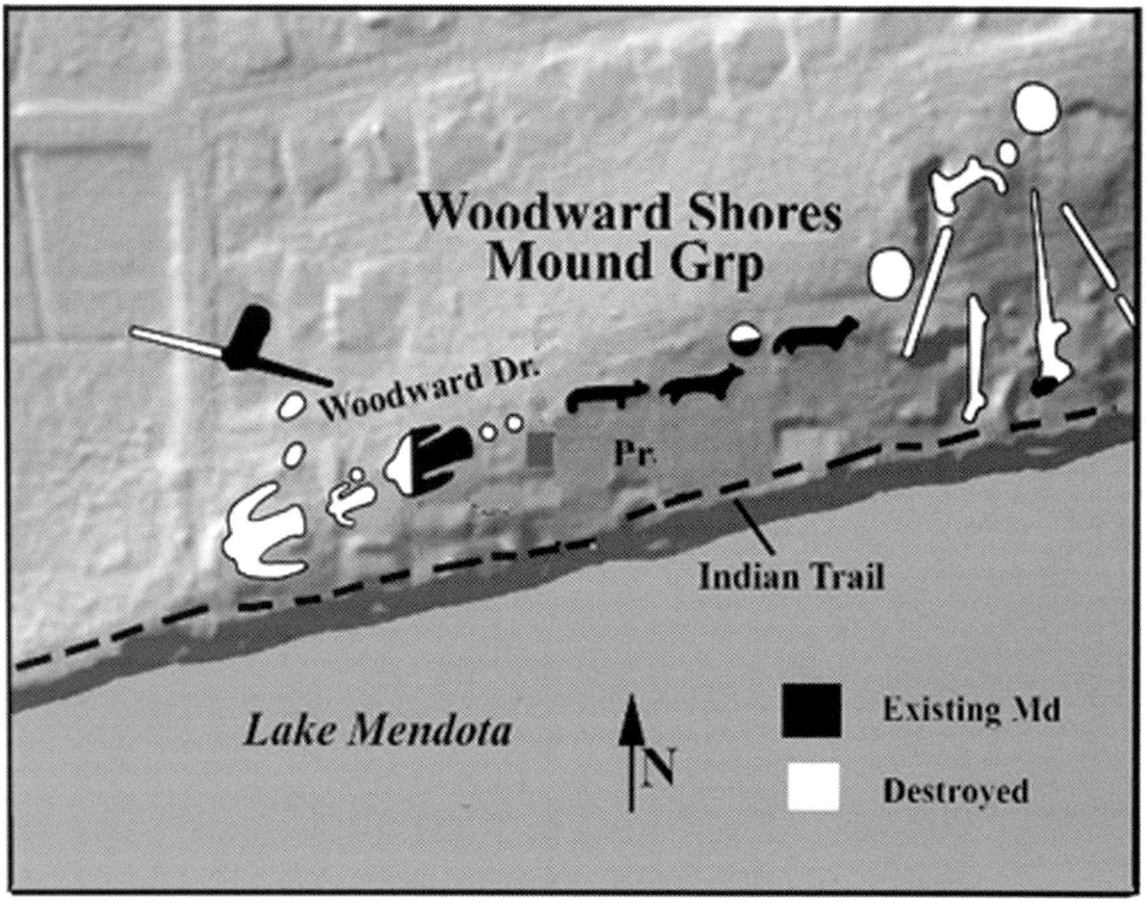

Woodward Shores
Mound Grp
Woodward Dr.
Pr.
Indian Trail
Lake Mendota
N
Existing Md
Destroyed

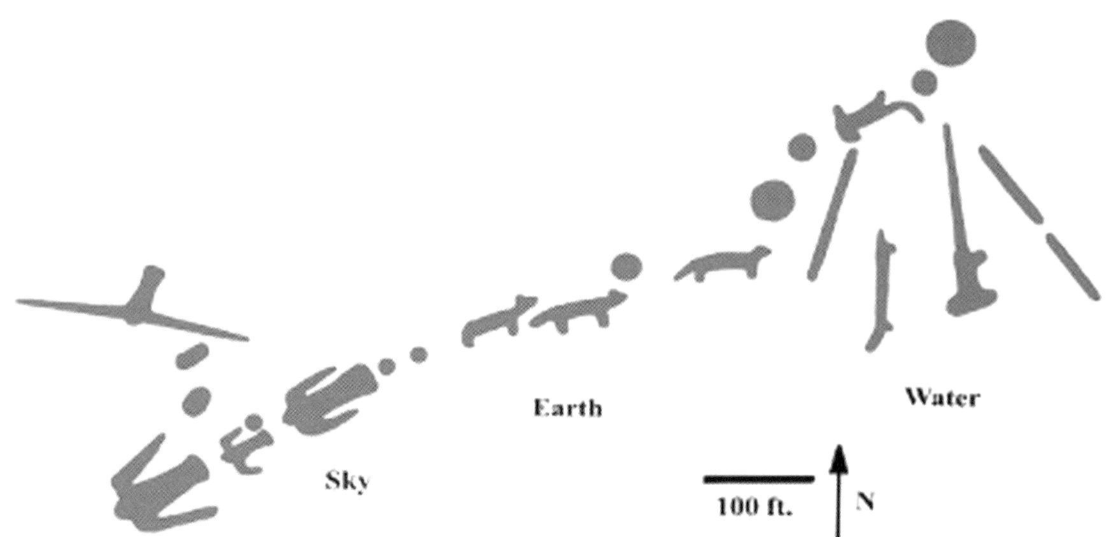
Earth
Water
Sky
100 ft.
N

Fig. 5.8 (*opposite*) The Woodland Shores Mound Group.

a Water Spirit and linear mounds radiating from a large, and probably earlier, conical mound (Fig. 5.8). The bird and mammal mounds follow a slight ridge but the Water Spirits and snake-like linear mounds are oriented down a steep slope to the water, following a familiar topographic pattern.

The birds, several of which survive on private land, are straight- and bent-winged, the former bearing clear resemblance to modern Native American depictions of standing Thunderbirds. The straight-winged bird seems to be a part of the arrangement of similar mounds partly encircling the Late Woodland village to the west. Utility trenching just south of a bird effigy on one house lot accidentally dug into a burial pit containing remains of several people. This, along with similar discoveries at other effigy mound sites, indicates that not all people were buried in the mounds.

West shore

Evidence of ancient Native activity extends down the west shore of Lake Mendota from the former inlet. Several mound groupings and a fortified habitation site are located at the present-day Governor Nelson State Park on the northwest shore (Figs 5.3 and 5.9). The Morris Park I Group, as mapped by T.H. Lewis, shows an impressive Water Spirit, a goose, a hawk, and four conical mounds arranged around a spring. A group of relatively large early conical mounds are found on a high ridge, part of the Morris II Group. Pottery found by archaeologists near the mounds of this group includes earlier Early and Middle Woodland types consistent with the types of mounds on the ridge (Dirst 1985). Effigy mounds, including large Water Spirits headed to the lake, were later built below. One measuring 300 ft (*ca* 91.5 m) in length can be viewed at the park. Immediately north is the Late Woodland fortified Camp Indianola site, almost certainly the home of the people that made this impressive mound. Occupied at the end of the Late Woodland phase it consisted of a circular, wood post enclosure surrounding a living place. An unusual number of arrow points emphasize its defensive nature (Dirst 1988). Ho-Chunk people continued use of this important spot in the 19th century and probably made the agricultural fields called 'corn hills' recorded among the effigy mounds (Fig. 5.9). The enigmatic Borchers Beach conical mounds were also found on the lake shore near the village and Morris II mounds, one reportedly with the possible evidence of Mississippian presence in the form of marine shells, unusual for the Four Lakes (Brown 1912). Another Water Spirit mound (panther form), called the YMCA mound, is located in the south of the park.

Further south, Charles E. Brown excavated a large, previously looted conical mound in the early 20th century, as it was about to be destroyed by a sub-division and found a circular burial enclosure (Brown 1912) similar to that of the possible Middle Woodland burial vault found at Farwell Point.

Continuing south, the West Point Group originally consisted of seven mounds: a bird effigy, four tapering linear mounds, and two conical mounds, as determined by various descriptions beginning in the late 19th century. Residential development destroyed a conical and part of the bird and shoreline erosion has impacted the ends of both linear mounds (Birmingham 2023).

Pheasant Branch creek flows from a large spring through wetlands to Lake Mendota at the southwestern end of the lake. Its mouth was once the location of a major Ho-Chunk village with an associated fur trading post which

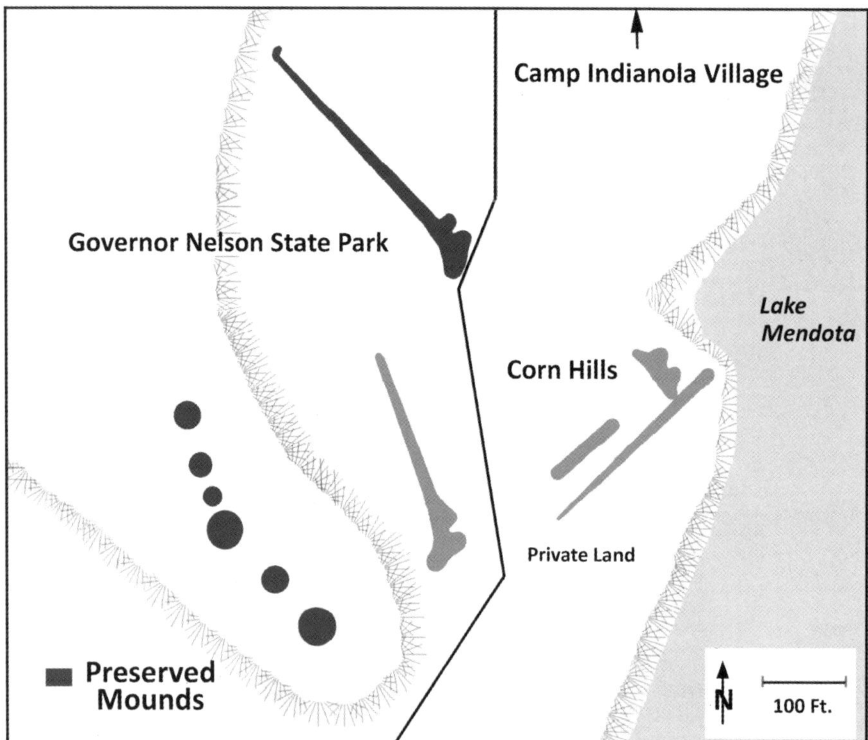

Fig. 5.9 Morris Park II Mound Group. The huge Water Spirit or water panther and the conical mounds on the ridge are preserved in Governor Nelson State Park.

operated into the 1830s. The spring was called *Mau e pinah* (beautiful spring) by the Ho-Chunk and now *Belle Fontaine.* Above the spring is a plateau and a large hill with a stunning view of the wetlands and the lake some distance to the east. As would be expected, mounds were and are a feature of the natural landscape, and now part of the Pheasant Branch Conservancy (Fig. 5.10). The Pheasant Branch Hill Mound group, on top of the high hill, is another example of mound construction just prior to zoomorphic mounds in that it consists only of low conical and short linear mounds. A later effigy group – two birds and several linear mounds at Pheasant Branch Grove – was once found on the plateau below, adjacent to the springs. Farming of the land obliterated all traces of these mounds.

East shore

One of the largest single concentrations of mounds in the Four Lakes spread across high limestone cliffs of Lake Mendota's northeast shore. These are now largely destroyed by residential construction. Over 80 mounds distributed in two adjacent groupings, Maple Bluff and Fuller's Woods, once occupied the elevations. Today this area is home to Madison's largest and most prestigious residences. The Maple Bluff Mound Group occupied the highest point of land on the lake. It once contained over 20 effigy and other mounds, but the exact location and arrangement of most of them had never been worked out because of confusion created by a map made by Charles E. Brown in 1922 and most mounds have been

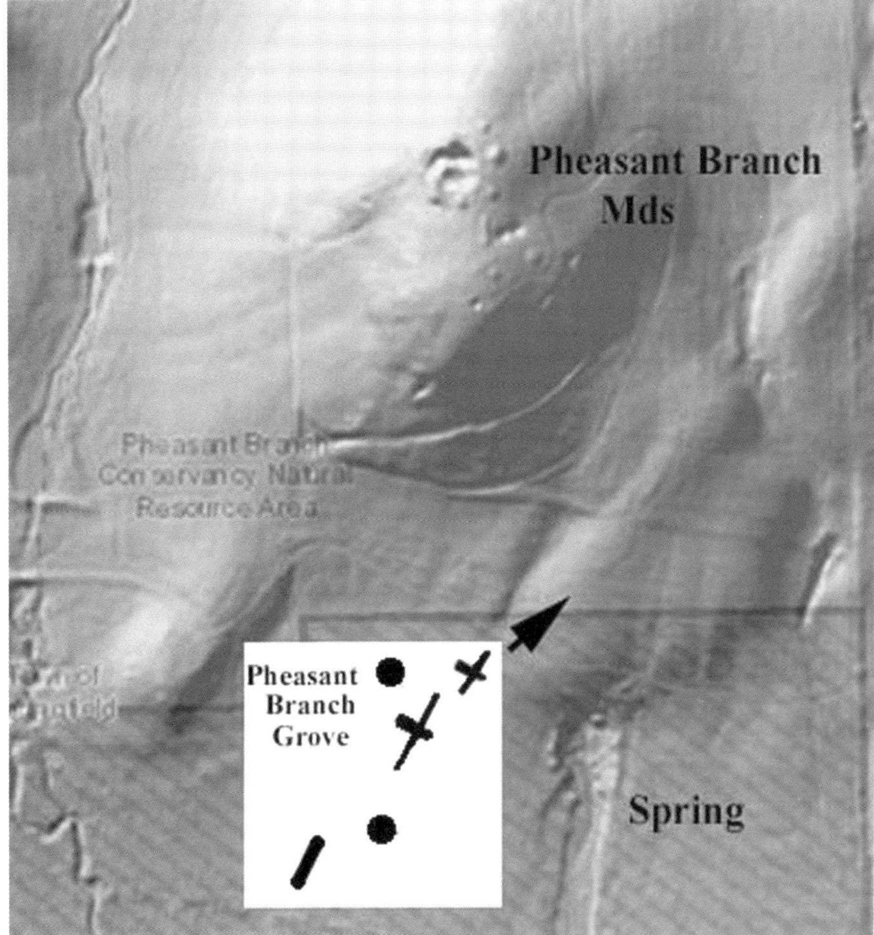

Fig. 5.10 LiDAR from the WisconsinView website of the Pheasant Branch Mound Group preserved on a high, isolated hill in an oak savanna overlooking a large spring in the Dane County Pheasant Branch Conservancy. The Pheasant Branch Grove once lay on the plateau below the hill but was lost to farming (map: Charles E. Brown).

destroyed by residential development. Two small surviving bird mounds, however, have been documented and cataloged by the Wisconsin Historical Society; Brown had evidently mapped the impressive grouping at different times and then pieced them together incorrectly. Using a previous map made by T.H. Lewis, unknown to Brown, we have been able to reconstruct the mound landscape more accurately on the modern landscape (Lewis maps birds, Water Spirits, tapering linear and linear mounds, and several conical mounds; Fig. 5.11). One key mound was an unusually large, eagle-like Thunderbird that had been constructed on the very top of the bluff overlooking the lake.

Conical mounds by far dominated the Fuller's Woods Group, suggesting that the area in the past, as now, maintained an identity or history slightly different from other parts of the Four Lakes. Among the more than 39 mounds were effigy mounds, including straight-winged birds. One zoomorphic mound was an unusual four-legged animal constructed in a flattened, aerial perspective. Brown (1912, 30–2) called it a frog, but more likely it is a bear with its legs extended forward.

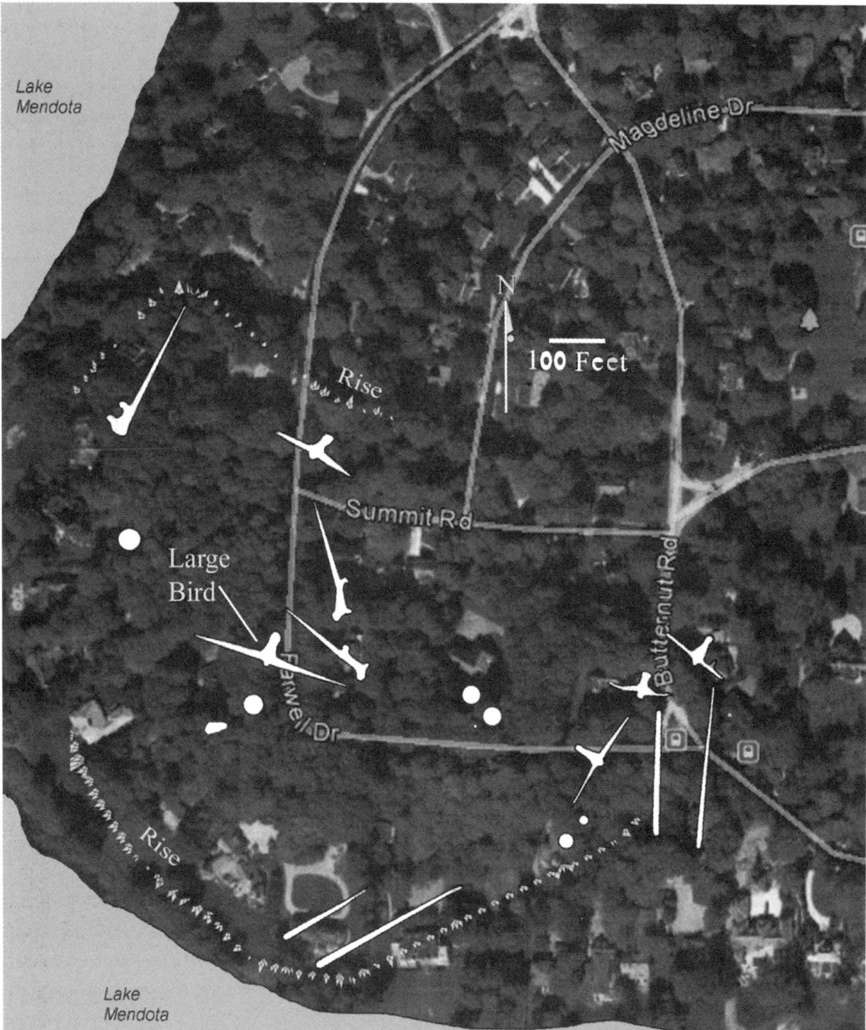

Fig. 5.11 The original Maple Bluff mound group mapped by T.H. Lewis superimposed on the modern landscape.

South of these groups, the city of Madison Burrows Park preserves a single bird mound headed in the direction of Lake Mendota (Fig. 5.12). Previously damaged, it had been partially reconstructed by Charles Brown with a Works Project Administration (WPA) crew in the 1930s. Another mound, referred to as a fox, was once located nearby but has since been destroyed by roadwork and house construction.

South shore

Moving over the once swampy isthmus that divides Lake Mendota from Lake Monona, a Water Spirit and other mounds once adorned the sides of a high hill now occupied by the present state capitol. Many more mounds were to be found on an adjacent elevation called Mansion Hill because of the stately residences built here (Fig. 5.3). Unfortunately, the desirability of the Mansion Hill location led to destruction of the mound landscape before accurate descriptions and maps could be made.

Fig. 5.12 Photo of Burrows Park bird flying down slope to Lake Mendota, looking east with drawing of mound.

The campus of the University of the Wisconsin extends along a large part of the south shore of Lake Mendota. At least one Water Spirit lived on Bascom Hill, a drumlin that is now the administrative center of the university, but many surviving mounds are found on the large, sprawling campus. Consisting of low conical and short linear mounds, the Picnic Point Mound Group (Fig. 5.3) stretches along a prominent peninsula extending into Lake Mendota. Some mounds may have been made during early Late Woodland, but archaeological excavation by Charles Brown of one conical mound, undertaken to repair previous damage, recovered a collared Woodland pottery rim in the mound fill of a type made late in the sequence of Late Woodland cultural activity, after about AD 1000. Maps made by Charles Brown show Native garden beds around the mounds, also indicating that this was a good place to grow corn. It is not possible today to determine the age of the beds since they have disappeared. The more recent Ho-Chunk also grew corn.

Perhaps the most unusual of the Lake Mendota mounds is the two-tailed, flattened or aerial, perspective Water Spirit mound on Observatory Hill, named for the historic UW observatory located there (Fig. 5.3). This is part of an effigy mound group that spread down the hill. Next to the Water Spirit is a small, southward flying bird, but a panther shape, long-tailed Water Spirit and a linear mound once lay low on the landscape near the lake (Fig. 5.13). Past farming obliterated surface features of the later mounds.

The two-tailed effigy mound is the only confirmed example recorded in the entire effigy mound region, perhaps lending great significance to Observatory Hill, the highest hill on a lake that was viewed as the residence of the Water Spirits by more recent Native people in historic times. Its form remains a mystery, but one possibility is that it represents not one spirit but two, shown in profile and joined at the back. Paired mounds of the different types, sometimes joined, have been recorded at other places in the effigy mound region. The unusual mound had been marred by sidewalks serving the campus community (Fig. 5.13, lower) but the university is now removing these intrusions. This adds another less dramatic possibility for the two tails that may occur to alert readers closely examining the map of the mound: Sometime early in the history of the university, well-meaning groundskeepers moved the tail of a single-tailed mound as campus pedestrian traffic began to obliterate it. This would not be the only case where land stewards reformed mounds to accommodate modern land use. In some mound groups, extra dirt seems to have even been added to make the features of the characteristically low effigy mounds more apparent to viewers. Since Lewis mapped two tails in 1888, this would have to have taken place before that date. The adjacent observatory and necessary land modifications were completed a few years earlier, in 1884. Further archaeological research is needed solve the mystery of the two-tailed effigy mound.

Some published information attaches additional significance to Observatory Hill, suggesting that the ancient Native Americans used a huge upright boulder on top of the hill, now called the Chamberlain Rock, for astronomical sightings or as part of a geometric pattern connecting other sites. The rock bears a 1926 plaque honoring pioneer geologist and university president Thomas Chamberlain. However, university records reveal that the rock, deposited by glaciers, is not at its original place or standing in its original position. Instead, it was found, lying flat, further down the slope of the hill and hauled to the present spot with great effort using cables and pulleys for the purpose of the dedication (McCoy *et al.* 1978). The Chamberlain Rock has now been removed from the site.

To the north of Observatory Hill, along a small creek, are three low lying mounds of the Willow Creek Group that appropriately seem to feature water symbolism (Fig. 5.3). A map made by T.H. Lewis in 1888 shows that, in the late 19th century, the mounds were located on an east–west trending ridge near the lake shore. By then already marred by early cultivation, Lewis mapped a goose, headed west to the lake shore, and several unusual forms including one that may have been a long-tailed Water Spirit or water mammal, mutilated by later land use. Charles Brown later reconstructed the goose but in the opposite direction shown by Lewis since Brown seemed to be unaware of Lewis's work.

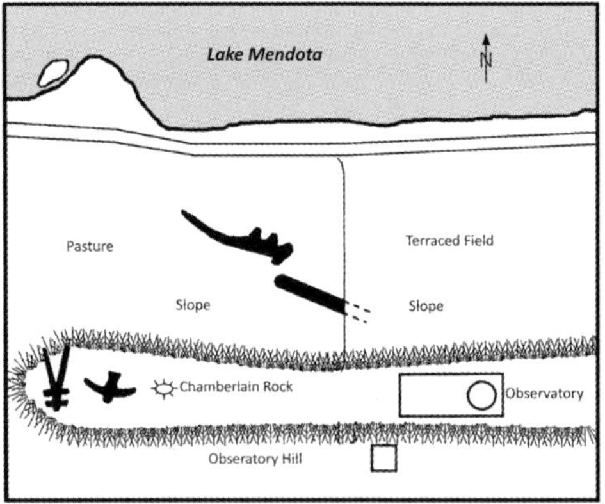

Fig. 5.13 Above: map of Observatory Hill Group as it appeared in the late 19th century; below: 20th century photo of the two-tailed mound on Observatory Hill outlined by snow (image: Wisconsin Historical Society archives).

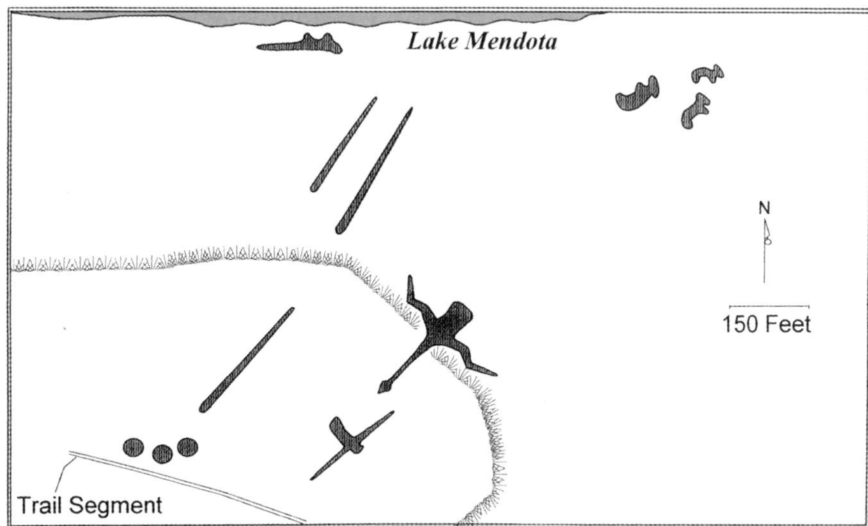

Fig. 5.14 Map of original mounds at the Blackhawk Country Club (by Amy Rosebrough).

Springs

Many major springs flowed from southwest and west of the shores of Lake Mendota. The Ho-Chunk, who still camped here in the 1850s, called one concentration *Mauelohanah,* literally 'group of springs'. Native people made offerings of various kinds to the waters of *Ma ka ma i* or medicine spring at present-day Spring Harbor. Another bore the name *E woo sanau* or 'he thirsts'. Clusters of mounds extended along the heights above the springs for over 1 mile (0.8 km), most since destroyed by residential development. A large bear is among the surviving mounds of the Spring Harbor Group and other mounds are found in residential yards.

At the eastern end of the complex, a remarkably well-preserved grouping provides more insight into effigy mound landscape organization. On the grounds of the privately run Blackhawk Country Club, groups of birds, including a third Lake Mendota goose, conical mounds, lake oriented linear and tapering linear mounds, and bears are all neatly segregated in clusters. A Water Spirit once ran parallel to the bank of the lake (Figs 5.3 and 5.14).

As is often the case for effigy mounds, the two birds fly perpendicular to a hill slope. In the book *The Eagle's Voice: Tales Told by Indian Effigy Mounds* (2001), Dr Gary Meier, formerly of the Mendota Mental Health Institute, argues that the direction of the birds may be explained in terms of the seasons. The goose of the Blackhawk Country Club Group points in the direction of the winter solstice sunset while the bird in front of the goose winged its way in the direction of the sunrise on the same day. Naturally, both concepts, solar orientations and topography, could have been artfully merged as the builders were no doubt capable of doing, given the close relationship of effigy mound symbolism and geography. One logical question emerges as to symbolism, however, in that the goose is flying up and away from the lake at a time when life would have been perceived as returning to the land after mid-winter.

Upland ponds

The ceremonial construction of mounds expanded during the Late Woodland away from major bodies of water, up small creeks and rivers, and sometimes to relatively small spring fed ponds in upland areas. Late Woodland people also used some of these locations for villages and burial mounds as population pushed from the lake shore.

Two mound groups located on or near upland ponds are the Kennedy Pond Group and what is called the Big Cross Group, also referred to as Hammersly Pond in state records (Fig. 5.3). Both these groups also share an unusual mound configuration – the joining and crossing of long linear mounds.

The Kennedy Pond Group once consisted of a spectacular array of effigy mounds: birds, a number of Water Spirits, and paired linear mounds built at an

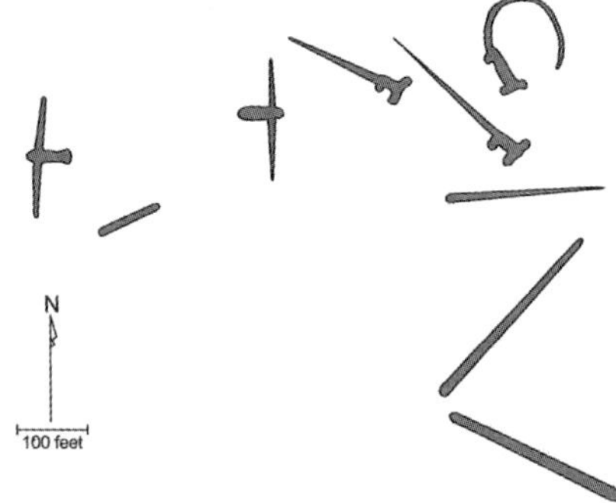

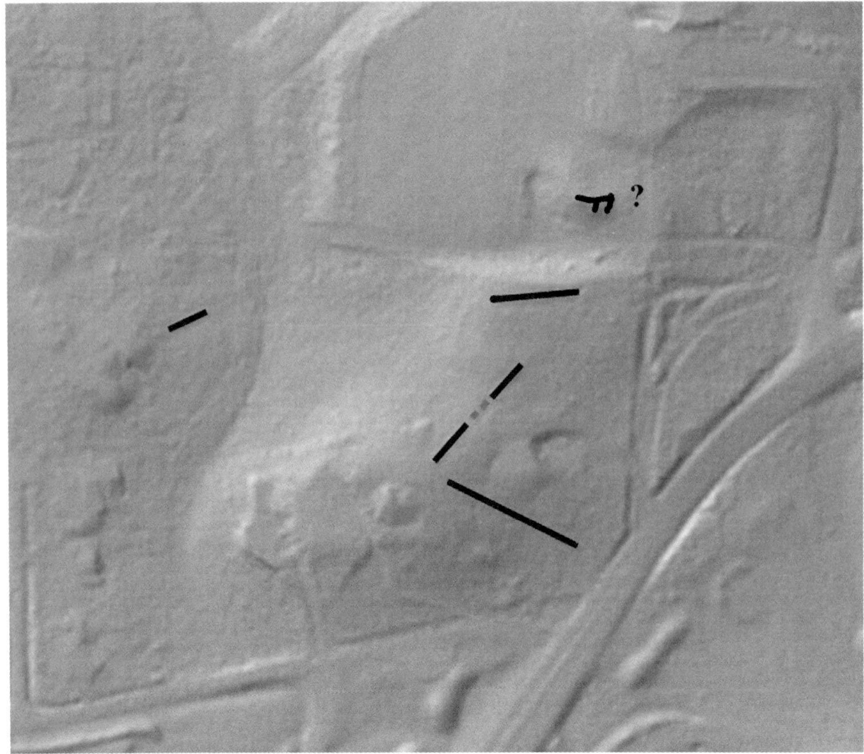

Fig. 5.15 Map of Kennedy Pond Mound Group (by Amy Rosebrough) and LiDAR from the WisconsinView website showing remaining mounds.

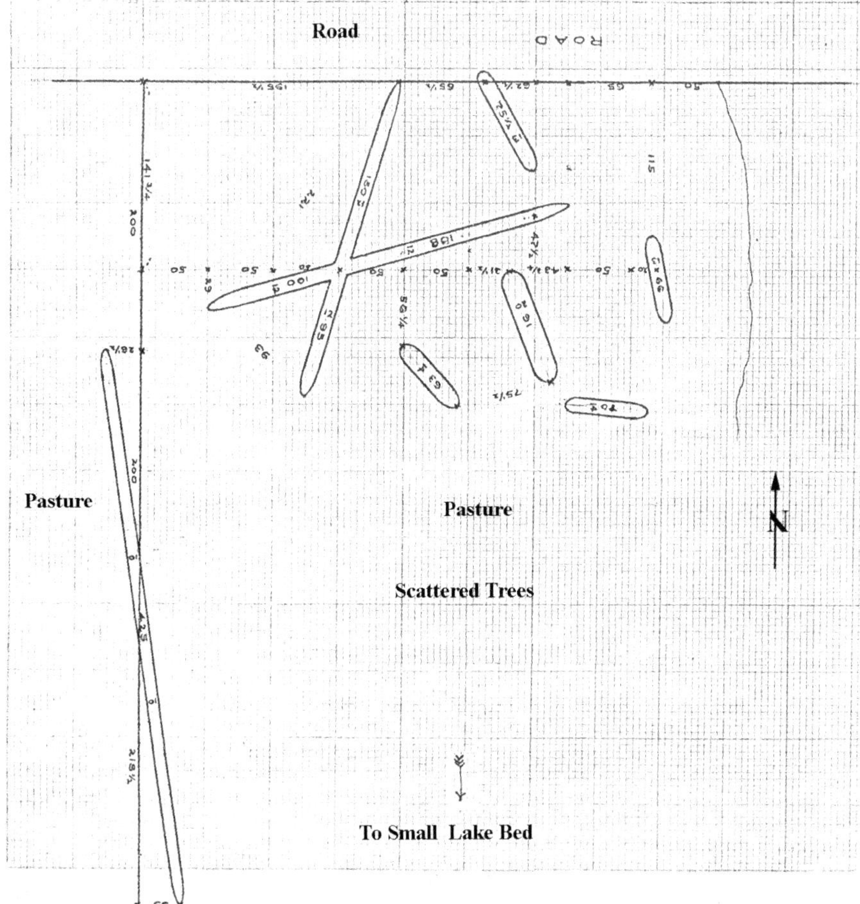

Fig. 5.16 The Big Cross Mound Group (Bachus, Hammersley) as drawn by Charles E. Brown (1872–1945, box 21 with additions by Robert Birmingham).

angle to one another (Fig. 5.15). One of the panther-like Water Spirits had a curved tail like the one at Farwell Point. This, and other mounds, have disappeared, but others are preserved in the grounds of the peaceful St Benedict Retreat Center, appropriately devoted to spiritual renewal.

The odd angling of the mounds of Kennedy Pond suggests possible celestial orientations, as do the two crossed mounds found elsewhere in the Four Lakes district. The reason here is again ambiguous. As mapped by modern surveyors, the southernmost mound comes close (within 10°) of a line that describes the winter solstice sunrise and summer solstice sunset, but the other mound has no directional significance, at least for solar and lunar standstill positions. Another linear mound at Kennedy aligns almost precisely east–west, the directions of the equinox, but this could also be a coincidence of topography since single linear mounds in the Fours Lakes are oriented in all directions.

The Big Cross Mound Group was located in what is now a residential area of Madison and all the mounds are gone (Fig. 5.16). It was once located on high ground at the edge of a large marsh and pond, now a part of a golf course. Mapped in the early 20th century, the group consisted entirely of long linear mounds, one 425 ft (129.5 m) long, though a bird was reported to have been in another grouping

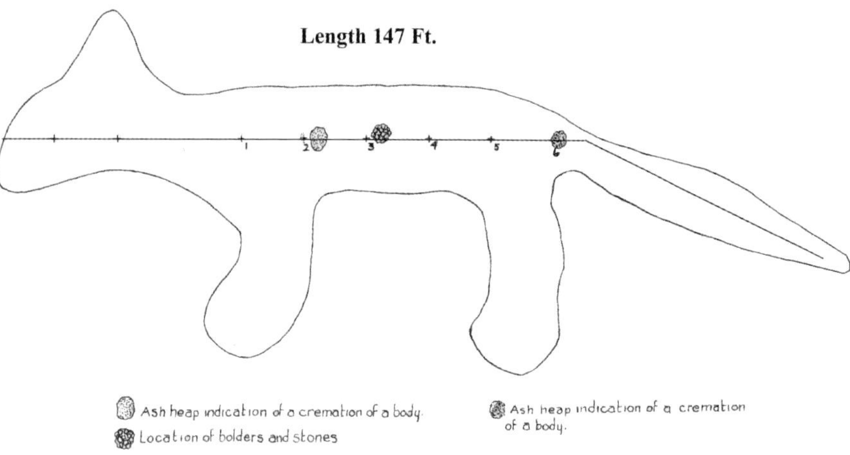

Fig. 5.17 1938 drawing of the Heim Mound (Brown 1872–1945, box 7).

nearby (Brown 1912). The site derives its name from the fact that two long linear mounds crossed each other. As mapped, the mounds do not have important solar alignments such as to the solstices and neither does another set of crossed linear mounds at the Eli Johnson Group near Lake Waubesa (see below). However, the repeated pattern of long crossed or angled linear mounds in various directions in this region suggests it was an important part of effigy mound cosmology even if the overall significance is not as yet understood.

A village without associated mounds was excavated in the 1980s at Sticker Pond, well south of Lake Mendota, where Late Woodland people grew a substantial amount of corn between *ca* AD 1116 and 1230 (Salkin 1987).

The Heim Mound

A large, running fox or wolf effigy mound is preserved near Lake Mendota on land owned by the Wisconsin Archeological Society (Fig. 5.3). Early in the 20th century it had been owned by Ferdinand Heim. Charles Brown examined and described it in 1915 when the area was still undeveloped. Brown subsequently wrote Heim a cordial letter extolling the uniqueness of the mound and urging him to preserve it and prevent others from digging into it. Brown predicted that the land would someday be threatened by housing development and suggested that the mound be preserved on a small public space. Two decades later, in 1937, Heim deeded the mound to the Wisconsin Archeological Society. Writing to Charles Brown, Heim said:

> It gives me a feeling of satisfaction to give this mound to your society and to know it will be preserved for the future. I want to thank you personally for the suggestion contained in your letter of more than twenty years ago. I still have your letter and a clipping from the Milwaukee Sunday Sentinel of August 29, 1915, which describes the mound in detail and published your tracing of it. Undoubtedly when you wrote the letter you thought you were looking a long way ahead in predicting that 'summer homes' would be located on the above property. Little did we then think that in about twenty years permanent homes would be built in this area. (Brown 1872–1945, papers 1937)

But the whole of the Heim Mound remains today on an undeveloped lot in a residential neighborhood in the City of Middleton, the only canine effigy mound form left near the shores of Lake Mendota (Fig. 5.17).

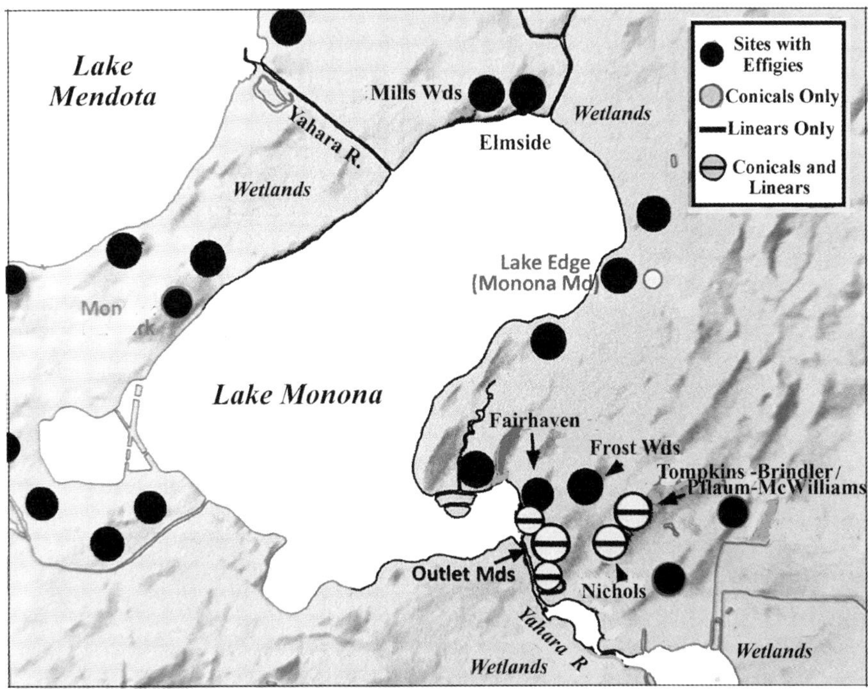

Fig. 5.18 Lake Monona Mounds.

Lake Monona

From Lake Mendota, the Yahara River flows through a formerly swampy isthmus to Lake Monona, called the Third Lake by early settlers, and Great Teepee or *Tchee-ho-bo-kee-xa kay-te-la* by the Ho-Chunk, who maintained camps here through the early 20th century (Brown 1922). The Wisconsin Historical Society documents 232 mounds that once existed at 27 locations on the shores of the lake (Fig. 5.18) or in the surrounding area, not including the Dividing Ridge Group that also overlooks Lake Wingra. Many of the Lake Monona records derive from the published works and files of Charles Brown.

Lake Monona geography and symbolism

The air, earth, and water effigy mound symbolism around Lake Monona was similar to that of lakes Mendota and Wingra, but for a large number of linear mounds near extensive marshlands on the southern reaches of the lake. The latter pattern continues on to Lake Kegonsa where linear mounds, some obviously snakes, are by far the most numerous mound form. One Lake Monona mound concentration that underscores the principles of effigy mound landscape organization extended along the northeast shore, adjacent to modern Olbrich Park: filled land that was once a swampy bay in Lake Monona (Fig. 5.19). At least 20 mounds covered two hills divided by a deep, wide valley and drainage. Most of the earthworks were destroyed by later home building in the 20th century, but T.H. Lewis had mapped a number in 1888 and Charles Brown later added maps and locations of others. The three that survive in two small city parks once again owe their existence to the preservation efforts of Brown.

The eastern grouping, called Elmside, included four large, straight-winged birds – eagles or Thunderbirds similar in form to the giant birds on the grounds of the Mendota Mental Health Institute on Lake Mendota described above. One huge bird here had a wingspan of 563 ft (171.3 m). Other mound forms include conicals, tapering linear, and two mammal effigies along the lake shore; a bear and unidentified tail-less animal. Across a low valley to the west is the Mills Woods Effigy Group with conical mounds, a small bird, a goose, tapering linear forms, and a Water Spirit.

The effigy mound forms in the related Elmside and Mills Woods groupings are typical of the Four Lakes and are spatially and geographically segregated, conforming to topography and cultural symbolism. Conical mounds once occupied the highest elevations, with the birds also on prominent high places. Lower down, along the lake and bluff edge, earth mammals can still be viewed in a park: a bear and another tail-less mammal with legs oriented down slope. On one side of the large birds, a tapering linear mound extended up a steep slope from the former marsh, a pattern repeated many times for these snake-like forms throughout the Four Lakes. Finally, low on the landscape in the western Mills Woods group, the panther-type Water Spirit with a slightly curved tail still crawls to the lake. A bent-wing goose in the Mills Woods group once flew east down the slope of the valley. It is the only one recorded for Lake Monona.

A bronze sculpture honors the memory of the effigy mound people. It was originally carved from a tree trunk by local Ho-Chunk artist Harry Whitehorse but was replicated in bronze as the wood decayed (Fig. 5.19, right).

Like Lake Mendota, the Wisconsin state capitol overlooks Monona from a high hill on the isthmus that divides the two lakes. As mentioned in the previous chapter, mounds were recorded for Capitol Hill. Near the base of this hill, and on a bluff overlooking Lake Monona, F. Hudson, a prominent early Madison settler, mapped a long-tailed effigy constructed in a flattened or aerial perspective, along with two conical mounds, in 1842. This map was subsequently published in Lapham's *Antiquities of Wisconsin* (Figs 5.18 and 5.20). Hudson's rendition shows an effigy with a rather long neck. It may have been either a Water Spirit or a water mammal. As noted by Lapham: 'Like most mounds of this general character, it has its head directed to the water' (Lapham 1855, 40, pl. 32). The earthworks were destroyed in the 19th century by urban development and the location is now the entrance to Madison's lake front community center at Monona Terrace.

The outlet

Like the Yahara River inlet on Lake Mendota, the Monona outlet was long an important ceremonial and living area for Native Americans. Here was the earliest dated mound group in the Four Lakes, the Outlet Mound Group. The site had been established as a ceremonial and burial place by earlier Hopewell-related Woodland people around 2000 years ago but continued to be used through the early part of the Late Woodland period, prior to the appearance of zoomorphic mounds. Extending north from the Outlet Mound Group, later effigy mound building spread across high elevations forming the Frost Woods and Fairhaven Groups (Fig. 5.21). Fearing destruction by encroaching residential development, Brown dug parts of two linear mounds and an unusual fork-tailed bird or bird-man mound at Frost Woods in the 1920s. In 1947 David Baerreis and the University of Wisconsin excavated a

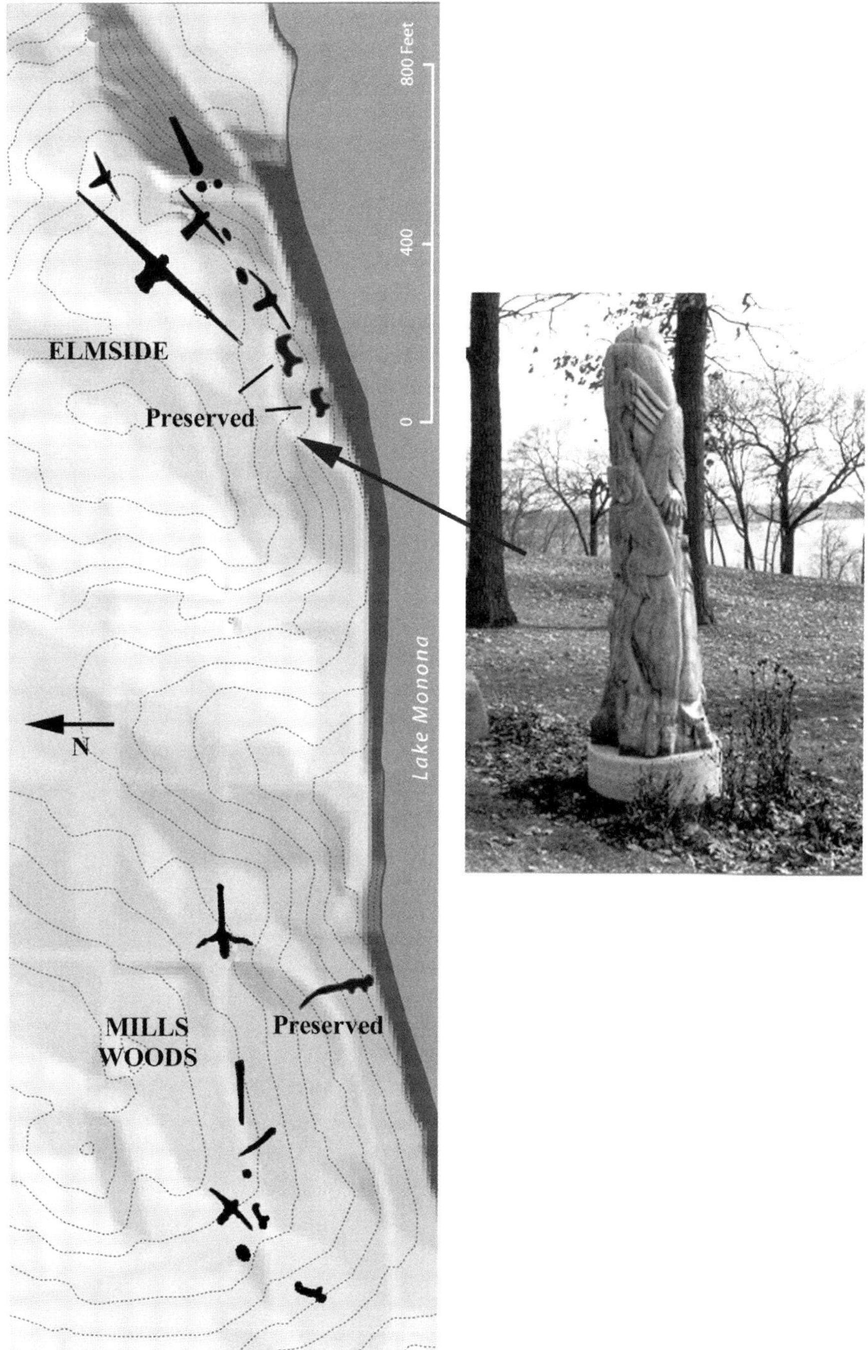

Fig. 5.19 Left: shaded relief map showing the original location of Elmside and Mills Woods (produced by Earth Information Technology based on information from T.H. Lewis (1880–1895, notebook 27) and Brown (1872–1947, box 7); right: bronze sculpture honoring the memory of the effigy mound people.

conical mound on the highest elevation of the grouping, just prior to development of the area. Brown found no burials or artifacts, supporting the conclusion that many mounds of the effigy mound period had a purely ceremonial function. On the other hand, Baerreis uncovered a burial pit below the conical mound but with only a few fragments of bone surviving. He also found a small, stone arrow tip in

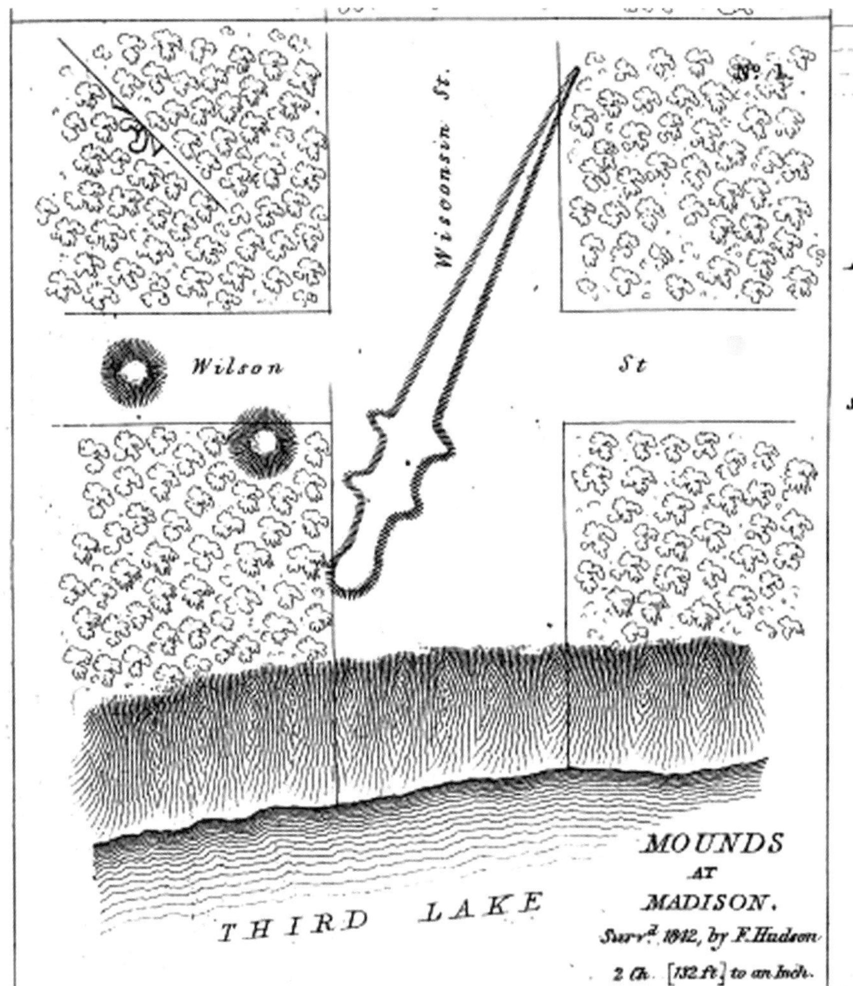

Fig. 5.20 The Monona Avenue Park Mound (destroyed), mapped by Frank Hudson, on the northwest shore of Lake Monona (from Lapham 1855).

the mound and a cut deer antler that he believed to be a digging tool. Perhaps the antler tool was used in loosing dirt for mound construction. The presence of the arrowhead dates the mound generally to the Late Woodland stage when the bow and arrow first come into use.

Drumlin mounds

Drumlins east of the outlet seemed to have been first used for mound building during the early part of the Late Woodland stage, mainly of linear and conical mounds. One notable group extended along a huge drumlin trending southwest through what is now downtown Monona for a distance of half a mile (0.8 km; Fig. 5.22). Part of the drumlin has been leveled for road construction and other development. The southwest part of the group was called the Nicholls Group and is separated from Tompkins-Brindler by Monona Drive, the main city thoroughfare. Combined, the original Tompkins-Brindler/Nicholls Mound Group contained at

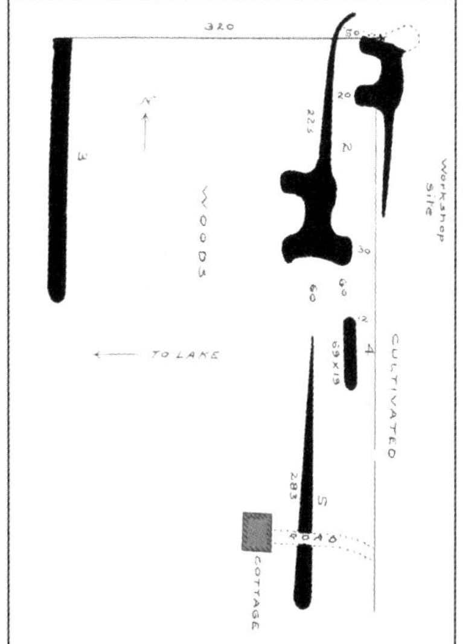

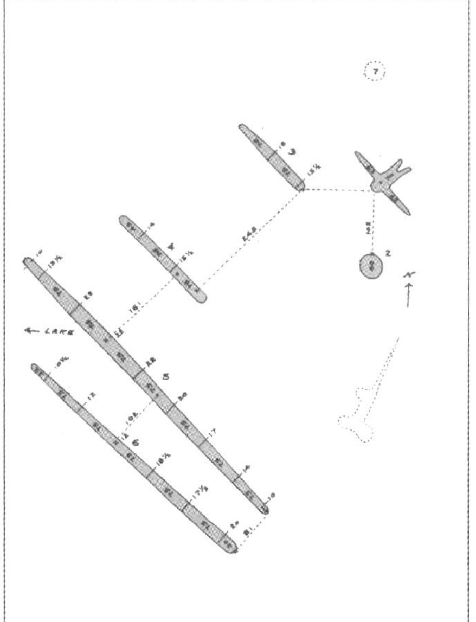

Fig. 5.21 Frost Woods and Fairhaven Mound Groups (from Brown 1922).

least 14 linear and one conical mound. Some had already been destroyed by road construction at the time of recording by Charles Brown in 1913, and the Nicholls part was entirely lost to sub-division development after that time.

The Monona water tower rises from one end of the Tompkins-Brindler group location. New water tower construction disturbed two graves in the late 20th century, probably originating from former mounds. Two linear mounds remain, 200 ft and 210 ft long (*ca* 61 m and 64 m) respectively, although the end of one had been truncated by farming. They are about 10 ft wide and 3 ft high (3.1 × 0.9 m). The mounds are now part of the city of Monona Woodland Park, a protected green space.

The theme of linear mounds, undoubtedly related to the watery Lower World, extends to another drumlin east of Lake Monona, also much compromised by modern development. The remaining mounds and remnants are now part of the Edna Taylor Conservation Park. The original group, called Pflaum-McWilliams, also closely followed the contours of the drumlin, overlooking a marsh about 1 mile (1.6 km) from the lake (Fig. 5.23). Three linear mounds, one over 700 ft (213+ m) long, ran along the crest with a curved linear and a conical mound on the southwestern end. The snake-like, curved linear followed the orientation of the ridge. Four shorter linear mounds and a long-tailed Water Spirit can still be found on the northwestern slope of the long high hill, the Water Spirit in its proper place just above a spring. Middle parts of the linear mounds had been flattened when the drumlin was used as a winter sledding hill. The grouping on the south part of the drumlin had been plowed down by farming in the late 19th and early 20th centuries leaving no visible evidence. Condominium development leveled this part of the drumlin in the 1990s, much to the distress of many local people.

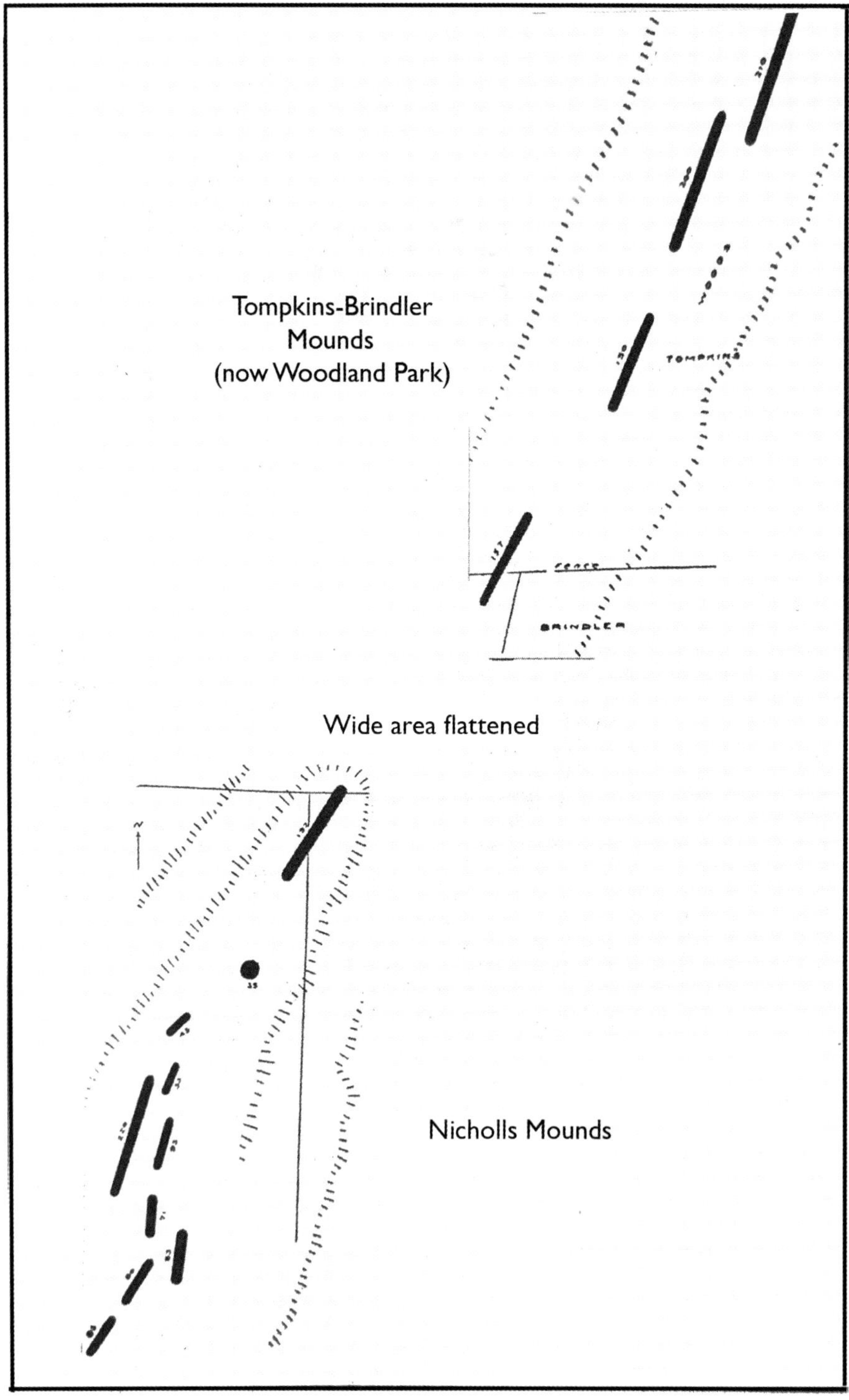

Fig. 5.22 The combined Tompkins-Brindler/Nicholls Mound Group (by Amy Rosebrough, derived from maps by W.G. McLachlan (1914)).

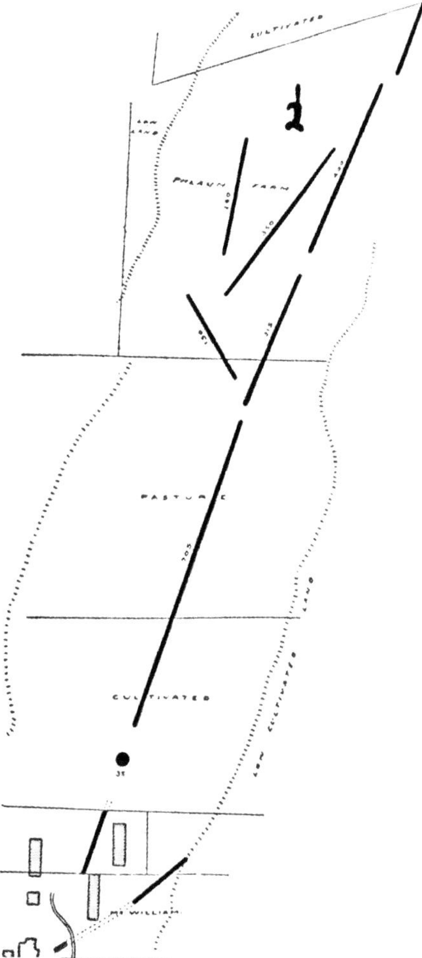

Fig. 5.23 The Phlaum-McWilliams Mound Group (from McLachlan 1914).

Wingra: lake of sacred springs

Lake Wingra, the fifth lake in the 'Four' Lakes district, had among the densest and most impressive effigy mound groupings found anywhere surrounding its shores (Fig. 5.24). Yet it is barely more than a large, shallow pond covering 300 acres (121 ha). Native people sculpted at least 233 mounds on the elevations around the small lake, creating a vast part of the Four Lakes ceremonial landscape covering several square miles. Urban expansion destroyed many, but the University of Wisconsin arboretum preserves three whole groups, and remnants of others are found at the Forest Home Cemetery (Fig. 5.24, 3), the Edgewood College campus (9), Vilas Circle Park (7), and Vilas Park (8). The Ho-Chunk families who camped here to fish, trap muskrat, and capture large turtles until about 1910 called the lake *Ki-chunk-och-hep-er-rah*, meaning 'where the turtle rises up', and maintained a village on the west side along a major trail (Brown 1915). The Ho-Chunk name *Wingra* was later used in the early 19th century, a reference to ducks.

Lake Wingra is surrounded by large wetlands although, at the time of the effigy mounds, increased moisture probably expanded the lake water to over twice the present size. This body of water differs from other lakes in that it is not an expansion of the Yahara River but one of its sources. Several large springs feed the lake and a small creek brings the water to Lake Monona and then to the Yahara. Because Wingra did not have the river flow like the other lakes, some early settlers also called Wingra 'Dead Lake' but, with the presence of so many springs, ancient Native Americans no doubt perceived it quite differently – as the source of life itself. The Ho-Chunk left offerings in one particular medicine spring, called the White Clay spring (exact location now unknown), for health and well-being (Brown 1927b). The white clay in the name no doubt refers to another physical characteristic of the lake important in Native American beliefs: like Lake Mendota, the shallow waters cover a thick deposit of white marl important in the beliefs of the Ho-Chunk and other Indian people.

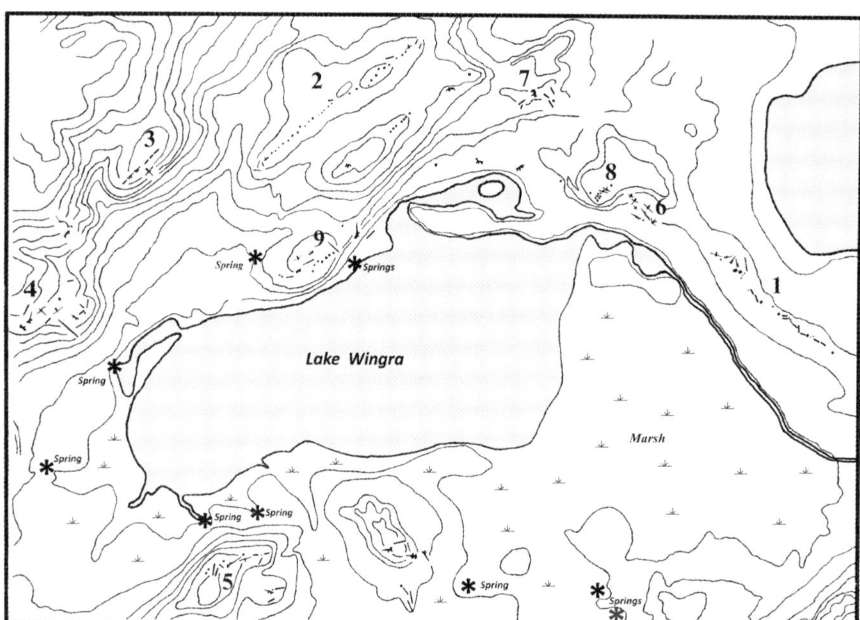

Fig. 5.24 Topographic map showing recorded Lake Wingra mounds. 1) Dividing Ridge; 2) Monroe Street; 3) Forest Hill Cemetery; 4) Wingra; 5) Lake Forest #1; 6) Greenbush; 7) Vilas Circle/Curtis; 8) Vilas; 9) Edgewood.

Fig. 5.25 Unusual effigy mound forms: above from Brown (1927b): below from Lewis (1889).

Because of the spiritual and symbolic importance of springs and marl, the small lake attracted much ceremonial activity. There are few other places in the effigy mound region that had this density of mounds in such a small area, an impression that Charles E. Brown also had from his early documentation.

Zoomorphic mounds of Lake Wingra are birds, geese, bears, canine forms, and Water Spirits, as well as snake-like, tapering linear and conical mounds. Among the effigy mounds are unusual forms. T.H. Lewis mapped a possible antler-less deer effigy in the 1880s, now gone, that is similar to the preserved deer mound at Mendota Mental Health Institute in that it shows all four legs. Other unusual mounds are a long-bodied water mammal (mink or otter?) and a mammal with two conical mounds built over or joining the legs, giving the mound a wheeled appearance (Lewis 1889; Fig. 5.25). The superposition of conical mounds on effigy mounds is documented elsewhere in the effigy mound region, for example in the Nitschke

I mound group at Burnett, Wisconsin, reflecting the continuing construction of conical forms during the final years of Late Woodland and/or the symbolic superposition of celestial Upper World forms over those of more earthly association. Neither of these unusual examples on Lake Wingra survived modern development, so their forms cannot now be verified.

Some of the most spectacular and interesting mound groups of Lake Wingra also no longer exist but fortunately drew the attention of early mound researchers and cartographers. The Dividing Ridge Group (Fig. 5.24, 1) lined the top of a 70 ft (21.4 m) high glacial ridge separating lakes Wingra and Monona, a Madison landmark until quarried away for gravel in the early 20th century. The mounds extended along the ridge, merging into adjacent mound groups. Increase Lapham, who had investigated the mounds in the 1850s, described the scene as 'conspicuous and beautiful' (Lapham 1860; Fig. 5.26).

Ancient people also found this ridge 'conspicuous and beautiful', beginning ceremonial and burial activity over 2000 years ago. Two main conical or oval mounds are large – 9 ft high and up to 60 ft in diameter (2.7 × 18.3 m) – consistent with Middle Woodland mound construction at that time. Excavation of one of them by Lapham revealed an extended 'in the flesh' skeleton, also typical of mound burials in the earlier part of the Woodland period. Effigy mound people expanded the landscape with the additions of straight-winged, eagle-like birds, panther-shaped Water Spirits, and a tapering linear mound. The eagle-like bird dramatically swooped upslope with its wings parallel to the ridge top. The Water Spirit and snake-like mound extend up the slope from Lake Monona. Linear and smaller conical mounds line the ridge top to the southeast. Destruction of the Dividing Ridge mounds began in the late 19th century as the growing city of Madison attracted people to the area who dug up the mounds out of curiosity or to develop their properties. Sand and gravel operations then leveled the ridge with the remaining mounds. Brown's notes record the destruction of the last remaining linear mound in 1915 where several wagonloads of dirt were removed, littering the ground with broken human bones and skull fragments. He called the destruction 'a crime that should never have been perpetrated' (Brown 1915, 89).

Another long line of conical mounds, the Monroe Street Group (Fig. 5.24, 2), once followed a high, long ridge overlooking the lake basin to the southeast with linear and effigy mounds found mainly at the two ends. The area is now an upscale commercial district. The conical mounds seem to be smaller than some of the Dividing Ridge examples and the overall lack of large conical mounds throughout the rest of the Lake Wingra basin suggests that, despite seasonal use of its shores by people for thousands of years, most ceremonial mound building took place during the Late Woodland, climaxing with the giant effigy mound landscape.

At least two, possibly four, geese were also part of the Lake Wingra landscape. One can still be viewed at Forest Hill Cemetery (Fig. 5.24, 3), flying down a steep slope in the direction of Lake Wingra (Fig. 5.27). Above are linear and Water Spirit mounds running in a straight line along the main orientation of a ridge. Several were destroyed to make space for later graves.

Water symbolism was further expressed by a large number of Water Spirit and linear mounds at the Wingra Mound Group (Fig. 5.24, 4) near the west shore, mapped by A.B. Stout in 1908 while attending the University of Wisconsin (Fig. 5.28). It has been since destroyed. The group included typical Four Lakes effigies such as a straight-winged bird, a goose, a bear, a canine, and a Water

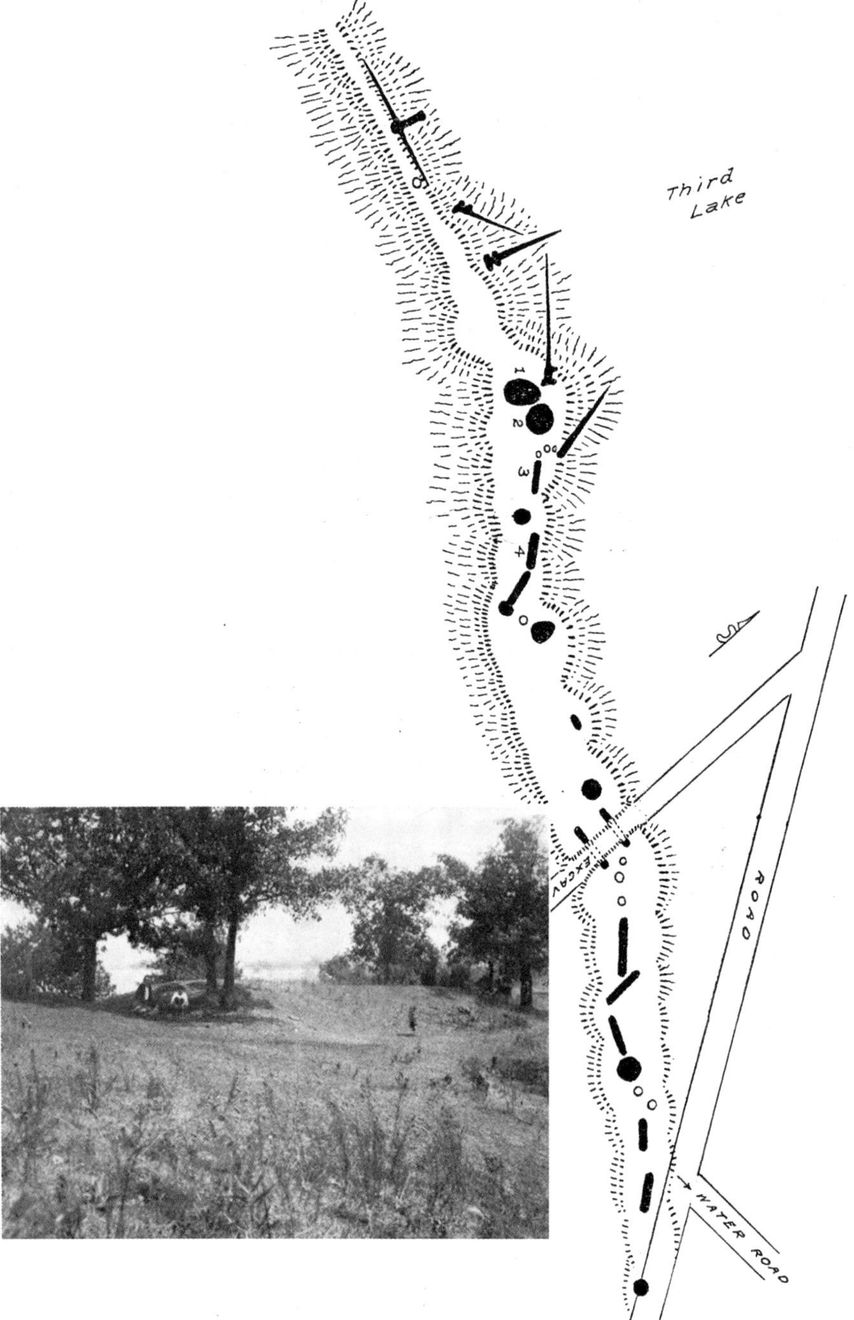

Fig. 5.26 The Dividing Ridge Mound Group mapped by Brown in 1905 before its destruction.

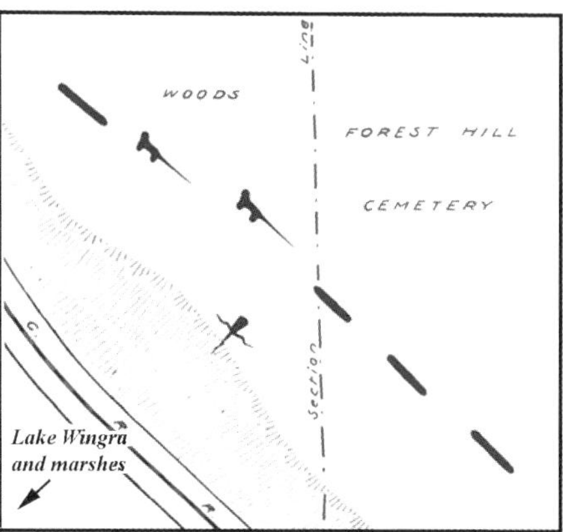

Fig. 5.27 The Forest Hill Cemetery Mound Group mapped by Brown (1915).

Spirit. Several of the long linear mounds assumed a tapering, snake-like form. The mound landscape illustrates the close connection between springs and effigy mound groups and major principles of effigy mound arrangements. It once spread across a high elevation, now home to a large school building, directly overlooking a prominent spring that still bubbles up near the shore of the lake in the University of Wisconsin arboretum. A straight-winged bird flew on the highest and most prominent elevation along with a large goose, while some of the tapering linear (snake) mounds, one measuring 291 ft (88.7 m), ran downslope towards the lake and springs. The goose flew down to the lake. A map by Stout implies that other mounds had been destroyed by plowing and other land use.

Another intimate connection between mounds and springs is at the Arboretum Woods Group, situated above two springs on the south shore, that were held in reverence by the early 20th century Ho-Chunk who camped here (Fig. 5.29). Brown excavated a portion of the panther-like Water Spirit form here when the mounds were being restored, finding that the earthwork covered a single bone bundle burial along with ash and charcoal.

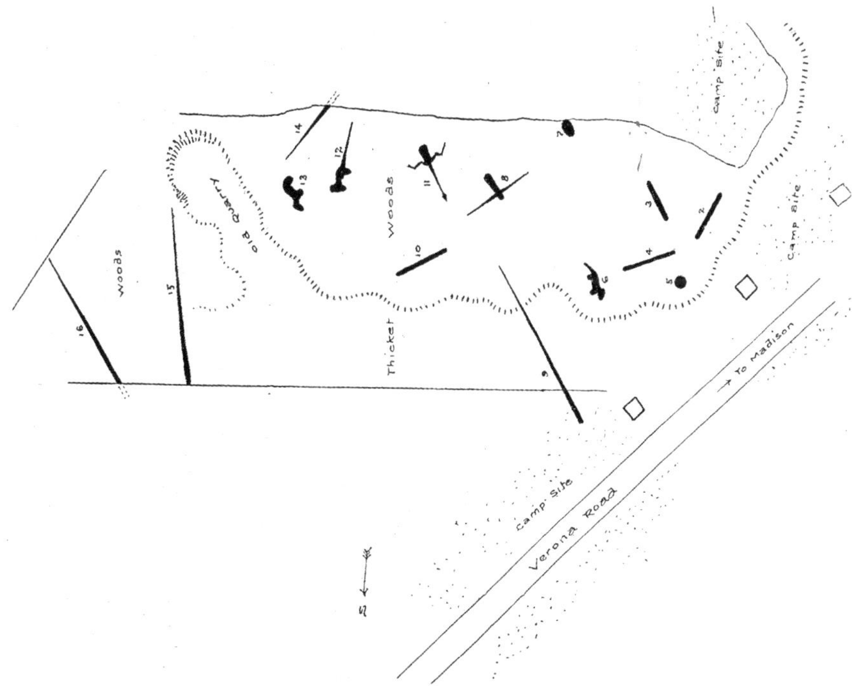

Fig. 5.28 The Wingra Mound Group (destroyed) as mapped by Stout in 1908 (from Brown 1915).

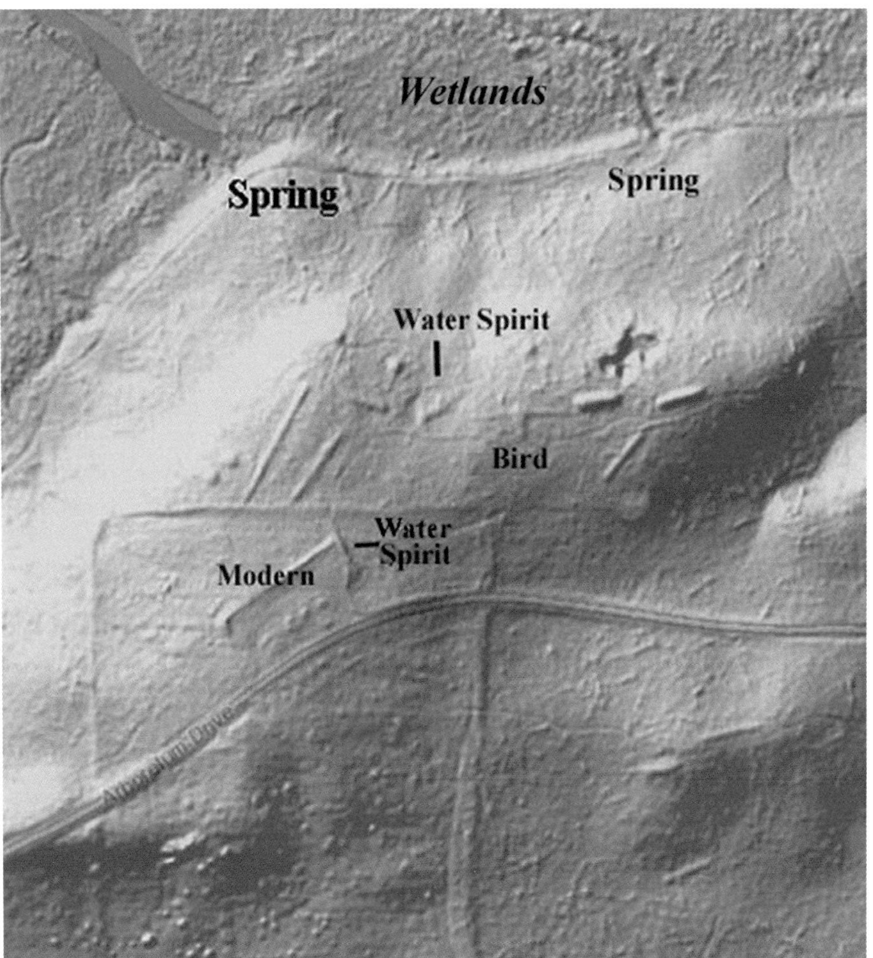

Fig. 5.29 LiDAR from the WisconsinView website showing Lake Forest #1 mound group.

Waubesa: lake of ancient serpents

The Ho-Chunk called Waubesa *Sa-hoo cha-te-la* or 'lake of reeds' because of its extensive marshlands. Much of what is known of Lake Waubesa mounds comes from the early works of T.H. Lewis, Charles Brown, and especially Dr McLachlan of McFarland, all of whom mapped mounds when much of the shoreline was still undeveloped. At least 183 mounds in 30 locations existed here, arranged along hills, drumlins, and high banks (Fig. 5.30). Like the southern end of Lake Monona, both Lake Waubesa and Lake Kegonsa differ from the northern part of the Four Lakes mound district, and other areas of the effigy mound region, in having a proportionally large number of linear mounds. Thirty-nine percent of the mounds on Lake Kenosha are straight or linear embankments, some of extraordinary length. Groups of linear mounds with a few small and low conical mounds were common. One example is the Bram Mound Group, now a part of Goodland County Park that consisted of an oval mound, two linears with hooked or bent ends, and a 240 ft (*ca* 73 m) straight, linear mound (Fig. 5.31).

Snake-like mounds are especially evident on and near Lake Waubesa. Some assume a curved or bent shape and several serpentine mounds are quite definitely the effigies of snakes. This Lower World symbolic pattern reflects the environment much dominated by marshes, especially on the south end and around an adjacent body of water called Mud Lake on the north end. Oddly, though, there are few Water Spirit mounds. As evident from the LiDAR image, the Uphoff Ridge Group (Fig. 5.30), originally mapped by Charles Brown, followed the top of a ridge 1 mile/0.3 km west of the lake, surrounded by marsh and open water.

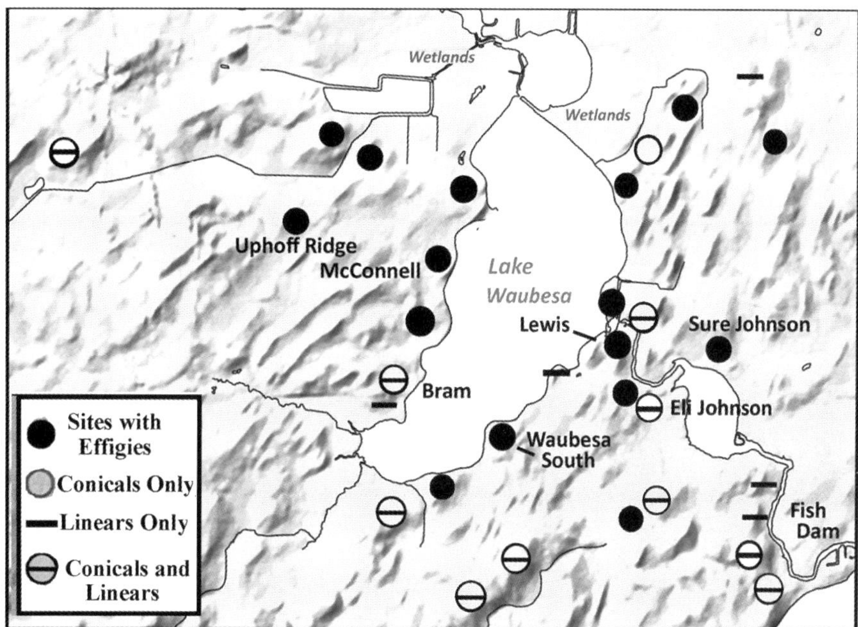

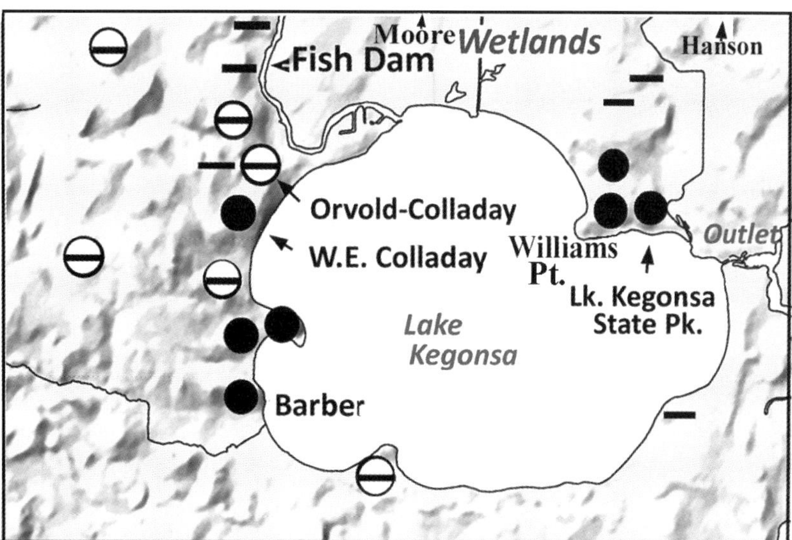

Fig. 5.30 Mound Groups of Lakes Waubesa and Kegonsa.

A snake mound, 333 ft (101.3 m) in length, runs along the curving ridge top along with an animal that Brown called a lynx and a short tear-drop shaped mound (Fig. 5.32).

Twenty-five bird and mammal effigy mounds are known to have existed on or near Lake Waubesa. The most spectacular clustering was the McConnell Group where remnants of 14 of the original 17 mounds survive among residential lots on the west shore (Fig. 5.30). Fortunately, the mounds drew the attention of early mound researchers and their maps, along with modern mapping, allow for a nearly complete reconstruction (McLachlan 1914; Fig. 5.33). Most of the mounds at McConnell run parallel or perpendicular to a long ridge above the lake shore. The arrangement included two sky birds, rare for this lake and now gone, and a large goose, also destroyed by property development. Mammals in the McConnell Group are tailed canine forms (wolf or

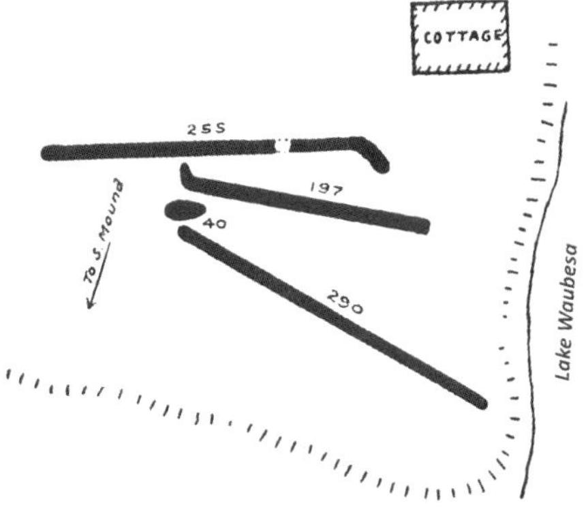

Fig. 5.31 Bram (Goodland Park) Mounds (from McLachlan 1914).

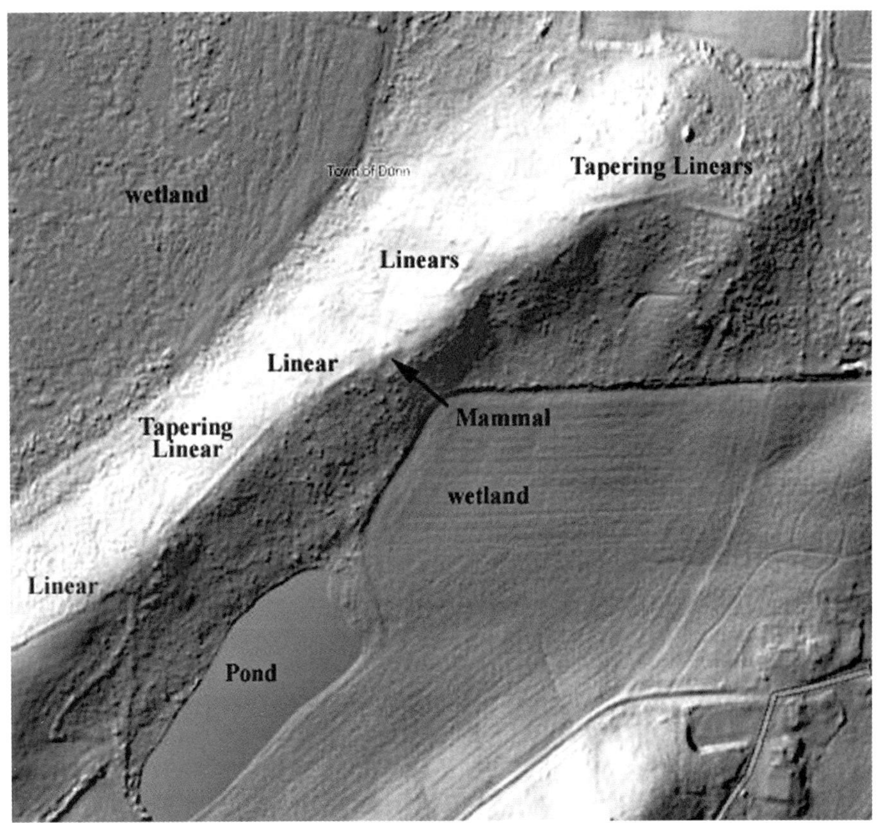

Fig. 5.32 LiDAR image from the WisconsinView website of the Uphoff Mound Group showing mounds along a curving ridge.

fox) as well as one that Brown later referred to as a rabbit. The short-tailed canines have a distinctive arched back found among other Waubesa mounds illustrated by McLachlan. A large tear-drop shaped mound of unknown symbolism occupied the center of the group with several large amorphous shapes following the ridge to the southwest. Three tapering linear mounds extend up the back or western part of the ridge from a wetland. Another linear mound runs parallel to the lake for an extraordinary distance of 645 ft (196.6 m).

Tapering linear mounds extend up a very steep bluff overlooking the east shore at Lake Waubesa South mound group as originally mapped by T.H. Lewis (n.d. c). Here, as with many groups in the Four Lakes, these snake-like forms ran up a slope from the water's edge (Fig. 5.34). Significantly, a large spring flowed from the base of the hill on the opposite or eastern side. Lewis mapped a lone hawk, representing the Upper World, flying across the west slope. A conical mound on top of the hill and a short, tapering, linear mound completed the grouping. None of the mounds of this interesting and informative group survives, so Lewis's mapping cannot be verified.

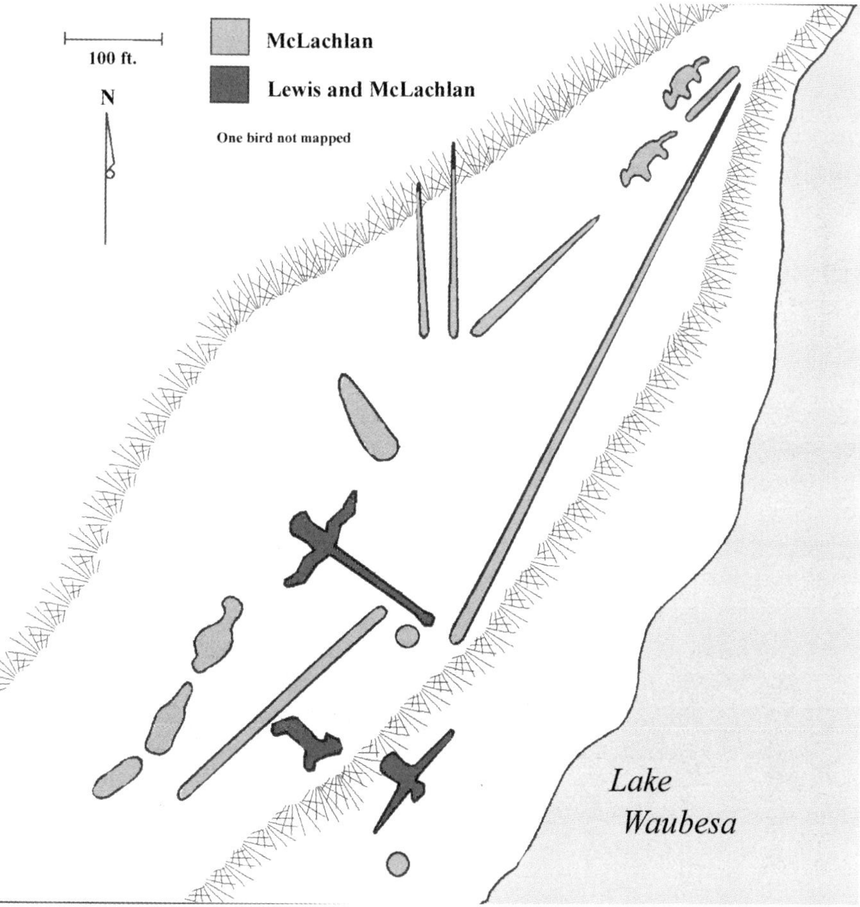

Fig. 5.33 The McConnell Mound Group (by Amy Rosebrough based on mapping by T.H. Lewis and W.G. McLachlan).

Outlet area mounds

As with the other lakes, notable mound building took place near the confluence with Yahara River. McLachlan (1914, 123) reported a mound complex just north of the outlet, which had already gone by the time of his research, with a conical mound reportedly of 'exceptional elevation'. This was probably an earlier Middle Woodland mound characteristically found near inlets and outlets of the lakes. A mile down the Yahara River from the outlet, adjacent to large wetlands, is the linear arrangement of the Sure Johnson Group (Fig. 5.30) that had probably also had its origins in earlier mound building phases (Fig. 5.35). Short and long linear mounds extend north from the Yahara River from an odd, partly enclosed earthwork that appears to have been damaged. It may have been a ceremonial enclosure or large, earlier conical mound that had been massively looted. Bear and bird effigies were positioned near the north end, among the last to be built.

The earthen ridged structure lies closest to the river on the south. It measures about 150 × 137 ft (45.7 × 41.8 m) in size with a 12 ft/3.7 m gap, and what McLachlan simply called 'a heap of dirt' extending to the west (McLachlan 1914, 112). The earthen walls stand about 5 ft (1.5 m) high. The structure has been interpreted as some type of sacred enclosure occasionally found at mound groups. However, the uneven banks enclose an area that is concave and dug out. Given its location near the outlet, a place where early conical mounds were built elsewhere in the Four Lakes, and the pattern of later mound building that extends from it, it is likely that the banks and depression are the remnants and spoil piles of a large Middle Woodland mound massively looted by people looking for bones and antiquities. McLachlan reported that when he visited the site the enclosure had been used for farm refuse and cattle carcasses, no doubt adding to the disturbance. Fortunately, the surviving Sure Johnson mounds are now part of a private conservancy.

Situated along a high drumlin, the Lewis Mound Group overlook the modern village of McFarland and the Yahara River outlet (Figs 5.30 and 5.36). The mound group is now part of Indian Mound Park, maintained by the village and volunteers. Conical and short linear mounds occupy the top, a common pattern; some were damaged by the construction of a water tower like that of the mounds along the high drumlin at Woodland Park, Monona, described above. Moving downslope, one encounters

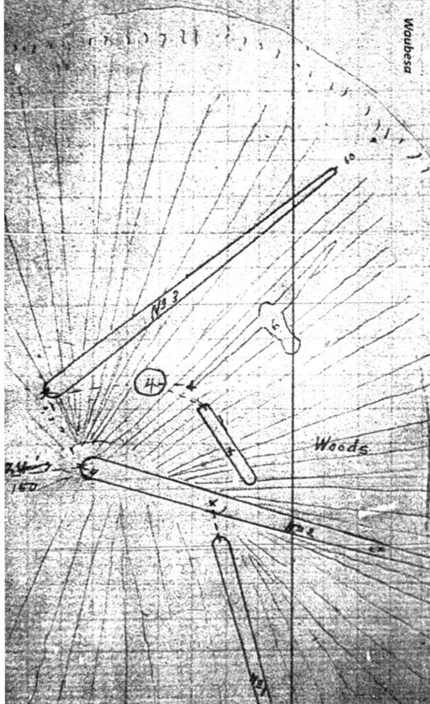

Fig. 5.34 Lake Waubesa South Mound Group as sketched by T.H Lewis (1880–1895, notebook 27, 56).

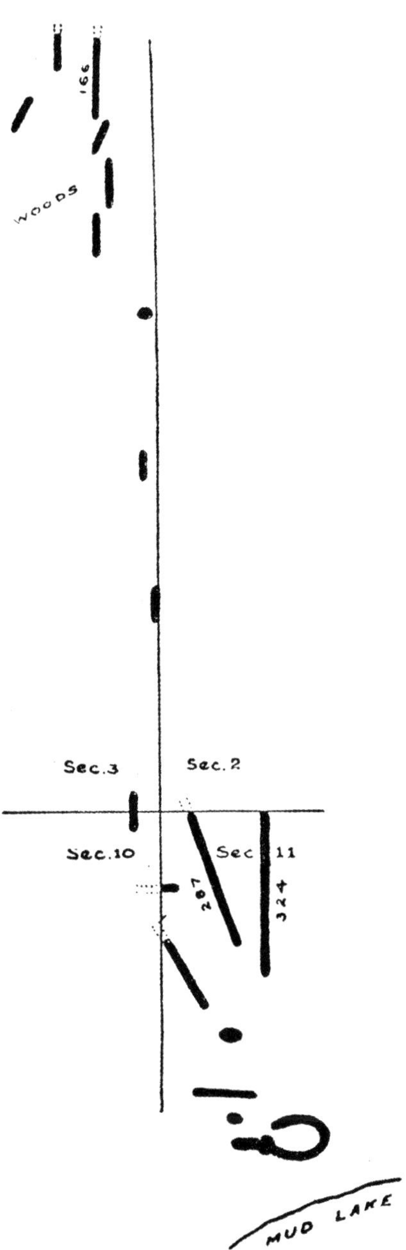

Fig. 5.35 Sure Johnson Mound Group mapped by McLachlan (1914).

a short-tailed fox or wolf, mistakenly mapped by McLachlan (1914) as a bear, a linear mound, and then a curved, 325 ft (99.1 m) long earthwork. As first mapped by T.H. Lewis and can be clearly seen today, the curved mound is a snake effigy with a slightly bulbous head and tapering tail. It appropriately 'snakes' its way down the lower part of the drumlin to a wetland.

Monitored by a professional archaeologist, installation of a new water pipe to the tower in the 1990s revealed that there had been burials made outside of the recorded mounds (Gilmore 1996). Workmen accidentally uncovered a burial accompanied by a large, unusual bone pendant made with two cut deer mandibles (lower jaws) that joined together. Holes in the upper part of the jaws had been drilled for a cord attachment. The burial is undated but it is quite likely these are the remains of one of the Late Woodland people who used the hill for mound building.

Linear mounds comprise most of the Eli Johnson Group arranged along the slope of a high hill overlooking the Yahara River as shown in a LiDAR image (Fig. 5.37). Here too, a tapering linear runs up the slope but, further up, is the other of the two mysteriously crossed mound arrangements in the Four Lakes mound district. Three oval and conical mounds top the hill. The directions of the crossed mounds here differ from Big Cross near Lake Mendota and may be the most compelling case in the Four Lakes for solar orientations as sketched, perhaps not precisely, by McLachlan in the early 20th century. The axes of the two long mounds seem to describe the general directions of both the summer and winter solstice sunrises and sunsets. The earthwork still exists in a wooded lot (on private land) so precise mapping and analysis of its positioning on the slope of the hill should tell whether or not there is good evidence that at least some ancient mounds were used to make celestial observations.

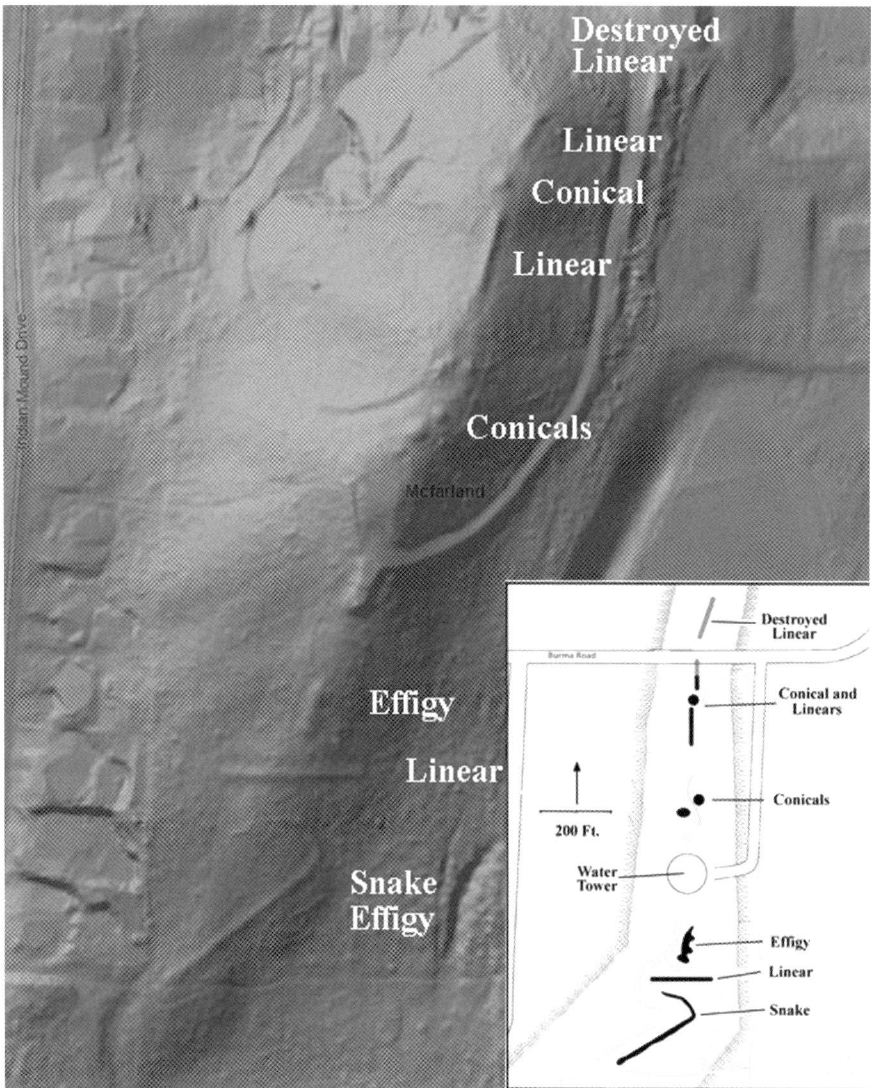

Fig. 5.36 LiDAR from the WisconsinView website of the Lewis group originally mapped by McLauglan (1914).

Lake Kegonsa and the mouth of the Yahara River

The Yahara River flows from the outlet of Lake Waubesa through wetlands called the Lower Mud Lake and on to the shores of Lake Kegonsa (Fig. 5.30). Remnants of a stone fish dam can still be viewed in a narrow part of the river that was most recently used by Ho-Chunk people into the 20th century to trap great quantities of fish. It was no doubt a fishing spot in prehistoric times too as it is situated right below the Skare site, a place used continuously by Native Americans for camps and villages from 11,000 BC to AD 1250. Several linear mounds on the opposite side of the river attest to the presence of Late Woodland mound builders.

This stretch of the Yahara River provided a natural ford and was an important trail crossing where a short iron bridge was later built. Early white settlers took advantage of this narrow and shallow stretch to build one of the first water-driven

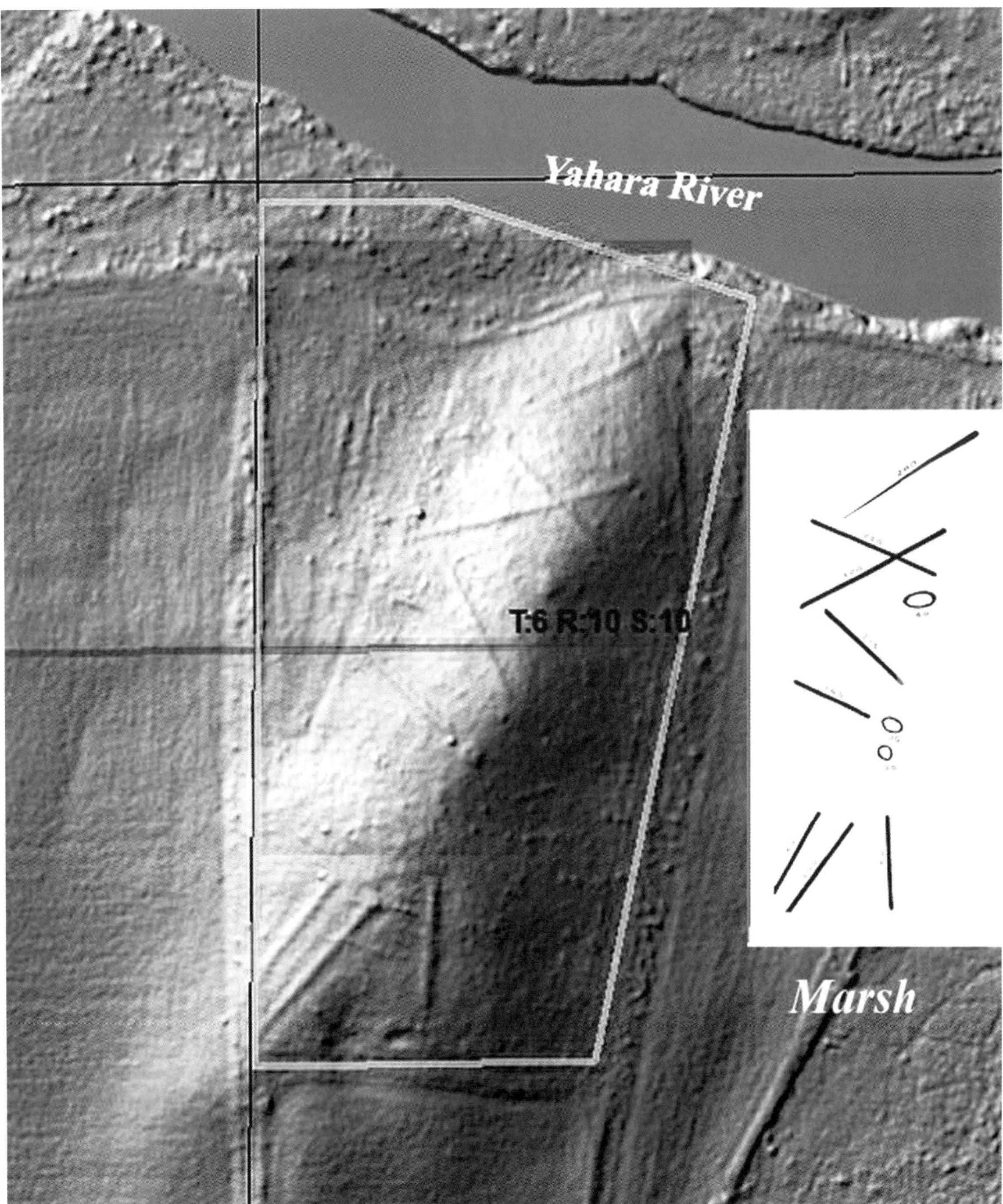

Fig. 5.37 LiDAR from Dane County Land Information of the Eli Johnson Mound Group first mapped by McLachlan (1914).

saw mills in the Four Lakes region. The unique complex of historic and archaeological sites represents nearly the entire span of human occupation of the Fours Lakes through to early white settlement and has been placed on the National Register of Historic Places as the Lower Mud Lake Archaeological Complex.

Kegonsa was called the 'First' lake by early settlers because it is closest to the confluence of the Yahara and Rock Rivers. The Ho-Chunk maintained camps or villages at several places on the lake. One, on Williams Point, is where Ho-Chunk people made maple sugar and near where Native garden beds could still be seen in the early 20th century (McLachlan 1925). The Ho-Chunk called the lake *Na-sa-koo-cha-tel-a* or 'hard maple groove lake'. Maple sugar was a seasonal staple of the Native American diet at the time and used as a trade item with American settlers. The spring sugaring time remains an important social occasion for many Native Americans of the Upper Midwest.

Being some miles from Madison, the mounds of Lake Kegonsa did not attract as much interest from early researchers and, therefore, many mounds disappeared under the plow before being recorded. T.H. Lewis mapped mounds here and modern mound surveys have been conducted but much of what is known is, again, due to Dr McLachlan's work.

Most of the 194 recorded mounds around the lake, however, appear to date to the Late Woodland period, among them at least 13 zoomorphic effigy forms, not including several that might be snakes. Large concentrations of mounds occurred near the west and northeast shores. Several smaller effigy mound groups lie several miles upstream along creeks that drain to the lake and provide insights into the expansion of mound ceremonial activity.

Like Waubesa, Lake Kegonsa is lower in elevation than the upper lakes and included large wetland areas. Reflecting this Lower World environment, only four sky birds are recorded here along with one goose, well away from the lake itself. Instead, the lake has a high proportion of linear mounds – 38% or nearly an identical proportion to that of Lake Waubesa. Other mound forms are Water Spirits; water mammals; bent, tapering, and curved snake-like forms; chain or compound mounds; and a great many conical mounds. At the Lee Group, McLachlan mapped an unusual mound he thought could be a 'swan' but its shape cannot be verified because it has since disappeared under the plow.

One large cluster of mounds, the Barber Group (Fig. 5.30), once spread across a high plateau southwest of the lake shore. Native garden beds were once located nearby, close to the lake shore. As mapped by Lewis in the 1890s, the site contained at least 50 mounds in two groups. Lewis mapped two effigies that resemble water mammals but noted the nearby existence of other effigies, as well as conical, linear, and compound mounds (Lewis 1890a, 6–8; Fig. 5.38). Springs flow from the edges of the plateau to an adjacent creek, accounting for the attraction to this place for purposes of ceremonial construction.

North of the Barber Group, 12 mounds of the Orvold-Colloday Group (Fig. 5.30) extended along the northwestern shore of Lake Kegonsa, onto a peninsula called Colloday Point. A close relationship to geography is evident here with one set of linear mounds following the east–west direction of the peninsula. On a ridge north of this, another set was oriented north–south (Fig. 5.39). Water Spirits, bears, and birds were among the few effigies found among linear and conical mounds in other larger groupings on this side of the lake. Another concentration of mainly linear mounds was found in the vicinity of Williams or Sugarbush Point on the northeastern shore near the Yahara River outlet and seven more linear mounds

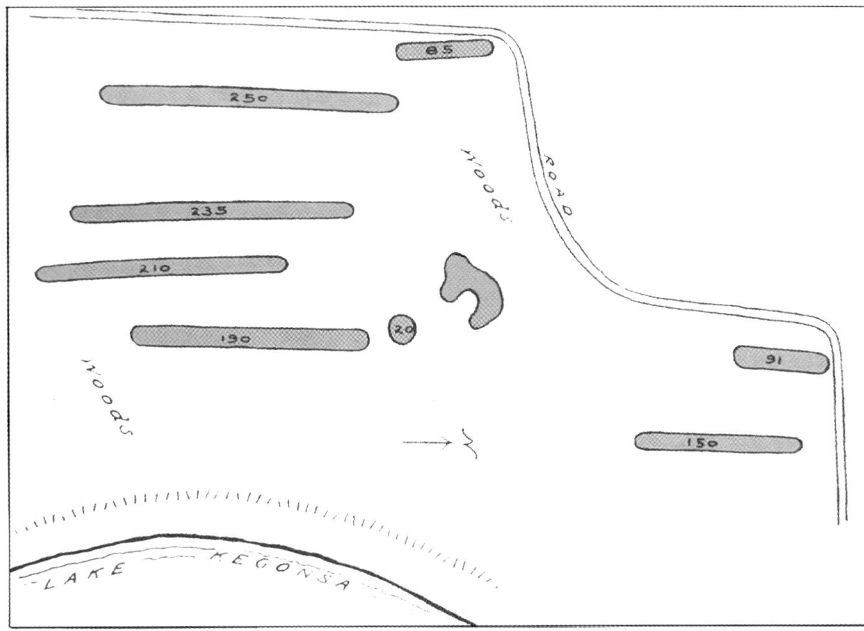

Fig. 5.38 Part of the Barber Site Effigy Mound Group mapped by T.H. Lewis (1880–1895, notebook 32, 6–8).

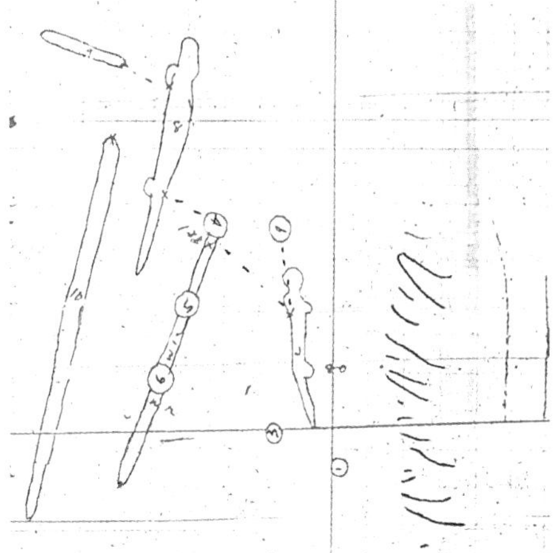

Fig. 5.39 The W.E. Colladay Mound Group (from McLachlan 1925).

are preserved in Lake Kegonsa State Park (Fig. 5.30), once part of a larger grouping. Ancient habitation sites and garden beds have been recorded in the vicinity.

Well away from the lake shore, smaller groups of mounds, all built during the Late Woodland, occupy drumlins. Three mounds of the Moore Group remain on private land at the edge of a large wetland bordering Door Creek to the east. McLachlan originally mapped the group in 1925 and it was remapped as part of the Dane County Mound Identification Project in 1991 using modern survey equipment (Salzer and Johns 1992). Figure 5.40 is a modern LiDAR image. A linear mound follows a north-east–southwest oriented drumlin while the Water Spirit and goose follow the slope down to a large wetland. The goose is perpendicular to the main axis of the land form as elsewhere in the area. Like much of the lower part of the Four Lakes ceremonial landscape, the effigy mounds belong to the Lower World water realm. The two mound Hanson Group, was once situated along a ridge at the edge of the Door Creek marsh (Fig. 5.41). The two mounds have forms uncommon for Four Lakes: one is a flattened or aerial perspective Water Spirit and the other is a compound mound comprising two conical mounds joined by a short linear. Aerial perspective Water Spirit mounds occur throughout the effigy mound

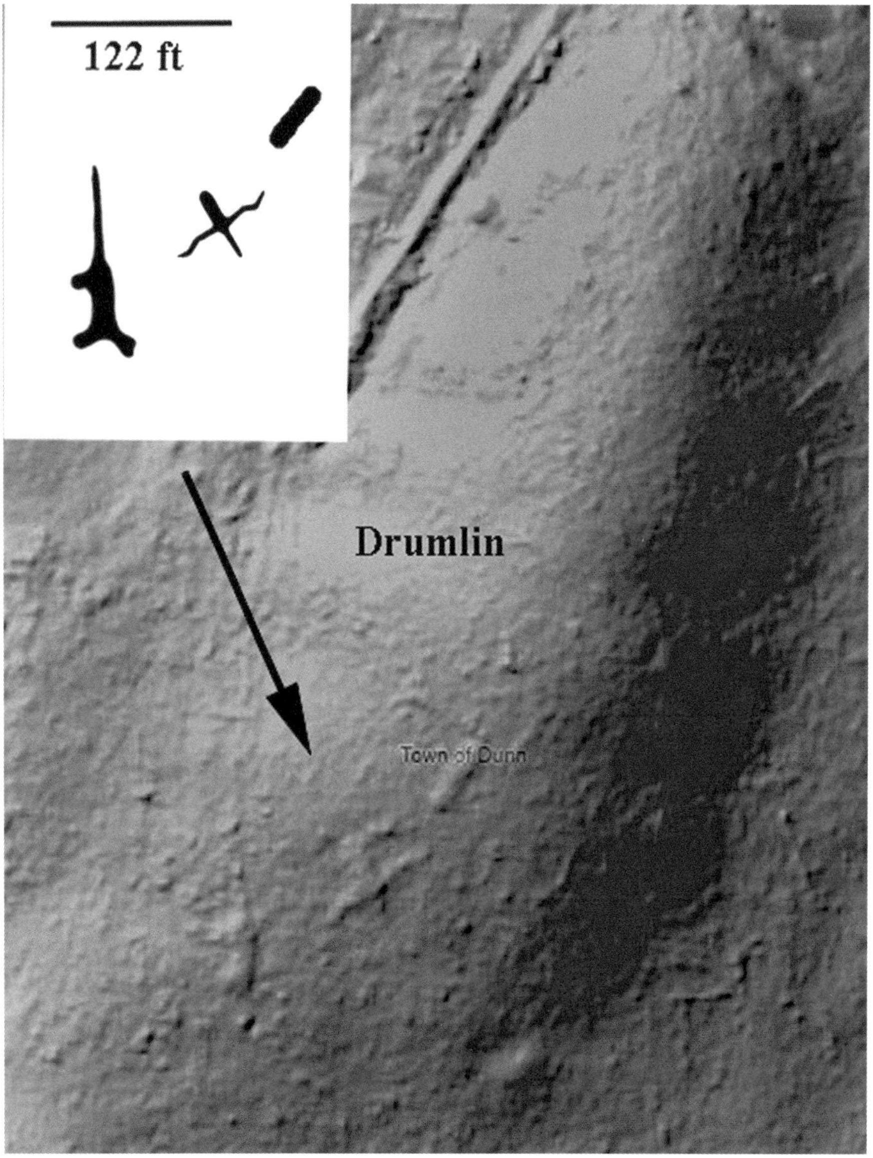

Fig. 5.40 Map and LiDAR image from the WisconsinView website of the Moore Group on a ridge overlooking wetlands (map from McLachlan 1925).

region, as we have seen, but are most common in the eastern part. Most of the Water Spirit mounds found here are shown in profile.

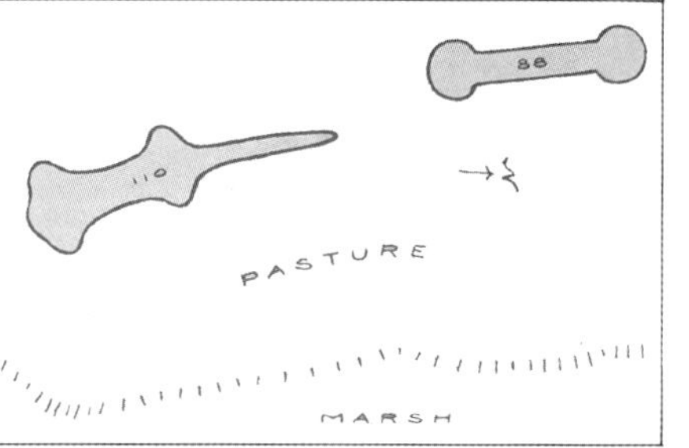

Fig. 5.41 The Hanson Mound (mapped by McLachlan 1925).

Compound or chain mounds are conical mounds joined with short linear earthworks, many times in a series. A total of 13 compound mounds occurred in the Four Lakes mound district, mainly in the south or lower part. They are common to the west along the Mississippi River where they seem to a part of initial Late Woodland mound ceremonial activity, as previously described. As yet, the symbolism of compound mounds is uncertain.

From Lake Kegonsa, the Yahara River meanders through the modern village of Stoughton and then for 20 miles (32 km) through typical southern Wisconsin farmlands to its confluence with the Rock River. Significantly, no mounds are found along this long stretch of the river, emphasizing the importance of the lakes in effigy and earlier mound ceremonial activity. The next mound group to be encountered is on a high, steep, hill along the Rock River 1 mile (0.8 km) north of its confluence with the Yahara River. The Indian Hill Group first drew the attention of Increase Lapham who provided a map and description in his 1855 *Antiquities of Wisconsin.* Lapham shows conical mounds on the top and base of the hill and three long, tapering earthworks extending from a cut-out along the river, possibly a former spring. Another remarkable snake-like mound extends up the steep, 80 ft high slope (Fig. 5.42, upper). Investigators after Lapham clarified

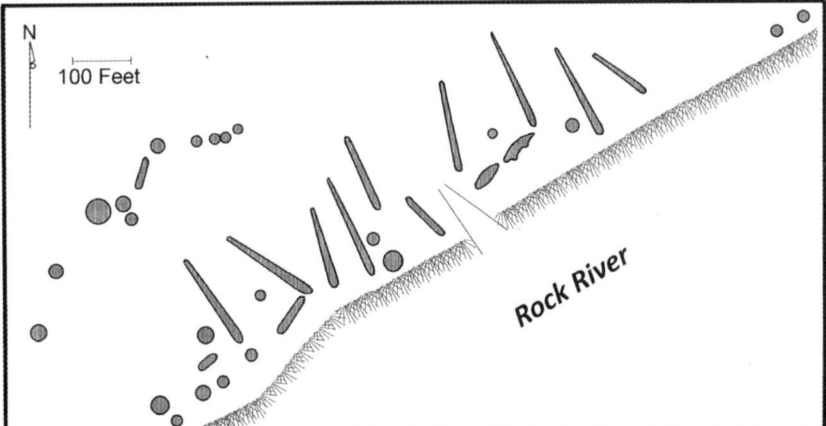

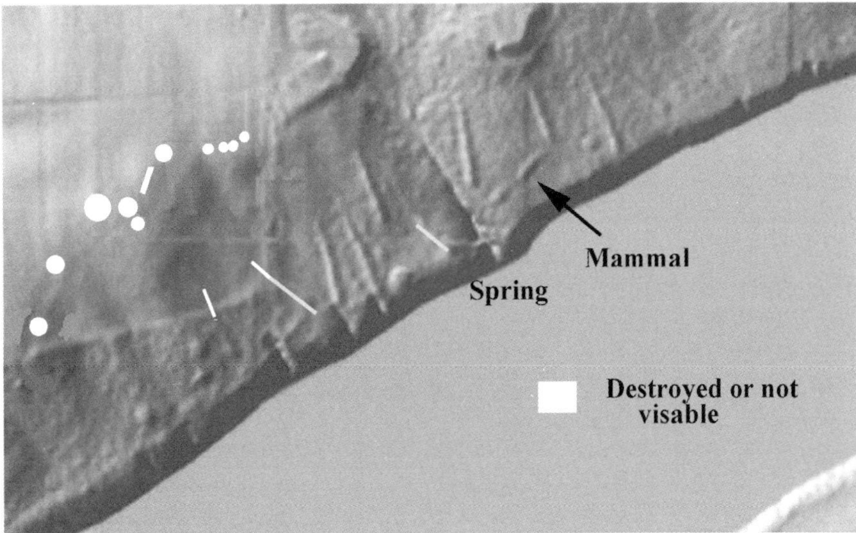

Fig. 5.42 Above: map of the Indian Hills Mound (by Amy Rosebrough); below: modern LiDAR image from the WisconsinView website.

some of his locations, adding more conical mounds and one effigy to one side of the group (Skavlem 1914; Brown and Brown 1925). A modern LiDAR map shows the current condition of the mound group with snake mounds arranged around the spring or drainage, heading down the steep slope to the Rock River (Fig. 5.42, lower). Conical mounds on top of the cliff had been plowed away.

One conical mound at Indian Hills dates back to the earliest mound building in the region, judging by its contents as reported by early mound diggers: red pigment (ochre) stained bones and a cache of 'blue hornstone' blades, referring to a stone traded from Indiana (Brown and Brown 1925). The use of red ochre and the presence of the Indiana hornstone are characteristic of the Red Ochre first mound building culture in the Upper Midwest during the end of the Archaic and beginning of the Woodland stage over 2500 years ago.

The Indian Hill site, then, is one of those rare places that trace the evolution of the mound building from its very start through to the time of the effigy mounds. We end our tour here near the entrance of the Yahara River watershed, which is a portal to the monumental Four Lakes effigy mound landscape that lies further up.

Appendix: Effigy mounds and effigy mound groups that can be viewed by the public

The following is a selection of effigy mounds and effigy mound groups that can be viewed by the public. These have been selected both because of ease of access and because they illustrate the different mound forms and arrangements found in each state, reflecting different cultures and periods of mound building. Many other mounds are on private lands or, if on public lands, are more difficult to view. Some sites have admission fees.

IOWA

Effigy Mounds National Monument

State Highway 76, Marquette, Iowa
Park open: dawn to dusk
Visitor center open: 8.00 am–5.00 pm (summer) 9.00 am–4.30 pm (winter), closed Thanksgiving Day, Christmas Day, and New Year's Day
Fees: admission free

The best interpreted effigy mound landscape is Effigy Mounds National Monument located along the Mississippi River on the western periphery of the effigy mound region, north of McGregor. This large, scenic national park contains lines of 'marching' bear effigies, bird effigies, conical and chain or compound mounds, linear mounds, and one conical mound dating to the earlier Hopewell-Middle Woodland stage. A total of 96 mounds have been preserved in the north and south units of the park. One effigy mound, the Great Bear, is 137 feet long and one unusually long compound or chain mound links together seven mounds. Most of the mounds are arranged in clusters along the tops of bluffs overlooking the Mississippi River. They extend north and south from the Yellow River, a major tributary of the Mississippi. Excavations of some mounds established that mound building began here during the Middle Woodland stage but expanded significantly during the Late Woodland. A visitor center is located off State Highway 76 north of McGregor with informative displays and trail maps.

Website: https://www.nps.gov/efmo/index.htm

ILLINOIS

Beattie Park, Rockford, Illinois

Riverside park off North Main Steet, Downtown Rockford, Winnebago County, Illinois
Park open: daily, 8.00 am–10.00 pm
Fees: admission free

The grouping represents the surviving remnants of a cluster that originally included nine conical mounds, a linear mound, an earthen embankment, and two effigy mounds: a bird and a turtle, of which three of the conicals, the linear mound, and the turtle effigy remain.

WISCONSIN

Calumet County

Calumet County Park
County Trunk Highway EE, off State Highway 55, Stockbridge, Wisconsin
Park open: daily, hours vary
Fees: admission free

Calumet County Park, located on the eastern shore of Lake Winnebago, is approximately 2 miles (3.2 km) north of the community of Stockbridge. Six effigy mounds that incorporate Lower World water symbolism – panthers or Water Spirits – are situated on top of a high escarpment that overlooks the lake. There are park trails, campgrounds and picnic areas.

High Cliff State Park
N7630 State Park Road, off State Highway 55, Sherwood, Wisconsin
Open: daily, 6.00 am–11.00 pm
Fees: State park and recreation fees

High Cliff State Park is situated along the scenic limestone cliffs of the Niagara Escarpment, paralleling the eastern shore of Lake Winnebago, south of the community of Sherwood. The central portion of a once far more extensive effigy mound group, which included a bird, an animal (probably a bear), a large concentration of Water Spirits or panthers, and small conical mounds, is located on the edge of the escarpment overlooking the lake. Some mounds at High Cliff were first featured in Increase Lapham's 1855 *Antiquities of Wisconsin*. The large number of Water Spirit mounds is characteristic of the many mound groups built on the eastern shore of Lake Winnebago and in eastern Wisconsin in general. Six of these long-tailed effigies, as well as several conical mounds, may be seen along an interpretive trail at the park. There are hiking, biking and horse trails, picnic areas, etc. in the park.

Website: dnr.wi.gov/topic/parks/highcliff

Columbia County

Kingsley Bend Mound Group
Off State Highway 16, 3 miles/*ca* 5 km south of Wisconsin Dells, Wisconsin
Park open: daily, 6.00 am–11.00 pm
Fees: State park and recreation fees

Overlooking the Wisconsin River in south-central Wisconsin, the well preserved and maintained Kingsley Bend Mound Group is owned and managed by the Ho-Chunk Nation. These mounds were formerly preserved within a Wisconsin Department of Transportation wayside along State Highway 16 but were transferred to the care of the Ho-Chunk Nation in 2006. The Ho-Chunk view these mounds, as with all mounds, as an important cultural and sacred place but welcome respectful visitation.

The mounds extend down the slopes of a hill to the Wisconsin River, bordered on the south by a spring-fed creek. A huge, classic, Water Spirit mound that is oriented towards nearby springs, and long linear mounds, are located next to the parking area, while a line of large conical mounds, two bear effigies, and a short linear occupy the bluff top overlooking the river. A large eagle-like bird effigy and a long straight tapering linear mound sometimes interpreted as a snake are situated on the opposite side of Hwy 16 but are not as easily visited.

Website: devilslakewisconsin.com/kingsley-bend-indian-mounds

Dane County: Madison area

Madison, with its surrounding lakes, was the center of mound building in Wisconsin. Between 800 BC and AD 1200, Native Americans built more than 1500 mounds in the Four Lakes area. A large number of them were preserved over the years through the efforts of Charles E. Brown of the State Historical Society and other area residents (see Chapter 5).

Burrows Park
Burrows Road, off Sherman Avenue, Madison
Park open: daily, 4.00 am–10.00 pm
Fees: admission free

Burrows Park, a small park on the shore of Lake Mendota, contains a bird effigy mound with a wingspan of 128 ft (39 m). A second effigy – a fox or canine-like animal – once stood alongside the bird but was destroyed. The bird was damaged by early looters but was restored by workers for the Works Progress Administration under the direction of Charles E. Brown.

Website: https://www.cityofmadison.com/parks/find-a-park/park.cfm?id=1148

Blackhawk Country Club Mounds
Blackhawk Country Club, 3606 Blackhawk Drive, Madison
Site open: for personal safety and to avoid interference with golfers, visitors should get permission to visit the mounds at the golf course clubhouse on Blackhawk Drive
Fees: admission free with permission

Arranged on the top and base of a drumlin along the shore of Lake Mendota, the mounds of the Blackhawk Country Club illustrate the basic symbolism of effigy mounds and the use of the natural landscape to emphasize that symbolism. Now on a golf course, three conicals occupy the highest elevation. A bird effigy on the top of the hill was destroyed during golf course construction but is memorialized by a half-scale replica built next to the clubhouse parking lot. A huge and impressive Madison-style winged goose flies across the upper slopes, between the top of the hill and Lake Mendota. Long linear mounds extend up the slope as though moving from the lake. One stretches up 200 ft (*ca* 61 m) from the base of the hill to the conical mounds on top. At the base of the hill and across Lake Mendota Drive, a cluster of three small bear effigy mounds, representing the earth, can be found near the golf course practice range. A long-tailed Water Spirit mound survives on private property along the lakeshore and is not publicly accessible. An excavation into the heart of the mound in the 1950s revealed the flexed remains of a young woman.

Website: https://www.blackhawkcc.com/

Forest Hill Cemetery
Regent Street and Speedway Drive, Madison
Cemetery open: daily, no hours stated
Fees: admission free

Established in 1858, the historic Forest Hill Cemetery is the final resting place of many of Wisconsin's most prominent citizens, including eight governors. Among the more modern graves is an effigy mound group that consists of most of a Madison-style, zig-zag winged goose, two Water Spirits or panthers, and a linear mound. The head of the goose effigy, which is on a slope that leads (appropriately) to adjacent wetlands, was removed when a railroad was built through the area in the 19th century. Part of the tail of one panther and three additional linear mounds were destroyed during the early development of the cemetery. Efforts by Charles E. Brown of the State Historical Society saved the remaining mounds. Fittingly, Brown himself is interred at Forest Hill. His grave can be found in Lot 1 next to a large granite monolith bearing a single word: archaeologist. A brochure for a self-guided walking tour of Forest Hill Cemetery is available at the cemetery office on Speedway Drive.

Website: foresthill.williamcronon.net/effigy-mounds/mounds-in-madison/

Governor Nelson State Park
County Trunk Highway M, Waunakee
Park open: daily, 6.00 am–11.00 pm
Fees: State park and recreation fees

The 422 acre (171 ha) Governor Nelson State Park is on the northern shore of Lake Mendota. A group of five conical mounds and a large panther or Water Spirit effigy mound can be found along trails that wind south of the main parking area and boat landing. The conical mounds may have been built during the Middle Woodland stage, while the effigy seems to have been added later. A stockaded Late Woodland village was located to the north of the mounds, in the vicinity of the showers and toilet near the beach. Native American cornfields were planted in this area, which also was the site of an early 19th century Ho-Chunk village.

Website: dnr.wi.gov/topic/parks/govnelson

Heim Mound
6314 Mound Street, Middleton
Open: daily, continuous, but please respect neighbors
Fees: admission free

The solitary Heim effigy mound is located on a small, wooded lot in a subdivision of Middleton, on the outskirts of Madison. The mound depicts a 147 ft (44.8 m) long canine such as a fox or wolf. The property is owned and maintained by the Wisconsin Archaeological Society and was donated to the Society by Ferdinand Heim at the urging of archaeologist and mound preservationist Charles E. Brown. Brown and the Society excavated a small part of the mound in the early 20th century. Though not a public park, the Wisconsin Archeological Society welcomes quiet visitation. Please make sure not to block the narrow road that leads to it and take care not to disturb the neighbors on adjacent lots or any of the many ephemeral wildflowers that grow on and near the mound.

Lewis Mound Group
Indian Mound Park, Burma Road, McFarland
Park open: daily, no hours stated
Fees: admission free

This Late Woodland mound group is located on a hill overlooking Lake Waubesa in Indian Mound Park. Called the Lewis Mound Group, after Tollef Lewis, the 19th century owner, it formerly consisted of a canine effigy, four linear, two conical, and one oval mounds. A long, curved earthwork sometimes identified as a 'snake' effigy crawls down a steep slope to wetlands. Portions of some mounds were damaged by construction of a water tower on the hill. Local volunteers have cleared the mounds and rerouted trails so they no longer pass over the mounds.

Observatory Hill Mound Group
Observatory Drive, University of Wisconsin, Madison
Site open: daily, 4.00 am–10.00 pm
Fees: admission free

Directly to the west of the observatory on the campus of the University of Wisconsin, overlooking Lake Mendota, are the Observatory Hill mounds: a bird effigy and the only known two-tailed Water Spirit effigy. One tail of the Water Spirit is barely visible and the other was partly destroyed by a sidewalk. The unusual two-tailed mound may represent two Water Spirits placed back to back, as paired effigies are found at several other mound groups. Other mounds at this site, including a long-tailed panther or Water Spirit, a linear mound, and conical mounds, were destroyed during development of the campus. Sidewalks that passed over portions of the mounds have been removed in recent years.

Website: https://lakeshorepreserve.wisc.edu/visit/places/observatory-hill/

University of Wisconsin Arboretum
McCaffrey Road, Madison
Arboretum open: daily, 4.00 am–10.00 pm
Visitor center open: 9.30 am–4.00 pm weekdays, 12.30 pm–4.00 pm weekends

Two Late Woodland effigy mound groups, including a bird, a panther, and linear and conical mounds, are located on both sides of McCaffrey Road at the University of Wisconsin Arboretum. One group is situated right above a prominent spring that was considered sacred by Ho-Chunk who camped nearby into the 20th century. Among other things, springs were considered entrances to the watery Underworld realm of the Water Spirits. These groups were restored by Charles E. Brown of the State Historical Society. Hiking and bike trails pass the mound groups and a map is available at the McKay Center at the arboretum, or to download from the website.

Website: www.arboretum.wisc.edu

Vilas Park
Erin and Wingra Streets, Madison
Park open: daily 4.00 am–10.00 pm
Fees: admission free (3 hour parking limit)

The Late Woodland effigy mound group in Vilas Park consists of a bird effigy, a linear mound, and six conical mounds. Two additional conical mounds and another bird effigy were destroyed when nearby houses were constructed. The plaque at the site is an example of the preservation efforts undertaken by Charles E. Brown and his colleagues at the Wisconsin Archeological Society.

Vilas Park Circle
1525 Vilas Avenue, Madison
Site open: 4.00 am–10.00 pm
Fees: admission free

The small (1.6 acre/0.65 ha) Vilas Park Circle was created to preserve a large effigy mound of a bear, which is located on the west side of the oval park. This mound was once part of a larger group that included seven linears and a conical mound. An unconfirmed early 20th century report claims that children digging in the mound found the remnants of a sword made during the period of the fur trade. If true, the sword was likely buried in or placed on the mound by Ho-Chunk living in the Madison area, centuries after the mound was built.

Yahara Heights County Park and Cherokee Marsh
Catfish Court, off Hwy 113/Northpoint Rd, Westport Township, Madison
Park open: 5.00 am–10.00 pm
Fees: admission free

Located along a large wetland called the Cherokee Marsh, north of Lake Mendota, this new Dane County park preserves two effigy mounds: a bear and a long-tailed Water Spirit that is oriented to the marsh. The mounds are part of the Yahara Heights Mound Group, which once included a short linear, a small conical, and a canine (fox or wolf) that had been plowed when the area was farmland. The effigies of the group are all Lower World forms but Upper World bird mounds were once found on hills further to the west. The bear and Water Spirit are easily viewed since park volunteers cleared brush and undergrowth over the area and returned them to oak savanna. Follow the trail northeast along the marsh a little over ½ mile (0.8 km). A second entrance to the park is located in a sub-division on Canton Lane where a short trail marked by a gate leads east a short distance to the mounds.

Website: parks-lwrd.countyofdane.com/park/YaharaCherokee

Dodge County

Nitschke Mounds Park
W5934 County Road East, just east of its intersection with Highway 26, Burnett, Wisconsin
Park open: daily, dawn to dusk
Fees: admission free

The Nitschke I mound group occupies a glacial drumlin several miles west of the great Horicon Marsh. It is now located in a Dodge County Park, created in the 1990s to preserve the large mound group for public interpretation. Another large mound group, Nitschke II, occupied an adjacent elevation a short distance to the southeast but was plowed away by farming. This two-part ceremonial mound landscape is unusual in both its remoteness and the fact that it is away from major bodies of water. Instead, the two mound groups had been arranged near two large springs.

Once consisting of at least 62 mounds crowded together to fit the narrow, low, southwest–northeast trending drumlin, the Nitschke I group now has 46 mounds. Many others were leveled by farming, including numerous undocumented mounds north of the present park. The effigy types are mainly water and earth related, but Nitschke II once included a single bird that was not a water bird. Effigy mounds preserved at Nitschke I include straight-winged geese, Water Spirits, a bear, and short-tailed canine-like mounds, all with heads pointing to the southwest following the direction of the drumlin. The group also featured several linear and unidentified mounds. As at many other effigy mound sites, a string of conical mounds extended along the very top of the ridge; several of these are superimposed on the long tail of a Water Spirit mound.

Many of the mounds of both groups were partly excavated by the Milwaukee Public Museum, revealing burials and a strikingly unusual number of ceremonial offerings – largely clay pots, arrows, tools, and food remains from a feast. Recent work by the University of Wisconsin-Milwaukee just east of the mounds in an area where a small plot of ancient garden beds was recorded in the early 20th century, identified a small campsite used by Late Woodland people during mound construction. Based on the ceramics recovered by the early Milwaukee Public Museum and modern radiocarbon dates derived from organic residue on the pots, the Nitschke mounds have been dated to the very end of the effigy mound era. The park has a trail, signage, and an interpretive display.

Website: https://www.co.dodge.wi.gov/departments/departments-e-m/land-resources-and-parks/parks-and-trails/nitschke-mounds-park

Grant County

Wyalusing State Park
County Trunk Highway C, Prairie du Chien, Wisconsin
Open: daily, 6.00 am–11.00 pm
Fees: State park and recreation fees

Wyalusing State Park is located near Prairie du Chien on the high bluffs overlooking the confluence of the Mississippi and Wisconsin Rivers. High vistas offer spectacular views of the rivers and surrounding countryside. More than 130 mounds were recorded within the park boundaries by various surveyors since the 1880s. Before the park was established by the State, many of the mounds were destroyed by farming or stone quarrying. However, 69 mounds survive and are carefully preserved, including the Sentinel Hill Mound Group and the Procession mound groups, which are composed of single lines of 28 mounds each that follow the crests of bluffs: small conicals, short linears, bears, and a single-tailed effigy. There are also examples of compound mounds at the park.

The mounds have not been professionally excavated but at least two separate periods of mound building seem to be represented. Cyrus Thomas's crews investigated several large conical mounds in the area and found burials in stone crypts, one with shell beads, a copper celt, and a stone platform pipe characteristic of the Hopewell influences of the Middle Woodland stage. Most other mounds in the park, however, appear to have been built during the early part of the Late Woodland stage. The park includes campsites, picnic areas, and hiking trails.

Website: www.dnr.wi.gov/topic/parks/name/Wyalusing

Nelson Dewey State Park
12190 Highway VV, Cassville, Wisconsin
Park open: daily, 6.00 am–11.00 pm. During the offseason, the main gate is closed, but visitors may park at the entrance and walk into the park.
Fees: State park and recreation fees

Groups of mounds can be viewed at Nelson Dewey State Park overlooking the Mississippi River, and opposite Stonefield Village Historic Site. The most prominent are located along the main park drive and include several massive compound mounds that were probably built just prior to the expansion of effigy mound groups and landscapes. The park includes campsites, picnic areas, and hiking trails.

Website: www.dnr.wi.gov/topic/parks/nelsondewey

Bird Effigy
Cassville Bluffs Natural Area, Sand Lake Road, off Highway 133, Cassville, Wisconsin
Site open: daily, no hours stated
Fees: admission free

Also near Cassville, a large bird effigy with a wingspan of 270 ft (82.3 m) flies down a bluff slope edge high above the Mississippi River at the Cassville Bluffs Natural Area. It was documented in the late 19th century by T.H. Lewis who did not mention any other associated mounds. The Natural Area incudes a variety of habitats and a wide range of flora and fauna. There are hiking trails but cycling is not allowed and the park literature does not mention the mound!

Website: https://www.mississippivalleyconservancy.org/sites/default/files/2017-10/Cassville%20Bluffs%20Brochure_Feb%202015.pdf

Jefferson County

General Atkinson Mound Group
Jefferson County Indian Mounds and Trail Park, Koshkonong Mounds Road, off State Highway 26, Fort Atkinson, Wisconsin
Park open: daily, no hours stated
Fees: admission free

The southern part of the General Atkinson Mound Group is preserved in the Jefferson County Indian Mounds and Trail Park, south of the community of Fort Atkinson. These 11 mounds consist of tapering linear, conical, bird, and 'turtle' mounds that represent panthers or Water Spirits as viewed from above, rather than from the side. The mounds range in length from 75 ft to 222 ft (*ca* 23–68 m).

The General Atkinson Mound Group originally consisted of 72 mounds, many of which were destroyed. The park includes one of the only surviving segments of the ancient trail system that once connected Wisconsin's mound-building communities. The trail was documented by a land surveyor in 1835 and is identified by signage within the park. In 1993, the late Hugh Highsmith of Fort Atkinson purchased the land containing the 11 mounds and, in cooperation with the Fort Atkinson Historical Society, donated it to Jefferson County.

Website: https://www.jeffersoncountywi.gov/park/_T9_R12.php

Panther Intaglio
Riverside Drive, State Highway 106, Fort Atkinson, Wisconsin
Site open: continuously
Fees: admission free

Just west of downtown Fort Atkinson, along the northern side of the Rock River, on a small plot of private land beside the road is the last remaining intaglio in Wisconsin. It was discovered by Increase Lapham in 1850 and is the only survivor of about a dozen intaglios recorded. It was once part of a large effigy mound group that was destroyed by residential development. The 125 ft (*ca* 38 m) intaglio is a scooped-out area in the form of a Water Spirit or panther about 2 ft (0.6 m) deep. The excavation of this reverse image of a panther mound may be related to the fact that such water spirits were believed to originate in a watery realm below the surface of the earth. In 1919, the Fort Atkinson chapter of the Daughters of the American Revolution leased the land to preserve the intaglio and it is now a (very) small city park.

Juneau County

Indian Mounds Park
Indian Mound Road off Highways 12/16, New Lisbon, Wisconsin
Park open: daily, 7.00 am–10.00 pm. Closed in winter, dates not stated
Fees: admission free

Indian Mounds Park, on the Lemonweir River on the south side of New Lisbon, preserves a mound group that consists of three conical, one linear, a compound or chain mound, and a Water Spirit or panther effigy. Originally, there were at least 10 other mounds, which have been destroyed. Chain or compound mounds are only occasionally found outside the Mississippi River valley. Some of the mounds were reconstructed by the Lion's Club of New Lisbon.

Richland County

Eagle Township Mounds
Close to the junction of State Highways 60 and 193, Muscoda, Wisconsin
Park open: daily, no hours stated. Contact Three Eagles foundation in advance if large groups wish to visit at 3eaglesinc@gmail.com
Fees: admission free

Along the Wisconsin River, vestiges of the once giant Eagle Township ceremonial landscape are preserved northwest and across the river from modern Muscoda in Richland County, Wisconsin. Virtually intact mound groups, called the Shadewald I and II mound groups, occupy two high adjacent hills just north of Hwy 60 and separated by Hwy 193 just north of their intersection. These were once part of the giant Eagle Township Effigy Mound Landscape along the Wisconsin River, most of which was destroyed by farming. The late landowner Frank Shadewald carefully preserved and maintained the mounds and encouraged visitors. On top of the westernmost hill, 12 conical mounds of the Shadewald I grouping are arranged in a line that follow the contours of the hilltop in a roughly north–south direction. Shadewald II occupies the eastern hill with effigies of a bird, bear, canine, as well as unidentified forms, and these also follow the contours of the hilltop, in this case in an east–west direction. The two groups are now managed by the Three Eagles Foundation of Muscoda.

To the south and overlooking the north bank of the Wisconsin River, the Schaeffer Bird effigy is located on Department of Natural Resources land along Hwy 60, a short distance west of its intersection with Hwy 80. The bird flies south to the river and is marked by a small sign. It is the last survivor of a grouping that also included bear and linear mounds and was part of the broad Eagle Mound ceremonial landscape. The mound is visible from the highway, but visitors should park on Effigy Mound Lane, off Hwy 60 and follow a trail to the mound.

Website: www.3-eagles.org

Rock County

Beloit College Mounds
Beloit College, 700 College Street, Beliot, Wisconsin
College campus open: weekdays 8.00 am–4.30 pm
Logan Museum open: 11.00 am–4.00 pm, closed Mondays
Fees: admission free

Twenty mounds dating to the Late Woodland period are located in the lawns in the heart of the historic and private Beloit College. This total includes conicals, short linears, and a flattened effigy that resembles a turtle. The latter is used as a symbol for the college. The Logan Museum, located on campus near the mounds, also features rare and unique archaeological objects from around the world and has interesting interpretative displays.

Totem Mound Park
1900–1998 Totem Rd, Beloit, Wisconsin
Park open: daily, no hours stated
Frees: admission free

Four mounds can be found in this city park along the Turtle River: an oval, two conical, and a ‘turtle’ mound depicting a long-tailed Water Spirit effigy from above. The effigy is one of the finest remaining in Rock County. The other mounds, particularly one conical, are lower and may be difficult to find.

Sauk County

Devil's Lake State Park
Park Road/North Shore Road, Baraboo, Wisconsin
Park open: daily, 6.00 am–11.00 pm
Fees: State park and recreation fees apply

Devil's Lake State Park, located 3 miles (*ca* 5 km) south of Baraboo, preserves a number of effigy mounds that represent both Upper World and Lower World symbolism. A 150 ft (45.7 m) long 'fork-tailed' bird effigy is located on the southeastern shore of the lake. It is also possible that this mound form represents a 'bird-man', combining characteristics of a bird and a human being. Effigy mounds at the northern end of the lake are from the opposing Lower World and include a bear, an unidentified animal, and a once huge Water Spirit or panther. The park is very busy in summer; it includes 30 miles of hiking trails, swimming beaches, picnic, and camping areas.

Website: https://dnr.wisconsin.gov/topic/parks/devilslake

Man Mound County Park
E13097 Man Mound Road, Baraboo, Wisconsin
Park open: continuously
Fees: admission free

Only one effigy mound in the shape of a human being has survived nearly intact. It is located near the base of a high hill in Man Mound County Park, to the northeast of Baraboo. Probably built more than 1000 years ago, this huge mound is in the form of a walking man who has horns or is wearing a horned headdress. The mound was first reported by W.H. Canfield in 1859 during a land survey. It was originally 214 ft (65.2 m) long, but road construction in 1905 destroyed the feet and lower legs of the figure. The remainder of the mound was saved from further damage by the Wisconsin Archeological Society and the Sauk County Historical Society, which purchased the mound in 1907. It is now the centerpiece of a small county park. The Man Mound was designated as a National Historic Landmark in 2016.

Website: https://saukcountyhistory.org/man-mound-nhl

Sheboygan County

Sheboygan Indian Mound County Park
South Ninth Street, Sheboygan, Wisconsin
Park open: April 1 to November 1, no hours stated
Fees: admission free

Sheboygan Indian Mound County Park preserves what was first known as the Kletzien Mound Group. The group originally consisted of 33 conical and effigy mounds, primarily deer and panthers, as well as one panther or Water Spirit intaglio. A number of mounds were excavated in 1926 by the Milwaukee Public Museum. Local garden clubs saved the mound group from development in the late 1950s by raising money to purchase the site. The land was subsequently donated to the city for an archaeological park, and 16 of the 18 existing mounds were restored under the supervision of the Milwaukee Public Museum. The Town and County Garden Club developed a nature trail with signage and a guide to the trail that is available at the park.

Website: https://wisconsinfirstnations.org/sheboygan-indian-mound-county-park/

Trempealeau County

Perrot State Park
South Park Road, off Hwy 35, Trempealeau, Wisconsin
Park open: daily, 6.00 am–11.00 pm
Fees: State park and recreation fees apply

Just north of the town of Trempealeau, mounds from the Trowbridge mound group can be found at Perrot State Park. The large group once consisted of 34 conical and oval mounds, two short-tailed mammal effigies, a Water Spirit effigy in an aerial or flattened perspective and a bird effigy. Most have been destroyed by previous land use but the park today preserves 16 mounds, including one of the tailed mammal effigies. Displays about area archaeology can be found at the Nature Center. The park includes hiking trails, campsites, and picnic areas.

Website: https://dnr.wisconsin.gov/topic/parks/perrot

Washington County

Lizard Mound State Park
Half mile east of intersection of State Highway 111 and County Trunk Highway A, West Bend, Wisconsin
Park open: daily, 6.00 am–11.00 pm
Fees: admission free

This mound group originally contained approximately 60 mounds dominated by long-tailed effigy forms that early investigators thought were lizards. They are undoubtedly versions of Water Spirits or panthers. Over the years, many of the mounds were obliterated by continued cultivation and others were reduced to a point where they are no longer visible. There are now 29 mounds: conical and oval shaped, short linears, tapering linears, Water Spirits, and two symmetrically paired water bird effigies that fly away from each other.

The location of the group is unusual. It is on a low, level plateau far from any major body of water. The plateau is, however, surrounded by springs, which have many spiritual associations for Native peoples, being the entrances to the Underworld of the Water Spirits. Thus the location and Underworld theme of the group may have been determined primarily by landscape features that have long-held spiritual connotations. An interpretive kiosk and shelter stands near the park entrance. A sign-posted trail winds around the mounds.

Website: https://dnr.wisconsin.gov/topic/parks/lizardmound

Quaas Creek Park
2500 County Creek Circle, West Bend, Wisconsin
Park open: daily, 6.00 am–11.00 pm
Fees: admission free

Near the Milwaukee River in West Bend, Wisconsin, are two bird mounds flying west together on a low ridge in the modern Quaas Creek Park. The birds have wingspans of 93 ft (28.3 m) and 134 ft (40.8 m) and are visible along a walking trail. Across the creek and lower on the landscape along the river there once stood effigies that had water and Lower World symbolism: long-necked water birds, similar to those at Lizard Mound, a long linear, and two probable Water Spirit mounds.

Website: https://westbendwi.gov/business_detail_T36_R49.php

Winnebago County

Smith Park
Park Street, off Keyes Street, Menasha, Wisconsin
Park open: daily, 8.00 am–10.00 pm
Fees: admission free

At least 17 mounds once spread across an area on Doty Island, which sits along the Fox River at the point where it exits Lake Winnebago in the city of Menasha, Wisconsin. Most were destroyed by farming and urban development but three long-tailed Water Spirit mounds are preserved in the south end of Smith Park.

Walworth County

Whitewater Effigy Mounds Preserve
288 Indian Mounds Parkway at intersection with Wildwood Rd, Whitewater, Wisconsin
Park open; daily, dawn to dusk
Fees: admission free

On the western side of the city of Whitewater, the municipally owned Effigy Mounds Preserve encompasses the Maples Mound Group. Fifteen mounds are found here: two types of birds, three Water Spirits, one water mammal, three tapering and two short linears, two conicals, an oval mound, and one mound of uncertain form. The group is arranged along a small creek with adjacent spring-fed wetlands. The preserve has informative signage, a picnic area, and a trail map.

Website: https://www.wwparks.org/park-guide/whitewater-effigy-mounds-preserve

Bibliography

Ahler, S.A, Thiesson, T.D. and Trimble, M.K. (1991) *People of the Willows: The Prehistory and Early History of the Hidatsa Indians.* University of North Dakota Press, Grand Forks ND.

Alex, L.M. (2000) *Iowa's Archaeological Past.* University of Iowa Press, Iowa City IA.

Bailey, G.A. (ed.) (1995) *The Osage and the Invisible World from the Works of Francis La Flesche.* University of Oklahoma Press, Norman OK.

Bakken, C.T. (1950) Preliminary investigations at the Outlet Site. *The Wisconsin Archeologist* 31(2), 43–70.

Barrett, S.A. (1933) *Ancient Aztalan. Bulletin of the Public Museum of the City of Milwaukee* 13.

Barrett, S.A. and Hawkes, E.W. (1919) The Kratz Creek Mound Group. *Bulletin of the Public Museum of the City of Milwaukee* 3(1), 1–138.

Barrett, S.A. and Skinner, A. (1932) *Certain Mounds and Village Sites of Shawano and Oconto Counties, Wisconsin. Bulletin of the Public Museum of the City of Milwaukee* 10(5).

Bascomb, W. (1965) The forms of folklore: prose narrations. *Journal of American Folklore* 78(307), 3–20.

Beer, J. (2016) The Catfish Creek Birdstone, Dane County, Wisconsin. *The Wisconsin Archeologist* 97(2), 7–8.

Bender, M.M, Baerreis, D.A, Bryson, R.A. and Steventon, R.L. (1982) University of Wisconsin Radiocarbon Dates XIX. *Radiocarbon* 24(1), 83–100. DOI: https://doi.org/10.1017/S0033822200004926.

Benn, D. (1979) Some trends and traditions in Wisconsin cultures of the Quad-State Region in the Upper Mississippi River Basin. *The Wisconsin Archeologist* 60, 47–82.

Benn, D. (1995) Woodland people and the roots of the Oneota. In *Oneota Archaeology: Past, Present and Future*, W. Green ed., 91–140. Office of the State Archaeologist, University of Iowa, Iowa City IA.

Benn, D.W. and Thompson, D.M. (1976) Preliminary Investigation of the FTD Site. Luther College Archaeological Laboratory unpublished report, Decorah IA.

Benn, D.W., Clark Mallam, R. and Arthur III Bettis, E. (1978) Archaeological Investigations at the Keller Mounds (13AM69) and Related Manifestations: Insights into Woodland Indian Mythology. Research Papers 3-1. Iowa, Office of the State Archaeologist, Des Moines.

Birmingham, R.A. (1994) An Archaeological Survey of Wisconsin Winnebago Land in Eagle Township, Richland County, Wisconsin. Unpublished manuscript on file Division of Historic Preservation-Wisconsin Historical Society, Madison, WI.

Birmingham, R.A. (1996) Charles E. Brown and the mounds of Madison. *Historic Madison: The Journal of the Four Lakes Region* 13, 17–29.

Birmingham, R.A. (2004) McKern, mound builders, and Upper Mississippians. *The Wisconsin Archeologist* 85 (2) 44–9.

Birmingham, R.A. (2010) *Spirits of Earth: The Effigy Mound Landscape of Madison and the Four Lakes.* University of Wisconsin Press, Madison WI.

Birmingham, R.A. (2015) *Skunk Hill, a Native Ceremonial Community in Wisconsin.* Wisconsin Historical Society Press, Madison WI.

Birmingham, R.A. (2023) Archaeological Monitoring of an Electrical Line Trenching at the West Point Mound Group (47 Da-0115) at 5109/5111 St. Cyr Rd, Middleton, Dane County, Wisconsin. Unpublished report on file, Wisconsin Historical Society Office of the State Archaeologist, Madison WI.

Birmingham, R.A. and Eisenberg, L. (2000) *Indian Mounds of Wisconsin.* University of Wisconsin Press, Madison WI.

Birmingham, R.A. and Rosebrough, A. (2003) On the meaning of effigy mounds. *The Wisconsin Archeologist* 84(1–2), 21–36.

Birmingham, R.A. and Rosebrough, A. (2017) *Indian Mounds of Wisconsin* (2nd edn). University of Wisconsin Press, Madison WI.

Birmingham, R.A. and Van Dyke, A.P. (1981) Chert and chert resources in the Lower Rock River valley. *The Wisconsin Archeologist* 62(3), 347–60.

Bowers A.W. (1950) *Mandan Social and Ceremonial Organization.* University of Chicago Press, Chicago IL.

Bowers A.W. (1992) *Hidatsa Social and Ceremonial Organization.* University of Nebraska Press, Lincoln NE.

Boszhardt, R.F. (1996) Angelo punctated: a Late Woodland ceramic type in western Wisconsin. *Journal of the Iowa Archaeological Society* 43, 129–37.

Boszhardt, R.F. (1998) Oneota horizons: a La Crosse perspective. *The Wisconsin Archeologist* 79(2), 196–226.

Boszhardt, R.F. (2003) *Deep Cave Art in the Upper Mississippi Valley.* Prairie Smoke Press, St Paul MN.

Boszhardt, R.F. (2006) An etched pipe from southeastern Minnesota. *Archaeology News* 24(2), 1–2.

Brain, J.P. and Philips, P. (1996) *Shell Gorgets: Styles of the Late Prehistoric and Protohistoric Southeast.* Peabody Museum of Archaeology and Ethnology, Cambridge MA.

Broihahn, J. (2003) Wisconsin's Pipestones: Comments on the History, Archaeology, and Cultural Aspects of Wisconsin's Pipestones. Unpublished, State Archaeology and Maritime Preservation Program Technical Report 03-0002, Wisconsin Historical Society, Madison WI.

Broihahn, J. and Rosebrough, A. (2014) Reconstructing Raisbeck: A Multi-Component Mound and Ritual Center in the Southern Driftless Area, Grant County, Wisconsin. Unpublished, State Archaeology and Maritime Preservation Program Techical Report 14-0001, Wisconsin Historical Society, Madison WI.

Brown, C.E. (1872–1945) Papers (53 Boxes). Wisconsin Historical Society Archives, Madison WI. https://digicoll.library.wisc.edu/cgi/f/findaid/findaid-idx?c=wiarchives;cc=wiarchives;view=text;rgn=main;didno=uw-whs-wis000hb

Brown, C.E. (1906) A record of Wisconsin antiquities. *The Wisconsin Archeologist* OS 5, 307.

Brown, C.E. (1908) The preservation of the Man Mound. *The Wisconsin Archeologist* OS 7(4), 140–54.

Brown, C.E. (1910) The intaglio mounds of Wisconsin. *The Wisconsin Archeologist* 9(1), 5–10.

Brown, C.E. (1911) The Winnebago as builders of Wisconsin earthworks. *The Wisconsin Archeologist* OS 10(3), 124–9.

Brown, C.E. (1912) Undescribed groups of Lake Mendota mounds. *The Wisconsin Archeologist* 11(1), 7–32.

Brown, C.E. (1915) Lake Wingra, *The Wisconsin Archeologist* 14(3), 75–117.

Brown, C.E. (1922) Lake Monona. *The Wisconsin Archeologist* 1(4), 119–67.

Brown, C.E. (1927a) *Lake Mendota Indian Legends.* University of Wisconsin-Madison, Madison WI.

Brown, C.E. (1927b) The springs of Lake Wingra. *The Wisconsin Magazine of History* 10(3), 298–303

Brown, C.E. (1936) Curve-tailed panther mounds. *The Wisconsin Archeologist* 16(1), 10–15.

Brown, C.E. (1938) The Helm effigy mound. *The Wisconsin Archeologist* 18(2), 39–41.

Brown, C.E. and Brown, T.D. (1925) Indian villages and campsites of the lower Rock River. *The Wisconsin Archeologist* 9(1), 7–93.

Brown, C.E. and Drexel, L.E. (1909) Signal Hill Mound Group. Unpublished, on file, Charles E. Brown Papers, November 2, 1909, Wisconsin Historical Society, Madison. WI.

Brown, C.E. and Drexel. L.E. (1921) Fox Lake. *The Wisconsin Archeologist* OS 20(4), 111–50.

Brown, D. (1937) Water monster inhabited lakes of Wisconsin. *The Wisconsin Archeologist* 17(2), 27–31.

Brown, D. (1947) *Wisconsin Indian Place-Name Legends.* Wisconsin Folklore Booklets, Madison WI.

Bruder, E.G. (1951) The Clark Mound Group of Dodge County. *The Wisconsin Archeologist* 32(4), 87–92.

Bryson, R.A. and Bryson, R.U. (2000) *The History of Woodland Climatic Environments: As Simulated with Archaeoclimatic Models.* University of Wisconsin Climatic Research Center, Madison WI.

Byers, A.M. (2011) *Sacred Games, Death, and Renewal in the Ancient Woodlands: The Ohio Hopewell System of Cult Sodality Heterarchies.* AltiMira Press, Walnut Creek CA.

Canfield, W.H. (1859) Map of the Greenfield Man Mound. W. H. Canfield unpublished survey notebook, on file, Charles E. Brown Manuscript Collection, Box 39, Wisconsin Historical Society, Madison WI.

Canfield, W.H. (1872) Map of the La Valle Man Mound. W. H. Canfield Survey Notebook, on file, Charles E. Brown Manuscript Collection, Box 39, Wisconsin Historical Society, Madison WI.

Carneiro, R. (2010) Pauketat's chiefdoms and other archaeological delusions: a challenge to social evolution. *Social Evolution & History* 9(1), 139–65, plus an answer to Pauketat's rejoinder, 172–6.

Chatters, J.C. (2001) *Ancient Encounters: Kennewick Man and the First Americans.* Simon & Schuster, New York.

Christiansen, G.W. III (2002) Archaeological Investigations along STH 60 between CTH W and STH 80 in Richwood and Eagle Townships in Richland County. Unpublished report, Great Lakes Archaeological Research Center, Milwaukee WI.

Christiansen, G.W. III (2004) Archaeological Investigations on the University of Wisconsin–Madison, City of Madison, Dane County. Unpublished report, Great Lakes Archaeological Research Center Reports of Investigation, Milwaukee WI.

Clark, C.P. and Martin, S.R. (2005) A risky business: Late Woodland copper mining on Lake Superior. In *The Cultural Landscape of Prehistoric Mines*, P. Topping and M. Lynott eds, 110–22. Oxbow Books, Oxford.

Clauter, J.A. (2011) Ceramic analysis from the Nitschke Mound Group (47DO27) and the Nitschke Garden Beds (47DO518) sites. *The Wisconsin Archeologist* 92(2), 3–26.

Cleland, C.E. (1966) *The Prehistoric Animal Ecology and Ethnozoology of the Great Lakes Region.* Anthropological Papers 29, Museum of Anthropology, University of Michigan, Ann Arbor MI.

Cole, H.E. (1920) *Baraboo, Dells, and Devil's Lake Region.* Baraboo Publishing Co, Baraboo WI.

Cornelison, J.B. (2013) Agents of Corporate Identity: Patterns and Variability of Effigy Mounds Social Organization. Unpublished Ph.D. Dissertation, Michigan State University.

Curtis, J.T. (1959) *The Vegetation of Wisconsin: An Ordination of Plant Communities.* University of Wisconsin Press, Madison WI.

Dewdney, S. (1975) *The Sacred Scrolls of the Southern Ojibway.* Glenbow-Alberta Institute, Calgary/University of Toronto Press, Toronto.

Diaz-Granados, C. (ed.) (2023) *Explanations in Iconography.* American Landscapes 9, Oxbow Books, Oxford.

Dirst, V. (1985) An Excavation near the Morris Park Mounds at Governor Nelson State Park, Dane County. Unpublished report, Wisconsin. Bureau of Parks and Recreation, Madison WI.

Dirst, V. (1988) Research in Pursuit of the Past at Governor Nelson Park, Dane County, Wisconsin. Unpublished report, Bureau of Parks and Recreation, Madison WI.

Dragoo, D.W. and Wray, C.F. (1964) Hopewell figurine rediscovered. *American Antiquity* 30(2), 195–9.

Duncan, J.R. and Diaz-Granados, C. (2000) Of masks and myths. *Midcontinental Journal of Archaeology* 25, 1–26.

Duncan, J.R. and Diaz-Granados, C. (2023) Son of the Sun: iconography in rock art and artifacts that reveal important associations between symbolism associated with Dhegiha religion, celestial bodies, and western Mississippian ideology. In Diaz-Granados ed. 2023, 13–37.

Egan, K.C. and Wier, D.J. (1992) Stage 2 of the Phase I Investigations on the Lizard Mound (47-WT-0001) and 47-WT- 0119 Sites. Unpublished manuscript on file Archaeological Site Inventory Files, Division of Historic Preservation and Public History, Wisconsin Historical Society, Madison WI.

Elarson, R.S. (1949) Vegetation of Dane County in 1935. *Transactions of the Wisconsin Academy of Science, Arts and Letters*, 39, 31–45.

Emerson, T.E. (1989) Water, serpents, and the Underworld: an exploration into Cahokia symbolism. In *The Southeastern Ceremonial Complex; Artifacts and Analysis: The Cottonlandia Conference*, P. Galloway ed., 45–92. University of Nebraska Press, Lincoln NE.

Fagan, B. (1998) *Ancient North America: The Archaeology of a Continent.* Thames & Hudson, New York.

Fagan, B. (2008) *The Great Warming: Climate Change and the Rise and Fall of Great Civilizations.* Bloomsbury Press, New York.

Finley, R.W. (1976) *Original Vegetation Cover of Wisconsin, Compiled from United States General Land Office Survey Notes (map).* University of Wisconsin Extension, Madison WI.

Finney, F. (ed.) (2006) The archaeological legacy of Theodore H. Lewis: letters, papers, and articles. *The Wisconsin Archeologist* 87(1–2).

Finney, F.A. and Johnson, D.I. (2010) Natural Prairie Mounds and a Taphonomic Assessment of Site 13AM79 at Harpers Ferry, Iowa: Contract Completion Report, no. 234. Unpublished report, Upper Midwest Archaeology, St Joseph IL.

Freckmann, K. (1942) The Hagner Indian mounds. *The Wisconsin Archeologist* 23(1), 1–16.

Funmaker, W.W. (1974) The Bear in Winnebago Culture: A Study in Cosmology and Society. Unpublished manuscript on file, Department of Anthropology, University of Minnesota, Minneapolis MN.

Gartner, W.G. (1999) Late Woodland landscapes of Wisconsin: ridged fields, effigy mounds and territoriality. *Antiquity* 43, 671–3.

Gerend, A. (1920) Sheboygan County. *The Wisconsin Archeologist* OS 19(3), 121–92.

Gilmore, W. (1996) An Archaeological Survey and Construction Monitoring Program Conducted at India Mounds Park for the Village of McFarland. Unpublished report, Water Main Project Great Lakes Archaeological Conservancy, Madison WI.

Goldstein, L. (1995) Landscapes and mortuary practices: a case for regional perspectives. In *Regional Approaches to Mortuary Analysis*, L.A. Beck ed., 101–20. Plenum, New York.

Green, W. (1988) The Turkey River Mound Group (13CT1.). Iowa Office of the State Archaeologist Research Paper 13 (1). Des Moines.

Green, W. (2014) Identity, ideology, and the effigy mound-Oneota transformation. *The Wisconsin Archeologist* 95(2), 44–72.

Green, W. and Schermer, S. (1988) *The Turkey River Mound Group (13CT1), Archaeological and Paleoenvironmental Studies of the Turkey River Valley, Northeastern Iowa.* Iowa Office of the State Archaeologist Research Papers 13(1), 131–98.

Green, W., Zimmerman, L.J., Lillie, R.M., Dawn Makes Strong Move and Sly-Terpstra, D. (2001) *Effigy Mounds National Monument Cultural Affiliation Report.* University of Iowa, Iowa City IA.

Hall, R. (1976) Ghosts, water barriers, corn, and sacred enclosures in the Eastern Woodlands. *American Antiquity* 41, 360–4.

Hall, R. (1979) In search of the ideology of the Adena–Hopewell Climax. In *Hopewell Ideology: The Chillicothe Conference*, D.W. Brose and N. Greber eds, 258–65. Kent State University Press, Kent OH.

Hall, R. (1993) Red Banks, Oneota, and the Winnebago: views from a distant rock. *The Wisconsin Archeologist* 74(1–4), 10–79.

Hall, R. (1997) *Archaeology of the Soul: North American Belief and Ritual*. University of Illinois Press, Urbana IL.

Hamilton, K., Tennesson, D., Slossman, S. and Bauman, M. (1995) *Archaeological Investigations of the Alternate Corridor Alignments for the Proposed Reconstruction of USH 12 between Middleton and Sauk County, Dane County*. Museum Archaeology Program Research Report 46, Wisconsin Historical Society, Madison WI.

Hansel, A.K. and Mickelson, D.M. (1988) A re-evaluation of the timing and causes of high lake phases in the Lake Michigan Basin. *Quaternary Research* 29(2), 113–28.

Harris, W.G. (2002) Upland abandonment during the Middle Archaic Period: a view from northeastern Illinois. *The Wisconsin Archeologist* 83(1), 3–18.

Haskins, R.W. (1903) The legend of the Winnebagos. *Wisconsin Historical Collections* 1, 86–92.

Henriksen, H.C. (1965) Utica Hopewell, a study of early Hopewellian occupation in the Illinois River valley. In *Middle Woodland Sites in Illinois*, E. Bluhm Herold ed., 1–67. Illinois Archaeological Survey Bulletin 5, University of Illinois, Urbana IL.

Henschel, G. (1996) Henschel Mounds (47 Sb 29) as possible solstice markers: a progress report. *The Wisconsin Archeologist* 77(1–2), 73–7.

Herrmann, E.W., Monaghan, G.W., Romain, W.F., Schilling, T.M., Burks, J., Leone, K., Purtill, M.P. and Tonetti, A.C. (2014) A new multi-stage construction chronology for the Great Serpent Mound, USA. *Journal of Archaeological Science* 50, 117–24.

Hoijer, P. (1959) Paul Radin, 1883–1959. *American Anthropologist* 61(5), 839–43.

Howey, M.C.L. and O'Shea, J.M. (2006) Bear's journey and the study of ritual in archaeology. *American Antiquity* 71(2), 261–82.

Hurley, W.M. (1975) *An Analysis of Effigy Mound Complexes in Wisconsin*. Anthropological Paper 59, University of Michigan Museum of Anthropology, Ann Arbor MI.

Hurley, W.M. (1986) The Late Woodland Effigy Mound Culture. *The Wisconsin Archeologist* 67(3–4), 283–301.

Iseminger, W. (2010) *Cahokia Mounds: America's First City*. History Press, Charleston SC.

Johnson, E., Overstreet, D.F., Joyce, D. and Clark, J.A. Jr. (2007) The Mud Lake mammoth and people in the southeastern Wisconsin. *The Wisconsin Archeologist* 88(1), 1–22.

Joyce, D.A. (2006) Chronology and new research on the Schaefer mammoth (*Mammuthus primigenius*) site, Kenosha County, Wisconsin, USA. *Quaternary International* 142–3, 44–57.

Kaufmann, K. (2005) Effigy Mounds as Cultural Landscapes: A Geophysical Analysis of Two Late Woodland Sites In Southeastern Wisconsin. Unpublished Ph.D. Dissertaton, University of Wisconsin-Milwaukee.

Kehoe, A. (1997) History of Wisconsin archaeology. *The Wisconsin Archeologist* 78, special issue, R.A. Birmingham, C.I. Mason and J.B. Stoltman eds, 78(1–2), 11–22.

Kidder, Rev. S.T. (n.d.) Part of Aboriginal Mounds – west of Mississippi on bluffs overhanging [*ca* 1911]. Correspondence on file in the Charles E. Brown Papers, Box 50, Wisconsin Historical Society, Madison WI.

Kuehn, S.R. (2007) The Crow Hollow site: a Middle Woodland Archaic campsite in southwestern Wisconsin. *The Wisconsin Archeologist* 88(1), 23–50.

Lackey-Cornelison, W. (2012) Constructing Community and Cosmos: A Bioarchaeological Analysis of Wisconsin Effigy Mound Mortuary Practices and Mound. Unpublished Ph.D. Dissertation, Michigan State University.

Lanfranco, L. and Eggers, S. (2012) Caries through time: an anthropological overview. In *Contemporary Approaches to Dental Caries*, M. yu Li ed., 1–39. IntechOpen, London.

Lankford, G.E. (1987) *Native American Legends: Tales from the Natchez, Caddo, Chickasaw, and Other Nations*. August House, Little Rock AR.

Lankford, G.E. (2007) The Great Serpent in eastern North America. In *Ancient Objects and Sacred Realms*, F. Kent Reilly III and J.F. Garber eds, 109–35. University of Texas Press, Austin TX.

Lapham, I. (1855) *Antiquities of Wisconsin, As Surveyed and Described.* Smithsonian Contributions to Knowledge 7. Smithsonian Institution, Washington DC.

Lapham, I. (1859) Man-shaped mounds in Wisconsin. *Report and Collections of the State Historical Society of Wisconsin for the Years 1857 and 1858*, 4, 365–8.

Lapham, I.A. (1860) Opening an ancient mound Near Madison, Wisconsin. *Milwaukee Daily Sentinel*, 2 January.

Larsen, C.E. (1985) Geoarchaeological Interpretation of Great Lakes Coastal Environments. In *Archaeological Sediments in Context*, J.K. Stein and W.R. Farrand eds, 91–110. Peopling of the Americas 1. Center for the Study of Early Man, Institute for Quaternary Studies, University of Maine at Orono.

Lepper, B.T. (2004) The Newark Earthworks, monumental geometry and astronomy. In *Hero, Hawk and Open Hand: American Indian Art of the Ancient Midwest and South*, R.F. Townsend and R.V. Sharp eds, 139–49. Yale University Press and Art Institute of Chicago, New Haven CO and London.

Lepper, B.T. and Frolking, T.A. (2003) Alligator Mound: geographical and iconographical interpretations of a late prehistoric effigy mound in central Ohio. *Cambridge Archaeological Journal* 13(2) 147–67.

Lepper, B.T., Duncan, J.R., Diaz-Granados, C. and Frolking, T.A. (2018) Arguments for the age of Serpent Mound. *Cambridge Archaeological Journal* 28(3), 433–50.

Lepper, B.T., Boszhardt, R.F., Duncan, J.R. and Diaz-Granados, C. (2023) Effigy mounds and rock art of Midcontinental North America. In Diaz-Granados ed. 2023, 69–92.

Levi-Strauss, C. (1969) *The Raw and the Cooked.* Mythologies 1, Harper and Rowe, New York.

Lewis, T.H. (1880–1895) *The Northwestern Archaeological Survey: Fieldbooks and Related Volumes.* The Minnesota Historical Society, St Paul.

Lewis, T.H. (n.d. a) *The Northwestern Archaeological Survey 1880-1895.* Notebook 20: 36–37. Minnesota Historical Society Archives, St Paul.

Lewis, T.H. (n.d. b) *The Northwestern Archaeological Survey 1880-1895.* Notebook 27: 7. Minnesota Historical Society Archives, St Paul.

Lewis, T.H. (n.d. c) *The Northwestern Archaeological Survey 1880-1895.* Notebook 27: 56. Minnesota Historical Society Archives, St Paul.

Lewis, T.H. (1885) Notice of Some Recently Discovered Effigy Mounds. *Science* Old Series 5(106), 131–2.

Lewis, T.H. (1886a) The 'Monumental' Tortoise Mounds of De-Coo-dah. *American Journal of Archaeology and History of the Fine Arts* 2, 65–60.

Lewis, T.H. (1886b) A New Departure in Effigy Mounds. *Science*, Old Series 13(318), 187–9.

Lewis, T.H. (1886c) *The Northwestern Archaeological Survey 1880-1895.* Notebook 25: 26–27. Minnesota Historical Society Archives, St Paul.

Lewis, T.H. (1886d) *The Northwestern Archaeological Survey 1880-1895.* Notebook 25: 47–48. Minnesota Historical Society Archives, St Paul.

Lewis, T.H. (1886e) *The Northwestern Archaeological Survey 1880-1895.* Notebook 25: 7. Minnesota Historical Society Archives, St Paul.

Lewis, T.H. (1886f) *The Northwestern Archaeological Survey 1880-1895.* Notebook 27: 34–35. Minnesota Historical Society Archives, St Paul.

Lewis, T.H. (1887) Snake and Snake-Like Mounds in Minnesota. *Science* 9 (220), 393–4.

Lewis, T.H. (1888) *The Northwestern Archaeological Survey 1880-1895.* Notebook: 23–24. Minnesota Historical Society Archives, St Paul.

Lewis, T.H. (1890a) *The Northwestern Archaeological Survey 1880-1895.* Notebook: 32, 6–8. Minnesota Historical Society Archives, St Paul.

Lewis, T.H. (1890b) Cave Drawings. In *Appleton's Annual Cyclopedia and Register of Import Events.* Vol. 20, Appleton & Co., New York.

Lewis, T.H. (1892) *The Northwestern Archaeological Survey 1880-1895.* Notebook: 32, 13. Minnesota Historical Society Archives, St Paul.

Lewis, W.D. and Pearce, D. (2005) *Inside the Neolithic Mind: Consciousness, Cosmos. and the Realm of the Gods.* Thames & Hudson, London.

Locke, J. (1840) Earthwork Antiquities in Wiskonsin [*sic*] Territory. House Executive Document No. 239. First Session, 26th Congress. U.S. House of Representatives, Washington DC.

Loebel, T.J. (2007) A survey of Wisconsin fluted points. *Current Research in the Pleistocene* 24, 118–19.

Loubser, J.H.N. and Bozhardt, R.E. (2004) Recordation, conservation, and management of rock imagery at Samuel's Cave, Wisconsin. In *The Rock-Art of Eastern North America: Capturing Images and Insights*, C. Diaz-Granados and J.R. Duncan eds, 219–38. University of Alabama Press, Tuscaloosa AL.

Lurie, N.O. (1978) Winnebago. In *Handbook of North American Indians, Vol. 15, Northeast*, B. Trigger ed., 690–707. Smithsonian Institution Press, Washington DC.

Lurie, N.O. (2002) *Wisconsin Indians.* Wisconsin Historical Society, Madison WI.

Lynott, M.J. (2014) *Hopewell Ceremonial Landscapes of Ohio: More than Mounds and Geometric Earthworks.* American Landscapes 1, Oxbow Books, Oxford.

Mallam, C.R. (1976) *The Effigy Mound Manifestation: An Interpretive Model.* Iowa State Archaeologist Office Report 9, University of Iowa, Iowa City IO.

Mallam, C.R. (1982) Ideology from the earth: effigy mounds in the Midwest. *Archaeology* 35(4), 60–4.

Mallam, C.R. (1984) Some views on the archaeology of the Driftless Zone in Iowa. *Proceedings of the Iowa Academy of Science* 91, 16–21.

Martin, F. (1922) The Milky Way and the moon at Lizard Mounds, West Bend, Wisconsin. *The Wisconsin Archeologist* 103 (1–2), 53–62.

Martin, S. (1999) *Wonderful Power: The Story of Ancient Copper Mining in the Lake Superior Basin.* Wayne State University Press, Detroit MI.

Mason, R.J. (1997) The Paleo-Indian Tradition. *The Wisconsin Archeologist* 78, special issue, R.A. Birmingham, C.I. Mason, and J.B. Stoltman eds, 78–111.

Mason. R.J. (2006) *Inconstant Companions: Archaeology and North American Indian Oral Traditions.* University of Alabama Press, Tuscaloosa.

Mason, R.J. (2014) Where Nicolet and the Winnebagos first met. *The Wisconsin Archeologist* 95(1), 65–74.

Mason, R.J. and Irwin, C. (1960) An Eden-Scottsbluff burial in northeastern Wisconsin. *American Antiquity* 26, 43–57.

McCoy, E., Fred, E.B. and Oimoen, E. (1978) *'Seeing' the University of Wisconsin-Madison Today.* University of Winsconsin Foundation, Madison WI.

McGrath, W. (1945) The North Benton Mound in Ohio. *American Antiquity* 11(1), 40–6.

McKern, W.C. (1928) The Neale and McCloughry Mound Groups. *Bulletin of the Public Museum of the City of Milwaukee* 3(1), 416–17.

McKern, W.C. (1930) The Kletzien and Nitchske Mound Groups. *Bulletin of the Public Museum of the City of the Milwaukee* 3(4), 417–572.

McKern, W.C. (1931) A Wisconsin variant of the Hopewell Culture. *Bulletin of the Public Museum of the City of Milwaukee* 10(2), 185–328.

McKern, W.C. (1939) The Midwestern taxonomic method as an aid to archaeological culture study. *American Antiquity* 4, 301–13.

McLachlan, W.G. (1914) The mounds of the Lake Waubesa region. *The Wisconsin Archeologist* 12(4), 106–66.

McLachlan, W.G. (1925) The Lake Kegonsa region. *The Wisconsin Archeologist* 4(4), 181–206.

Mead, B. (1979) The Rehbein I Site (47-Ri-81). *The Wisconsin Archeologist* 60(2), 91–182.

Meier, G. (2001) *The Eagle's Voice; Tales Told by Indian Effigy Mounds.* Trails Books, Madison WI.

Meinholz, N. and Kolb, J. (1997) *The Statz Site: A Late Woodland Community and Archaic Workshop in Dane County Wisconsin.* Museum Archaeology Program, Archaeology Research Series 5. Wisconsin Historical Society of Wisconsin, Madison WI.

Newberg, A., d'Aguili, E.G. and Rause, V. (2001) *Why God Won't Go Away: Brian Science and the Biology of Belief.* Ballantine Books, New York.

Orr, E. (1938) Sundry Archaeological Papers 1938. Unpublished, Iowa Archaeological Reports 8, on file, Effigy Mounds National Monument, McGregor IA.

Overstreet, D.F. (1980) The Convent Knoll site (47Wk327): A Red Ochre cemetery in Waukesha, Wisconsin. *The Wisconsin Archeologist* 61(1), 34–90.

Overstreet, D.E. (1993) McCauley, Astor, and Hanson – candidates for the provisional Dandy Phase. *The Wisconsin Archeologist* 74(1–2), 120–96.

Overstreet, D., Doebert, L., Henschell, G., Sander, P. and Wasion, D. (1996) Two Red Ocher mortuary contexts from southeastern Wisconsin—the Henschell site (47 SB 29), Sheboygan County and the Barnes Creek site (47 KN 41), Kenosha County. *The Wisconsin Archeologist* 77(1), 36–62.

Overstreet, D., Doebert, L., Henschell, G., Sander, P. and Wasion, D. (1997) Oneota prehistory and history. *The Wisconsin Archeologist* 78, special issue, R.A. Birmingham, C.I. Mason, and J.B. Stoltman eds, 250–97.

Overstreet, D., Doebert, L., Henschell, G., Sander, P. and Wasion, D. (2000) Cultural dynamics of the late prehistoric period. In *Mounds, Modoc and MesoAmerica: Papers in Honor of Melvin F. Fowler*, S.R. Ahler ed., 405–38. Illinois State Museum Scientific papers, Springfield Il.

Overstreet, D., Joyce, D.J., Blazina-Joyce, R., Wasion, D. and Sverdrup, K.A. (1993) FY 1992 Historic Preservation Survey and Planning Grant: Early Holocene Megafaunal Exploitation, Kenosha County, Wisconsin. Unpublished, Great Lakes Archaeological Research Center, Reports of Investigations, no. 325. Great Lakes Archaeological Research Center, Milwaukee WI.

Parker Pearson, M. (2013) *Stonehenge; Exploring the Gretest Stone Age Mystery.* Simon & Schuster, London.

Parker Pearson, M., Pollard, J., Richards, C., Thomas, J., Tilley, C. and Welham, K. (2022) *Stonehenge for the Ancestors: Part 2 Synthesis.* Sidestone, Leiden.

Pauketat, T. (2007) *Chiefdoms and Other Archaeological Delusions: Issues in Eastern Woodlands Archaeology*. AltaMira Press, Walnut Creek, CA.

Pauketat, T. (2012) *An Archaeology of the Cosmos: Agency and Religion in Ancient America.* Routledge, London.

Peet, S.D. (1890) *Emblematic Mounds and Animal Effigies.* Prehistoric America 2. American Antiquarian Office, Chicago IL.

Peet, S.D. (1892) The clan centers and clan habitat of the effigy builders. *Transactions of the Wisconsin Academy of Sciences, Arts, and Letters* 8, 299–311.

Penny, D.W. (1985) Continuities in imagery and symbolism in the art of the woodlands. In *Ancient Art of the American Woodland Indians*, D.S. Brose, J.A. Brown and D.W. Penny eds, 147–98. Harry N. Abrams, New York.

Phillips, P. and Brown, J.A. (1984) *Pre-Columbian Shell Engravings from the Craig Mound at Spiro, Oklahoma* 2. Peabody Museum Press, Cambridge MA.

Pidgeon, W. (1853) *Traditions of De-coo-dah and Antiquarian Researches; Comparing the Extensive Explorations, Surveys, and Excavations of the Wonderful and Mysterious Earthen Remains of the Mound Builders of America; the Traditions of the Prophet of the Elk Nation Relative to their Origin and Use; and Evidence of an Ancient Population More Numerous Than the Present.* Thayer, Bridgeman, and Fanning, New York.

Pleger, T.C. (1992) Functional and temporal analysis of copper implements at the Chautauqua Grounds site (47-Mt-71): a multicomponent site at the mouth of the Menominee River. *The Wisconsin Archeologist* 73(3–4), 160–76.

Pleger, T. (2000) Old Copper and Red Ochre social complexity. *Midcontinental Journal of Archaeology* 25(2), 169–90.

Pleger, T.C. and Stoltman, J.B. (2009) The Archaic Tradition in Wisconsin. In *Archaic Societies: Diversity and Complexity Across the Midcontinent,* T.E. Emerson, A.C. Fortier and D. McElrath eds, 697–723. State University of New York Press, Albany NY.

Quilter, J. (2006) Introduction. In *The Pre-Columbian World*, J. Quilter and M. Miller eds, 7–19. Dumbarton Oaks, Washington DC.

Radin, P. (1923) *The Winnebago Tribe*. Thirty-Seventh Annual Report of the Bureau of American Ethnography, Washington DC.

Radin, P. (1945) *The Road to Life and Death*. Bollingen Series 5, Pantheon Books, New York.

Radin, P. (1948) *Winnebago Myth Cycles: A Study in Aboriginal Myth Cycles*. Waverly Press, Baltimore ML.

Radin, P. (1954) *The Evolution of an American Indian Prose Epic*. Special Publication 3. Bollingen Foundation, Princeton NJ.

Rajnovich, G. (1994) *Reading Rock Art: Interpreting the Indian Rock Paintings of the Canadian Shield*. Natural Heritage/Natural History Inc., Toronto.

Reardon, R. (2014) Oldest carbon-14 dated copper projectile points from Wisconsin. *The Wisconsin Archeologist* 95(1), 86–7.

Romain, W.F. (2000) *Mysteries of the Hopewell: Astronomers, Geometers, and Magicians of the Eastern Woodlands*. University of Ohio Press, Akron OH.

Romain, W.F. (2011) *Shamans of the Lost World: A Cognitive Approach to the Prehistoric Region of the Ohio Hoepwell*. Altimira Press, Walnut Creek CA.

Romain, W.F. (2013) *LIDAR Assessment of Earthworks at Effigy Mound National Monument*. Ohio State University Newark Earthworks Center, Newark OH.

Romain, W.F. (2015) *An Archaeology of the Sacred: Adena-Hopewell Astronomy and Landscape Archaeology*. The Ancient Earthworks Project, Newark OH.

Rosebrough, A.L. (2010) Every Family A Nation: A Deconstruction and Reconstruction of the Effigy Mound 'Culture' of the Western Great Lakes of North America. Unpublished Ph.D. dissertation, University of Wisconsin, Madison.

Rosebrough, A.L. (2014) Monuments and mysteries: social geography of the effigy mound builders. *The Wisconsin Archeologist* 95(1), 5–28.

Rosebrough, A.L. (2021) Inter-Mound and Off Mound Features at Mound Sites: Considerations for Site Preservation and Management. State Archaeology and Maritime Preservation Program. Unpublished, State Historic Preservation Office, Wisconsin Historical Society, Madison WI.

Rowe, C.W. (1956) *The Effigy Mound Culture of Wisconsin*, Milwaukee Public Museum Publications in Anthropoplogy 3, Milwaukee WI.

Salkin, P. (1986) The Lake Farms Phase: the Early Woodland stage in central Wisconsin as seen from the Lake Farms Archaeological District. In *Early Woodland Archaeology*, K. Farnsworth and T. Emerson eds, 92–120. Kampsville Seminars in Archaeology 2, Center for American Archaeology Research, Kampsville IL.

Salkin, P. (1987) Archaeological Mitigation Excavation Excavations at the Sticker Pond I Site (47DA424 in Middleton, Dane County. Wisconsin. Reports of Investigations No. 353. Unpublished report, Archaeological Consulting and Services, Inc. Verona WI.

Salkin, P. (1988) Archaeological Studies at Two Proposed Recreational Sites at the Mendota Mental Health Institute in Dane County, Wisconsin. Unpublished report, Archaeological Consulting and Services Report of Investigations 1073, Verona WI.

Salzer, R.J. and Johns, L.A. (1992) Report of the Dane County Identification Project, Dane County Park Commission. Unpublished report on file, Office of the State Archaeologist, Wisconsin Historic Society, Madison WI.

Salzer, R. and Rajnovich, G. (2000) *The Gottschall Rockshelter: An Archaeological Mystery*. Prairie Smoke Press, St Paul MN.

Saunders, D. (1947) *When the Moon is a Silver Canoe. Legends of the Wisconsin Dells*. Wisconsin Dells Events, Wisconsin Dells WI.

Scherz, J.P. (1991) *Wisconsin's Effigy Mounds*. Ancient Earthworks Society, Madison WI.

Service, E. (1962) *Primitive Social Organization*. Random House, New York.

Sibley, D.A. (2000) *The Sibley Guide to Birds*. National Audubon Society, New York.

Silverberg, R. (1986) *The Mound Builders*. Ohio University Press, Athens OH.

Skavlem, H.L. (1914) Indian Hill mounds. *The Wisconsin Archeologist* 13(2), 93–6.

Skinner, A. (1913) Social life and ceremonial bundles of the Menominee Indians. *Anthropological Papers of the American Museum of Natural History* 13(1), 1–165.

Skinner, A. (1926) Ethnology of the Ioway Indians. *Bulletin of the Public Museum of the City of Milwaukee* 5(4).

Snead, J.E. (2008) *Ancestral Landscapes of the Pueblo World.* University of Arizona Press, Tucson AZ.

Sneed, J.E. and Preuce, R.W. (1999) The ideology of settlement: landscapes in the northern Rio Grande. In *Archaeologies of Landscape: Contemporary Perspectives*, W. Asmore and A.B. Knapp eds, 169–200. Blackwell, Malden MA.

Spindler, L.S. (1978) The Menominee. In *Handbook of North American Indians, Vol. 15, Northeast*, B.G. Trigger ed., 708–24. Smithsonian Institution Press, Washington DC.

Squier, E. and Davis, E.H. (1848) *Ancient Monuments of the Mississippi Valley* 1. Smithsonian Institution, Washington DC.

Stevenson, K.P., Boszhardt, R.F., Moffat, C.R., Salkin, P.H., Plegar, T.C., Theler, J.L. and Arizigian C.M. (1997) The Woodland Stage. *The Wisconsin Archeologist* 78, special issue, R.A. Birmingham, C.I. Mason, and J.B. Stoltman eds, 140–201.

Stiles-Hanson, C. (1987) Rock art of the Coulee Region. In Wisconsin Rock Art. *The Wisconsin Archeologist* 68, special issue, R.A. Birmingham and W. Green eds, 287–340.

Stoltman, J.B. (1997) the Archaic tradition. *The Wisconsin Archeologist* 78, special issue, R.A. Birmingham, C.I. Mason and J.B. Stoltman eds 78, 112–39.

Stoltman, J.B. (2000) A Reconsideration of the cultural processes linking Cahokia to its northern highlands during the period A.D. 1000–1200. In *Mounds, Modoc, and MesoAmerica: Papers in Honor of Melvin L. Fowler*, S. Ahler ed., 439–54. Illinois State Museum Scientific Papers 28, Springfield IL.

Stoltman, J.B. (2005) Tillmont (47CR460): a stratified prehistoric site in the upper Mississippi River valley. *The Wisconsin Archeologist* 86(2).

Stoltman, J.B. and Christiansen, G.W. (2000) The Late Woodland stage in the Driftless Area of the Upper Mississippi Valley. In *Late Woodland Societies: Tradition and Transformation Across the Continent*, T.E. Emerson, D.I. McElrath and A.C. Fortier eds, 497–524. University of Nebraska Press, Lincoln NE.

Stoltman, J.B. and Pleger, T. (2009) The archaic in Wisconsin. In *Archaic Societies: Diversity and Complexity across the Midcontinent*, D.I. McElreth and A.C. Fortier eds, 697–723. State University of New York, Albany NY.

Stout, A.B. (1906) Antiquities of eastern Sauk County. *The Wisconsin Archeologist* OS 5(2), 26

Stout, A.B. (1911) The Winnebago and the Mounds. *The Wisconsin Archeologist* OS 9(4), 101–3.

Tanner, J. (1830) *A Narrative of the Captivity and Adventures of John Tanner (U.S. Interpreter At the Saut De Ste. Marie) During Thirty Years Residence Among the Indians in the Interior of North America.* Carvili, New York.

Taylor, R.C. (1838) Notes respecting certain Indian mounds and earthworks in the form of animal effigies, chiefly in Wisconsin Territory, U.S. *American Journal of Science and Art* 34, 88–104.

Taylor, S.S. (1843) Description of ancient remains, animal mounds, and embankments, principally in the counties of Grant, Iowa, and Richland, in Wisconsin Territory. *American Journal of Science and Art* 44, 21–40.

Theler, J.L. (1986) The Early Woodland component at the Mill Pond site. In *Early Woodland Archaeology*, K. Farnsworth and T. Emerson eds, 137–57. Kampsville Seminars in Archaeology 2. Center for American Archaeology Research, Kampsville IL.

Theler, J.L. and Boszhardt, R.E. (2006) Collapse of critical resources and culture change: a model for the Woodland to Oneota transformation in the Upper Midwest. *American Antiquity* 71(3), 433–72.

Thomas, C. (1885) *Report on the Mound Explorations of the Bureau of Ethnology*. Twelfth Annual Report of the Bureau of American Ethnology, Smithsonian Institution Press, Washington DC.

Thomas, C.R., Carr, C. and Kerr, C. (2005) Animal totemic clans of Ohio Hopewell. In *Gathering Hopewell: Society, Ritual, and Ritual Interaction*, C. Carr and D. Troy Case eds, 339–85. Springer Science-Business Media, New York.

Tiffany, J.A. (1981) A compendium of radiocarbon dates for archaeological sites in Iowa. *Plains Anthropologist* 26, 55–73.

Tigerman, K. (ed.) (2006) *Wisconsin Indian Literature: Anthology of Native Voices*. University of Wisconsin Press, Madison WI.

Van Langden, H. and Kehoe, T.F. (1971) Hilgen Springs Park Mounds. *The Wisconsin Archeologist* 52(1), 1–19.

Volkert, W.K. and Sampson, K.A. (2023) *Indian Mounds of the Horicon Marsh and Upper Rock*. Puffbird Press, Cambellsport WI.

West, G. (1907) The Indian authorship of Wisconsin antiquities. *The Wisconsin Archeologist* OS 6(4), 167–256.

Whittaker, W.E. and Green, W.W. (2010) Early and Middle Woodland earthwork enclosures in Iowa. *North American Archaeologist* 31(1), 27–57.

Whittaker, W.E. and Storey, G.R. (2008) Ground-penetrating radar survey of the Sny Magill Mound Group, Effigy Mounds National Monument, Iowa. *Geoarchaeology* 23(4), 474–99.

Winkler, M.G., Swain, A.M. and Kutzbach, J.E. (1986) Middle Holocene dry period in the northern Midwestern United Site: Lake levels and pollen stratigraphy. *Quaternary Research* 25, 235–50.

Wittry, W.L. (1959) The Wakanda Park Mound Group, DN-1, Menomonie, Wisconsin. *The Wisconsin Archeologist* 40(3), 95–115.

Wittry, W.L. and Bruder, E.G. (1955) Salvage operations at the Kolterman Mound Group, Dodge County, Wisconsin. *The Wisconsin Archeologist* 36(1), 3–12.

Zamencnik, A.M. (2009) An Osteological Investigation of Lake Woodland Raisbeck Effigy Mound Group, Grant County, Wisconsin. Unpublished Masters Thesis, Department of Anthropology, University of Wisconsin-Milwaukee.